*Encyclopedia of Black Radio
in the United States,
1921–1955*

Also by Ryan Ellett

Radio Drama and Comedy Writers, 1928–1962
(McFarland, 2017)

Encyclopedia of Black Radio in the United States, 1921–1955

RYAN ELLETT

McFarland & Company, Inc., Publishers
Jefferson, North Carolina

The present work is a reprint of the illustrated case bound edition of Encyclopedia of Black Radio in the United States, 1921–1955, first published in 2012 by McFarland.

LIBRARY OF CONGRESS CATALOGUING-IN-PUBLICATION DATA

Ellett, Ryan, 1975–
Encyclopedia of black radio in the United States,
1921–1955 / Ryan Ellett.
p.   cm.
Includes bibliographical references and index.

ISBN 978-1-4766-9339-2
softcover : acid free paper ∞

1. African Americans in radio broadcasting—Encyclopedias.
2. Radio programs—United States—Encyclopedias.
I. Title.
PN1991.8.A35E45 2023
384.54089' 96073003—dc23   2011035286

BRITISH LIBRARY CATALOGUING DATA ARE AVAILABLE

On the cover: Cab Calloway, 1947
(William P. Gottlieb Collection, Library of Congress)

Printed in the United States of America

McFarland & Company, Inc., Publishers
Box 611, Jefferson, North Carolina 28640
www.mcfarlandpub.com

For Dennis Ellett

Acknowledgments

A book of this sort cannot be created by one individual. I am first and foremost indebted to those scholars who laid the foundation of African American radio scholarship. Their work is duly noted throughout. Dr. Thomas Cripps provided information and encouraging words in the earliest stages of research for this work. Melanie Aultman proved herself invaluable in critically reviewing most of this text, questioning some findings, and pushing me to follow up on new leads. Martin Grams, Jr., scoured NBC files in New York City and the Library of Congress for information that could be found nowhere else. Doug Hopkinson provided key early research into some of the jazz musicians profiled in these pages and, with David Siegel, shared leads and sources throughout the development of this project.

Writing this book has been a daunting task, and Jim Cox was quick to share his experiences and insights into the processes of seeing such a project through to completion. He, along with Laura Leff and Elizabeth McLeod, were generous with their time in reviewing entries and fact-checking key portions of the text. Don Frey provided important audio interviews while Derek Teague, Ivan Schreive, Larry Jeannette, and Joe Webb supplied information and suggestions. Jim Beshires kept my nose to the grindstone with his regular contacts by phone and Internet. The staff at the University of Kansas libraries were tireless in tracking down the books, articles, and other sources utilized in these pages. Similarly, the staff at Emory University's Manuscript, Archives, and Rare Book Library were prompt and helpful in copying rare material.

Bob Burchett, editor of *The Old Time Radio Digest* and *The Old Radio Times*, Jack French, editor of *Radio Recall*, Patrick Lucanio, editor of *Radiogram*, and Frank Rosin, editor of *Air Check*, published some of the original findings which were incorporated into this book. I'm grateful for their support in shining light on these previously unknown topics.

I didn't always follow the suggestions offered by those mentioned, and their searches were not always as fruitful as hoped; this is no reflection on their hard work, and the book is better for their contributions. Despite the hard work of everyone involved, mistakes will surely be discovered. They are entirely mine.

Most importantly, I am indebted to my family for giving me the time and space to write this book. My wife, Joanna, and children, James, Jasmine, and Grace, never complained about the countless hours I was hidden behind my books and computer. In feigning interest in the book's topic all four demonstrated their boundless love.

Thank you, everyone.

Table of Contents

Preface

Radio records from the industry's first decade are sketchy and rare; documentation that may reveal more insights to the work of early black radio men and women is especially scarce since their programs were rarely sponsored. Thus there are few paper trails to follow through advertisers' archives. In addition, many black programs appeared on small local stations which are unlikely to have extant records. As a result, in-depth information on black performers in the first decade of commercial radio is uncommon, and the era generally has received little more than cursory reviews in works on radio history.

This volume, while far from comprehensive, attempts to shed light on the breadth and variety of black programming during radio's Golden Age, considered by historians of the medium to stretch generally from the debut of *Amos 'n' Andy* in 1928 to the late 1950s, though 1962 is widely accepted as the firm end of the era of dramatic radio. Most of the programs and performers I have included have received very little attention in prior works on African American radio. I believe several are examined for the first time. Though the emphasis is black-centric radio, some white performers have been included. While I have made every effort to make clear when an individual is known not to be African American, it is possible, even likely, that some of the entries intended to reflect black participation in fact featured white or predominantly white casts. The race of particular performers was not always clear to listeners and reviewers of the era. Still, the material I have chosen to include is either known to have had African American actors or writers or was based on themes and content that were of interest to the black press, its readers, and black listeners.

While the work of many black artists and series from the late 1930s onward has been better covered than those of earlier years, the information is scattered. This book attempts to synthesize that research in a single source. Similarly, there are no comprehensive works on black musicians and radio. A comprehensive review of this topic is beyond the scope of this text, but every attempt has been made to note the earliest instances of black concert broadcasts, to highlight such broadcasts in a variety of geographic areas, and to bring attention to the variety of African American musicians on the air. Therefore, the reader will find information on the radio work of some of the most prominent black musicians as well as some of the most obscure, but not exhaustive coverage of either. Similarly, a thorough review of the development of the disc jockey is too big to be covered here.

1

However, several of the most prominent pioneers in the field are discussed. In addition, African American broadcasts of special interest which may not fit in a convenient category, such as those of early amateur radio operators and Harlem Renaissance artists, have been included to emphasize the diversity of content aimed at black listeners.

In addition to reviewing the major literature on early African American radio, this book provides copious original material to those interested in black culture, black media and radio history, and offers a greater appreciation for the work of countless long-overlooked and oft-forgotten African Americans radio artists. Where the data provided is less than scholars and readers would like, it is my hope that others will be inspired to search out new information that will add to the ever-growing body of literature on black involvement in radio's early years.

Introduction:
The Beginning of Radio

In order to fully understand the contributions of African Americans to early radio, it is helpful to have a basic understanding of the beginnings of the technology. The discovery of radio technology began in the late nineteenth century and developed quickly through the first two decades of the twentieth century, but it was not until after World War I that the commercial prospects for radio began to brighten. In 1920, KDKA in Pittsburgh, a station developed by Westinghouse, broadcast the results of the Harding-Cox presidential election. While there is some debate as to whether this was the true beginning of commercial broadcasting, it serves as a convenient marker for the beginning of what would become a powerful and profitable industry within a decade.

The early money in radio came from selling receiving sets; broadcasts were simply a by-product of broadcasters' needing a reason for the public to purchase these new radios. Hence, during the early 1920s, program quality was relatively poor. Desperate to fill air time, stations accepted about any "talent" that walked through their doors. There was little money at the time to pay for quality performers, and in the earliest years the sheer novelty of the technology sufficed to enthrall listeners.

While advertising over the airwaves was initially scorned and condemned by the government and public alike, it became apparent within a few years that there was no other workable way to pay the growing expenses of radio. Government funding early on was discarded as an option. Listener donations did not prove a satisfactory source of income. Finally, in 1922, WEAF aired what is generally considered the first paid advertisement, a ten-minute talk selling apartments in Jackson Heights, New York City. Thus, the radio commercial, so familiar to radio listeners today, was born.

From the earliest years of broadcasting, stations had attempted to link together to deliver programming to the widest possible audience. In 1926 various technological and commercial barriers were surmounted and the National Broadcasting Company was born from a partnership between RCA, General Electric, Westinghouse, and AT&T. The network soon became two networks, identified as the Red and Blue, which were owned and operated by the same company but aired competing programming.

Radio's African American Pioneers

During these formative years for the industry African Americans played only incidental roles. None of the inventors credited with contributing to radio development were black, nor were any of the primary businessmen that led the companies that would make fortunes from it. That is not to say, however, that African Americans were entirely uninvolved with the new technology. In one of the most thorough retrospectives of blacks on radio, Henry Sampson identifies pioneering black broadcasts by W. C. Handy (1916), the Umbrian Glee Club (1922), and Bessie Smith (1923).[1]

A review of contemporary African American newspapers, one of the best sources of information on early black radio, reveals other black pioneers. Robert Gillespie may be the earliest identified African American wireless operator, working the airwaves in 1910. La Frantz Jones in 1913 was one of the first black radio amateurs after the government began licensing the hobby in 1912. That same year, 1913, Kansas City's Sumner High School was believed to be the only school in the country training black youth in the technology. Other pioneers include Alonzo Thomas, who sent a message from Chicago's Emancipation Exposition to President Woodrow Wilson in 1915. That same year another African American youth, Boy Scout Roland Carrington (whose amateur call letters were 3BA, then 3CY), was recognized as the only African American amateur radio operator in Maryland. He later went on to organize the Banneker Radio Club of Maryland. *The Chicago Defender,* a major black newspaper, further recognized the importance of radio that year and began publicizing the regular meetings of the Woodlawn Radio Association. By 1918 the military was opening radio training programs at black institutions such as Howard University.

It may be impossible to identify radio's first African American performer, but we can cite some of the earliest radio appearances by African Americans. Historians Donna Halper and the previously mentioned Henry Sampson note singer W. C. Handy as having broadcast in 1914 or 1916 respectively. Bernice Ellis is also in contention for earliest black radio performer, having sung over a Fort Smith, Arkansas, station in 1921. Earl Hines and Lois Deppe are known to have broadcast on KDKA in 1921 as well. Charles Gilpin, a prominent black actor, recited some lines from *The Emperor Jones* over a Boston station on April 3, 1922. Other black broadcasters that year included the duo Farrell and Hatch, Maud George, James Mundy and a company of singers, Cecilia Hubert, who accompanied some white singers, and Maude Hall, perhaps the first African American with an ongoing weekly program, which covered fashion.

Jack Cooper is frequently cited as the first African American to make a career in radio. He debuted at Washington, D.C.'s WCAP in the early 1920s and worked there until moving to Chicago in 1926, where he pursued other opportunities in the industry. His *All-Negro Hour* debuted in 1929 and was on the air until 1935, a run that outlasted all other black programming of the time.[2]

These accomplishments, as impressive as they were, still only represented a very small portion of broadcasting time. By the latter half of the 1920s the black presence on radio was undoubtedly most prominent in the area of music, primarily jazz. Much radio content during the 1920s was music, whether live or recorded, and the growing popularity of jazz provided an opportunity for many black performers to reach the larger white audience. Duke Ellington, Fletcher Henderson, and Louis Armstrong all managed to get their share of air time.

Traditional spirituals, though less popular than jazz, also created opportunities for African American singers and choirs to reach the airwaves. By 1925 various choirs were appearing on the air and getting attention from the black press, among them the Hampton Institute Quartet, the Hampton Glee Club, the Tuskegee Quartet, and Harrod's Jubilee Singers. That same year saw one of the first lecture and music programs featuring black talent; this would be a prototype for series to come. The YMCA sponsored a talk over WGBS about the Harlem community and included various musical selections. WGBS, incidentally, would be the home of the *Pittsburgh Courier Hour*, black radio's first ongoing series, in 1927.

Besides musical acts, early black radio acts included live stage plays such as *Shuffle Along* (1923) and *Black Boy* (1926). Comedy routines, too, were popular. African American duos such as Flournoy Miller and Aubrey Lyles entertained black audiences. Minstrel and black-face acts—primarily performed by whites—were popular with white audiences and received mixed reactions from black listeners. Charles Correll and Freman Gosden created a radio act called *Amos 'n' Andy* (originally *Sam 'n' Henry*) which rocketed them to national fame by decade's end. Intentionally or not, these two white actors set the boundaries within which most black radio actors and actresses would perform for years to come, roles of generally undereducated men and women in menial positions. White minstrel teams such as Charles Mack and George Moran (the Two Black Crows) and a troupe featuring Hal Gilles and Henry Moeller proved popular as well, though they could not compete with *Amos 'n' Andy*.[3]

The reasons for the relatively small black participation in radio are varied. Historians J. Fred MacDonald and William Barlow have offered three primary reasons for the limited black presence on radio. First and perhaps foremost was the rise of the networks. To maximize benefit for sponsors, content had to be increasingly aimed at the largest possible audience. This meant appealing as much as possible to middle-class whites, the dominant demographic in radio ownership.

Obstacles to African Americans on the Radio

African American radio ownership was disproportionately small compared to whites, one source citing urban black ownership at 14 percent compared to a white ownership of 56 percent. Rural ownership was even lower. With such a small listening audience, there was little incentive for the networks to create programming for African Americans; with so few black professionals in the industry there were few insiders to advocate for a larger black voice, and thus a catch-22 was created. With a black audience finding few reasons to tune in, the networks saw few financial benefits for creating material appealing to that audience, thus perhaps reinforcing low black listenership. Similarly, advertisers wanted to avoid scandal whenever possible lest it cost them sales. Therefore, they actively avoided sponsoring any content that might raise the specter of race. To avoid offending Southern audiences, the networks minimized the black radio presence and ensured what presence there was appropriately servile.[4]

A second reason for low participation of African Americans in the radio industry was the lack of an organized source for black talent. During the 1910s and 1920s a strong base of performing talent developed from the black recording studios and Theatre Owners' Booking Association (a black vaudeville circuit) which could sustain what little black-oriented programming existed. Both of these industries were devastated by the Great Depression and had virtually disappeared by the mid–1930s. Thus, the talent pipeline that may have fed new black broadcasts on the networks during the 1930s and 1940s dried up.

A third roadblock to African American participation in radio was white co-workers.

Since much of radio's content during the 1920s was music, this offered an ideal opening for black musicians. However, beyond the headliners mentioned, it was difficult for blacks to make inroads on the music programs. Many of the early radio bands were made up of members of the American Federation of Musicians, which did not encourage African American membership. Since union musicians booked most of the major hotels and theaters (from where many musical broadcasts originated), they increased their presence with radio as it grew and effectively blocked entrance to this area of radio to blacks.[5]

Black Radio's Golden Age, Decline, and Renaissance

Despite these obstacles, black men and women succeeded in getting a variety of programming on the air. In fact, the golden age of African American radio is appropriately identified as the years between 1927, when Floyd Calvin's *Pittsburgh Courier Hour* debuted, and 1933, when *John Henry* went off the air after a nine-month run on CBS, on which it became the first black series to meet with widespread network success. During this span, African Americans presented broadcasts of diversity and variety that would not be matched until a resurgence in the 1940s and 1950s. From lecture and music programs (*The Courier Hour, The Negro Achievement Hour*) to variety programs (*The All-Negro Hour*) to drama (*Careless Love, John Henry*) to special interest shows (*Negro Business Hour, National Negro Forum*), African Americans could find nearly as wide a mix of radio content geared to them as could their white counterparts, if not in as much quantity.

Bolstering the value of these African American–oriented programs was their frequent use of black writers and creators; these were programs for a black audience, created by black artists and black performers. Even

when African Americans gained greater access to airwaves after World War II, the variety of programming would not match that of two decades earlier, nor would African Americans ever again have so much control over so much radio content until the rise of the disc jockey.

After black radio's golden age, African American performers found themselves primarily relegated to supporting roles during the rest of the Depression years, from 1933 into the early 1940s. Ironically, the black presence was diminished as network radio matured and the broader radio industry entered the peak of its own golden age, generally identified by historians as the mid–1930s to the end of World War II. During the 1930s and 1940s, when network radio was run by whites for the enjoyment of a white listening audience, a handful of African Americans gained a degree of prominence, including Eddie Anderson (Rochester on *The Jack Benny Program*), Lillian Randolph (Birdie on *The Great Gildersleeve*), and Hattie McDaniel (*Beulah*). These prominent actors were exceptions, however, and African Americans in behind-the-scenes roles such as writer and producer were all but nonexistent.

A third stage of black radio history can be identified beginning in the early 1940s; this reemergence of radio programming with a black identity and strong African American characters parallels the nation's struggle through and emergence from World War II. Reflecting the nationwide desire of African Americans to shake off Jim Crow and receive the freedom and opportunity for which a global war had just been fought, black writers and actors again began creating their own material for the airwaves. *Freedom's People* premiered in 1941 and *Native Sons* in 1942. Debuting in 1944, *New World A' Coming* was a series focused on black themes and based initially on a book by Roi Ottley. Between 1946 and 1948 Richard Durham penned three black dramatic series for Chicago-area radio, *Democracy—USA, Here Comes Tomorrow,* and *Destination Freedom.*

In her 1954 master's thesis, Estelle Edmerson claims that interviews with (then) contemporary black performers and white executives did not lead to the identification of any African Americans in non-acting jobs.[6] This final era of early black radio would have one last gasp between 1954 and 1955 with the black serial *The Story of Ruby Valentine.* Produced by the National Negro Network, the program was to be at the vanguard of a new black-centric radio enterprise. The timing was poor; dramatic radio in general was in rapid decline with the meteoric rise of television and new dramatic programming—let alone programming which took a serious look at black life—had trouble finding an audience. The brief revitalization of black radio drama represented by *Ruby Valentine* disappeared by the middle of the decade.

The small opening blacks had in radio to develop an independent radio voice between 1927 and 1933 was firmly closed at the network level by the middle 1930s. The resurgence of black drama in the 1940s remained confined to urban stations and rarely, if ever, reached a large audience. The broader demise of radio drama during the 1950s resulted both from the ascendency of television and the relatively inexpensive alternative of music and disc jockey programs. In this area black radio professionals found the opportunities and successes that had eluded them for so long. Many of these record-spinners gained large followings and played a major role in the development of popular music and commercial formats through the 1950s and 1960s. DJs such as Al Benson, Eddie Honesty, and Hal Jackson ensured that African Americans would have a greater influence on the airwaves in the decades to come than they ever dreamed of having through radio's earliest years.

*   *   *

The contents of this book are arranged alphabetically, by last name of individuals and first word of the radio series. Each entry is cross-referenced with other entries indicated with bold lettering. Sources are cited after each entry while full bibliographic information is at the back of the book.

Notes

1. Henry T. Sampson, *Swingin' on the Ether Waves: A Chronological History of African Americans in Radio and Television Broadcasting, 1925–1955, Volume 1* (Lanham, MD: Scarecrow, 2005), p. 7.

2. Mark Newman, *Entrepreneurs of Profit and Pride: From Black Appeal to Radio Soul* (New York: Praeger, 1988), pp. 60–75. Also see Newman's "On the Air with Jack L. Cooper: The Beginnings of Black-Appeal Radio," *Chicago History* 12 (Summer 1983).

3. Elizabeth McLeod, *The Original Amos 'n' Andy: Freeman Gosden, Charles Correll and the 1928–1943 Radio Serial* (Jefferson, NC: McFarland, 2005). McLeod wrote perhaps the authoritative treatment of the original *Amos 'n' Andy* series in her book. More sympathetic than most accounts, she argues that Correll and Gosden certainly did not intend for the characters of Amos Brown and Andrew Jones to set a precedent for negative black radio characters. Regardless, it is clear that many popular black characters for years afterwards shared many stereotypical attributes of the groundbreaking duo.

4. J. Fred MacDonald, *Don't Touch That Dial! Radio Programming in American Life, 1920–1960* (Chicago: Nelson-Hall, 1979), p. 333.

5. William Barlow, *Voice Over: The Making of Black Radio* (Philadelphia: Temple University Press, 1999). MacDonald touches on some of these themes in his volume *Don't Touch That Dial!*, pp. 333–334, one of the first radio histories to devote a section to African Americans on the air. Barlow expands and develops these ideas in his text, pp. 25–28.

6. Estelle Edmerson, "A Descriptive Study of the American Negro in United States Professional Radio, 1922–1953," (master's thesis, University of California at Los Angeles, 1954).

Station List

To maintain the narrative flow of the text, the locations of radio stations are not specified in every entry. The following list of stations will assist the reader in determining the broadcast location of particular programs and performers. The cities and towns cited reflect the market served by a particular station and not necessarily the exact location of the station facilities. Such information is frequently difficult and even impossible to find. Further, over the years, broadcasting stations moved to different locales in a metropolitan area.

AFRS—Armed Forces Radio Service
BBC—British Broadcasting Corporation
CFCF—Montreal
CKGW—Toronto
KBLF—Red Bluff, CA
KCOH—Houston
KDAY (formerly KOWL)—Los Angeles
KDKA—Pittsburgh
KECA—Los Angeles
KEGF—Los Angeles
KENT—Shreveport, LA
KFAC—Los Angeles
KFI—Los Angeles
KFKF—Shenandoah, IA
KFWB—Los Angeles
KGPJ—Los Angeles
KHJ—Los Angeles
KING—Seattle
KLZ—Denver
KMBC—Kansas City
KMPC—Los Angeles

KNBC—San Francisco
KNX—Los Angeles
KOA—Denver
KOL—Portland, OR
KOWL (later KDAY)— Los Angeles
KPOL—Los Angeles
KPRS—Kansas City
KRKD—Los Angeles
KSTL—St. Louis
KWBR—San Francisco
KYW—Chicago
WAAM—New York
WAAT—New York
WABC—New York
WANT—Richmond, VA
WBBM—Chicago
WBBR—New York
WBCN—Chicago
WBCO—Bessemer, AL
WBMD—Baltimore
WBMS—Boston
WBNX—New York
WBYN—New York

WBZ—Boston
WCAE—Pittsburgh
WCAO—Baltimore
WCAU—Philadelphia
WCBM—Baltimore
WCCO—St. Paul, MN
WCFL—Chicago
WCGU—New York
WCIN—Cincinnati
WCNW (later WLIB)— New York
WCRW—Chicago
WDAD—Nashville
WDAR—Philadelphia
WDAS—Philadelphia
WDBH—Worcester, MA
WDIA—Memphis
WDT—New York
WEAF (later WNBC and WRCA)—New York
WEAM—Arlington, VA
WEAR—Baltimore
WEBH—Chicago
WEBJ—New York

9

WEBK—Tampa, FL
WEEI—Boston
WENR—Chicago
WERD—Atlanta
WESC—Greenville, SC
WEVD—New York
WFAA—Dallas
WFBR—Baltimore
WFDR—New York
WGAR—Cleveland, OH
WGBA—Baltimore
WGBS—New York
WGES—Chicago
WGIV—Charlotte, NC
WGN—Chicago
WGY—Schenectady, NY
WHAT—Philadelphia
WHDH—Boston
WHFC—Chicago
WHN—New York
WHOD—Pittsburgh
WHOM—New York
WHP—Harrisburg, PA
WIBC—Indianapolis
WIBO—Chicago
WIND—Chicago
WINS—New York
WINX—Washington, D.C.
WIP—Philadelphia
WJAR—Providence, RI
WJJD—Chicago
WJLB—Detroit
WJMO—Cleveland

WJOB—Hammond, IN
WJOL—Joliet, IL
WJR—Detroit
WJY—New York
WJZ—New York
WKBC—Fort Worth, TX
WKRC—Cincinnati
WLIB (formerly
    WCNW)—New York
WLNA—New York
WLOU—Louisville
WLS—Chicago
WLTH—New York
WLW—Cincinnati
WMAQ—Chicago
WMBC—Detroit
WMBM—Miami Beach
WMC—Memphis
WMCA—New York
WMFS—Chattanooga, TN
WMOZ—Mobile, AL
WMRO—Chicago
WMRY—New Orleans
WNEW—New York
WNJ—Newark
WNJR—Newark
WNYC—New York
WOBS—Jacksonville, FL
WOCS—Columbia, SC
WOL—Washington, D.C.
WOO—Philadelphia
WOOK—Washington,
    D.C.

WOR—New York
WOV—New York
WOWO—Fort Wayne, IN
WPAL—Charleston, SC
WPAP—New York
WPC—Washington, D.C.
WPCH—New York
WPEN—Philadelphia
WPG—Baltimore
WPIX (television)—New
    York
WPNX—Columbus, GA
WQJ—Chicago
WQV—Pittsburgh
WRBC—Jackson, MS
WRC—Washington, D.C.
WRMA—Montgomery,
    AL
WRNY—New York
WRVA—Richmond, VA
WSAI—Cincinnati
WSB—Atlanta
WSID—Baltimore
WSM—Nashville
WSMB—New Orleans
WSOK—Nashville
WTAM—Cleveland, OH
WTAR—Norfolk, VA
WVON—Chicago
WWRL—New York
WXYZ—Detroit

The Encyclopedia

Abbey, Leon

Leon Abbey was an early radio operator in the Minneapolis, MN, area. He and **Earl Duncan** were reported to be the only two African American amateurs in the city's radio club in 1915. Abbey's skills were notable: he won a prize of distinction and first honors at a local public library for his wireless set-up.

Source: *Chicago Defender*, September 25, 1915, p. 5.

All-Negro Hour

While **Jack Cooper**'s *All-Negro Hour* (which was a full sixty minutes, unlike many shows which used "Hour" in their title) cannot claim to be the first regularly scheduled African American radio series, it can lay legitimate claim to being the first black series focused primarily on entertainment rather than education (as were predecessors *The Floyd Calvin Hour* and *The Negro Achievement Hour*). It is very possibly the first black production that attempted to compete with white productions on pure entertainment value, as noted by Cooper historian Mark Newman. *The All-Colored Hour* (as the series was originally named) debuted on Chicago's WSBC November 3, 1929. Details of the earliest broadcasts are unknown but the De-

cember 9, 1929, broadcast included "everything from 'pop' and novelty to grand opera." J. Berni Barbour, who was associated with Zieffield, Arnold Wiley, Turner and Hanks (Bud and Buddy), and others, provided the entertainment. Cooper himself took care of announcing duties.

A short profile of *The All-Negro Hour* written ten months after its debut included a list of creative staff and performers. They included Estella Patton-Cooper, executive secretary, Lonnie L. Stratton, program director, and Claude Rhodes, musical director. Performers included Buddy Burton, David Mozee, Catherine Wade, Lucretia Knight, Odella Nelson, E. Milton Johnson, James McQueen, Gernell Grumley, Ann Cooper-Edwards, Baby June Rhodes, Ezra Shelton, "Big Boy" Edwards, Myrtle Allen, A. B. Brooks, Claude Rhodes, Haiite Andres, and D. E. Milton, a preacher. Guest stars included Lovie Austin, Rose Summerville, and the Original Cotton Pickers.

One interesting feature of Cooper's *Hour* was a sketch devoted to two characters named Luke and Timber which debuted February 27, 1930. The pair was played by Cooper and Arnold Wiley respectively. Newman convincingly argues that Cooper's duo lacked the crudeness, dialect, and stereotypes that many African Americans found disturbing about *Amos 'n' Andy* and represented a more authentic picture of African American life. Later that year two more serials were introduced on the program, "Mush and Clorinda, the Alabama Sunflowers" and "Horseradish and Fertilizer." Cooper not only played Horseradish but is credited with writing the serial which lasted an astonishing twelve years. Whether these qualify as the first black-written radio sketches remains unconfirmed. In addition to these groundbreaking skits, *The All-Negro Hour* included interviews, choirs, news announcements, and music records.

As much as Cooper wanted his program to be an all-black endeavor, he relied on a white-owned station to broadcast the show, white engineers, and primarily white advertisers. *The All-Negro Hour* was a great success, nevertheless, airing until 1935.

Sources: Barlow pp. 50–57; Newman, *Entrepreneurs*, pp. 60–65; Spaulding pp. 71–72; *Chicago Defender*, December 14, 1929, p. 7, January 25, 1930, p. 6, August 2, 1930, p. 5.

The Alpha and Omega Opera Company de Luxe

The Alpha and Omega Opera Company de Luxe was an early black comedy based on the antics of an inept opera troupe. J. Rosamond Johnson was the author and leader of this fictional outfit and played the part of Deacon Simon Pure on the all-black endeavor. Gregory Williamson wrote the scripts and Paul Dumont handled production matters.

The debut broadcast over WEAF, New York, on February 7, 1930, featured a farcical rehearsal of Bizet's famous opera *Carmen*. The following week focused on the troupe's efforts to find a suitable basso for the role of Mephistopheles in Gounod's *Faust*. When a local clergyman objects to the choice of an opera featuring the devil in the lead, Deacon Pure suggests that the pastor might make a good Mephistopheles because of his fine bass voice.

Clarence Williams took over director's

duties the fourth week when the cast bumbled through Verdi's *Rigoletto* in which popular arias turned into down home blues tunes. The company also ran into difficulty with their stage which is set up on a pool table at the defunct Alpha and Omega Pool and Billiard Parlor. Saint-Saëns' *Samson and Delilah* was spoofed in another episode. Apparently the premise was not enough to capture the audience's attention and the program left the air after two months. Critics were cool to the show, complaining that the star power was wasted in the slap-stick comedy that was supposedly produced by a white writer. Cast members included **Eva Taylor** and Alvin Simmons, the latter of whom was billed as an NBC hatboy.

Sources: *Baltimore Afro-American*, February 22, 1930, p. 9, March 1, 1930, p. 9, March 8, 1930, p. 8, 9; *New York Amsterdam News*, February 5, 1930, p. 11, February 12, 1930, p. 11, February 26, 1930, p. 11, March 5, 1930, p. 11.

Ambrose Smith's Orchestra

Ambrose Smith jumped into radio in early 1932 on Baltimore-area stations where he had a twice-weekly program with River Chambers as the **Twenty Harlem Fingers** piano duo over WFBR. By February 1932, Smith had formed the self-named Ambrose Smith's Orchestra which was playing daily (except Sundays) over WCBM. By July 1932, the band was engaged at the Rio Rita Club and WCBM, Baltimore, where they played every night of the week at 9:30. Zerita Stepteau, graduate of Baltimore's Douglass High School and Howard University, was the outfit's director. Smith faded from the aural spotlight by the end of 1932.

Sources: *Baltimore Afro-American*, February 13, 1932, p. 9, March 26, 1932, p. 8, April 23, 1932, p. 20, May 14, 1932, p. 11, June 25, 1932, p. 18, July 9, 1932, p. 16.

Amos 'n' Andy

Amos Jones, played by **Freeman Gosden**, and Andrew Brown, played by **Charles**

Correll, were the most famous African American characters in the history of radio which was ironic because Gosden and Correll were, of course, white. Much has been written about the pair and their contributions, both positive and negative, to the portrayal of blacks in electronic media. While an in-depth analysis of the controversies that surrounded the program (especially the 1950s television incarnation) is beyond the scope of this book an overview of the radio program is pertinent as is a history of the program and the employment afforded to numerous black performers over the years.

The *Amos 'n' Andy* radio serial grew out of *Sam 'n' Henry*, the story of two black men (Sam Smith and Henry Johnson) who moved to Chicago from rural Alabama, a situation familiar to many African American men and women who made the same journey during the first decades of the twentieth century. Debuting on January 12, 1926, over the powerful Chicago station WGN, Sam and Henry slowly gained a following in the region as Gosden and Correll arduously mastered the tasks of writing and performing a daily radio program which had no real precedent.

After recording for Victor Talking Machine Company in the spring of 1926, Gosden and Correll began to realize *Sam 'n' Henry* could be heard by listeners beyond the range of WGN via record. When approached about the idea, however, WGN brass would have none of it. Why create potential competition by selling a hit feature to other stations? Meanwhile, the two actors took further note of various *Sam 'n' Henry* merchandise being snapped up by fans of the show. Their popularity only grew after nationwide exposure during a gala broadcast from New York's Astor Hotel in 1926 and again in 1927. Under contract until the end of 1927, however, the men had no recourse but to endure their present situation.

On December 18, 1927, after 586 broadcasts and nearly two years on the air, *Sam 'n' Henry* disappeared. Gosden and Correll immediately set about negotiating with another Chicago station, WMAQ. Recognizing the value of their creations, the pair were careful to hold on to all future copyrights and trademarks. Even so, WMAQ station signed them in a whopping $25,000 package (which included their announcer, Bill Hay), a considerable improvement over their weekly $300 salary at WGN. Most important, however, Gosden and Correll were guaranteed the right to syndicate their show to any interested station.

In the meantime, *Sam 'n' Henry* suddenly reappeared on January 10, 1928, this time played by Hal Gilles and Hank Moeller, two other white men. Gilles and Moeller were acquaintances of Gosden and Correll going back to their days with the traveling Bren minstrel troupe. The newcomers didn't click with the audience and *Sam 'n' Henry* permanently left the air just a few weeks later. Gilles and Moeller ended up making nice careers (if less famous and prosperous) out of their follow-up effort, *Louie's Hungry Five*, a German act. In many ways the new six-a-week serial was simply an adaptation of the black Sam and Henry to a German immigrant setting with the principle characters Herr Louie and the Weasel backed up by a small traditional German band. Both men stayed busy with other WGN efforts including minstrel programming that aired into the 1930s.

Settling on the new names Amos and Andy, Gosden and Correll returned to the air March 19, 1928. Via their syndication method, *Amos 'n' Andy* was heard coast-to-coast by the end of the year and by the middle of 1929 they'd attracted both a sponsor, Pepsodent, and a network, NBC. It was at this point that Amos and Andy relocated from Chicago to Harlem, their home for the next thirty years of broadcasting. The result was a program whose popularity at the turn of the decade cannot be overstated. The duo spawned countless imitators and can fairly be given credit for helping boost radio's popularity to new heights as the Depression dawned. Sources indicate 75% of the listening audience tuned them in and nearly one-fourth to one-third of the nation's population listened in at the height of the show's popularity in 1931.

While reaction to *Amos 'n' Andy* was overwhelmingly positive, the show had its detractors. Elizabeth McLeod, in her masterful history of the program through 1943, reviews *The Pittsburgh Courier*'s campaign against the duo which began in 1931. While many African Americans no doubt had mixed reactions to them, McLeod points out that there is strong evidence to suggest that the *Courier*'s crusade was as much a marketing ploy to increase readership as it was a genuine outrage against Gosden and Correll. Not only was the *Courier* in poor financial straits at the time but publisher Robert Vann had earned a reputation as a crusader against dubious causes for which he'd later been known to retract accusations and allegations. The timing was also questionable considering Gosden and Correll had been on radio playing black characters for five years, three of those years on the nationwide airwaves as Amos and Andy after they implemented their syndication network.

The African American newspaper of record for Gosden and Correll's hometown, Chicago, was *The Chicago Defender*, and it proved to be supportive of the pair during their early years, especially in regards to their participation with the annual Bud Billiken parade. In 1931 Gosden and Correll attended in person and for years afterward donated thousands of *Amos 'n' Andy* candy bars to be given away. That Amos and Andy received comparatively little attention from the other major black newspapers is indicative that the *Courier*'s ire was not broadly shared.

Though the popularity of *Amos 'n' Andy* peaked in 1931, the program still maintained a healthy listenership of fourteen million by decade's end and twelve million by 1943 when it underwent a heavy format change.

On February 19, 1943, after more than 4,000 broadcasts *Amos 'n' Andy* left the air until October. For fifteen years the series was a minimalist production with just a handful of cast members (Gosden and Correll played all the characters the first few years), the announcer Bill Hay, and an orchestra that played the introductory theme "The Perfect Song." Significantly, Gosden and Correll had written every word of the program.

While Gosden and Correll played all the male characters during the fifteen-year serial run, they finally brought in female cast members in 1936. Two of the nine women that McLeod identifies as appearing over the years were African American, **Ernestine Wade** and **Lillian Randolph**. Wade was the more active of the two, appearing as the Kingfish's wife Sapphire from 1939 until the end of the fifteen-minute serial in 1943. During that same four-year span she also appeared less regularly as Clara Van Porter, a society matron. She made additional appearances as Valada Green, Andy's fiancé in 1939, and Sara Fletcher, a neighborhood busybody. Lillian Randolph is credited with just a single role in *Amos 'n' Andy*, that of Widow Armbrister between 1941 and 1942.

When Amos and Andy returned to the air the show was nearly indistinguishable in format from other popular comedy programs of the time such as *The Jack Benny Show* and *Fibber McGee and Molly*. Scripts were churned out by a team of professional writers, the cast expanded, an orchestra provided music throughout, and a boisterous studio audience roared at the snappy jokes. These changes alone would have altered the tone of the program drastically; that it was switched from a daily fifteen-minute serial format to a weekly half-hour sitcom format ensured that the days of subtle character development and light dramatic comedy on which the show was built were over. Listeners loved the new *Amos 'n' Andy Show* and it ran another dozen years until 1955. The audience increased dramatically, reaching nearly 37 million listeners in the 1947-48 season, a number comparable to their 1931 heyday though less so as a percent of the overall population.

By 1955 listeners dwindled to less than 12 million and *The Amos 'n' Andy Show* was cancelled. To an extent their decline reflected that of dramatic radio in general; the so-called Golden Age of radio was coming to an end, bowing to an ascendant medium called television. Still, the entertainers who had done so much to spur enthusiasm for radio soldiered on for five more years in a format called *Amos 'n' Andy Music Hall*, a nightly segment of varying length over the years consisting mainly of contemporary musical hits interspersed with light patter between Amos and Andy. There were thin attempts at a story but in truth it was little more than a stylized disc jockey show. On November 25, 1960, Amos and Andy left the air for the final time after 32 years.

Sources: Andrews & Julliard pp. 13–20, 31; Dunning pp. 31–35; Ellett pp. 16–17; Ely pp. 54–60; Hopkinson & Ellett, pp. 12–13; MacDonald, *Don't Touch That Dial!*, pp. 340–344; McLeod pp. 29–58.

Amos 'n' Andy Music Hall

The final radio series featuring Amos Jones and Andy Brown was the *Amos 'n' Andy Music Hall*, a program of prerecorded music interrupted by a feeble storyline and occasional patter between the two long-time friends. Premiering September 13, 1954, the program ran for six years but is not widely remembered today among old time radio fans or historians, existing primarily as a postscript to the *Amos 'n' Andy* legacy. Few of the episodes are in circulation among hobbyists and, indeed, there is little interest in the series.

By today's standards of continuity used in television and film the *Music Hall* stands outside the *Amos 'n' Andy* canon. There was little in the way of storyline and no evidence of character development; it was merely a musical vehicle attached to two familiar voices which had entertained a nation for three decades. John Dunning, noted old time radio historian, describes *Amos 'n' Andy Music Hall* simply as "embarrassing." Other *Amos 'n' Andy* scholars have not felt the need to add or detract from this assessment, though Jim Cox concedes it was a profitable venture for CBS.

Amos 'n' Andy Music Hall left the air November 25, 1960, along with most of the remaining daytime radio serials including *The Couple Next Door*, *The Right to Happiness*, and *Ma Perkins*. Among old time radio enthusiasts the day is frequently referred to as the "day radio drama died" though a handful of programs lived on a couple more years. William Paley, head of CBS where Amos and Andy ended their radio run, recalled in his memoirs that he recognized the significance of the cancellations and wrote to Gosden and Correll: "I just wanted you to know what a depressing feeling it gives me to face up to the fact." He added "it was sad to see ... [the] old-timers go."

Sources: Cox, *Music Radio*, pp. 152–153; Cox, *This Day in Radio History*, pp. 152, 214; Cox, *The Great Radio Sitcoms*, pp. 45–46; Dunning pp. 31–36; McLeod p. 150; Paley pp. 227–228.

The Amos 'n' Andy Show

On October 8, 1943, Amos Jones and Andy Brown returned to the air in *The Amos 'n' Andy Show* after their original daily program, simply titled *Amos 'n' Andy*, was retired. While the new title was only slightly modified, the content of the program was nearly unrecognizable to those who had listened faithfully to the subdued and understated daily fifteen-minute installments for a decade and a half. Under the sponsorship of Lever Brothers' Rinso, the longtime chums returned to a glitzy, polished, half-hour extravaganza packed with gut-busting gags and occasional celebrity guests. While perhaps disappointing to diehard *Amos 'n' Andy* fans, the change was a success. Ratings popped and new listeners eagerly began to tune in. Within five seasons the number of sets tuned in every week tripled over the final season of the earlier daily format.

The characters did not change much, their personalities having been carefully crafted by **Freeman Gosden** and **Charles Correll** since 1928. But gone were the long story arcs that swept up the American public in earlier years. Now the staff of writers whipped through a set-up, problem, and solution in 30 minutes all while keeping the newly added studio audience laughing in the aisles. Interestingly, Amos all but became a supporting character, giving way to the antics of the scheming George "Kingfish" Stevens (played by Freeman Gosden) and ever-gullible Andy. Stars such as Peter Lorre and Edward G. Robinson stopped by to spice up some broadcasts during the first year of the revamp.

Numerous African American actors and actresses played regularly on the program. **Ernestine Wade**, who had been featured on the serial beginning in 1939, continued in her role as Sapphire Stevens, Clara Van Porter, and Sara Fletcher. Black performers with ongoing roles who joined the cast included James Baskett, **Ernest Whitman, Hattie McDaniel, Eddie Green, Johnny Lee, Jester Hairston, Ruby Dandridge, Amanda Randolph, Horace (Nick) Stewart**, and **Lillian Randolph** (who had appeared briefly in the original version of *Amos 'n' Andy*). African Americans in minor roles included **Roy Glenn, Dorothy Dandridge, Vivian Dandridge, Wonderful Smith**, Millie Bruce, Corny Anderson, **Vince Townsend**, and Amos Reece. While all were unquestionably talented, the sudden influx of black performers surely was at least partly an effort to deflect growing discontent with Gosden and Correll's roles as the leading black characters. Protests comparable to the *Courier* outcry mounted in 1931 never arose again in regard to the radio show but such race mimicking, no matter how well-intentioned, was increasingly out of favor

through the 1940s and into the 1950s. When the role of Beulah on *The Beulah Show* was finally taken over by Hattie McDaniel in 1947, Gosden and Correll may have been left as the only white actors of any consequence still impersonating African Americans on radio.

It was during the weekly version of the *Amos 'n' Andy* radio show that the characters made their way to television as was common with many top-rated aural comics including Jack Benny, Fibber McGee and his wife Molly, and Red Skelton. Realizing it would not be remotely acceptable in the late 1940s for white actors to portray blacks on screen, Spencer Williams, Jr., was cast as Andy, Harry (Tim) Moore as Kingfish, and Alvin Childress as Amos. Production began in 1950 and *Amos 'n' Andy* debuted on television in 1951. It aired on the CBS network through 1953 then went into syndication in 1954 where it remained popular until its 1966 shelving. Though the episodes are easily available on bootleg DVDs, the *Amos 'n' Andy* television program has reportedly never been officially broadcast since 1966 nor have licensed copies been released in the video marketplace.

This second aural incarnation of *Amos 'n' Andy* lasted a dozen years, a good run for any radio program by any measure, let alone one that had aired in an alternate format for a decade and a half prior. After six years of sponsorship Rinso released *Amos 'n' Andy* which was promptly picked up by the Rexall drug company until the series' second demise on May 22, 1955. While Amos and Andy would find a third life with the *Amos 'n' Andy Music Hall* from 1954 to 1960, the Amos and Andy of popular imagination really passed on with the end of the second series. For twenty-seven years—through the Great Depression, World War II, and the Korean War—the exploits and joys and trials of Amos Jones, Andrew Brown, and their cast of friends entertained America. Their six-year stint as "glorified disc jockeys" on the

Music Hall was an uneventful coda for two matchless radio careers.

Sources: Cox, *The Great Radio Sitcoms*, pp. 34, 71; Cox, *This Day in Radio History*, p. 152; Dunning pp. 31–36; Ely pp. 203–243; Edmerson pp. 27–32, 34–40, 49; McLeod pp. 147–150, 179–185; numerous recorded programs 1943–1948.

Anderson, Eddie

Edmund Lincoln Anderson, Jr., was born September 18, 1905, in Oakland, CA. A career in show business was perhaps inevitable; his father, "Big" Ed Anderson (Sr.) was a minstrel performer who had spent time with the Richards and Pringle George Minstrels, Howe's Greater London Circus, and Fordham's Medicine Show while his mother, Ella Mae, had worked as a circus tightrope walker before being seriously injured.

Anderson's distinctive sandpaper voice was not an acting gimmick but came from selling newspapers as a child. At the age of 12 he took a job selling the *San Francisco Bulletin* on street corners and to out-do his competition would yell louder than the others. As a result his vocal chords were permanently damaged. There may be some question as to whether he made his voice a little extra raspy on the air; one interviewer claimed that, in fact, his voice was "pleasing, clear, deep" while another acknowledged his out-of-character voice was deeper but still gravelly.

At fourteen Anderson worked in an all-black review and within a few years was on the vaudeville circuit with his brother Cornelius as the Anderson Brothers, a song-and-dance team. By the early 1920s he was touring with an act billed as the Three Black Aces. Throughout the decade Anderson worked any shows he could, primarily singing and dancing but throwing in some humor as his show business sense matured. As the Depression set in during the early 1930s stage work became harder to come by and Anderson began appearing in motion pictures. There's no evidence that he ever appeared on radio until March 28, 1937.

Jack Benny and his troupe were on a cross-country train trip when they met an eccentric Pullman porter they couldn't forget. Upon getting back to work Benny insisted that his scripters write in a character based on this porter for one episode. Anderson won the part and debuted on that Easter broadcast in 1937. Audience reaction was overwhelming and he was written into more episodes. On June 20, 1937, Rochester made his first appearance and thus Anderson would be associated with Jack Benny on radio and television for the next three decades.

To a considerable extent Rochester defined Eddie Anderson's radio work. When he broadcast away from Jack Benny's program he was often still in character and even if he wasn't specifically playing the Rochester role his persona came across as Rochester. On the air the man and the character became virtually inseparable. Several programs survive of Eddie Anderson in character on programs other than Jack Benny's. Some of them are: *The Fred Allen Show* (April 24, 1940, June 16, 1946, and June 8, 1947), *Behind the Mike* (August 24, 1941), *Time to Smile* (June 24, 1942 and June 2, 1943, January 3, 1945), *Command Performance* (#12 May 7, 1942, #41 November 10, 1942, unnumbered episode from May 29, 1947), *The Army Show* (February 14, 1943), *The Camel Comedy Caravan* (June 11, 1943), *Your All-Time Hit Parade* (June 11, 1944), *The Amos 'n' Andy Show* (November 10, 1944, November 6, 1949), *The Elgin Christmas Day Greeting to America* (December 25, 1944), *The Eddie Cantor Show* (May 23, 1945, February 6, 1946, November 28, 1946), *Mail Call* (March 7, 1945), *Atlantic Spotlight* (September 8, 1945), *Pabst Blue Ribbon Town* (October 26, 1945), *Request Performance* (January 20, 1946), *Truth or Consequences* (March 23, 1946), *Teentimers' Inc* (May 25, 1946), *Bill Stern's Sports Newsreel of the Air* (June 7, 1946), *Radio's Biggest Show* (June 18, 1946), *A Day in the Life of Dennis Day* (October 10, 1946), *Santa Claus Parade* (November 22,

1946), *Hollywood Open House* (January 1, 1948), *Community Chest of America* (September 30, 1948), *Opportunity U.S.A.* (May 16, 1949), *Salute to the 1954 Easter Seal Campaign* (1954), and *The Nutrilite Show Starring Dennis Day* (September 26, 1954).

David Goldin, long-time collector of old time radio programs, has identified at least one broadcast from 1943 on the *Treasury Star Parade* in which Anderson had the opportunity to play a straight dramatic role. Coincidentally, that same year he also starred in MGM's *Cabin in the Sky*. While Rochester was not an infrequent guest star along with Jack Benny or a regular from that program, the following broadcasts all feature Eddie Anderson separate from Benny and the regular *Jack Benny Show* cast. However, it is possible that Anderson either appeared in character on many of the programs or acted with Rochester-like mannerisms: *Jubilee* #1 (Recorded October 9, 1942), #21 (recorded April 19, 1943), #39 (recorded August 23, 1943), #48 (recorded October 25, 1943), #49 (recorded November 2, 1943), #59 (recorded January 3, 1944), #63 (recorded January 31, 1944), #75 (recorded April 17, 1944), #99 (aired January 20, 1945), #103 (aired February 5, 1945), #109 (aired March 31, 1945), #111 (recorded December 5, 1944), #124 (recorded March 12, 1945), #129 (recorded April 16, 1945), #157 (recorded November 19, 1945), #160 (recorded November 30, 1945), #206 (aired February 14, 1947), #295 (aired November 1948), *G. I. Journal* #5 (April 14, 1943), #17 (November19,1943), #24 (January 14, 1944), #31 (February 18, 1944), #36 (March 24, 1944), #46 (June 2, 1944), #92 (May 4, 1945), *Command Performance* #67 (May 15, 1943), #73 (recorded 7/3/43), #218 (August 26, 1944), #142 (October 14, 1944), #222 (July 1946), *Treasury Star Parade* #255 (September 12, 1943), *Mail Call* #68 (December 8, 1943), #94 (June 2, 1944), and *Salute to Canada Lee* (October 5, 1941).

While Jack Benny took pains to make sure Anderson was treated fairly and didn't suffer from discrimination in regard to his employment with Benny, when the cast went on a tour of military bases in 1945 Anderson did not accompany them because of the complications his housing would have caused in segregated military facilities. This is a bit puzzling because Benny's long-time manager Irving Fein emphasized that whenever the troupe went on the road they would only stay in hotels where Anderson could stay with them. Perhaps Benny felt in this instance that helping troop morale took priority over a civil rights cause.

The Jack Benny Show cast members Dennis Day and Phil Harris both received their own radio series in 1946, and in 1950 an attempt was made to give Rochester his own program as well. NBC records indicate that Anderson made his television debut on Los Angeles' KTTV on March 8, 1949; the next year there was movement toward creating a solo radio vehicle for Anderson. Per the records of Goldin, four audition episodes were made, some of which are in circulation among collectors. However, neither proposal (*The Rochester Show*, audition dated February 18, 1950, and *The Private Life of Rochester Van Jones*, dated May 12, 1950) was turned into a network broadcast. Estelle Edmerson in her review of early black radio actors claims that rumors swirled that the American Tobacco Company's Lucky Strike cigarettes—the sponsor of *The Jack Benny Show*—had "nixed the deal" for Anderson to receive a program under any other sponsor. When she raised this question with James Fonda, then a CBS program supervisor, he gave no reply.

Even without his own program Eddie Anderson was wildly successful financially, despite Benny's on-air cheapskate reputation for nickel-and-diming his cast members. Anderson had a luxurious home in Los Angeles with a swimming pool and full movie theater in his basement, race horses, a yacht, and, appropriately enough, three servants.

Anderson's unique voice fell permanently silent on February 28, 1977, just over two years after Jack Benny's death.

Sources: NBC records, Library of Congress (hereafter LOC); Balk pp. 146–148; Benny pp. 76–79; Berry & Berry p. 9; Dunning pp. 356; Edmerson pp. 32–34; Fein p. 106; Leff vol. 1 p. 271; Nachman pp. 62–65; Wertheim pp. 155–156; Woll p. 38; *Baltimore Afro-American*, August 19, 1939, p. 11, February 3, 1945, p. 5, August 11, 1945, p. 8, October 6, 1945, p. 10, December 25, 1948, p. 7, March 12, 1977, p. 7; *Los Angeles Times*, May 18, 1950, B1; *New York Amsterdam News*, May 30, 1936, p. 8, April 2, 1938, p. 16, June 8, 1940, p. 1, December 18, 1948, p. 23.

Anderson, Marian

Marian Anderson was born in 1897 to a hard-working but not impoverished Philadelphia family. She played with a toy piano at age two and got her first violin at six. Denied many opportunities to pursue music which were available to whites, Anderson found her talents fostered in the black church community.

Through the 1920s Anderson rehearsed and practiced endlessly while slowly growing her reputation. By the end of the decade her performance fee had tripled from $100 to $300. Her first known radio performance was December 3, 1929, when she appeared on *Around the World with Libby* over WJZ. Further work on the air continued to be rare for some time. During the first half of 1931 manager Arthur Judson was only able to arrange a single radio booking. At the time, biographer Allan Keiller recounts that Anderson even considered a radio career in place of her faltering concert career but opportunities for black classical singers had become scarce as the Depression worsened. A March 6, 1932, broadcast sponsored by Vigoro over a New York area station represents the other known radio appearance during the early 1930s.

By decade's end, as the Depression was easing, radio prospects were looking up for Anderson. Beginning in 1936 she began to perform infrequently on NBC, bringing her voice to the nation. In 1936 Anderson sang over the network on February 2 and then again November 29 on the *RCA Magic Key* program while on tour in Europe. The *General Motors Hour* featured Anderson in March 1937, and a year later NBC brought her back to the *RCA Magic Key* show on April 18, 1937, July 18, 1937, May 29, 1938, and December 11, 1938. Broadcasts picked up in 1939 beginning with guest appearances on NBC's *The Circle* program on February 12 and March 12. The next month proved to be one of her most defining moments when on April 9, 1939—Easter afternoon—she sang before an estimated 75,000 people from the steps of Washington, D.C.'s Lincoln Memorial. Since the beginning of the year Anderson had been connected to controversy surrounding her manager's attempt to book her at D.C.'s Constitution Hall. The Daughters of the American Revolution had steadfastly refused to back down from their denial of permission for Anderson to perform at the Hall despite public protest that reached to the First Lady Eleanor Roosevelt. That Easter day Anderson sang from the Lincoln Memorial, just across the street from the Constitution Hall. The concert, which Mary McLeod Bethune claimed allowed African Americans to make a "triumphant entry into the democratic spirit of American life," was carried over NBC.

Anderson graced the airwaves later in the year, always under less dramatic circumstances than her Easter concert. WOR featured her songs on May 30, 1939, and finally NBC's prestigious *Ford Hour* invited her to appear November 26. For a year and a half *The Baltimore Afro-American* newspaper had been urging readers to write Ford and encourage them to invite Anderson onto their Sunday night *Hour*. Later that year she performed in Springfield, IL, in honor of the premier of *Young Mr. Lincoln*. Demonstrating how far she had come since the 1920s, Anderson earned the handsome sum of $6,000 for singing five numbers at the Springfield engagement. The *Bell Telephone Hour* would be one of Anderson's most popular engagements and she appeared on it at least nearly 37 times between 1942 and 1958 (September 14, 1942, November 2, 1942, January 18, 1943, March 29, 1943, May 3, 1943, July 19, 1943, October 11, 1943, December 13, 1943, April 24, 1944, June 26, 1944, September 11, 1944, November 6, 1944, December 11, 1944, April 9, 1945, August 6, 1945, October 22, 1945, December 10, 1945, March 18, 1946, June 17, 1946, September 23, 1946, November 11, 1946, December 2, 1946, January 6, 1947, March 31, 1947, January 12, 1948, April 12, 1948, November 22, 1948, January 10, 1949, December 5, 1949, March 13, 1950, November 20, 1950, February 5, 1951, April 16, 1951, November 5, 1951, March 10, 1952, August 11, 1952, January 19, 1953, November 2, 1953, and January 18, 1954, and January 3, 1955). Other notable programs on which she sang were *The Ford Sunday Evening Hour* (November 26, 1939, December 24, 1939, and March 31, 1940), *Command Performance* (recorded February 27, 1943), *New World A' Coming* (June 11, 1944), General Motors' *Symphony of the Air* (October 15, 1944), and *Kraft Music Hall* (February 22, 1945).

Radio schedules reveal many additional concerts broadcast by a variety of stations: WJZ—September 29, 1942, May 13, 1944; WEAF (later WNBC and WRCA)—March 21, 1937, March 16, 1940, May 16, 1953, July 25, 1953, January 3, 1955, January 23, 1956, September 10, 1956 (*Tex & Jinx Show*), November 30, 1958 (*Monitor*); WABC (later WCBS)—November 26, 1939, December 24, 1939, April 14, 1940, September 10, 1941 (*Treasury Hour*), September 27, 1945, December 16, 1950, December 10, 1955, June 14, 1956, December 25, 1956; WQXR—November 17, 1942, December 12, 1945, August 8, 1952, June 24, 1953, July 22, 1953, September 1, 1954, April 6, 1955, June 4, 1957; WNYC June 28, 1943, December 10, 1950, June 23, 1952, March 11, 1955, June 18, 1956, January 15, 1957, July 15, 1959; WOR—September 11, 1943.

Sources: LOC; Arsenault pp. 157–164; Cox, *This Day in Radio History*, p. 44; Dunning pp. 155, 655; Grams, *Radio Drama*, p. 358; Keiler; Vehanen; *Baltimore Afro-American*, December 2, 1939, p. 14, July 31, 1943, p. 1; *New York Amsterdam News*, November 27, 1929, p. 11, February 1, 1936, p. 13, December 5, 1936, p. 27, March 27, 1937, p. 9, December 10, 1938, p. 18, March 11, 1939, p. 16, May 27, 1939, p. 21, April 15, 1939, p. 20, June 17, 1939, p. 17; *New York Times*, March 21, 1937, p. X9, November 26, 1939, p. X11, December 24, 1939, p. X11, March 16, 1940, p. 22, April 14, 1940, p. X11, September 10, 1941, p. 46, September 14, 1942, p. 31, September 29, 1942, p. 43; November 2, 1942, p. 37, November 17, 1942, p. 47, January 18, 1943, p. 31, March 29, 1943, p. 31, May 3, 1943, p. 35, June 28, 1943, p. 39, July 19, 1943, p. 31, September 11, 1943, p. 27, October 11, 1943, p. 39, December 13, 1943, p. 39, May 13, 1944, p. 31, April 24, 1944, p. 35, June 26, 1944, p. 31, September 11, 1944, p. 27, December 11, 1944, p. 33, September 27, 1945, p. 41, December 12, 1945, p. 32, September 23, 1946, p. 37, December 2, 1946, p. 51, January 6, 1947, p. 41, March 31, 1947, p. 38, January 12, 1948, p. 38, November 22, 1948, p. 42, January 10, 1949, p. 38, December 5, 1949, p. 42, March 13, 1950, p. 25, November 20, 1950, p. 32, December 10, 1950, p. X16, December 16, 1950, p. 15, February 5, 1951, p. 36, April 16, 1951, p. 39, November 5, 1951, p. 39, March 10, 1952, p. 28, June 23, 1952, p. 27, August 8, 1952, p. 15, August 11, 1952, p. 22, January 19, 1953, p. 30, May 16, 1953, p. 16, June 24, 1953, p. 35, July 22, 1953, p. 35, July 25, 1953, p. 17, November 2, 1953, p. 34, September 1, 1954, p. 37, January 3, 1955, p. 33, March 11, 1955, p. 33, April 6, 1955, p. 41, December 10, 1955, p. 41, January 23, 1956, p. 49, June 14, 1956, p. 67, June 18, 1956, p. 49, September 10, 1956, p. 55, December 25, 1956, p. 39, January 15, 1957, p. 44, June 4, 1957, p. 54, November 30, 1958, p. X11, July 15, 1959, p. 61; *Pittsburgh Courier*, March 12, 1932 p. 7; www.radiogoldindex.com.

Armstrong, Louis

Despite Louis Armstrong's legendary status in the annals of jazz music, he had a relatively minor presence on radio in person. While the playing of his countless recordings over stations nationwide certainly gained him no small amount of fame, Armstrong only performed on radio for relatively short engagements over the years. Because it was very rare for black radio performers—even those of Armstrong's stature—to gain commercial sponsorship, he likely found it more lucrative to tour than to tie himself down to regular broadcasts.

Very possibly Armstrong's first radio experiences came between 1924 and 1928 as a member of **Fletcher Henderson**'s band in New York (where he spent most of the 1920s) which was occasionally broadcast from the Club Alabam and then the Roseland Ballroom. In 1928 his gigs at the Savoy Ballroom with Carroll Dickerson were aired on WCFL. Records indicate some appearances over WPAP (October 30, 1929, and November 6, 1929), New York, before he relocated to Los Angeles where he spent about one year engaged at the city's Cotton Club. These concerts were regularly broadcast over West Coast radio as were those from Chicago's Showboat Club, Armstrong's next stop in 1931, which aired on WIBC. He made at least one further broadcast that year over WSMB, New Orleans, when Armstrong introduced himself to listeners because a white announcer refused to do so.

Armstrong then spent time touring Europe before returning to the United States in 1935 where he was a guest on Walter Winchell's *Shell Gasoline Hour* (October 5, 1935, and October 19, 1935, WEAF). Early 1936 found him playing three times a week over WMCA and at least once (March 12, 1936) on WOR. While booked in Pittsburgh Armstrong made an appearance on WQV's *Club Celebrity* on April 24, 1936. Such broadcasts while on the road were likely common but have not necessarily left much of a record, thus making their documentation very difficult. Perhaps the high point of Armstrong's radio career was a 1937 stint on network radio sponsored by Standard Brands' Fleischmann Yeast while Rudy Valley went on a summer vacation.

Loudly heralded in the press as the first commercial all–African American program on network radio (which is a questionable claim), *The Fleischmann Yeast Hour* (also referred to as *Harlem* during Armstrong's run as host) in fact was panned by critics and many listeners and quietly disappeared after a thirteen-week run. The thirty-minute program over NBC featured Armstrong's music and **Eddie Green** and **Gee Gee James** in various skits. One critic was "inclined to the opinion that the material furnished them could be considerably improved" and claimed Green and James were "hampered by a very poor script" which was written by Octavus Roy Cohen. Guest stars included Billy Baily, tap dancing star, **Amanda Randolph**, and the Four Nuts of Rhythm. Three other documented radio broadcasts by Armstrong during 1937 include May 7 (KECA), July 8 (*The Rudy Vallee Program*), and December 30 (*Kraft Music Hall*). Armstrong had at least one network appearance in 1939 on the October 14 edition of *Camel Caravan*.

Jubilee, a black program created by the Armed Forces Radio Service and distributed to overseas troops, featured Armstrong over a dozen times both during the years of World War II and through the late 1940s while it was still in production. He is credited with appearing on the following episodes: #16 (recorded March 14, 1943), #19 (recorded April 5, 1943), #21 (recorded April 19, 1943), #24 (recorded May 3, 1943), #25 (recorded May 17, 1943), #26 (recorded May 24, 1943), #49 (recorded November 2, 1943), #58 (recorded December 27, 1943, broadcast June 11, 1944), #80 (recorded May 14, 1944), #146 (recorded September 6, 1945), #337 (broadcast August 6, 1949), #339 (broadcast August 20, 1949), #344 (broadcast September 24, 1949), #347 (broadcast October 15, 1949), and the 1947 Christmas broadcast.

Armstrong opened the 1940s with a sustained broadcast on March 29, 1941, called *Song of Your Life* (NBC) followed by a five-month string of weekly broadcasts on WHN from May to September 1941. Though he made numerous guest appearances on radio programs after that throughout the 1940s, he is not known to have had a regular spot on any shows. The wide variety of his guest slots is demonstrated by the following broadcasts, many of which are known today because they were recorded and exist in the collections of old time radio and jazz enthusiasts: *The Norge Program* (1937), *Hot Jazz Excerpts* (January 11, 1939, but possibly December 14, 1938, Blue Network), *The Camel Caravan* (October 14, 1939, NBC), remote broadcast (March 30, 1940, WBBM), *The Pursuit of Happiness* (multiple appearances between October 22, 1939, and May 5, 1940), "The Negro and National Defense" (March 30, 1941); remote broadcast (November 26, 1941, WBBM), *Tune Up America* (March 26, 1942, WGN), *The Jack Benny Program* (May 9, 1943, NBC), *Spotlight Bands* (December 15, 1942, February 3, 1943, July 8, 1943, August 17, 1943, August 21, 1943, December 7, 1943, March 25, 1944, October 26, 1944, and November 1944, Blue Network), *The Chamber Music Society Of Lower Basin Street* (November 7, 1943, Blue Network), *One Night Stand* #186, 187, 188 (January 18, 1944, AFRS), *Million Dollar Band* (March 18, 1944, NBC), *Command Performance* #120 (recorded May 20, 1944, AFRS), *Downbeat* (September 23, 1944, AFRS), remote broadcast (December 11, 1944 WMCA), *Esquire Jazz Concert* (January 17, 1945, Blue Network), *One Night Stand* #485 (January 17, 1945, Blue Network), *Second Annual American Swing Festival* (February 11, 1945, WNEW), remote (February 12, 1945, and February 17, 1945, WNYC), remote broadcasts (July 20, 1946, August 3, 1946, August 10, 1946, WBBM), *This Is Jazz* #12 hosted by Rudi Blesh (April 26, 1947, WOR), *Louis Armstrong and The Original All-Stars* from the Winter Garden Theatre (June 19, 1947, NBC), *The Sealtest Village Store* (September 11, 1947), *My Best Records* (February 15, 1948, WMCA), a remote from Ciro's in Philadelphia (June 5, 1948), *Swingin' at the Savoy* (Summer, 1948, NBC), *Damon Runyon Memorial Concert* (December 11, 1948,

ABC), a remote from New York's Hickory House (1948), *Philco Radio Time* (March 16, 1949, ABC), *The Bing Crosby Show* (March 16, 1949, January 25, 1950, December 27, 1950, January 17, 1951, April 11, 1951, April 25, 1951, May 23, 1951, November 21, 1951, November 28, 1951, CBS), *The Big Show* (December 17, 1950, NBC), *A Salute to Bing Crosby* (January 9, 1951, CBS), *Jazz Saga* (April 21, 1951, WFDR), a remote from the Blue Note in Chicago (July 31, 1953), *Here's To Veterans* #342 (1953), *Basin Street* (1954–1956), *Hear America Swingin'* (August 13, 1954, August 20, 1954, WNBC), *Americana* #21 (March 5, 1955, NBC), *The Freeway Club* (December 1956, KMPC, Los Angeles), and *Parade of Bands* (May 7, 1955, WRCA).

Sources: LOC; Barlow p. 23; Cox, *Music Radio*, pp. 16–51; 67; Dunning pp. 556, 603; Hickerson (2nd ed.) p. 195; Leff vol. 2 p. 58; Lotz & Neuert; MacDonald, *Don't Touch That Dial!*, p. 335; Savage, *Broadcasting Freedom*, p. 161; *Baltimore Afro-American*, December 1, 1928, p. 9; *Chicago Defender*, April 11, 1931, p. 5; *Chicago Tribune*, March 30, 1940, p. 6S, November 26, 1941, p. 16, March 26, 1942, p. 18, July 20, 1946, p. 15, August 3, 1946, p. 6, August 10, 1946, p. 20. *Los Angeles Times*, May 7, 1937, p. 11; *New York Amsterdam News*, October 30, 1929, p. 11, November 6, 1929, p. 11, October 5, 1935, p. 15, October 19, 1935, p. 5, January 4, 1936, p. 5, March 14, 1936, p. 5, April 17, 1937, p. 16, May 15, 1937, p. 19, May 24, 1941, p. 21, November 18, 1944, p. B1, February 10, 1945, p. 4, April 26, 1947, p. 21, February 14, 1948, p. 13, August 7, 1948, p. 9; *New York Times*, December 30, 1937, p. 22, November 21, 1951, p. 25, January 9, 1952, p. 36, August 13, 1954, p. 22, p. 14, May 1, 1955, p. 10X; *Pittsburgh Courier*, September 13, 1930, p. 6, May 2, 1936, p. 16; www.radiogoldindex.com.

Aunt Mandy's Chillun

Aunt Mandy's Chillun was a vehicle for the **Dixie Jubilee Singers** led by **Eva Jessye** that premiered in July 1929, and ran through April 1930. Besides directing the choir Jessye also scripted the continuity, thus becoming one of the first African American women to write for radio. Though containing a good portion of traditional African American music, contemporary accounts indicate the series also contained sketches both of humorous and dramatic natures. The series lasted approximately ten months and spent its entire run on Newark's WOR. Similar to most black programs that included sketches, the settings for *Aunt Mandy's Chillun* were frequently in the south, though it was intended to "depict the life and characteristics of the Negro people in all parts of the United States." Though dialect frequently made black radio critics cringe, one reviewer admitted the dialect for this program was "done with dignity and racial respect."

So far, details of only four episodes have been uncovered, three of which were early in the series' run during late July and early August 1929. One week's sketch dramatized the life of a "Native" family in Oklahoma, descendants of mixed African American and Native American ancestors. The following week was set in Virginia and the week after that in Houston. No storylines were revealed. While the goal of the show clearly was to entertain, Jessye wanted the broadcasts to be informative as well, "thus rais[ing] the status of the Negro in the minds of those who listened." The fourth identified broadcast is from 1930 and presented events at a Georgia camp meeting which included a short sermon on the Prodigal Son by Singers' bass James Brown. Outside of the choir and Eva Jessye, only one cast member of the program, Essie Queen, is known.

By December 1929, there was talk of the Dixie Jubilee Singers appearing on the big screen. Their first film work was in King Vidor's *Hallelujah* (1929) but there's no indication the choir appeared in any motion pictures after 1929. A few months later, in 1930, the Singers released a record on the Columbia Phonograph label. Entitled "Adam and Eve in the Garden," it included a sermon and excerpts from five spirituals, a mainstay of their song repetoire. The group released one more record as Aunt Mandy's Chillun in December 1930, eight months

after going off the air. Again on Columbia, this record featured a sermon on the Prodigal Son, possibly a reworking of the episode outlined above.

Sources: *Baltimore Afro-American*, July 13, 1929, p. 9, August 10, 1929, p. 13, November 30, 1929, p. 9, December 28, 1929, p. 11, April 5, 1930, p. 9, December 6, 1930, p. 9; *New York Amsterdam News*, September 11, 1929, p. 11, November 27, 1929, p. 11.

Aunt Mandy's Kitchen

Details are few, but *Aunt Mandy's Kitchen* is believed to be a follow-up to *Aunt Mandy's Chillun* which went off the air six months earlier. The *Kitchen* program appeared from October to December 1930, on WPAP, New York.

Sources: *New York Amsterdam News*, October 1, 1930, p. 10, November 12, 1930, p. 12, December 10, 1930, p. 10.

Baltimore Achievement Hour

Broadcast over Baltimore's WFBR during 1930, the *Baltimore Achievement Hour* is presumed to have been similar to the *Negro Achievement Hour* aired from New York. The March 23, 1930, episode featured the Sharp Street Memorial M. E. Church choir.

Source: *Baltimore Afro-American*, March 22, 1930, p. 18.

Banneker Radio Club of Maryland

Officially organized in August 1922, the Banneker Radio Club of Maryland was one of the first such organizations in the state. The club's first officers were **Roland Carrington**, president, Clarence Facts, vice-president, Tecumseh Woodland, secretary, Ralph Recktling, treasurer, and John Hebron, chairman executive committee. The organization's purpose was "to stimulate interest in radio and promote the art of radio communication among its members." Throughout 1922 and 1923 the club provided regular news updates to *The Baltimore Afro-American* which they had gleaned from their radio operations. In 1923 the club gave a concert over WEAR in Baltimore consisting of a variety of classical and contemporary songs, then a few months later they celebrated their first anniversary with a concert over that same station.

Sources: *Baltimore Afro-American*, September 1, 1922, p. 11, June 29, 1923, p. 6, August 31, 1923, p. 8.

Basie, William "Count"

William "Count" Basie was a native of New Jersey but came to prominence as part of Kansas City's jazz scene in the early 1930s. He is first known to have taken to the airwaves as part of Benny Moten's band around 1934 when KMBC, Kansas City's small CBS affiliate, aired their concerts from the El Torreon Ballroom three nights a week. During the latter half of the decade Basie's orchestra began to make semi-regular appearances on New York radio including an early run on WABC in the fall of 1937. Two years later the band was still plugging away on local stations like WNEW despite its increasing national fame. While out on tour the Basie Orchestra received radio coverage as evidenced by regular broadcasts over WMAQ and WENR during an extended stay in Chicago in the fall of 1937.

In the late 1930s Basie's reputation was such that he was called to guest on such sponsored network programs as the *Fitch Bandwagon* (October 8, 1939), *We, the People*, *Chamber Music Society of Lower Basin Street*, and Benny Goodman's show. By 1941 he had earned his own weekly spot on WHN but continued to make guest appearances on NBC series such as *Chamber Music Society* (January 27 and May 5), and *Freedom's People* (October 19). Still, one commentator couldn't help but note in 1942 that it seemed strange that Basie, then one of the top swing leaders in the country, continued to be denied his own sponsored spot by the networks or even a regular sustained spot at a plum time. This was an obstacle faced by many premier

African American musicians in the 1940s as their white counter-parts proliferated over the air. Nevertheless, the Count continued to receive irregular invitations to white programs through the decade, notably the *Kate Smith Show* (1943–1946).

Between 1943 and 1949 Count Basie was a guest on approximately 30 episodes of *Jubilee*, an AFRS series transcribed for military listeners. His list of appearances includes: #28 (recorded June 7, 1943), #30 (recorded June 21, 1943), #32 (recorded July 5, 1943), #55 (recorded December 1943), #96 (broadcast December 30, 1944), #97 (broadcast January 4 or 6, 1945), #98 (recorded September 25, 1944), #99 (broadcast January 20, 1945), #112 (recorded December 11, 1944), #140 (recorded July 5, 1945), #141 (recorded July 9, 1945), #142 (recorded July 16, 1945), #143 (recorded July 23, 1945), #147 (recorded September 10, 1945), #148 (recorded September 17, 1945), #149 (recorded September 24, 1945), #150 (recorded October 1, 1945), #206 (broadcast February 14, 1947), #223 (material originally used in #149), #224 (material originally used in #150), #245 (broadcast October 24, 1947), #269 (broadcast April 1949), #270 (broadcast April or May 1949), #287 (broadcast August 20, 1948), #295 (broadcast October 1948), #310 (broadcast January 14, 1949), #329 (broadcast June 11, 1949), and the 1945 and 1948 Christmas episodes.

William Basie continued to appear on radio well into the 1950s, long after the swing craze had passed and jazz had entered the American mainstream but a signature radio series eluded him throughout his career. Later broadcasts included *The Dave Garroway Show* (February 13, 1950), *Stars in Jazz* (July 29 and 31, 1952, August 3 and 5, 1952, and January 1–14, 1953), *All Star Parade of Bands* (December 31, 1953, May 29–July 3, 1954, and June 11, 1955), and numerous episodes of *Monitor* during 1955 and 1957.

Sources: LOC; Cox, *Music Radio*, pp. 16–51;

Dance, *Count Basie*, p. 331; Murray p. 119; Lotz & Neuert; *Chicago Tribune*, November 29, 1936, p. SW7, November 30, 1936, p. 15; *New York Amsterdam News*, October 7, 1939, p. 16, February 15, 1940, p. 20, May 10, 1941, p. 16, January 17, 1942, p. 16; *New York Times*, November 24, 1937, p. 18, July 20, 1939, p. 11, April 22, 1941, p. 42, November 19, 1943, p. 39, March 31, 1944, p. 37, February 1, 1946, p. 30.

Beale Street Nightlife

Beale Street Nightlife was a short-lived quarter-hour sketch on WEAF set in an African American boarding house on Memphis' Beale Street. Airing April 18, 1932, to May 14, 1932, from 11:45 until midnight, the series portrayed "rough and tough Negroes" who, deep down, had "kind and philosophic hearts." The cast appears to have been all black, featuring **Frank Wilson**, **Carlton Moss**, Rose McClendon, and **Georgia Burke**. The **Hall Johnson**'s Choir provided music. Moss wrote several all-black series but records do not indicate he assumed writing chores on this daily (except Sundays) program. A network memo indicates that executives planned on having the series return May 23 but for unknown reasons *Beale Street Nightlife* was never aired again.

Sources: NBC archival material; Sampson, *Swingin' on the Ether Waves*, p. 80; *New York Amsterdam News*, May 4, 1932, p. 9.

Beavers, Louise

Louise Beavers was one of the most prominent African American actresses of Hollywood's Golden Age, 1934's *Imitation of Life* being the crown jewel of her career. She appeared in nearly 200 films from the late 1920s until her death in 1962 and her stature was such that in late 1945 or early 1946 she was appointed to the board of directors of the Screen Actors Guild. Beavers' television career was punctuated by the title role of *Beulah* in the early 1950s. She did make a handful of radio appearances to add to her resume including *The Gulf Screen Guild Theatre* (January 22, 1939), *Family Theatre* (June

17, 1948 and July 22, 1948), and some parts on radio's *Beulah*. In March 1954, Beavers received her own daily radio show, *The Louise Beavers Show*, on KOWL from 11:30 to noon. The series lasted seven months before she was replaced by **Lillian Randolph** when Beavers left Los Angeles to tour.

Sources: Berry and Berry p. 21; Bogle, *Bright Boulevards*, pp. 150–152; Cox, *The Great Radio Sitcoms*, p. 71; Grams, *Radio Drama*, p. 214; Sampson, *Blacks in Black and White*, p. 500; *Los Angeles Sentinel*, January 31, 1946, p. 17, March 20, 1952, p. B2, March 4, 1954, p. 10, October 7, 1954, p. 10; www.radiogoldindex.com.

Benson, Al

Al "Old Swingmaster" Benson made his radio debut as the Reverend Arthur Leaner over Chicago's WGES in 1945. His preaching proved popular enough that he soon was able to sell that broadcast time and expand from fifteen minutes to a full hour. Realizing there was more money in playing popular records than ministering, Leaner became Al Benson on the air and subsequently made a small fortune. Within three years he was selling ten hours of time per day on his broadcasts over three stations, WAAF, WGES, and WJJD.

A generation younger than pioneer **Jack Cooper**, Benson held great appeal to youthful listeners and his shows were among the most popular through the 1950s. He was one of the first disc jockeys to use street slang mixed with a Southern accent on the air, endearing him to his black audience. Like Cooper before him, Benson began farming out his contracted time to "satellite jockeys" who, in turn, eventually made their own names in the radio field. His success during this time parlayed itself into a television program and a record label, Parrot Records. In 1962 Benson had moved to WHFC which was later renamed WVON. Benson's career was winding down by then and he left broadcasting in 1964 after earning millions of dollars over the lifetime of his career.

Sources: Barlow pp. 98–103; Newman pp. 82–85; Passman p. 185; Spaulding pp. 78–82.

Beulah (also The Marlin Hurt and Beulah Show, The Beulah Show, and The New Beulah Show)

The character of Beulah was created by white actor **Marlin Hurt** for a series called *Home Town Unincorporated* which aired over NBC from November 1939, to April 1940. The character then appeared during the summer of 1940 on *Show Boat* over NBC Blue. Four years later writer Don Quinn wrote the Beulah character into *Fibber McGee & Molly* beginning January 1944. She was typical of other black maids and housekeepers who populated many series of the time; jovial, overweight, and deferential to her white employers. With such catchphrases as "Somebody bawl for Beulah?" and "Love that man!" (in the excited black dialect common to most African American characters on network programs), Beulah proved a popular addition to the McGee cast of characters and earned her own series, *The Marlin Hurt and Beulah Show*, beginning as a summer replacement for *Fibber McGee & Molly* in 1945. In August the program switched from NBC to CBS where it ran weekly until Hurt suffered a heart attack and died suddenly on March 21, 1946. The role was picked up by another white man, Bob Corley, but he lasted only six months as Beulah while the show moved to yet another network, ABC.

After Corley's failed run the part of Beulah was given to Academy Award–winning actress **Hattie McDaniel** in 1947. Thus, after several years on the air, the part of Beulah was finally played by a black woman. McDaniel's interpretation of Beulah followed that of the character's creator, a "bubbling, chuckling, ever happy domestic whose good spirits and laughter echo through the whole house." During McDaniel's tenure the show became a daily quarter-hour comedy serial. She played Beulah for four full seasons before becoming ill in the fall of 1951 at which point she was succeeded by **Lillian Randolph**. Lillian's sister, **Amanda Randolph**, took over for the 1952-1953 season and portrayed Beulah for two seasons until the program left the air in 1954.

Despite the rather stereotypical nature of the Beulah character, the program was never as controversial as *Amos 'n' Andy*. While many African Americans may have wanted more positive black characters on the air, at least a number of black actors and actresses (**Louise Beavers, Ruby Dandridge, Roy Glenn, Jester Hairston, Butterfly McQueen,** and **Ernest Whitman** to name some) received parts on the show. Still, times were changing and by mid-century such roles were openly criticized. For one reviewer in 1949 Beulah was little more than "'the old mammy type,' so dear to the hearts of the Dixiecrats, the Ku Klux Klan, and the opponents of decent citizenship for colored Americans." Similarly, by 1951 the army had had enough. Acknowledging the numerous complaints from black servicemen, AFRS director Major William Tarrance removed the program from their broadcasting schedule commenting, "I wondered when somebody would protest that damned program." That same year another commentator complained that "Beulah says yassuh and yassum more revoltingly than anybody on earth."

Sources: Cox, *The Great Radio Sitcoms*, pp. 71–85; Dunning pp. 83–84; Nachman pp. 238–240; Stumpf and Price p. 171; *New York Amsterdam News*, January 31, 1948, p. 13, February 17, 1951, p. 22, August 4, 1951, p. 6; *Pittsburgh Courier*, April 30, 1949, p. 19.

Billy Page's Broadway Syncopaters

Billy Page's Broadway Syncopaters was a jazz group which was broadcasting from Loew's State Theatre over WHN in September 1924.

Source: *Pittsburgh Courier*, October 4, 1924, p. 15.

Black Cameos

Black Cameos debuted on WOR, Newark,

on July 16, 1928, at 8:30 P.M. This program was more than just a musical program, featuring skits of a more serious nature. The storylines revolved around a "southern Negro's Main Street," a gathering spot where men and women from all walks of life could meet. This "Main Street" was on an old Virginia plantation and some of the characters had lived on that plantation since the time of slavery. In what appears to be a direct dig at *Amos 'n' Andy*, *The Baltimore Afro-American* stated that it was "not merely another southern sketch with a Harlem setting." The series' premise was to "portray the folk lore, racial joys and sorrows ... and the music ... of the Negro's life" in stories that were promoted as based on true events. One paper indicates that at least some humor "was promised." As was a part of every African American program from that era, plenty of music was also included with a focus on black folk tunes. *Black Cameos* lasted three months, going off the air after its October 20 broadcast.

Sources: *Baltimore Afro-American*, July 14, 1928, p. 13, August 4, 1928, p. 8; *New York Amsterdam News*, July 11, 1928, p. 8, August 29, 1928, p. 8.

Bordentown Male Quartet

The anonymous foursome who made up the Bordentown Male Quartet performed over a station run by Westinghouse in Newark, as early as May 1922. The quartet consisted of students from the Bordentown Industrial and Manual Training School in Bordentown, NJ.

Source: *Chicago Defender*, May 20, 1922, p. 9.

Bostic, Joe

Writer and director Joe Bostic was a native of Mt. Holly, NJ, but graduated from a Philadelphia high school and then attended Morgan College in Baltimore. Bostic's first radio work was as host of *The Negro Business Hour* from 1932 to 1935 over WCBM, Baltimore. He took care of writing, producing, and announcing chores. From Baltimore he spent a short period in Philadelphia broadcasting over WIP before moving to New York radio. There Bostic produced *Harlem on Parade* over WHN in 1935 and 1936 and *Man About Harlem* over WBNX in 1936. From December 1937 to early 1939 he was the writer and producer for *Tales from Harlem*, a variety-type show which aired first over WMCA and then WNEW. According to biographer George Hiss, Bostic spent the next quarter-century as a radio disc jockey on one station, first WCNW (1939–1942) and then WLIB (1942–1963) after a change of call letters. Through his long radio career he was a big promoter of gospel music. He retired from radio in the early 1970s and died at age 79 in 1988.

Sources: Hiss p. 3; Jaker, et al. p. 55; McNeil pp. 46–47; Southern p. 485; *New York Amsterdam News*, December 11, 1937, p. 1.

Bowers, William

William Bowers, a baritone who started his career with the **Hall Johnson Choir**, sang light classics weekly on WOR in 1934. The station also allowed him to write his own continuity.

Source: *Baltimore Afro-American*, August 25, 1934, p. 9.

Broadice, Annette White

Annette White Broadice, supervisor of music and voice instructor at Jarvis Institute, sang over radio at the Texas state fair in 1925. It is recorded that she was the only African American to sing at the fair that year.

Source: *Chicago Defender*, February 13, 1926, p. 5.

Brown, Euless

Euless Brown was a songwriter, composer, and performer with a decades-long career. Brown was on the radio by 1930, playing piano selections over New York's WEVD. Two years later he was featured on the CBS network as "The Blues Chaser." Some of Brown's original compositions included

"Trice Love," "Love and Romance," "Your Sweetheart," and "My Darling." Outside of music Brown appeared on stage (*The Black King*) and film (MGM's *Hallelujah*) and as a member of the Red Devil Stompers orchestra.

Sources: *New York Amsterdam News*, June 25, 1930, p. 11, July 2, 1930, p. 2, June 29, 1932, p. 7.

Brown, Oscar, Jr.

Oscar Brown, Jr. was born October 10, 1926, in Chicago, the city where he spent most of his life. Brown began acting at age 11 with a group called The Peter Pan Players and did dramatic training with the renowned teacher LaVerne Officer. At 15 he was selected from the Southside Boys' Club to appear on a Blue network juvenile detective serial called *Secret City*. The program ran less than a year from November 1941, to September 1942. As a young man Brown went on to study at the University of Wisconsin and then Lincoln University in Pennsylvania where he majored in English and minored in dramatics. He later studied radio writing and acting at Columbia College of Drama and Speech in Chicago.

Brown's primary radio years were 1946 to 1950 when he starred in four separate series. The first was **Richard Durham**'s debut effort *Democracy—USA*, a weekly dramatization of the lives of notable African Americans over Chicago's WBBM. The next year he joined the cast of another Durham program, *Here Comes Tomorrow*, which is regarded as the first black soap opera and on which he played Chickie. Both series left the air in early 1948. In 1947 Brown started a daily morning radio news program called *Negro Newsfront* on WJJD which focused on stories of interest to the African American community and ran until approximately 1952. Though it started on WJJD, Brown claimed the series ended up on several stations, including WVON and WHFC, because he would get himself kicked off the air. In June 1948, Brown earned starring roles on Dur-

ham's final radio series *Destination Freedom* which, similar to *Democracy—USA*, featured dramatizations of black and white civil rights leaders. *Destination Freedom* lasted until 1950. There is no record of notable radio work by Brown after this time.

Brown is more widely remembered for his post-radio years as a musician and songwriter. In later years he scored the film *Buck White* (1969) featuring Muhammad Ali and did some television work including roles on *Brewster Place* and *Roc*. He passed away at 78 in 2005.

Sources: Cox, *Radio Crime Fighters*, p. 220; Dunning pp. 604–605; Porter and Wojcik; Southern p. 502; Woll p. 36; *Chicago Defender*, January 8, 1949, p. 9, February 19, 1949, p. 22; *New York Times*, May 25, 2004, p. A23, May 31, 2005, p. D8.

Brown Women in White

Brown Women in White was a public affairs program aired over NBC in April 1949. The program dramatized the story of the National Association of Colored Graduate Nurses. *Harlem, USA* creator and producer Jack Caldwell wrote the script and original music was scored by Herman Baron. **Maurice Ellis** and Charles McRae assumed the lead roles while Alma Vessells, Executive Secretary of the Association, was cast in a lead female role.

Source: *New York Amsterdam News*, April 9, 1949, p. 24.

Bryant, Willie

Born in New Orleans and raised in Chicago, Willie Bryant fell in love with show business early and worked for many years with the Whitman Sisters show. He formed a band in 1934 and by the fall they were on the radio over WMCA of the American Broadcasting System. The band soon earned a spot on NBC's WEAF. At the time Bryant was credited with being the first black bandleader to do his own announcing over the NBC network during his broadcasts with the

Harlemanians. Listeners loved their music saying it had "plenty of rhythm" and that they played "beautiful dance music." Bryant and his band debuted on NBC in December 1934, when Chick Webb's orchestra left to go on tour. Slotted on Tuesdays and Thursdays for fifteen minutes they were soon bumped up to thirty minutes. Meanwhile, they continued to air over WHDH and WMCA, and between the three stations Bryant was heard on the radio six days a week. Bryant began providing the vocals on their second broadcast and in January 1935, the Harlemanians began recording with Victor. The group was so popular they received a third spot on NBC in April. By the end of 1935 Bryant and his band were down to just a single broadcast per week, instead favoring a heavier touring schedule.

On February 26, 1944, Bryant appeared on NBC's *Negro Newspaper Week* where he talked about his overseas tour to entertain the troops. Bryant was later a disc jockey over WHOM in the 1950s.

Sources: LOC; Jaker, et al. p. 90; Peterson pp. 202–203; Sampson, *Blacks in Black and White*, p. 505; *New York Amsterdam News*, January 4, 1936, p. 5; *Pittsburgh Courier*, December 1, 1934, p. 9, December 22, 1934, p. 8, January 5, 1935, p. 9, January 12, 1935, p. 8, January 19, 1935, p. 9, January 26, 1935, p. 9, April 13, 1935, p. 8, May 25, 1935, p. 21; Oxford Music Online.

Burdette, Clifford

Clifford Burdette called Atlanta, Georgia, home and studied at Morehouse College but had trouble getting into the field of dramatic arts. He was denied a position with the Federal Theater Project because he was African American so he took a job digging ditches with the WPA instead. Around 1940 Burdette relocated to New York where he quickly got involved with radio. His first effort was a series called *Those Who Made Good*, dramatic profiles of important black Americans aired over WNYC from 1941 to 1942. At the same time Burdette got involved with the theater where his jobs included directing a version of *The Emperor Jones* at the Harlem YWCA. In December 1941, after *Those Who Made Good* proved more popular than WNYC originally expected, Burdette began negotiations with the Mutual Broadcasting System about airing his series to a national audience. The talks didn't pan out and Burdette's series continued to run on WNYC until June 1942.

Soon after *Those Who Made Good* left the air Burdette was back with a new series called *All Men Are Created Equal*, this time over WNEW. Guests who appeared on the show included Leon Ames, Vincent Price, Earl Robinson, Zero Mostel, Benny Baker, Allen Reed, George Jessel, and **Cab Calloway**. This second effort aired through 1942 and into 1943, switching to station WINS in February 1943, while gaining the sponsorship of the National Negro Congress. In July 1943, it was announced that Burdette had accepted a production position with WOR, New York's Mutual Broadcasting Network outlet.

When war came Burdette served in the army and arranged entertainment for the troops. In 1946 he was discharged with a certificate for Meritorious Service and returned to radio where he took the reins of *Freedom Ladder*, a series over WNYC "designed to combat prejudice and discrimination" which featured stars such as **Nat King Cole** and the **Charioteers**. By 1947 he added a second series to his weekly radio duties when he debuted yet another show called *Of Thee We Sing*, a program consisting of music and poetry selections, over WHN. In 1948 Burdette resurrected his original show, *Those Who Made Good*, over WNYC, this time as a variety show.

Sources: *Baltimore Afro-American*, March 6, 1943, p. 8, September 14, 1946, p. 15; *New York Amsterdam News*, June 28, 1941, p. 20, December 27, 1941, p. 16, June 20, 1942, p. 11, February 27, 1943, p. 8, April 3, 1943, p. 8, July 24, 1943, p. 20, June 10, 1944, p. B6, November 2, 1946, p. 6, April 19, 1947, p. 21, June 21, 1947, p. 25, December 4, 1948, p. 25.

Burke, Georgia

There is considerable discrepancy as to when actress Georgia Burke was born. Sources cite dates between February 27, 1878, and February 27, 1894, a considerable discrepancy. No less uncertain is her birthplace. Most sources claim Atlanta, GA, as her hometown while one source claims she came from La Grange, GA, a town about 70 miles southwest of Atlanta. Sources agree that after attending college at Claflin University and New Orleans University, Burke served as a public school teacher for ten years in Wilson City, NC, before heading to New York for a summer course at Columbia University to study music.

While in New York her professional ambitions took a dramatic turn. Though in earlier years Burke had helped with Sunday School productions as well as school plays while teaching, there's no indication she had dreamed of a career on the stage. Nevertheless, during her 1927 New York sojourn she became hooked on show business. She took an interest in theater and by 1928 was singing in the choir of *Blackbirds of 1928*. This led to a variety of stage work before being discovered for radio.

In 1931 Burke was visiting her friend **Edna Thomas**, a fellow stage performer, when **Carlton Moss** stopped by. He heard Burke singing a song that happened to be connected to a play he was rehearsing (whether this was a stage work or his radio series *Careless Love* is not clear) and immediately invited her to try out for a role on his historic all-black series *Careless Love*. She won a spot and went on to feature for eleven months in the Moss production which was broadcast out of the NBC studios. This was the beginning of a radio career that would last through the entire Golden Age of radio.

Radio work during the 1930s was plentiful and included roles on the popular series *The Rise of the Goldbergs* and the *Maxwell House Show Boat* on which she played Aunt Jemima. Other early-30s work included *Maud &*

Cousin Bill, a Booth Tarkington series on NBC, from October 17 to 28, 1932, as well as *John Henry* (on which she played Julia Ann next to leading man **Juano Hernandez**). A virtually unknown program on which Burke starred was *Beale Street Nightlife* which aired nightly (except Sundays) over WEAF at 11:46 during April and May of 1932. This series, set on Memphis's Beale Street, featured Burke along with **Frank Wilson**, Carlton Moss, and Rose McClendon in uplifting scripts that depicted the rougher side of black life in that neighborhood. She also appeared in an episode of the *Theatre Guild* (exact series title unknown) which adapted the 1932 Spencer Tracy film *20,000 Years in Sing Sing*.

Carlton Moss was sufficiently pleased with her work on *Careless Love* to call Burke back on his second series, *Folks from Dixie*, in 1933. Here she played the lead role of Aunt Jenny, a poor woman from Abbeville, GA, who inherited $50,000 and had to contend with not only her own desires for using the money but the needs of her family.

Later in 1933 after *Folks from Dixie* had left the air, Burke had a one-shot appearance on **John B. Kennedy**'s Saturday evening show, sometimes called *The John B. Kennedy Hour* over NBC. The December 9 broadcast featured Burke, along with several other notable black actors and actresses, who took listeners on an aural tour of everyday life in Harlem. By this time Burke was appearing in an average of three programs a week over CBS and NBC. Sometime during 1933-34 she was featured on a program sponsored by the A&P stores. Similarly, she did a year-long stint three times a week for the American Stores Company. The sources for these two radio references are years apart but possibly refer to the same job. In 1935 Burke appeared with **Eva Taylor** on the *Log Cabin* broadcast which began October 2. Two months later she was a guest on General Foods' *Maxwell House Show Boat* (January 2, 1936).

The soap operas would be a source of steady paychecks for many years for Burke. She made her first sudsy appearance on *Betty and Bob* playing Gardenia in 1932. Five years later she made her big break in the genre when she won the part of Leonia, the "Voodoo Woman," on the popular *Ma Perkins*. Her role was a 12-week part which lasted from December 20, 1937, to March 11, 1938. Beginning September 29, 1941, she took the role of Lilly, a maid, on *When a Girl Marries*, a job that would run at least fourteen years. During the mid–40s she also played on *Bright Horizon*. Burke stayed busy enough during the War years that in a 1945 interview she claimed "I have quite a job running from my matinees to radio broadcast. Most of the time, I don't have a chance to get my stage make-up off, and I just run out and grab a cab to the studio."

Burke appeared in an unusual broadcast February 11, 1945, on the *New World A' Comin'* series over WMCA. With **Canada Lee** and Frank Wilson they dramatized the stories of three African Americans who knew Abraham Lincoln in an episode entitled, appropriately enough, "They Knew Lincoln." Burke played a free black who shoots a Confederate soldier, saving the life of the president. She also appeared on the program on March 11, 1945, April 22, 1945, and May 6, 1945.

Even while enjoying a healthy radio career, Burke continued to make steady stage appearances. These included Sada Cowan's *Defiance*, produced by Arch Selwyn (1931), and *Savage Rhythm* in 1932 which also featured **Inez Clough** and **Ernest Whitman**, both of whom would later work on Carlton Moss radio productions. One of her biggest stage roles was in *Mamba's Daughters*, written by Dorothy and DuBose Heyward with music by Jerome Kern. She would star in this show both in New York and on the road for some time, eventually taking over the lead role. In 1950 she appeared alongside a young Ossie Davis in the play *Wisteria Trees*.

Though Burke never made much of a mark in television she had high hopes for the new medium in the mid–40s. In an interview she said "colored artists will have their greatest success in television ... [because] colored people show up much better on the screen than whites." She also admitted that the pay was much better and work "less gruelling" than the stage. By 1945 she had participated in a few experimental broadcasts including one with **Ethel Waters** and Fredi Washington. The only mainstream program with which she has been identified is "The Little Foxes," an episode of NBC's *Hallmark Hall of Fame*. This particular episode aired Sunday, December 16, 1956, and featured Greer Garson and Franchot Tone. Burke filmed at least one motion picture, an adaptation of the long-running *Anna Lucasta*, by Todd-AO studios which also featured Sammy Davis and Eartha Kitt. Among Burke's other accomplishments were a charter membership in the Negro Actors Guild and the Donaldson Award (as third best supporting actress) for her work in *Decision* during the 1943-44 season.

Despite her impressive stage and radio credentials, Burke was always haunted by racism. One particularly painful period occurred while on tour in London where she recalled "Not once, but hundreds of times, I was refused accommodation because of my color. I have had doors slammed in my face and all sorts of insults." She was ready to give up her role with the company and return to New York before an anonymous Londoner stepped up and offered free quarters until the play's run was complete.

Reflecting on her radio career, Burke echoed the sentiment of many other radio performers during the medium's Golden Age: "The work [radio] is so much easier and much better paying. It's the highest paying profession as far as I know. Do you know that I get more money for a fifteen-minute radio broadcast than for one night's work in [the stage play] 'Anna Lucasta'?" Burke's career covered the length of radio's Golden Age, from 1930's *Careless Love* all the way to 1965 when she appeared in perhaps her last radio role. On May 28, 1965, she is credited in the *Theater Five* story "Protective Circle." For a career path that began with a chance run-in with Carlton Moss, to appear on the air along side such legends as Eddie Cantor, Al Jolson, and Rudy Vallee and broadcast across four decades was no small accomplishment.

Sources: LOC; Dunning p. 717; Grams, *Radio Drama*, p. 358; Southern p. 451; Woll pp. 9, 31, 37, 102; *Baltimore Afro-American*, August 15, 1931, p. 9, October 10, 1931, p. 8, January 9, 1932, p. 9, December 16, 1933, p. 18, January 6, 1934, p. 18, October 5, 1935, p. 9, December 25, 1937, p. 11, January 14, 1939, p. 9, February 3, 1940, p. 14, May 25, 1940, p. 14, September 19, 1942, p. 15, December 19, 1942, p. 10, May 6, 1944, p. 6, January 6, 1945, p. 6, May 15, 1948, p. 6, May 17, 1952, p. 6, December 22, 1956, p. 7; *Chicago Defender*, August 22, 1936, p. 6, March 19, 1938, p. 18, December 8, 1956, p. 15; *New York Amsterdam News*, May 4, 1932, p. 9, June 29, 1932, p. 7, December 18, 1937, p. 9, April 30, 1938, p. 16, August 30, 1941, p. 20, February 17, 1945, p. B6, December 30, 1950, p. 22, December 7, 1985, p. 22.

Bush-Washington, Beatrice

Violin teacher Beatrice Bush-Washington played Simonetti's *Romand* and Godrad's *Bercuese* over WCAE February 14, 1925.

Source: *Pittsburgh Courier*, February 14, 1925, p. 4.

Byron, Mayme Calloway

Mayme Byron was a Chattanooga, TN, native and Fisk University graduate who made a career as a dramatic soprano singer, primarily in Europe. She made at least one early radio appearance over the Post-Intelligencer's radio station while performing in Seattle, WA, in April 1922. Her rendition of the Depuis le Jour aria from the opera *Louise* composed by Gustave Charpentier was a hit with listeners.

Sources: *Chicago Defender*, April 29, 1922, p. 5.

The Cabin Door

The *Cabin Door* featured Ethel Park Richardson, a white actress, as Mandy, the lead character of the series which was described by one reviewer as a "dramalogue." Mandy was joined by brother Willie and husband Ezie in impersonations of Southern African American characters. The racial make-up of the cast is not clear though it appears to be primarily Caucasian. Phil Cook, white, appeared as one of the men and it is also possible "Uncle" Don Carney, white, had an early radio role on the program. Evidence suggests the episodes featured Broadway tunes and spirituals built around a general story, such as one that satirized black lodge culture. Broadcast first from New York's WEAF then later on WJZ, *Cabin Door* was picked up by various NBC stations including WRC, Washington, D.C., WCAE, Pittsburgh, and WGY, Schenectady. *Cabin Door* premiered March 22, 1928, and left the air a year later in April 1929. In September 1929, the show was reborn with the same characters (though Ezie became Easy) as *Cabin Nights*. A few episode descriptions survive:

April 12, 1928—While Mandy and the rest of the cast go see a motion picture, her brother, Willie, stays home to baby-sit. He is caught singing the baby to sleep when the movie goers return unexpectedly.

April 19, 1928—Willie's latest escapade to ensure he doesn't get trapped with a job was chronicled this week.

August 13, 1928—Trouble ensues when Willie must find a "sufficiently gorgeous" outfit for his campaign to be elected head of a newly forming lodge, the Esteemed and Contemporous Brothers and sisters of the Grand and Exalted Protective Order of Sunburnt Blondes.

August 20, 1928—Willie's campaign for the post of High Almighty Mystic and Magnified Sunbeam continues.

August 27, 1928—Willie is victorious in his quest for leadership of the lodge. Now he's responsible for directing rehearsals of a play to raise money for the lodge's new treasury.

September 3, 1928—Willie's mule, Is, creates hassles for Willie, Mandy, and Ezie.

Sources: DeLong pp. 108–109, 117–118; *Baltimore Afro-American*, June 9, 1928, p. 9, August 4, 1928, p. 8; *New York Amsterdam News*, March 28, 1928, p. 5, April 11, 1928, p. 10, April 18, 1928, p. 8, June 13, 1928, p. 6, August 8, 1928, p. 8, August 15, 1928, p. 8, August 22, 1928, p. 8, August 29, 1928, p. 8, August 28, 1929, p. 11.

Cabin Nights

Cabin Nights, sponsored by the Ken-Rad (Kentucky Radio) Company out of Owensboro, KY, debuted Monday, September 2, 1929, over NBC's WJZ. It was a half-hour program described as a serial by some sources that brought listeners "musical scenes in a typical Negro cabin." Written by Don Bernard, a program manager with NBC's Chicago Division, it was billed as a sequel of sorts to *Cabin Door*, a program that went on the air in 1928 and featured some of same characters and similar musical selections.

The series focused on three main characters: Willie, a piano player, his sister Mandy, and Mandy's husband Easy. After a stint in New York where he claims to have been "as famous on Broadway as the lights," Willie returns to his sister's Kentucky home for a visit. The visit, it seems, turned into an extended stay which led to numerous conflicts between Mandy and Easy.

Easy was described as "an easygoing, lovable chap" as his name might imply who loved music but was just as passionate about finding a job for his brother-in-law Willie. Every time Easy confronted Willie about his lack of income, Willie would play a top-notch tune and Easy's anger melted away. Easy "forgets the bills ... and joins the melodies." The musical selections varied from "plantation" melodies to brand-new tunes from New York. Rosamond Johnson, musical comedy writer, and concert and radio performer, performed with one of his quartets on occasion on the program. *Cabin*

Nights appears to have run for four months, from September to December 1929.

Ken-Rad, the sponsor of *Cabin Nights*, was a long-time manufacturer of radio tubes. Founded in 1899 as Kentucky Electric Lamp Co., the company produced electric generators, motors, and light bulbs. They turned to radio tubes in 1922 with a sister company called the Ken-Rad Corporation which was combined with the Lamp Co. to form Ken-Rad Tube & Lamp Corp. in 1936. This company lasted less than a decade before selling itself off to General Electric and Westinghouse. In 1993, MPD, Inc., the final descendant of the Kentucky Electric Lamp Co., produced its last vacuum tube.

Sources: Baron; *New York Amsterdam News*, August 28, 1929, p. 11.

Calloway, Cab

Though Cab Calloway began cutting his performing chops in Chicago in the 1920s, his first known radio appearances originated from New York in August 1930, over the NBC network. His band was one of several in a salute to Harlem on *RKO Theatre of the Air* over affiliate WEAF. Calloway's first ongoing radio series premiered in February 1931, and originated from Harlem's famed Cotton Club. His performances were aired twice a week over WJZ and a third time over WEAF. This engagement lasted through July 1931, and then the band left for a short tour, the bread and butter of the era's jazz bands. Upon returning to New York, Calloway's outfit resumed broadcasting on NBC in September and aired three times a week through the end of the year.

On December 29, 1931, Calloway was a guest on the *Lucky Strikes Radio Hour*, making him one of the first African Americans to play on a sponsored show. After a hiatus from the air NBC brought him back in the spring of 1932 for a thrice-weekly routine that lasted through mid-summer when the band again went on tour. After returning to New York in the fall Calloway's orchestra was engaged on WMCA daily in October and within weeks they'd added three slots on NBC on top of their five on WMCA. By the new year they were performing up to ten broadcasts per week between WMCA and NBC. A gruelling six-month tour from March to September 1933, interrupted the orchestra's regular broadcasts but the NBC appearances were resumed three times a week until January 1934. While Calloway and company made at least a small handful of broadcasts in 1934, their prime radio years were over. Calloway's band was an airwaves mainstay through the 1940s but it would only have a couple more long-running steady gigs on one station.

After a short stay on NBC again in January 1935, Calloway's band signed with New York's WOR and were featured regularly from September 1936, through February 1937. During this span they also made their final appearance on Rudy Vallee's Standard Brands-sponsored program (November 5, 1936). Calloway's reputation among African American performers was such that in 1937 he was elected chairman of the executive board of the newly-formed Negro Actors Guild. Beginning July 1941, Calloway starred in a musical quiz program called *Cab Calloway's Quizzicale*, a gig that lasted thirteen months until August 1942. During this run he is also credited with a four-month run on the Blue network as well as the November 23, 1941, episode of *Freedom's People*. Calloway and his orchestra were guests on *Fitch Bandwagon* on February 1, 1942, but regular broadcasts for Calloway became more rare after this time. In the spring of 1943 his orchestra appeared on WJZ twice a week for several weeks and then it was three years of sporadic appearances (including spots on *Time to Smile*, *For the Record*, and *Bill Stern Sports*) before becoming a radio regular again during the second half of 1946.

A handful of these scattered appearances were on the AFRS series *Jubilee* produced for overseas service personnel. They included:

#6 (recorded January 17, 1943), #12 (recorded February 7, 1943), #14 (recorded February 28, 1943), #49 (recorded November 2, 1943), and #65 (recorded February 14, 1944). His domestic performances were spread across the dial on WOR, WJZ, and WABC. At times the broadcasts were his own and at other times he was a guest. By the end of the 1940s his radio appearances, like many black jazz players, had dwindled to occasional spots.

Among his post-war radio work were bookings on *Teentimers' Club* (January 29, August 3, and September 21, 1946), *Bill Stern's Sports Newsreel* of the Air (August 23, 1946), and *King Cole Trio Time* (June 14, 1947). Appearances on NBC's *Monitor* lasted as late as 1957.

Sources: LOC; Calloway and Rollins; Dunning p. 66; Grams p. 112; Hickerson (3rd ed.) p. 72; Lotz and Neuert; *Baltimore Afro-American*, August 23, 1930, p. 9; *Chicago Defender*, September 6, 1930, p. 5; *New York Amsterdam News*, July 22, 1931, p. 7, September 16, 1931, p. 7, December 16, 1931, p. 7, June 9, 1932, p. 7, October 19, 1932, p. 16, November 30, 1932, p. 14, January 11, 1933, p. 16, September 27, 1933, p. 7, November 17, 1934, p. 11, December 18, 1937, p. 18; *New York Times*, August 29, 1930, p. 24, February 9, 1931, p. 27, July 26, 1931, p. XX9, January 4, 1934, p. 15, May 3, 1934, p. 27, September 24, 1936, p. 26, February 11, 1937, p. 32, August 11, 1942, p. 37.

Careless Love

Careless Love represents writer **Carlton Moss'** first dramatic work for radio. It is also likely the first African American radio drama ever aired. The series debuted in November 1930, and ran until May 1932. According to a contemporary newspaper review, "the themes for the sketches were suggested by W. C. Handy's 'blues' and Negro plantation life." The program's moniker likely reflected the classic blues tune of the same name, the melody of which was used by Handy in his song "Loveless Love."

The show opened with an announcer proclaiming "[These are] stories of Negro life in the South—stories of yesterday and today—

simple stories that throb with heart-beat and emotion—the character and feeling of Negro people, written by a Negro pen." *Careless Love* was not reviewed on a regular basis and only scattered references provide insight to its content.

February 16, 1931—"Tinsel Preferred" A young girl gives up her dream of stage stardom to return to her husband toiling away on their farm. Upon discovering he's had to have a leg amputated she returns to the stage.

September 29, 1931—"Big Eddy's Partner" This episode related the story of an African American boy who leaves his family's farm to work on the rough and tumble docks of New Orleans.

April 24, 1932—"Susie's Solitaire" Susie Jackson returns home after working a stint in the large city of Nashville. Trying to distance herself from the provincial townsfolks, Susie rejects her old beau Simon in favor of the flashy "Jelly Roll" Williams, whom she met in Nashville. Williams, however, does not measure up to the vanilla Simon and Susie is rejected by the Nashville bigwig who slaps her, reclaims his diamond ring, and blows town.

Other episodes featured folk-lore and legends, including "Stack-o-Lee," "John Henry," "Hard Trials," "Corn Cob Roll," "The Ghost Wrestlers," "The Fall of the Conjure," "The Ways of Satin," and "Aaron's Conjure Scare." Uplifting stories included the aforementioned "Big Eddy's Partner," "Easter Parade," and "A Son of the Soil." Moss also tried his hand at comedy with "Callie's Santa Clause," "A Good Woman," and "Luke's Courtship." One other episode is identified as "Hard Trials."

Careless Love appeared first over WEAF and later was switched to WJZ. Its broadcast time also fluctuated between 15 and 30 minutes. Over an eighteen-month run it aired nearly every night of the week at some point. Despite these inconsistencies, the series was picked up by NBC's Red Network and broadcast in cities as diverse as Seattle, Houston, New York (its originating city), Council Bluffs, IA, Portland, ME, and Covington, KY.

Across his various radio ventures Moss used many of the same African American performers, most of whom worked with him first on *Careless Love*. These actors and actresses included **Georgia Burke** (whom he discovered while visiting mutual friend **Edna Thomas**), Edna Thomas, singer **Eva Taylor**, **Frank Wilson**, **Wayland Rudd**, **Richard Huey**, **Ernest Whitman**, **Inez Clough**, **Georgette Harvey**, and **Clarence Williams**. The **Southernaires**, a black gospel quartet formed in New York City in December 1930, provided incidental music for much of *Careless Love*'s run.

Sources: Swartz and Reinhehr p. 267; All broadcasting stations identified in various issues of the industry magazine *Radex* between May 1931, and Midsummer, 1932; *Baltimore Afro-American*, November 21, 1931, p. 23; *Chicago Defender*, September 5, 1931, p. 5; *New York Amsterdam News*, November 19, 1930, p. 10; *Pittsburgh Courier*, April 30, 1932, p. A7.

Carpenter, Thelma

Born in 1922, Thelma Carpenter grew up idolizing **Ethel Waters**. She started on children's radio shows and then as a teenager had her own program on WINS during 1938. At the end of that year she won a talent contest on *Tales from Harlem* over WNEW. In 1939 Carpenter began fronting the Teddy Wilson Band, Wilson having just left Benny Goodman's band. She spent a year with Wilson and then another year with Coleman Hawkins before going solo. In 1942 she sang over WMCA's *The 63 Club*, a weekly program featuring only black singers.

Through the 1940s Carpenter was featured on AFRS programs *Jubilee* and *One Night Stand*. Her *Jubilee* credits include #28 (recorded June 7, 1943), #55 (recorded December 1943), #96 (broadcast December 30, 1944), #97 (broadcast January 4 or 6, 1945), #98 (recorded September 25, 1944), #99 (broadcast January 20, 1945), #174 (undated), #206 (broadcast February 14, 1947), and #295 (broadcast October 1948). Though credited by some writers with appearances on Eddie Cantor's network program during the late 1930s and early 1940s, recordings, news reports, and NBC records confirm her first string of appearances was from September 26, 1945, to March 13, 1946, on his *Time to Smile* show when she replaced white singer Nora Martin. Carpenter was dropped after her 26-week contract expired. She later claimed the contract was not renewed because she would not agree to the comic lines the writers wanted to give her, which Carpenter considered degrading. Between 1947 and 1952 she is credited with another four radio spots on *King Cole Trio Time* (January 11, 1947), *Stars & Starters* (August 18, 1950), *The Dave Garroway Show* (March 5, 1951), and *Jazz Arts Concert* (October 4, 1952).

Sources: LOC; Balk p. 142; Dunning p. 224; Gourse pp. 119–123; Lotz and Neuert; Patterson p. 269; *Baltimore Afro-American*, October 13, 1945, p. 10 April 13, 1946, p. 8; *New York Amsterdam News*, December 31, 1938, p. 17, January 7, 1939, p. 17, July 29, 1939, p. 16, October 17, 1942, p. 13, July 13, 1946, p. 17.

Carrington, Roland

Roland Carrington was one of the first African American amateur radio operators in Maryland and among the earliest on the East Coast. He was granted the call sign 3BA (later 3CY) and in 1915 per the office of Radio Inspector, was identified as the only black ham in Baltimore. In a letter at the time he noted there was a black operator in Washington, D.C., and one formerly in Philadelphia who had stopped operating. As of 1916 he was the only African American youth in the entire state of Maryland engaged in amateur radio. As a youth he was a member of the United Colored Boy Scout Troops of Baltimore and very active in promoting interest in radio technology. After growing to young adulthood Carrington had earned his Amateur's First Grade License by

1922, the first African American in Maryland to qualify for such a license. Around the same time he helped organize Baltimore's **Banneker Radio Club**.

Sources: *Baltimore Afro-American*, October 23, 1915, p. 2, November 27, 1915, p. 6, September 1, 1922, p. 11.

Cellar Knights

WABC premiered a weekly comedy skit called *Cellar Knights* in July 1928. Set in the cellar of a New York apartment house, the series focused on the exploits of two janitors, Ham and George. The pair sang and joked in sketches that even the black press considered "highly humorous." Station staff member Bradford Browne was credited with creating and directing the program. It's possible that Ham and George were played by Browne and Al Lewellyn, a comedy duo hired by WABC in 1928 and may be an example of the era's aural blackface shows.

Sources: *Baltimore Afro-American*, July 28, 1928, p. 14; *New York Amsterdam News*, September 18, 1929, p. 11; *Stand By ... On the Air* #5 (undated, ca. 1970).

Chadwick, Sadye-Cochrane

Soprano Sadye-Cochrane Chadwick was featured on several radio broadcasts during a West Coast tour in the winter of 1922-23.

Source: *Chicago Defender*, January 13, 1923, p. 18.

The Charioteers

The Charioteers was one of several African American quartets who got their start on Cincinnati's WLW before getting an opportunity on New York radio. The foursome was originally composed of Howard Daniels, William Williams, John Harewood, and George Leuber; later Harewood and Leuber were replaced by Ira Williams and Edward Jackson. The quartet emerged while the young men were students at Ohio's Wilberforce University in the early 1930s. In the mid–30s they were granted a spot on WLW when the **Southern Singers** left for the greater promises of New York.

After honing their skills for two years on Powel Crosley, Jr.'s, WLW superstation, the Charioteers left for New York in 1935. There the quartet debuted on WOR on the program of Jean Goldkette, their manager. The move paid off and on August 15, 1935, they appeared on Rudy Vallee's hit program. By the end of the year they were a sustaining program on NBC and as 1936 began CBS signed them to a commercial series, a series they held for over a year. The Charioteers racked up over one half dozen appearances on NBC throughout 1937 on both the *Fleischman Yeast Program* and a show sponsored by Firestone Tire and Rubber. During 1939 they appeared four times a week over NBC and three times over the Mutual chain via WOR.

The quartet's popularity endured into the 1940s. They were guests on a dozen episodes of *Jubilee*; #3 (recorded November 5, 1942), #8 (recorded January 28, 1943), #13 (recorded February 21, 1943), #23 (recorded May 10, 1943), #30 (recorded June 21, 1943), #39 (recorded August 23, 1943), #59 (recorded January 3, 1944), #60 (recorded January 10, 1944), #66 (recorded February 21, 1944), #73 (recorded April 3, 1944), #77 (recorded May 1, 1944), and #131 (recorded April 30, 1945). Network records indicate the Charioteers were regulars on *Kraft Music Hall* from October 1, 1942, to August 24, 1944, from November 9, 1944, to June 28, 1945, and from October 4, 1945, through May 9, 1946.

The Charioteers were guests on the *Chesterfield Supper Club* numerous times (July 24, 1945, August 13, 1945, September 6, 1945, June 26, 1946, August 19, 1946, and February 6, 1947), and *The Dave Garroway Show* (July 15, 1948, and November 28, 1948), during the late 1940s. Into the 1950s the quartet could still command guest appearances on programs hosted by Bing Crosby, Jack Smith, and Vaughn Monroe.

Sources: LOC; Cox, *Music Radio*, p. 69; Lotz and Neuert; Patterson p. 269; *Baltimore Afro-American*, September 2, 1933, p. 18, September 14, 1935, p. 9, January 11, 1936, p. 10, January 2, 1937, p. 11, February 14, 1948, February 21, 1948, p. 8.

Chicago South Side Opera Company

The Chicago South Side Opera Company was a small troupe of eight black classical singers, led by **James Mundy** and managed by Mary Maxwell. The Company made at least one broadcast for the Westinghouse Radio Company on March 12, 1922.

Source: *Chicago Defender*, May 27, 1922, p. 4.

Clough, Inez

Inez Clough started her stage career around the turn of the century after a quiet upbringing in Worcester, MA. She spent a season with Isham's Oriental America in the late 1890s then spent ten years performing in England before working with the Cole and Johnson troupe, Williams and Walker, the Lincoln Players, and the Lafayette Players. Clough worked only one known radio series, **Carlton Moss'** *Careless Love*, a black dramatic anthology series that ran from November 1930, to May 1932, on NBC. Clough died in Chicago in 1933.

Sources: Haskins pp. 55–56; Smith and Phelps pp. 112–113; Southern p. 247; *Baltimore Afro-American*, November 21, 1931, p. 23; *Chicago Defender*, April 3, 1920, p. 7; *New York Amsterdam News*, November 29, 1933, p. 1.

Cohen, Cecil

Cecil Cohen, a professor at Howard University's School of Music, teamed with fellow Howard professor Wesley Howard to participate in an aural vaudeville broadcast. The pair had good chemistry and made multiple radio broadcasts by the end of 1922.

Source: *Chicago Defender*, January 6, 1923, p. 19.

Cole, Nat King

Nat King Cole and his trio, which consisted of guitarist Oscar Moore and bassist Wesley Prince, began on radio as the King

Cole Jesters in October 1938, over Hollywood's NBC station. In their early radio years the trio also made numerous appearances on New York's municipal station WNYC in the early 1940s. Cole's radio career is highlighted by an eighteen-month run on NBC between October 1946, and April 1948. While the King Cole Trio was not the first black group to gain a sponsor (Wildroot hair tonic) on network radio (the **Mills Brothers** were sponsored in the early 1930s), it was among the few African American performers to achieve such status. Cole was also featured on the AFRS series *Jubilee* and the long-running *Kraft Music Hall*. During the 1940s Cole made multiple appearances on AFRS's *Jubilee*, including #5 (recorded January 17, 1943), #10 (recorded February 7, 1943), #29 (recorded June 14, 1943), #36 (recorded August 2, 1943), #45 (recorded October 4, 1943), #51 (recorded November 1, 1943), #65 (recorded February 14, 1944), #85 (recorded June 26, 1944), #89 (recorded July 24, 1944), #126 (recorded March 26, 1945), #129 (recorded April 16, 1945), #133 (broadcast September 1, 194 5), #144 (recorded August 3, 1945), #171, #172, #184, #186, #207, #220 (all undated) #256 (broadcast January 16, 1948), #297 (broadcast October 1948), and the 1947 Christmas episode. Over the years his band was credited with appearances on the radio programs of the Andrew Sisters, Jack Smith, and Frank Sinatra as well as *Supper Club* and the *Chamber Music Society of Lower Basin Street*.

Sources: Cox, *Radio Music*, p. 66; Dunning p. 69; MacDonald, *Don't Touch That Dial!*, p. 359; Patterson p. 269; Sampson, *Swingin' on the Ether Waves*, pp. 279, 317; *Chicago Defender*, November 5, 1938, p. 19, December 10, 1938, p. 19, January 17, 1942, p. 20, October 27, 1945, p. 17, November 2, 1946, p. 10; *New York Amsterdam News*, February 10, 1945, p. 11, February 17, 1945, p. B5, February 1, 1947, p. 21.

Colonial Orchestra

Like many bands of the era, the Colonial Orchestra derived its name from its home base of employment, the Colonial Theatre of Portsmouth, VA. When the group broadcast over WTAR, Norfolk, VA, in March 1924, they were reported to be the first black orchestra in the region to play over radio. The orchestra consisted of Edward Gatewood, pianist, W. F. Keeth, cornet and leader, Ed Cuffe, trombone, Prince Robinson, clarinet, and William Savage, drums.

Source: *Norfolk Journal and Guide*, March 15, 1924, p. 4.

Colored Kiddies' Radio Hour (also Colored Kiddies of the Air)

One of the few children's programs aimed at African Americans, the *Colored Kiddies' Hour* aired for at least a year out of Philadelphia from 1932 to 1933. Hosted by Louis Garcia and sponsored by the Lincoln Parisian Tailors, the *Hour* aired over WPEN at various Sunday times between 10:00 in the morning and 1:00 in the afternoon.

Sources: *Philadelphia Tribune*, March 24, 1932, p. 7, March 31, 1932, p. 7, April 7, 1932, p. 7, June 1, 1933, p. 9.

Cooper, Jack

Born in 1888, Jack Cooper entered the workforce at the turn of the century, two decades before radio began growing into a profitable new industry. He worked at race tracks, as a newsboy, porter, and even baseball before entering show business on the black stage. Cooper sang, danced, wrote, and even produced for his own company of actors, the Cooper and Lamar Music Company, which worked the black vaudeville circuit. In 1924 he took a job writing for *The Chicago Defender* and the next year he relocated to Washington, D.C., as a correspondent.

Cooper finagled his way into the studio of radio station WCAP and ended up performing three times a week for five dollars a show. This first radio gig lasted just a year when, tired with the limitations placed on him, Cooper returned to Chicago and possibly took a job with WWAE producing religious fare for the Supreme Liberty Life Insurance Company. He was assisted in this job by Leon Kirkpatrick. Accounts are not clear, but if he was engaged by WWAE the position was short-term and it would be over a year before he got a more permanent position on the air. On November 3, 1929, Cooper's show *The All-Negro Hour* debuted over WGBS. Drawing on his years in vaudeville, Cooper created one of the first black-oriented entertainment programs for the medium. Audiences approved and the series ran weekly until 1935.

Building on the success of *The All-Negro Hour*, Cooper began creating additional shows as early as 1933. His formula was so successful that by 1935 Cooper was responsible for ⅙th of WGBS' broadcasting time. Nevertheless, Cooper biographer Mark Newman emphasizes that the would-be radio mogul could never get programmed on the station's prime time hours. He was consistently relegated to late night and weekend slots. Among his numerous creations in addition to *The All-Negro Hour* during the early to mid–1930s were *The Colored Children's Hour*, *The Defender Newsreel*, *Midnite Accommodation*, *Timely Tunes*, *Midnite Ramble*, and *Nite in Harlem*.

Cooper managed to produce so much programming by using prerecorded music, a gimmick he didn't originate but one that he eventually used to his immense benefit. As early as 1931 he came to the realization that playing so-called race records (which were exempt from the ASCAP ban on playing such recordings) was considerably cheaper than paying live talent. The format was so successful that even his flagship show, *The All-Negro Hour*, cut most of its live singing, skits, and serials (only "Horseradish and Fertilizer" lived on).

Despite Jack Cooper's apparent success as measured by airtime, financial security was elusive as long as he was blocked out of the best broadcasting times. In 1938, fourteen

years after his first radio work and celebrating his 50th birthday, Cooper finally caught a break and had the opportunity to buy mid-afternoon time on WSBC and WHFC. He immediately programmed some new disc jockey shows called *Rugcutter's Special*, *Gloom Chasers*, and *Jump, Jive, and Jam*. Cooper was off and running. A listing of his productions from a 1942 *Chicago Defender* illustrates his proliferation across the airwaves:

SUNDAYS

WSBC: 6:00 A.M. Little Wooden Church, 6:30 A.M. Missing Persons, 7:00 A.M. Mother of Friendship, 7:15 A.M. Gospel Music, 7:30 A.M. Spiritual Varieties, 8:00 A.M. L. Wafford, Arkansas Four, Midwest Wonders, 9:00 P.M. Variety Hour, 11:00 Church of God Apostles.

WEDC: 8:30 A.M. New Optimist Singers, 8:45 A.M. Blue Jay Singers.

MONDAY

WSBC: 2:00 P.M. Blue Monday Jamboree.

TUESDAY

WSBC: 2:00 P.M. Rugcutters Special, 11:00 P.M. Midnite Ramble.

WEDNESDAY

WSBC: 2:00 P.M. Rugcutters Special.

THURSDAY

WSBC: 2:00 P.M. Hot 'N Bothered Music, 11:00 P.M. Defender Newscast, 11:15 P.M. Quiz program, 11:30 P.M. Gospel and Folklore.

FRIDAY

WSBC: 2:00 P.M. Rugcutters Special, 11:00 P.M. Missing Persons, 11:15 P.M. Musical Varieties, 11:30 P.M. Dramatic Guild, 11:45 P.M. Monotones & Music.

In June 1947, he debuted *Wardrobe Derby* on WAAF sponsored by National Credit Clothiers. Participants competed for items of clothing including a complete wardrobe for the grand prize winner. He had two other shows at the time including *Jivin' With Jack*, a daily record program. That year, according to Newman, represented the highpoint of Cooper's radio enterprise whereupon he was weekly selling 40 hours of air time across four stations. Between 1946 and 1952 he produced *Listen Chicago* over WAAF, a public affairs program focused on topics of interest to black listeners. Other series created by Cooper over the years included *Bible Time*, *Know Your Bible*, *Song of Zion*, *Songs By Request*, *Tomp Time*, *Evening Heat Wave*, and *Tips and Tunes with Trudy*. The aforementioned *Missing Persons* claimed to have helped reunite thousands of black families separated during the migrations of the early 20th century. Another, *Your Legal Rights*, offered legal advice to listeners. Cooper was well compensated for his tireless work, pulling in a reported $200,000 per year.

Cooper was responsible for nurturing the radio careers of many other African Americans as early as 1930 including D. S. B. Bellamy, Gertrude Roberts Cooper, Trudy Cooper, Lucky Cordell, Oliver Edwards, William Kinnison, Corkie Lott, Manny Mauldin, Sonny Parker, Eddie Plique, Robert Robertson, and Joseph Robinson. After a career on the air that stretched from 1924, one of the earliest years of commercial radio, across four decades to the early 1960s, Jack Cooper died in 1970.

Sources: Barlow pp. 50–58; Newman, *Entrepreneurs*, pp. 55–77; Passman pp. 78–79; Spaulding pp. 71–78; *Baltimore Afro-American*, March 18, 1933, p. 8, June 28, 1947, p. 6; *Chicago Defender*, January 25, 1930, p. 6, April 12, 1930, p. 7, September 13, 1930, p. 5, March 16, 1935, p. 10, March 21, 1942, p. 19, June 7, 1947, p. 3, March 13, 1948, p. 12, December 29, 1951, p. 15, May 14, 1963, p. 9; *New York Amsterdam News*, February 7, 1948, p. 11.

Correll, Charles

Born in 1890, Charles Correll was the first of three radio superstars who would call Peoria, IL, home. The others were Jim Jordan and Marian (Driscoll) Jordan (born 1896 and 1898 respectively) who would have careers nearly as legendary as Correll's under the monikers Fibber McGee and Molly McGee. Correll developed a love for show business while a high school student when he got a job at a local vaudeville theater. He soon got involved in various talent and stage shows but pursued his acting on the side while he entered the construction business.

When business was slow Correll began performing publicly at movie houses and with small minstrel troupes where he earned his first money as an entertainer. In 1917 he hooked up with a representative of the Joe Bren Theater Company and in 1918 took a job with them as a coach. His career in show business was set. Correll met fellow Bren employee **Freeman Gosden** in 1920; little did either know a brief assignment together would turn into a forty-year partnership that was both professional and personal. During the first few years of the 1920s they worked closely together both onstage and behind stage in administrative positions.

Correll and Gosden made their first tentative forays into radio while working for Bren, appearing first on a Louisiana transmitter in 1920 to publicize a Bren show then, in 1925, over four stations in the Chicago area, KYW, WLS, WEBH, and WQJ. Despite miserable pay (free daily supper but no salary) the pair spent seven months performing various acts over WEBH. After a short sojourn away from Chicago they returned and began broadcasting over the Tribune's WGN as a harmony duo. In addition they did some writing and announcing, skills that would be useful down the road.

Approached by station executives about creating a radio version of the newspaper's serial *The Gumps*, Correll and Gosden countered with an idea about two black men, content with which they were much more familiar. WGN was convinced and *Sam 'n' Henry* debuted January 12, 1926. Two years later they switched to competitor WMAQ for contractual reasons and rechristened their program *Amos 'n' Andy*.

For the next 32 years Correll played Andrew H. Brown, loud-mouthed braggart and owner of the Fresh Air Taxi Company. He also played nearly four dozen other roles over the years according to Elizabeth McLeod's seminal study of the *Amos 'n' Andy* program. Despite Correll's versatility on *Amos 'n' Andy*, outside of guest appearances on various shows in character as Andy there's no record that Correll did any other radio work. Gosden, too, does not appear to have done any radio work outside the *Amos 'n' Andy* characters.

Charles Correll had one acting job left in him after the demise of *Amos 'n' Andy Music Hall* in 1960, voicing an animated television series called *Calvin and the Colonel* with old pal Freeman Gosden. They used the voices of Amos and Andy and the plots were recycled elements of old *Amos 'n' Andy* radio programs. *Calvin and the Colonel* lasted one season (1961-1962) and Correll and Gosden retired from show business afterward. Correll lived the final decade of life quietly in Los Angeles where he enjoyed spending time with old friends and his family (second wife Alyce and four grown children Dorothy, Barbara, Charles, Jr., and Richard) before succumbing to a heart attack in 1972.

Sources: Cox, *The Great Radio Sitcoms*, pp. 45–46; Ely pp. 11–56; McLeod pp. 7–22, 150, 179–181.

The Cotton Pickers

The Cotton Pickers, led by Robert "Bobbie" Lee, was a popular Philadelphia-area jazz band that received significant air play. The ten Pickers were Bobby Lee, pianist and band leader, Charles Lee, bass, Wilbert de Paris, trombone, Sidney de Paris, trumpet, "Coxie" White, trumpet, Herbert Faulkner, banjo, Dick Ward, drummer, Percy Glasscoe, saxophone and clarinet, Andrew Meade, saxophone, and Albert Hughes, saxophone and clarinet. Lee had gotten his start in music playing in Richmond, VA, years before the Cotton Pickers formed. In the early

1920s they earned a Saturday afternoon air slot over WDAR, Philadelphia. By 1924 the Pickers were airing nightly over Wanamakers' station, WOO, also in Philadelphia.

Sources: *Baltimore Afro-American*, January 11, 1924, p. 2, January 25, 1924, p. 5, February 1, 1924, p. 10, May 30, 1924, p. 4.

Crawford, Robert

Robert Crawford was a pioneering African American amateur radio operator in Chicago. While a 17 year-old student at Wendell Phillips High School in Chicago, Crawford built a fully functioning wireless station including a homemade transmitter, receiver, and telegraph key. Crawford was the only black member of the local Wireless Club in 1916.

Source: *Chicago Defender*, January 8, 1916, p. 1.

Cross, Ellen Montague

Ellen Montague Cross was a classical singer who performed on WHN, New York, in the mid–1920s.

Source: *Baltimore Afro-American*, October 9, 1926, p. 5.

Cullen, Countee

Countee Cullen was one of the pillars of the Harlem Renaissance during the 1920s and remains a highly influential black poet. Research does not indicate that he or any of the major Renaissance writers ever made regular appearances on radio, but they did so occasionally either to read their work or discuss literary matters. A small number of broadcasts with Cullen have so far been discovered, most all in New York in 1928, the year he married his first wife, Nina Yolande DuBois.

On March 3, 1928, Cullen read some of his works over WMCA. Three weeks later on March 22, 1928, Cullen appeared on the pioneering *Negro Achievement Hour* over WABC. What he contributed to the programs is not clear. On May 18, 1928, Cullen again read selections from his writings, this time on station WEVD.

Years later on May 22, 1942, Cullen was a guest on Mary Margaret McBride's popular NBC program. Two years later he was involved in a curious radio project which does not appear to have come to fruition and about which little is known. In 1944, just two years before he died unexpectedly, Cullen began work on a series entitled *The Sunny Side of the Street*. Written with Hughes Allison, the scripts were an adaptation of a radio serial written by Leston Huntley and Natalie Johnson.

Sources: LOC; *New York Amsterdam News*, February 29, 1928, p. 5, March 21, 1928, p. 10, May 16, 1928, p. 8; Guide to the Microfilm Edition: Papers of Countee Cullen 1921–1969, retrieved from http://microformguides.gale.com/Data/Download/8350000C.pdf on November 8, 2010.

Daily, Harry

Harry Daily was an early black radio operator from Chicago who was proficient with radio technology after learning the skills while serving in the navy. In 1914, after multiple rejections for government radio jobs due to his race, he applied successfully for a wireless job with the Red Star Line. Daily was subsequently denied the position when he showed up for work and the Atlantic liner discovered he was black, a fact which had not been clarified on the job application.

Source: *Chicago Defender*, October 17, 1914, p. 1.

Dandridge, Dorothy

Dorothy Dandridge was born November 9, 1922, in Cleveland, OH, to a struggling single-mother, **Ruby Dandridge**. Dorothy started entertaining early with sister **Vivian Dandridge** as The Wonder Kids or The Wonder Children. For three years in the late 1920s the sisters toured the South, especially the black churches aligned with the National Baptist Convention. The act's exhausting touring was the family's initiation into the world of show business; Ruby wrote the girls' routines and did her own performances while the girls performed night after night, in good health and bad.

In the early 1930s Dorothy's family (Dorothy, Vivian, Ruby, and Ruby's friend Geneva Williams who the girls called Aunti Ma-ma) moved to Chicago. Finding little opportunity there Ruby soon moved them on to Los Angeles where the girls got bit parts in MGM motion pictures. The Wonder Kids were sporadically resurrected whenever money ran low in the house but by 1934 the act was expanded when Etta Jones joined them and the three became the Dandridge Sisters. All three appear to have made their radio debut over Los Angeles' KNX on an amateur contest. Sister Vivian recalled "there was a great deal of prejudice. We were shocked that we won."

While the Dandridge Sisters were making a name for themselves, Dorothy continued to earn small roles in films such as *Going Places*, *Snow Gets in Your Eyes*, *It Can't Last Forever*, and *A Day at the Races*. The Sisters found enough success that around 1936 they were invited to perform at New York's famed Cotton Club with a small part in **Cab Calloway**'s show. Three years later their fame was such that they were booked in London's Palladium and performed through numerous bombings. The trio finally broke up around 1940 when Vivian married a member of Jimmie Lunceford's band and decided to quit the Dandridge Sisters act. Thereafter Dorothy began to find regular work in Hollywood.

In 1942 Dorothy married Harold Nicholas of the Nicholas Brothers. The marriage quickly went south and in her autobiography she did not look back fondly on it. It was during the 1940s that Dandridge did most of her radio work. Her most notable appearances were on *Beulah* and *The Amos 'n' Andy Show*, both programs her mother worked regularly. She also made a couple appearances on *The Jack Benny Program* in late 1949. Film was to be this Dandridge's route to stardom, the pinnacle of which was reached in the 1950s and included an Oscar nomination for Best Actress in 1954's *Carmen Jones*.

Dorothy Dandridge died September 9, 1965, and her death was never satisfactorily explained. The initial autopsy indicated she died of a blood clot but a few weeks later it was declared that she died from an overdose of anti-depressant medication. A three-person psychiatric team concluded the death had been a "probable accident." Dandridge's legacy continues and her work has been influential with an entirely new generation of African American actresses.

Sources: Bogle, *Dorothy Dandridge*; Dandridge and Conrad; Dunning p. 83; McLeod pp. 145, 184; *Baltimore Afro-American*, April 22, 1939, p. 11, August 30, 1941, p. 13, August 22, 1942, p. 10.

Dandridge, Ruby

Ruby Dandridge's origins are not clear. Some print sources indicate she was born in 1900 or 1904 in Nashville, TN, or Kansas City, KS. Donald Bogle, the authoritative historian of the Dandridges, indicates that her marriage certificate from Cleveland, OH, states 1899 as her year of birth though her grave marker states 1900. Similarly, Bogle is the source of claims that Wichita, KS, was her place of birth.

Christened Ruby Jean Butler, she was born to George Butler and Nellie Simmons. Dandridge liked to claim that her father was a minstrel actor and entertainer but reality may not have been so interesting. It seems that later in life Dandridge liked to embellish her early years, making it difficult to tease out fact from fiction. Bogle concedes it's very possible that Butler was a performer but he was also a janitor and minister. As a child in Wichita she sang and acted when possible and then, in her late teens, moved to Cleveland, OH. There she met and, in 1920, married Cyril Dandridge and eventually bore two girls, **Vivian Dandridge** and **Dorothy Dandridge**, both of whom would follow Ruby into show business.

While living in Cleveland, Dandridge participated in various church performances and recalled attending the Cleveland School of Dramatics for six years, after which she began to win parts in various stock companies. When her daughters were seven (Vivian) and five (Dorothy), Ruby arranged for them to tour southern black churches under the auspices of the National Baptist Convention. Vivian and Dorothy were dubbed The Wonder Kids or sometimes The Wonder Children. Ruby and her partner Geneva Williams (called Aunti Ma-ma by the girls) wrote their scripts, choreographed their skits, and even participated at times. Dorothy recalls touring all over the South before the family "headed northward to Chicago." Finding little opportunity in early 1930s Depression-era Chicago, Ruby, Geneva, and the girls relocated to Los Angeles where she began taking what acting parts she could find. Some of her earliest documented roles were in *Silver Threads*, a romantic drama by Frederick Stower, and *Blessed Lamb* a melodrama set in Harlem featuring an all-black cast. The productions ran in June and September 1935, respectively in L.A. theaters. By 1942 she was still receiving regular roles such as those in *Hit the Deck* (June) and *Nudist* (October).

In an interview with Estelle Edmerson, Dandridge recalled being involved with radio "since its infancy" and that she first worked over the air on a WPA project. Further details of this early work have so far not been uncovered but she did do a lot of stage work with the WPA through the 1930s. It wasn't until 1943 that Dandridge began receiving parts on major radio programs and was able to make a decent career alongside her stage and film work. That year landed her a job with *The Amos 'n' Andy Show*, now a revamped weekly production, on which she would play various parts over the years. She also was cast in the June 28, 1943, episode of *Lux Radio Theatre*. The next year she won the role of Mammy Brown on *The Gallant Heart*, a daily serial that was an attempt by NBC to begin originating soap operas from Hollywood. It ran only during 1944.

Around this same time Dandridge took the part of Geranium, a fat maid on *The Judy Canova Show* which ran nearly uninterrupted from 1943 to 1953. Records indicate Dandridge was cast from January 13, 1945, through September 28, 1953, on the series. One black newspaper, voicing the increasing displeasure at menial roles so many African Americans continued to receive on radio, described Geranium as an "'Uncle Tom' maid." Despite the criticism, Dandridge claimed this was her first contract job and she would be associated with the role for years to come. Another character during these years was that of Ella Rose, part of *The Hoagy Carmichael Show* (also called *Tonight at Hoagy's*) which ran from 1944 to 1946, first on Mutual and then on NBC. The nature of the role is not clear nor is the length of her tenure on this musical variety program.

In 1947 Dandridge earned the role of Oriole on *The Beulah Show* (later *Beulah* and *The New Beulah Show*), her most famous radio role along with that of Geranium. If Oriole, friend of Beulah and maid to the next-door neighbors, wasn't the most prestigious job it was a steady one, keeping her busy the entire length of the series until 1954. When the program left the air she and **Ernest Whitman**, who played Beulah's boyfriend Bill, were the only original cast members still around. Two years after being cast as Oriole she won the part of Raindrop on *The Gene Autry Melody Ranch* soon after Pat Buttram took over writing duties. Yet another servile role, one author described Raindrop as a "Rochester-meets-Aunt Jemima" character. Shrugging off the slight, Dandridge would later simply say that "Negroes are used mostly in comedy, on the radio."

For some time at the end of the 1940s she was regularly working four series: *The Amos 'n' Andy Show*, *The Judy Canova Show*, *Beulah*, and *Melody Ranch*. Through the years she made many appearances on programs such as Bing Crosby's *Philco Radio Time*, *The Red Skelton Show*, *Lux Radio Theater* (March 2, 1941, February 15, 1943, June 28, 1943, October 9, 1944, November 27, 1944, February 19, 1945, May 28, 1945, November 5, 1945), *Eddie Cantor Show* (January 9, 1947), *Mr. Blandings Builds His Dreamhouse* (July 1, 1949), *Screen Guild*, *The Jimmy Durante Show*, *The Spam Show*, *The Olson and Johnson Show*, and *Deep South*. Even though Dandridge kept busy on radio, it's interesting to note that in 1949, while starring as Queenie in a Los Angeles stage version of *Show Boat*, one critic suggested her "sparkling eyes, and excellent acting ability seem lost on the radio."

Dandridge joined countless other radio performers in attempting to transition to television in the early 1950s. She and Ernest Whitman were the only two actors on *Beulah* to be cast in the new video version which was filmed (not aired live) on Stage 5 at Hal Roach studios. Similarly, she was hired as Henrietta Smith on the small screen version of *Amos 'n' Andy*, a show that would quickly become mired in controversy. Like *Beulah*, *Amos 'n' Andy* was shot at the Roach studios.

Despite steady radio and film work throughout the 1940s and into the early 1950s, Dandridge never achieved financial security. In 1954 she became a real estate agent working for Dorothy Foster Real Estate. Newspaper ads regularly played on her radio career with captions such as "Give your listings to Oriole." Dandridge worked in the industry until at least 1960. On the side she made appearances in local L.A. clubs such as in 1956 when she sang and played with the Rythmanians, an ensemble she formed. These small acts seem to be her final contributions to a decades-long show business career.

Both daughters achieved notable success as performers though Dorothy became considerably better known. Dorothy died unexpectedly September 8, 1965, under somewhat mysterious circumstances. Ruby Dandridge lived another 22 years, passing away quietly in a nursing home on October 17, 1987.

Sources: LOC; Billups and Pierce pp. 267, 286, 295, 318, 321, 326, 331, 340; Bogle, *Dorothy Dandridge*, pp. 1–41, 118; Cox, *The Great Radio Sitcoms*, pp. 71, 84; Dandridge and Conrad pp. 12–35; Dunning pp. 83, 276, 321, 377; Edmerson pp. 27–28; George-Warren p. 246; Grams, *Radio Drama*, p. 421; McLeod pp. 142, 148; *Baltimore Afro-American*, October 19, 1946, p. 19, January 17, 1948, p. 11, July 23, 1949, p. 8, August 11, 1951, p. 8, August 18, 1951, p. 8, November 13, 1965, p. 1, September 22, 1984, p. 12; *Los Angeles Sentinel*, March 6, 1947, p. 18, November 5, 1953, p. 5, January 14, 1954, p. B1, March 18, 1954, p. B5, September 9, 1954, p. B8, February 16, 1956, p. 10, December 22, 1960, p. D12, October 29, 1987, p. 1; *Los Angeles Times*, June 9, 1935, p. A11, September 22, 1935, p. A2, June 7, 1942, p. C4, October 13, 1942, p. 14.

Dandridge, Vivian

Vivian Dandridge was the older sister of **Dorothy Dandridge** and first daughter of **Ruby Dandridge**. Though never the prolific radio actress that her mother was, Vivian can claim a few aural credits. The first was a 1934 appearance on Los Angeles station KNX when, as a member of the Dandridge Sisters (with sister Dorothy and friend Etta Jones), they won first place in an amateur contest broadcast. Vivian recalled being "shocked that [they] won." The rest of the decade was successfully spent performing with the Dandridge Sisters before they broke up in 1940. Like her sister, Vivian is credited with supporting roles on *The Amos 'n' Andy Show* and *Beulah*. She passed way in obscurity in 1991.

Sources: Bogle, *Dorothy Dandridge*; Cox, *The Great Radio Sitcoms*, pp. 33, 71; Dandridge and Conrad.

Dean, Viola

Viola Dean is a little-known actress active from the 1930s to 1950s. It appears Dean started in theater in the early 1930s in productions such as *Never No More* (1932), *Brain Sweat* (1934), *Turpentine* (1936), and Orson Welles' *Macbeth* WPA play in 1936. Though primarily a stage actor, Dean made a handful of radio broadcasts through the 1940s. Two were episodes of *Cavalcade of America*, December 25, 1940, ("The Green Pastures" with **Juanita Hall** and **Emory Richardson**) and November 15, 1948 ("The Burning Bush"). She also appeared in a pair of broadcasts of *The Theatre Guild on the Air* (sometimes referred to as *The United States Steel Hour*), March 23, 1947 ("The First Year"), and September 14, 1952 ("The Wisteria Tree). Other broadcasts include a rendition of "Green Pastures" aired over the BBC in 1945 with Emory Richardson, **Juano Hernandez**, and **Amanda Randolph,** and an episode of *The Ford Theatre* also based on "Green Pastures" with **Maurice Ellis**, Emory Richardson, and **Elwood Smith**. Dean's most notable work was on *The Story of Ruby Valentine*, an African American soap opera broadcast over the forty stations of the National Negro Network from 1954 to 1955.

Sources: Grams, *Cavalcade*; Woll pp. 32, 114, 173; *Baltimore Afro-American*, April 25, 1936, p. 10, November 3, 1945, p. 10; *Los Angeles Sentinel*, March 18, 1943, p. A10; *New York Amsterdam News*, April 7, 1934, p. 7, December 28, 1940, p. 5.

Dee, Ruby

Ruby Ann Wallace was born in 1924 in Cleveland, OH, the third child born to her teenage parents. Her father remarried soon after her birth and the family relocated to Harlem, then swinging in the midst of the Harlem Renaissance. From Hunter High School she went on to attend Hunter College where she studied French and Spanish, not seeing much future in an acting career. In 1940, one year into college, Dee auditioned with the American Negro Theatre and won a role in their production of *On Striver's Row*.

Later that year in August, Dee made what is believed to be her first radio appearance in an unidentified skit on New York's WNYC. She indicated at the time that she hoped it would turn into a weekly gig but there's no evidence that occurred. Every year through college she appeared in American Negro Theatre productions (*Starlight* in 1942 and

Three's a Family in 1943) before graduating in 1944. That year she appeared in *Walk Hard* and returned to the air in two episodes of *New World A' Coming*, a series of broadcasts of station WMCA (December 10, December 31) that were based on Roi Ottley's book of the same name published the year before. Dee appeared on further episodes of that series on February 25, 1945, and March 18, 1945.

Dee steadily began working the stage and then motion pictures but the evidence indicates it would be nearly a decade before she returned to radio. In 1954 she was cast in *The Story of Ruby Valentine*, an all-black soap opera featuring **Juanita Hall** and aired over the National Negro Network. Dee was written in as the "vivacious" daughter of the Reverend Rockwell, played by **Emory Richardson**. It's not known how long her role lasted but *Ruby Valentine* left the air in April 1955, so it could have been no longer than a few months. She continued her radio work in June when she received a role on the CBS soap *This Is Nora Drake*. Her role was to last approximately three weeks; sources differ on the character's name, either Claudia Morgan or Florence.

The radio roles Dee won in 1956 and 1957 would be her last documented aural parts for another decade. On February 15, 1956, she appeared in a broadcast of the classic science fiction program *X Minus One*. The script ("The Skulking Permit") was repeated on July 4, 1957, and Dee was again cast. At the end of the year she appeared in an episode of *The Eternal Light*, a program featuring dramatized events from Jewish history. That same month she was featured in an episode of *The CBS Radio Workshop* called "The Big Event." She was cast in another episode of *Radio Workshop* in March 1957, in addition to another broadcast of *The Eternal Light*. In her co-autobiography penned with husband Ossie Davis, Dee makes no mention of these jobs which must pale in significance in her memory next to the *Brown v. Board*

of Education Supreme Court decision, the murder of Emmett Till, and Rosa Park's bus ride, all from the same era.

Old time radio enthusiasts generally consider 1962 as the end of radio drama's Golden Age though a variety of comedic and dramatic program continued to be aired sporadically in the following years. Dee acted in a handful of post–1962 dramatic broadcasts, the first being *The Eternal Light* on April 10, 1966. The episode was titled "Let There Be Light" and dramatized the story of Sol Finestone, a conservationist. Dee acted alongside husband Ossie Davis among others that day. Debuting in 1944, the Sunday morning religious program was considered a "prestige show" by actors of the time. Finally, between 1974 and 1975 Dee was featured in four episodes of *The CBS Radio Mystery Theater*, regarded as the pinnacle of the radio drama revival of the 1970s. She appeared January 13, 1974, March 25, 1974, July 11, 1974 and June 24, 1975. From 1974 through 1978 Dee appeared with her husband on the *Ossie Davis and Ruby Dee Story Hour*. Her work as an actress and activist continues as of this writing.

Sources: Davis and Dee pp. 3–6, 88–98, 452; Grams, *Radio Drama*, pp. 358, 525, 528; Haskins pp. 135–138; Payton and Grams pp. 11, 17, 42, 98; Sampson, *Blacks in Black and White*, pp. 517–518; Segal pp. 13, 96, 97, 114; *Chicago Defender*, September 18, 1954, p. 6; *Jet*, June 9, 1955, p. 62, June 30, 1955, p. 62.

Democracy—USA

African American writer **Richard Durham** made his radio debut with *Democracy—USA*, a weekly feature broadcast over Chicago's WBBM. The fifteen-minute episodes debuted May 4, 1946, and ran almost two years until February 22, 1948. Each production dramatized the life of a prominent African American until about halfway into its run. At that point *Democracy—USA* also began to include the stories of white men and women who worked for black civil rights.

When the series premiered many of the regular cast members were also involved in a local troupe called the Skyloft Players, including Charles Griffin, Dorothy Van Zandt, Thomas Irons, and Margie McClory. Other actors who appeared over the two-year run were Helen Spaulding, Harris Gaines, and **Fred Pinkard**. Hooper White worked as producer and writing was primarily done by Richard Durham though Robert Lucas receives some writing credit in one source. In the fall of 1946 after just six months on the air *Democracy—USA* won a special award for merit from the NAACP. The award was given for the opportunities the show gave black writers and actors and for "informative narratives about the lives of those Negro Americans who are seeking the answer to life's problems and inspiring others to follow in their paths or to hew new trails of achievement." Just a few months later, in March 1947, no less than the president of the United States, Harry Truman, presented the *Chicago Defender* and WBBM with a certificate of merit for their work with the series. *Democracy—USA* was also cited by The Chicago Council Against Racial and Religious Discrimination and at the end of its run by the National Conference of Christians and Jews. Four months after its February 1948, departure from radio Durham's series *Destination Freedom* hit the airwaves and featured several performers and subjects from *Democracy—USA*.

Subjects of the weekly *Democracy—USA* dramatizations included Robert Abbott, founder of *The Chicago Defender*, A. A. Alexander, Emma Clarissa Clement, Col. B. Davis, Jr., **Duke Ellington**, Captain Charles Hall, Dr. Lloyd Hall, Lionel Hampton, **W. C. Handy**, Lucius Harper, Matthew Henson, **Lena Horne**, Langston Hughes, Joe Louis, Pruth McFarlin, Ralph Metcalfe, Dorie Miller, **Paul Robeson**, Rabbi Jacob Weinstein, Dr. Charles Wesley, Walter White, Dr. J. Ernest Wilkins, Jr., Dr. Dan Williams, and Dr. James Yard.

Sources: *Baltimore Afro-American*, May 2, 1953, p. 6; *Chicago Defender*, June 8, 1946, p. 3, 13, October 5, 1946, p. 4, February 22, 1947, p. 14, March 8, 1947, p. 1, May 10, 1947, p. 12, February 14, 1948, p. 2, March 7, 1948, p. 1, 20.

Deppe, Lois

Lois Deppe is widely credited with being one of the first African Americans to appear on radio when he and **Earl Hines** performed on Pittsburgh's KDKA in 1921. Their set included the songs "Isabel" and "For the Last Time Call Me Sweetheart." Years later Deppe sang for the popular Don Redman Orchestra, and in 1932 he received a weekly singing spot on WCAH, Columbus, OH. Deppe appeared in at least one stage production, 1931's *Fast and Furious*.

Source: Balk p. 38; Woll p. 62; *Pittsburgh Courier*, November 26, 1932, p. 16.

Des Moines, Iowa

African American residents of Des Moines, IA, put on an entire radio broadcast July 7, 1922. Two local newspapers, the *Register* and the *Tribune*, directed the events. The broadcast included performances by the YWCA quartet, Regina Crawford, Roberta Maupin, Ophelia Washington, Mabel Atwood, and Joe Brown, an attorney who gave a lecture.

Source: *Chicago Defender*, July 8, 1922, p. 5.

Destination Freedom

Despite a modest, but not insubstantial, run from June 27 (originally scheduled to debut June 20), 1948, to August 13, 1950, and the fact that it was never picked up by one of the national radio chains, *Destination Freedom* remains one of the most prominently remembered African American radio programs during the medium's Golden Age. Radio historian John Dunning attributes this to the discovery of a large stash of the recorded shows around 1980. Now the series is widely circulated and recognized by old time radio enthusiasts.

Destination Freedom aired over Chicago's WMAQ (the same station on which *Amos 'n' Andy* debuted in 1928) on Sunday mornings, a time in which it was guaranteed to attract a meager audience. Originally intended to run for only thirteen weeks, the program was sponsored by the black newspaper *The Chicago Defender*. After that initial sponsorship WMAQ decided to retain the show on a sustaining basis. *Destination Freedom* remained an unsponsored feature until it went off the air except for a short period in early 1950 when the Urban League of Chicago provided some funding.

The brainchild of African American writer **Richard Durham**, *Destination Freedom* was, to an extent, an outgrowth of Durham's earlier effort, *Democracy—USA* (1946–1948), which dramatized the lives of African Americans in various walks of life. Durham's new show began as an effort to dramatize the lives of individuals of African descent. Stories covered both historical (Harriet Tubman, Crispus Attucks) and contemporary (black World War II soldiers, **Lena Horne**) topics. **Fred Pinkard** and **Oscar Brown, Jr.** played many of the male lead characters and **Wezlyn Tilden** and **Janice Kingslow** took many of the female leads during the series' run. They, along with supporting cast members (which included Studs Terkel), were drawn from the W. E. B. Du Bois Theater Guild. Homer Heck and Dick Loughran handled directing duties and Hugh Downs served as the announcer. All three were white. Durham declared in an interview that his goal was to "cut through the false images of black life propagated through the popular arts." He became, in a way, the successor to the fragile line of black-centric radio writers that stretched back to **Carlton Moss**.

Recognition of the series' social importance is not new; even while it was on the air the black community and others lauded the merits of *Destination Freedom*. The South Central Association of Chicago praised it as "one of the finest programs of its kind" and

the Ohio State University called it "vital" and "compelling." Adlai Stevenson, Illinois governor and future Democratic presidential nominee, commemorated the program's first anniversary in 1949. Norman Corwin, one of classic radio's most highly regarded writers, recognized its value.

Controversy was perhaps inevitable for a series that glorified African American history and boldly denounced Jim Crow. WMAQ had final approval of all scripts and not infrequently would require modifications and changes. The American Legion and Knights of Columbus took issue with specific broadcasts. J. Fred MacDonald and William Barlow point out that Durham was at the forefront not only of the developing black civil rights movement but of supporting women's equality and the concept of self-determination for colonized populations of the time, especially in Africa and Asia. Durham wrote 91 scripts which were aired until August 1950. A few further episodes—not penned by Durham—were broadcast through September but they were generic dramas of American history with no connection to African Americans. In the spring of 1951, six months after the program left the air, station WMAQ was awarded second place by *Billboard* magazine in its 13th annual competition for public service promotion due to its work supporting *Destination Freedom*.

Sources: Barlow pp. 83–89; Dunning pp. 196–198; MacDonald, *Richard Durham*, pp. 1–11; *Baltimore Afro-American*, June 26, 1948, p. 6; *Chicago Defender*, June 19, 1948, p. 8, April 7, 1951, p. 21; Interview recording, John Dunning and Richard Durham, January 16, 1983.

Dewey, Ida Mae

Ida Mae Dewey, a contralto singer, left her mark on radio when she played the Creole Lady on *It's From Harlem*. This series was broadcast Friday nights at 8:00 P.M. over New York's WPCH in 1932.

Source: *Baltimore Afro-American*, July 16, 1932, p. 16.

Dextra Male Chorus

The Dextra Male Chorus performed over WJZ in May and June 1925. The group was under the leadership of William Elkins and made numerous concert appearances around New York. Their repertoire was primarily spirituals and jubilee songs.

Sources: *New York Amsterdam News*, May 20, 1925, p. 9, June 17, 1925, p. 10.

Dinah and Dora

Dinah and Dora were a radio comedy pair played by Ann Freeman and **Artie Bell McGinty**, respectively. The scripts revolved around their "affairs of the heart" with boyfriends Lucius White and Spud Johnson, also known as Goldie and Dusty, the Gold Dust Twins (in deference to the sponsoring Gold Dust Corporation). *Dinah and Dora* aired on New York's WEAF for several months in 1930 before they were granted a second weekly spot Friday evenings on WOR in October. The second broadcast was not a repeat of the morning show; both were unique scripts. There is no indication that the series was related to *The Gold Dust Twins* program of the mid–1920s, sponsored by the same company.

Sources: *Baltimore Afro-American*, October 24, 1931, p. 9; *New York Amsterdam News*, October 15, 1930, p. 12, October 22, 1930, p. 4.

Dismond, Geraldyn Hodges

A graduate of the University of Chicago and the Chicago Teachers' College, Geraldyn Dismond went on to work in various capacities at *The Pittsburgh Courier*, *Pittsburgh Guard*, *Baltimore Afro-American*, *Chicago Bee*, *Washington World*, and *Inter-State Tattler*. In 1924 she relocated from Chicago to New York and became generally known as a gossip reporter. There she founded the Geraldyn Dismond Bureau of Specialized Publicity while continuing her reporting. At least one source cites her as the first African American female radio announcer after a stint with New York's WABC in which she

hosted the *Weekly Review of Events*. She was reported to have belonged to various organizations from the Urban League to the Little Art Theatre to the Communist Party.

Source: *Baltimore Afro-American*, February 1, 1930, p. 5.

Dixie Jubilee Singers

The Dixie Jubilee Singers was one of several outfits who performed jubilee songs over the air. This group broadcast as early as January 1925, over WGY. Their popularity was such that in November of that year they reportedly earned ten dollars a minute for a broadcast over WEAF, New York, for the Ambassador's Orchestra program. This performance was aired over a mini-network with nine other stations hooked up to WEAF. The response to this broadcast was so strong that they returned two days later for another broadcast and then again the next day, a Sunday, with the Metropolitan Brass Quartet. The Dixie Jubilee Singers sang "John Saw the Holy Number" and "Stand Steady, Brethren" with the Ambassador's Orchestra and then "Negro Love Song," "All Over This World," and Down Yonder in "Virginia" without accompaniment. The only member known from that time was Alta Melba Brown, soprano. The Singers' director was **Eva Jessye** who went on to have a long and distinguished career directing musical choirs. The Dixie Jubilee Singers were later renamed the Eva Jessye Choir and became radio regulars.

Sources: *Baltimore Afro-American*, January 10, 1925, p. 5, November 7, 1925, p. 4.

Dixie Nightingales

The Dixie Nightingales starred Ona Welsh and sisters Laura and Ida Duncan. With a repertoire made up of a mix of spirituals and pop melodies, the trio got its break over Newark's WOR with a Saturday evening spot in 1932. Before putting the Nightingales together Welsh had moved from Baltimore to Long Island where she then got a part in an unidentified production by Irvin Miller.

Sources: *Baltimore Afro-American*, May 28, 1932, p. 18, July 16, 1932, p. 16.

Dixie Stompers

The Dixie Stompers was a five-member band who received air time over Philadelphia's WDAS in 1933. The Stompers could not be considered a traditional jazz band; along with Eddie Braford on piano, Creed Bogan on jazz horn, and George (Bud) Fisher on guitar, they featured Teddy Abel on the banjo and Bill Brown on the washboard. Brown was noted for his **Louis Armstrong**-esque vocals.

Source: *Baltimore Afro-American*, April 15, 1933, p. 8.

Duncan, Earl

Along with **Leon Abbey**, Earl Duncan was one of two African American radio operators who had membership in a Minneapolis-area wireless club in 1915.

Source: *Chicago Defender*, September 25, 1915, p. 5.

Durham, Richard

Richard Durham was born in Raymond, MS, on September 6, 1917, but he spent most of his childhood in Chicago. One source claims he studied first at Wilberforce and Central YMCA College before attending Northwestern University in suburban Chicago where he participated in the first NBC-Northwestern University summer radio institute in 1942. Some of Durham's earliest writing work came as a dramatist with the WPA's Writers Project and as national editor for the black newspaper *The Chicago Defender*.

Durham's first known radio work was a weekly series entitled *Democracy—USA*, aired on Chicago's WBBM beginning May 4, 1946. It was a fifteen-minute series of Sunday morning broadcasts that dramatized the life of prominent African Americans.

Sixteen months later in September 1947, while *Democracy—USA* was still on the air, Durham's second effort, *Here Comes Tomorrow*, premiered on WJJD. Considered the first black soap opera, this story followed the Redmond family and their son, Milton, who returned with amnesia after fighting in Italy during World War II. Both *Democracy—USA* and *Here Comes Tomorrow* went off the air in the spring of 1948.

Destination Freedom, Richard Durham's most enduring radio legacy, debuted June 27, 1948, over Chicago station WMAQ. The basic premise of *Destination Freedom*, dramatizing the lives of individuals of African descent and prominent events in black history, was an extension of his original work *Democracy—USA*. *Destination Freedom* ran for two years, a decent run for a program that never attracted a commercial sponsor, was not picked up by a network, and focused on the interests of African Americans. In 1956, six years after the program left the air, Durham filed suit against NBC for $250,000 claiming the network had continued to air episodes in the years since despite his claims to all copyrights concerning the show.

The extent of Durham's post–WMAQ writing is not clear. In a 1983 interview with John Dunning, Durham recalled leaving *Destination Freedom* to work on the Irna Phillips show *What's New?* starring Don Ameci. According to Durham, the pay differential between the sustained *Destination Freedom* and a sponsored Phillips work was too much to pass up. He also commented in the same interview that frequently his name was not associated with scripts in order to avoid causing problems with Southern sponsors. One other known Durham script was the August 31, 1957, episode of *CBS Radio Workshop* which featured a story concerning Denmark Vesey, a slave who led an uprising in 1821. Vesey had been the subject of *Destination Freedom* on its July 18, 1948, broadcast.

During the 1950s Durham worked for the

Packinghouse Workers' Union doing publicity and in 1958 served as the press agent for GOP Congressional candidate Dr. T. R. Howard. He followed these jobs with an editorship at *Muhammad Speaks* through most of the 1960s. In 1969, while he continued to work for *Muhammad Speaks*, Durham returned to writing for the electronic media. He was hired to script *Bird of the Iron Feather* (originally called *More from My Life*), an African American soap opera set in the Chicago ghetto that was broadcast over WTTW, Chicago's public television station, beginning in January 1970. Bill Quinn, assistant writer at *Playboy*, worked as an associate writer on the project. The effort lasted just seven weeks before going off the air due to a premature and unexplained disappearance of funds. In the late 1970s Durham worked with Mohammad Ali on the boxer's autobiography which was released in 1977. Richard Durham passed away April 27, 1984, and was inducted into the National Radio Hall of Fame in August 2007.

Sources: Barlow pp. 83–89; Dunning pp. 196–198; MacDonald, *Richard Durham*, pp. 2–3, 9; *Chicago Defender*, June 19, 1948, p. 8, October 15, 1956, p. 18, August 5, 1969, p. 10, August 29, 1957, p. 19, October 21, 1958, p. 8, February 14, 1966, p. 10, January 12, 1970, p. 11, February 26, 1970, p. 4, October 13, 1975, p. 26; Richard Durham Papers, 1939–1999 online finding aid, Chicago Public Library www.chipublib.org accessed July 23, 2010; Interview recording, John Dunning and Richard Durham, January 16, 1983.

Echoes of Harlem

In February 1938, station WBNX premiered a daily program called *Echoes of Harlem*, a half-hour human interest program. A significant portion of the show was dedicated to Harlem social activities such as weddings, birthdays, and club happenings. Arthur Knight served as director and announcer. The series was cut to twice a week in March then returned to nightly in April. *Echoes of Harlem* left the air in May after a four-month run.

Sources: *New York Amsterdam News*, February 5, 1938, p. 7, February 26, 1938, p. 17, March 12, 1938, p. 17, April 9, 1938, p. 21.

Edmondson, William

William Edmondson was one of the four founding members of the **Southernaires** quartet and the only original member still singing with the group when it disbanded in the early 1950s. Born October 15, 1902, in Spokane, WA, details of Edmondson's life are unknown until he reached college, presumably in the early 1920s. He studied at Spokane College, a Northwest Norwegian Lutheran institution that closed its doors in 1929.

After leaving Spokane College, Edmondson joined touring troupes in 1923 and spent much of the decade honing his singing and acting skills before settling in Harlem at the end of the decade as the Harlem Renaissance was winding down. There he got involved with the Lafayette Players, a notable black theater troupe which was based out of the Lafayette Theater. Around the same time he appeared in two films by Oscar Micheaux, regarded as the first African American producer of feature-length films. Edmondson's film credits under Micheaux include *The Millionaire* (1927) and *Thirty Years Later* (1928). He also appeared in *The Midnight Ace* (1928), the only production by Oscar Micheaux's brother, Swain Micheaux.

The seeds of the Southernaires quartet, the band with which Edmondson would perform for over two decades, were sewn years before the group's formation when the members' paths crossed while singing on the college circuit and while working in Harlem's black theater industry. Edmondson's connection came when working a production with future Southernaire **Lowell Peters**. Peters, incidentally, had earlier met future quartetmate **Homer Smith** while on a college vocal tour. In late 1929 Edmondson ran into Smith in front of the Lafayette Theater, a prominent Harlem theater which staged all-black productions for black audiences to mixed success. The two shared their ideas of forming a musical quartet. The aforementioned Lowell Peters was invited to join as was **Jay Stone Toney**, Smith's roommate.

In December 1929, Smith (tenor), Peters (tenor), Toney (baritone), and Edmondson (bass) locked themselves away for three months, forsaking all other responsibilities to rehearse and hone their vocal teamwork. Emerging from their practices in the basement of the Williams Institutional C.M.E. Church in Harlem, the quartet almost immediately landed a slot on radio. After a couple live concerts they hit the airwaves on WMCA's *Goodwin's Goodtimers* in February 1930. Over the next few months they also appeared on WRNY, WGBS, WOR, and most importantly WEAF, NBC Red's New York affiliate. Their relationship with NBC and then ABC after the Blue network was sold off, would last into the early 1950s.

During their first three years on the air the Southernaires appeared at different times on *RKO Theatre of the Air*, Major Bowe's *Capitol Family*, *Visits with Uncle Ben in His Cabin*, *Slow River*, *Harlem Fantasy*, *The New Molle Show*, and *Rocking Chair Memories*, along with various slots under their own name. The Southernaires also provided the music for three programs written by **Carlton Moss**, radio's first black drama writer. These Moss productions were *Careless Love*, *Folks From Dixie*, and *Meetin' House* which aired between 1930 and 1936.

The Southernaires' Sunday morning gospel show, originally entitled *Southland Sketches* and later simply taking the quartet's name, was their core broadcast, the showcase for their gospel harmonies for which they were so fondly remembered. After their fame had subsided somewhat and the group was no longer in multiple programs every week, they held on to their Sabbath slot against all comers.

Despite the Southernaires' success, Edmondson did not give up all acting aspira-

tions. In 1933, when the Southernaires won a spot providing music for *The New Molle Show* which aired Mondays, Wednesdays, and Thursdays over WEAF, Edmondson earned an additional role as the show's master of ceremonies. He was also chosen to present a feature on the show entitled "The Comic Side of the News." A year later the Southernaires provided music for a short **Ethel Waters** film called *Bubbling Over*. Edmondson won a small acting part in the picture.

In addition to song and comedy Edmondson tried his hand at dramatic roles. The first such documented role was on an episode of NBC's *Magic Key*, a series relayed to over 100 stations. The particular episode was "David the Giant Killer," aired June 5, 1938, and was based on the biblical story of David and Goliath. The broadcast featured William Edmondson as Jonathan as well as fellow Southernaire Homer Smith as David along with Pauline Palmer, **Frank Wilson**, and **Juano Hernandez**. A few days later on June 23, Edmondson once again received a prime time role on a broadcast called "In Abraham's Bosom" broadcast over the Blue network. The program was directed by James Church and featured music by the Southernaires and the **Juanita Hall** choir. The script was based on a Pulitzer Prize-winning play from the mid–1920s.

"In Abraham's Bosom" is the story of Abe McCranie, an African American man bent on providing educations to black boys in the oppressive environment of the Reconstruction-era South. The radio play was cast entirely by members of the Negro Actors' Guild of America, three of whom were also members of the Southernaires. William Edmondson was cast as Bud Gaskins, Homer Smith as Puny Avery, and Jay Stone Toney as Douglass McCranie. Their parts were minor and critics called their performances "creditable." Such an underwhelming response perhaps explains why they were not featured in more future dramatic productions.

Despite these forays, singing remained the

focus of Edmondson's career through the 1930s, 1940s, and into the early 1950s. As membership turned over, Edmondson slowly became the center of the Southernaires. In 1940 the group's accompanist and arranger, **Clarence Jones**, fell ill and was replaced by **Spencer Odom**. In 1942 Homer Smith was drafted into the Coast Guard and would forge a separate musical career after leaving the armed forces. His replacement was **Ray Yeates**, an old friend of Edmondson's from their days on the stage's *Blackbirds of 1928*. In 1948 Jay Toney died of a heart attack while the band was touring in Iowa. He was soon replaced with **William Franklin**, a graduate of the Chicago Conservatory of Music.

The Southernaires sang on, finishing out the decade on radio and on tour before being ignominiously dropped by the networks in 1950. In 1951 the Southernaires returned briefly to the airwaves, by now featuring only William Edmondson of the four founding members. The new program dropped their tried-and-true spirituals and reworked their repertoire with popular ballads and more modern tunes. The final works of the quartet were a 1952 radio appearance and a record released in 1953 on Rudder Records featuring the songs "Baby What You're Doing to Me" and "For You, for You, for You."

There is no evidence at this time that Edmondson continued to pursue music after the final incarnation of the Southernaires faded from the musical scene. He pursued at least one dramatic radio project entitled *Opportunity Unlimited*. Broadcast around New York state in 1953, the show was a series of scripts dramatizing episodes of African American employment discrimination. In 1954 he worked a few months as a disc jockey over station WLIB. Beyond these radio efforts, Edmondson resumed his acting career, this time on the small screen, making the first of a string of television appearances on an episode of a New York police show called *The Naked City*. He went on to make scattered appearances on such television classics as *Richard Diamond, Private Detective*, *The Twilight Zone*, and *Bonanza*. He seems to have closed out a ten-year television run at the age of 66 with an appearance on a 1968 episode of *The Flying Nun*. William Edmondson passed away on May 28, 1979, in Los Angeles.

Sources: Bowser, Gaines and Musser; Funk and Grendysa; Sampson, *Blacks in Black and White*, p. 519; Wintz; *New York Amsterdam News*, September 26, 1953, p. 17, November 27, 1954, p. 1; Internet Movie Database.

Ellington, Duke

Duke Ellington, perhaps the most famous jazz performer of his time, was a pioneer on radio and had a consistent presence on the air from the 1920s into the early 1950s. Ellington's first known radio appearance was on a small New York station WDT on August 25, 1923, on which his band shared time with singers **Trixie Smith** and Rosa Henderson. The two were accompanied by Fats Waller and **Fletcher Henderson**, both of whom would make their own name in the music industry. Ellington's next documented broadcasts were during January 1927, over WHN while his band was booked at New York's Kentucky Club, a venue they would play steadily for a few years. Ellington's broadcasts from the Kentucky Club over WHN lasted well into 1929 three or four times a week.

In the summer of 1929 Ellington was broadcasting over WABC three times a week, a schedule that was reduced to once weekly by October. His band aired over the station intermittently until February 1930, either once or twice a week. Off the air during the spring, Ellington was picked up again by WABC two nights a week at midnight through the summer of 1930. One of his first network pick-ups—if not the first—began in September 1930, originating in WEAF and distributed via NBC. Weekly to start, the broadcasts were increased to three times a week split between WEAF and WJZ.

While touring outside New York, Ellington would at times get engagements over an out-of-town station if the band was booked into a long-term gig. Such was the case during the summer of 1931 when *The Chicago Tribune's* station WGN regularly broadcast their concerts from the city's Lincoln Tavern. After a three-times-weekly program over NBC during spring 1932 the band returned to Chicago in the summer of 1932 for another series of concerts and broadcasts over WGN. The rest of the year was quiet, however, outside a few appearances on WABC leading one commentator to complain in early 1933 that Ellington needs to "return to the air before he is completely forgotten."

Though it appears that Ellington did not have a regular series during the mid–1930s, it's very likely that his outfit aired locally while on their many tours. For example, while playing engagements at Cincinnati's Castle Farms on July 23 and 29, Powel Crosley, Jr.'s WLW aired both 1934 performances. Similarly, when they played an early January 1936, concert from Chicago's Hotel Sherman it was picked up by the CBS network. From December 1936, until January 1937, the band headed West and was on the air multiple times a week on stations KFAC and KHJ in Los Angeles. It was back to New York when that booking was done for a string of weekly broadcasts over WOR.

Though Ellington was not a stranger to the airwaves, the next three years seemed to consist of one-shot performances or very short stints. Notable network appearances during the late 1930s and early 1940s included *RKO's Theatre of the Air* (October 24, 1939), *Quaker Party* (February 26, 1940), and *Kraft Music Hall* (January 16, 1941, May 29, 1941, and October 9, 1941). Chicago's Hotel Sherman again hosted the band in September 1940, concerts which were subsequently sent to a weekly NBC hook-up. Through October Ellington also was featured more often on the city's WMAQ and WENR in addition to the NBC spot. The

early years of the 1940s provided prolific broadcasting opportunities for the band; four spots a week on WNEW and WHN during the summer of 1941 and then a daily program from July to August on WENR in 1942. A weekly slot on Chicago's WCFL rounded out the busy year. Four months later in April 1943, he started a series of six-times-a-week broadcasts from the Hurricane over WOR, the number of which was down to once a week by May but the series ran until September. Despite gaps between extended series runs, Ellington received plenty of air time as suggested by a sample week from July 1943: WEVD (July 24, 29, 31), WMCA (July 24), WBYN (July 27), WWRL (July 28 and July 30). Though his broadcasting schedule was not so full week in and week out, such a routine was not uncommon. The band closed 1943 with regular appearances on WWRL and WBNX. For six months in 1944, from January until July, he was a regular guest on CBS' *Orson Welles Almanac.*

While World War II wound down Ellington and his band continued to grace the airwaves with one-shot guest appearances (*Bill Stern Sports, Music America Loves Best,* and *Kraft Music Hall*), and with an ongoing series, *A Date with the Duke,* on the ABC network from March 1945, until January of the following year. The series was restarted in April 1946, for another run until September. WCFL, the Chicago station which had hosted prior series of Ellington's music, welcomed him back for a weekly stint in December 1946, and January 1947. Nearly a year later his longest running program, simply called *The Duke Ellington Show,* premiered December 29, 1947, on WMCA. Initially the program was daily (except Sundays) though the Saturday broadcast was dropped by the summer of 1948. In total the show ran for eighteen months until April 1949. Even by the century's mid-point and after a quarter-century of broadcasting, Ellington continued to entertain the radio audience with a series of weekly concerts in July and August 1951.

Jubilee, a series recorded by the Armed Forces Radio Service and beamed to overseas soldiers, featured Ellington as a guest throughout its entire run, from its debut in 1942 until 1950, close to its demise. He is credited with appearances in the following episodes: #1 (recorded October 9, 1942), #49 (recorded November 2, 1942), #69 (recorded March 11, 1944), #117 (broadcast May 26, 1945), #314 (broadcast March 5, 1949), #315 (broadcast March 12, 1949), #317 (March 26, 1949), #320 (broadcast April 9. 1949), #323 (broadcast April 29, 1949), #336 (broadcast July 30, 1949), #342 (broadcast September 10, 1949), #349 (broadcast October 29, 1949), #352 (broadcast November 19, 1949), #356 (broadcast December 17, 1949), #360 (broadcast January 14, 1950), #361 (broadcast January 21, 1950), Christmas 1947.

Ellington and band had at least two regular broadcasts during the 1950s. The first was a series of concerts from Chicago's Blue Note club between July 30 and August 19, 1952, and then from June 12 to June 26, 1953, on an NBC program called *Music for Mothers*. As late as 1956 and 1957 Ellington performed regularly on the *Monitor* program.

Sources: LOC; Balk pp. 58, 210; Cox, *Music Radio*, pp. 16–51; Dunning pp. 66, 72, 91, 525; Hickerson (3rd ed.) pp. 115, 134; Lawrence pp. 34, 409; Lotz and Neuert; Savage pp. 138, 161; *Chicago Tribune*, May 24, 1931, p. G6, May 15, 1932, p. G8, September 1, 1940, p. NW4, October 9, 1940, p. 21; *New York Amsterdam News*, January 23, 1929, p. 10, January 30, 1929, p. 10, February 20, 1929, February 27, 1929, p. 9, March 6, 1929, p. 9, March 27, 1929, p. 10, April 3, 1929, p. 10, April 10, 1929, p. 11, April 17, 1929, p. 11, June 5, 1929, p. 11, October 2, 1929, p. 11, November 20, 1929, p. 11, January 1, 1930, p. 11, February 5, 1930, p. 11, May 21, 1930, p. 10, June 4, 1930, p. 12, September 24, 1930, p. 10, October 29, 1930, p. 12, February 10, 1932, p. 9, April 6, 1932, p. 9, January 11, 1933, p. 16, July 21, 1934, p. 6, January 11, 1936, p. 15, March 27, 1937, p. 10, July 5, 1941, p. 21, April 10, 1943, p. 16, May 29, 1943, p. 8; *New York Times*, December 18, 1940, p. 50, September 4, 1943, p. 18, July 24, 1943, p. 25, July 27, 1943, p. 35, July 28, 1943, p. 35, July 29, 1943, p. 35, July 30, 1943, p. 31, July 31, 1943, p. 25; www.fatswaller.org.

Ellis, Bernice

Bernice Ellis was a St. Louis native who finished her education at the Lincoln Institute in Jefferson City, MO. After graduating from the Institute she taught in the Chandler, OK, public schools for four years. During her summer breaks Ellis began singing publicly. She is believed to be one of radio's first black performers, singing over a Fort Smith, AR, station in 1921. In November 1923, Ellis joined the Whitman Sisters vaudeville troupe which eventually counted such luminaries as **Eddie Anderson** and **Count Basie** as alumni. She returned to radio, at least briefly, in 1924.

Sources: *Pittsburgh Courier*, August 2, 1924, p. 10, September 20, 1924, p. 14.

Ellis, Maurice

Born and raised in Providence, RI, Maurice Ellis made his way to New York at the age of 19. There he worked to break into show business and by 1930 was working in Broadway productions such as *Brown Buddies*. The famous choir director J. Rosamond Johnson one day heard Ellis playing piano and singing in a the basement of an apartment complex where he was working. Impressed, Johnson gave him an audition and Ellis was soon singing with the Dixie Echoes on stage and on radio. Ellis' first documented radio work was in 1933 when he sang with the Dixie Echoes over WEAF's *General Motors Hour*. Radio work kept coming in 1933; he was featured in a radio tour of Harlem hosted by **John B. Kennedy** over WJZ. Most notably Ellis was cast in *John Henry, River Giant*, the first all-black dramatic series to gain wide publicity. There is also evidence that he made the first of several appearances on *Maxwell House Show Boat* that year. The following year in 1934 he played Uncle Hannibal on the little-known *The Story of Wheatenaville*. During these early years Ellis also recalled playing on the programs of Rudy Vallee, Eddie Cantor, and Paul Whiteman.

Stage productions such as *The Case of Philip Lawrence* (1937) seem to have occupied most of Ellis' time through the rest of the 1930s. His next known radio roles came in 1939 when he appeared on NBC's *Magic Key* with comedian **Eddie Green** and on a sustaining series called *Ideas That Came True*. Radio work was still sporadic and Ellis' steady work continued to be in theater in such plays as *Hot Mikado* (1939) and *Cabin in the Sky* (1940). Broadcasting jobs began to pick up though the 1940s, however, when he received a wide variety of roles. In 1941 he is known to have worked WEAF's *Regular Fellers*, an NBC Blue tribute to African American soldiers, and an all-black episode of *Forecast* on CBS. That year Ellis was elected president of the new Negro Radio Workshop, an organization dedicated to producing African American radio works for the networks and advertising agencies and to create more black jobs in radio. Such a position indicates Ellis had a strong reputation in the industry.

Though Ellis didn't make a fortune in radio, he received more regular work on the air than most black actors during this period. In 1942 Ellis was cast as a lawyer in the daily soap opera *Young Widder Brown*. Other black performers **Juano Hernandez** and **Venzuela Jones** were playing on the serial as well. Sources confirm that he received parts on other soaps including *Hilltop House, Valiant Lady, Woman of America* (on which he played Sam beginning August 20, 1943), *Young Dr. Malone,* and *Portia Faces Life* in the series' later years. In 1944 Ellis received a role on *Mr. District Attorney* (July 12) as a white forest ranger, a rare casting decision and one that raised some eyebrows. Other well-known series on which Ellis earned parts during the decade were *Dick Tracy, Grand Central Station, Casey, Crime Photographer, Crime Doctor, Jungle Jim,* and *Arch Obler's Plays.* Which

roles Ellis took and how long they lasted is not known for all programs.

In addition to these prime-time programs Ellis starred in several broadcasts on issues of importance to African Americans. One was a February 24, 1945, NBC broadcast celebrating the 118th anniversary of black newspapers by the Negro Newspaper Publishers' Association. Another was a 1946 program called *When He Comes Home* that included an episode devoted to the problems faced by black soldiers returning from war. Ellis won parts on *Freedom's People* and several episodes of *New World A' Coming*, a series based on Roi Ottley's book of the same name. Credits on *New World A' Coming* include broadcasts on April 9, 1944, May 28, 1944, and March 25, 1945. Later in 1945 Ellis was cast in a series of four broadcasts called *World's Great Novels* which aired October 26 and November 2, 9, and 16.

As the 1940s wound down Ellis found his radio work diminishing. Still, he managed to get cast on *Eternal Light* (March 2, 1947, February 6, 1949, September 23, 1951, February 15, 1953, February 28 and March 14, 1954, and March 17, 1957) and on close to a dozen episodes of *The Cavalcade of America* (September 20, 1948, September 20, 1949, September 19, 1950, October 10, 1950, January 16, 1951, February 20, 1951, March 13, 1951, January 8, 1952, January 15, 1952, April 1, 1952, October 7, 1952). Nevertheless, one critic complained: "Ellis mentioned more than a dozen shows he once appeared on regularly. None of them now use Negroes at all. As a result of the few spots he gets on the radio, Ellis devotes much of his time to the legitimate theater." Radio roles had all but dried up for Ellis when he took the part of Walter Williams, "lawyer and man-about-town," when **Elwood Smith** left *The Story of Ruby Valentine*, an all-black soap opera which ran from 1954 to 1955. Around that time he began making forays into television, his first appearance on the small screen being a 1953 episode of *Hall of Fame*. Maurice Ellis continued to take roles on stage in his later years and passed away in 2003 at the age of 97.

Sources: LOC; Scripts August 1, 1932, and May 14, 1933 (*John Henry* scripts, Deliah Jackson Papers, Manuscript, Archives, and Rare Book Library, Emory University); Cox, *Radio Soap Operas*, p. 71; Dunning p. 37; Grams, *Cavalcade*; Grams, *Radio Drama*, pp. 357–358; Sampson, *Swingin' on the Ether Waves*, pp. 104, 144, 529; Woll pp. 33, 36–37, 40, 80; *Baltimore Afro-American*, September 27, 1930, p. 8, March 12, 1932, p. 8, December 16, 1933, p. 18, March 3, 1945, p. 15, March 10, 1945, p. 8, May 19, 1945, p. 4, July 20, 1946, p. 6, May 16, 1953, p. 7; *Chicago Defender*, June 10, 1939, p. 20, July 29, 1944, p. 6; *New York Amsterdam News*, November 18, 1939, p. 20, November 2, 1940, p. 20, April 5, 1941, p. 20, May 31, 1941, p. 20, August 9, 1941, p. 21, August 16, 1941, p. 20, June 27, 1942, p. 8, February 12, 1944, p. 9, April 1, 1944, p. 9B, July 29, 1944, p. 8B, April 23, 1949, p. 24, November 19, 1949, p. 13, September 23, 1950, p. 25, August 21, 1954 p. 20; *Pittsburgh Courier*, December 16, 1944, p. 13; *New York Daily News*, February 13, 2003 http://www.nydailynews.com/archives/ accessed July 27, 2010; Some episode descriptions from the collection of David Goldin www.radiogoldindex.com.

Ernie Moore's Terrace Garden Orchestra

Little is known about Ernie Moore or this orchestra, presumably based out of Chicago's Terrace Garden. Nevertheless, they were an early black band on radio appearing April 1925, over Denver's KLZ.

Source: *Chicago Defender*, April 18, 1925, p. 8.

Evans, Leonard

Leonard Evans was born in Kentucky in 1914 but spent his childhood and young adult years in Chicago. It was here that he got involved in the advertising industry. With an eye toward tapping the large African American radio audience, Evans relocated to New York and established the **National Negro Network** with Jack Wyatt and Reggie Schuebel in late 1953. Their first program, *The Story of Ruby Valentine*, went on the air in January 1954. The National Negro Network lasted just over a year, going defunct in April 1955, when Philip Morris stopped sponsoring *Ruby Valentine*.

Years later in 1965 Evans founded *Tuesday*, a black-interest magazine, which was circulated in *The Chicago Sun-Times* and later in many additional papers. In 1971 he added a second magazine to his business, *Tuesday at Home*. Evans retired in the mid–1970s and passed away in 2007.

Sources: *New York Amsterdam News*, April 17, 1971, p. 5; www.targetmarketnews.com accessed July 30, 2010.

The Evelyn Preer Memorial Program

In February 1933, Los Angeles' KRKD committed to broadcasting a weekly program for one year in the memory of Evelyn Preer, an African American film actress who died unexpectedly at a young age that year. Placed in charge of *The Evelyn Preer Memorial Program* was **Clarence Muse**, a prominent black actor of the era who himself went on to work in over 200 films. He became so connected with the program that it was at times referred to as *The Clarence Muse Entertainers.*

Muse, Gus Robinson, and Muse's daughter Mae arranged all the talent. *The Preer Memorial Program* was a variety show broadcast with plays, songs, and speakers. The half-hour series was heard Monday evenings from its debut in 1933 until March 1936, when it moved to Friday nights. After four years on KRKD the program moved to KFAC on March 8, 1937, where it was subsequently heard coast-to-coast. Not long after the move Muse had to give up managing the broadcasts because of his work with the commercial *Paducah Plantation.*

Sources: Berry and Berry p. 264; *Chicago Defender*, February 4, 1933, p. 5, August 25, 1934, p. 8, March 2, 1935, p. 8, March 23, 1935, p. 10, July 20, 1935, p. 7, June 6, 1936, p. 11, March 20, 1937, p. 20, March 27, 1937, p. 20.

The Fair's Syncopaters

When *The Fair's Syncopaters* program, sponsored by a company simply known as

Fair's, went on the air in May 1931, it became one of the first African American broadcasts to find a sponsor. The *Syncopaters* program featured pianist Louis Brown and weekly guest artists. The first guest of the new series was tenor James Lee. WOL, Baltimore, broadcast the program twice a week, Tuesday and Friday, at 6:30.

Source: *Baltimore Afro-American*, May 16, 1931, p. 19.

Farrell and Hatch

Farrell and Hatch were an African American duo who sang over radio in San Diego as early as June 1922.

Source: *Chicago Defender*, June 24, 1922, p. 8.

Fielding's Orchestra

John Fielding led this self-named orchestra which had a thrice weekly spot on Dallas' WFAA in 1925.

Source: *Baltimore Afro-American*, January 31, 1925, p. 4.

The Fleischmann Yeast Hour

Standard Brand's Fleischmann Yeast sponsored an hour-long broadcast featuring **Louis Armstrong** during May and June of 1937 on Friday nights over NBC Blue. The exact title of the program is not known but it was referred to as *The Fleischmann Yeast Hour* in some sources and *Harlem* in others. Primarily a musical program, **Eddie Green** and **Gee Gee James** were cast as an engaged couple from Harlem who performed sketches which were continued from week to week. Storylines revolved around the husband's inheritance of $3,000 which got the couple into various comedic situations.

The program featured numerous guest stars as well as Armstrong, James, and Green. **Amanda Randolph** sang on the premier episode and the Four Nuts of Rhythm, the Beale Street Boys, tenor Sonny Woods, Cleo Brown, and the incomparable **Ethel Waters** all showed up on the broadcast along with

tap dancers Billy Bailey and Alma Turner. Despite all the talent writer Octavus Roy Cohen had at his disposal, he was blasted for poor scripts. This may not be surprising considering other efforts of his were not overly successful, none lasting over ten months. *The Townsend Murder Mystery* (1933) aired for eighteen weeks, *The Personal Column of the Air* (1936–1937) lasted ten months, and a later stint on *The Amos 'n' Andy Show* ended after six weeks.

Prominent African American composer Will Marion Cook was so incensed by the effort that he belittled the show and called for a boycott, insisting "the Jews of Hollywood, the stage and NBC only exploit the worst and basest of my race." Cook's tongue lashing was probably not necessary as the tepid reviews and lukewarm audience reception ensured a quick demise for the program after just a few broadcasts.

Sources: Dunning p. 541; McLeod pp. 196–197; *New York Amsterdam News*, April 17, 1937, p. 16, May 1, 1937, p. 19, May 15, 1937, p. 19; *Philadelphia Tribune*, April 15, 1937, p. 16.

Floyd Calvin Hour (originally The Pittsburgh Courier Hour)

Evidence strongly indicates that *The Pittsburgh Courier Hour*, which traces its roots to 1927, was the first African American radio series. On September 8, 1927, the prominent African American newspaper *The Pittsburgh Courier* sponsored a 15-minute talk over New York radio station WGBS owned by the Gimbel Brothers department stores. The talk, given by Ruth R. Dennis who contributed religious features to the *Courier*, was "Some Notable Colored Women." Though the talk was not labeled *The Pittsburgh Courier Hour*, response was so positive that the paper and WGBS scheduled a follow-up talk a month later.

WGBS, incidentally, had a history of broadcasting black men and women despite not being a station or a company (Gimbel Brothers) that catered especially to that audience. Before Dennis' talk, artists and writers such as the Creole Six, Carmen Shepard, **Ethel Waters**, Lydia Mason, Ruth R. Dennis, **Countee Cullen**, James Weldon Johnson, Alyse Frazier, **Paul Robeson**, Mike Jackson, a group from the Harlem YMCA, and Lucky Roberts had all appeared on the station.

Through Ms Dennis, Terese Rose Nagel, manager of day programs at WGBS met Floyd Calvin, the *Courier*'s special features editor in New York. Dennis and Nagel were acquainted even before Dennis' "Women" talk, she having made various religious talks over the station. Responding to the success of Dennis' talk, Nagel offered Calvin the opportunity to discuss a topic of interest to African Americans. Calvin seized the opportunity and wrote "Some Notable Colored Men" which was broadcast October 8, 1927, and covered black leaders in business, industry, education, the arts, and the press. The speech was received enthusiastically across the Hudson River in Newark, NJ, Washington D.C., and even as far as Houston, TX. The talk was so successful that WGBS offered Calvin a monthly slot on which to discuss issues of importance to African Americans.

Floyd Calvin was not a radio veteran (nor were many individuals) in 1927. His background was in the press and he saw radio as a natural extension of that work. He was born in Washington, AR, to a farmer and school teacher. In 1920 he graduated from the Shover Street Teacher Training School in Hope, AR, where he had become familiar with all aspects of the print world while working for *The Southwestern Outlook*. Soon after graduating he took a job as a printer for *The New York Age* where he joined the paper's first African American typesetting crew. In four short years Calvin moved on to *The Harlem Daily Star*, *The New York Dispatch*, *The Messenger Magazine*, then finally *The Pittsburgh Courier*, all along the way honing his writing and editorial skills. The

Courier assigned him to serve in New York City in May 1924.

Calvin almost immediately began preaching the power radio could have in the black search for equality. "Over the radio we can reach vast audiences," he proclaimed, "a large percentage of whom have been hitherto untouched by the flood of literature on the subject [black achievement]. We should lose no opportunity to avail ourselves of this newest opportunity." And Calvin didn't lose the opportunity, following up his debut radio effort with a speech on November 26. In it he celebrated the 100th anniversary of the black press, bringing attention to John B. Russworm, the first African American to graduate from an American college and who also founded New York City's *Freedom Journal* paper, and *The Colored American*, the first Southern black paper published out of Augusta, GA. Also on the night's bill were piano and vocal numbers.

Per the agreement, Calvin again brought *The Courier Hour* to the public on December 15. This time his topic was the Durham Conference, a contemporary meeting of black educators. Musical guests included Vivian Abbott, Ernest Hemby, and the **Georgette Harvey** Runnin' Wild Four, a quartet performing in *Porgy and Bess* and formerly on the Keith vaudeville circuit. Whether due to less-than-stellar public response, racial pressure, or some other reason, WGBS dropped *The Courier Hour* after the third edition, nearly bringing to a premature end the first black effort at an ongoing program.

Soon after the announcement by WGBS, Andy Razaf, a popular African American song writer and recording artist, arranged for Calvin to meet with J. P. Coulon, the general manger of WCGU. It didn't take long for Coulon to agree to air Calvin's show so Calvin moved his program to WCGU on the corner of Broadway and 48th St. in New York. Owned by Charle Unger, WCGU broadcast a modest 500 watts. While his hour was cut in half, he now would go on the air every other week instead of just once a month. Calvin didn't miss a beat and was back on the air January 12, 1928, at 5:30 to talk about "The Negro in Art," a lecture given in conjunction with a black art exhibit at the International House. Music was provided by Ernestine Covington and Elizabeth Sinkford, both Oberlin Conservatory graduates. For the rest of the program's run it would be known as *The Floyd J. Calvin Program* (or *Hour*).

About this same time *The Negro Achievement Hour* started on station WABC with a format very similar to *The Calvin Hour*. This program should be regarded as the second black series. Calvin continued on, unfazed by the competition. His January 26, 1928, program featured his own lecture on Negro History Week and musical entertainment by Vivian Abbott. For a change of pace he also brought in actor **Richard Huey**, then starring in stage's *Porgy and Bess*, to do a dramatic reading of "Creation," a piece from James Wheldon Johnson's "God's Trombones." Huey, who would appear in several radio efforts over the next few years, performed at the last minute, replacing Leigh Whipper who had a bad throat at the time.

Thus in this manner did Calvin settle into a routine for the next several months, sandwiching a serious lecture in between generous musical numbers. The February 16 program featured Charles Johnson, editor of *Opportunity* magazine, talking about a new book of essays called *Ebony and Topaz* while music was provided by Lillian Gauntlett and Vernal Matthews. The speech of March 8 was by Dr. George Haynes with music by Olyve Jeter. On March 22 the Rev. John Robinson of St. Mark's M. E. Church talked on the state of African American youth. The May 24th broadcast featured W. R. Valentine, principal of Bordentown Manual Training School who talked about the need for vocational training among black youth. The next week, May 31, soprano Fay Cany was featured.

In September 1928, WCGU program manager William Melia notified Calvin that his show was being granted a weekly slot at 5:30, its regular time since January. While Calvin took pride in the "high type" of artists used on his show, he was very excited to use the broadcast as a vehicle to promote new black talent and actively encouraged performers to contact him about getting a chance to go on the air. His first musical guests as a weekly host were Milliard Thomas, music arranger for the Handy Brothers Music Company, W. C. Handy, Jr. with his xylophone, and Vivian Abbott, a pianist who made repeated appearances. Other speakers included Dr. George E. Haynes, Roscoe Conkling Bruce, James Hubert, Ira Reid, T. Arnold Hill, and A. M. Wendell Malliet, though specific air dates could not be identified. The weekly format apparently did not boost the program as was envisioned. *The Floyd J. Calvin Hour* disappeared from the radio listings in the black newspapers in October 1928, just one year after its debut without the slightest mention of Calvin's historic broadcasting effort.

Sources: Spaulding p. 23; *New York Amsterdam News*, March 14, 1928, p. 10; *Pittsburgh Courier*, September 10, 1927, p. 8, October 8, 1927, p. 1, October 15, 1927, pp. 4, 8, 20, November 5, 1927, p. 1 second section, November 19, 1927, p. 1, November 26, 1927, p. 13, December 3, 1927, p. 3, December 10, 1927, p. 1, 5, December 31, 1927, p. 1, January 28, 1928, p. 2, February 4, 1928, p. 1, February 11, 1928, p. 1, April 14, 1928, p. 6, May 26, 1928, p. 4, June 9, 1928, p. 1, September 15, 1928, p. 4.

Folks from Dixie

Carlton Moss' second ongoing series was entitled *Folks from Dixie* and it debuted May 7, 1933, over the NBC network on WEAF. The show replaced *Moonshine and Honeysuckle*, a "dramatic series of the Kentucky mountains" which had run for nearly two years. Like most of Moss' work, details of *Folks from Dixie* are sketchy. One newspaper account described it as "a series of comedy sketches using colored performers." The premise of the show was a "negro mammy" named Jenny Jackson who inherits a sizable fortune. At least one critic who was initially skeptical of the programming change said "it'll have a tough job" replacing *Moonshine and Honeysuckle*. He later admitted after hearing the premier of *Folks from Dixie* that the show was "a worthy successor to the Moonshine and Honeysuckle skit."

Roi Ottley of *The New York Amsterdam News* summarized the premise of the series in one of his columns, providing more insight to the story lines of this program than of any of Moss' other works. Set in Abbeville, GA, and later in Oklahoma, stories revolved around Aunt Jenny Jackson (**Georgia Burke**) who inherits $50,000 from a deceased relative. Episodes revolved around Aunt Jenny's management of the fortune, balancing her wishes with the needs of her nephew, Ozzie (Moss), and Ozzie's beau, Amber. The wealthy villain, Jasper, provided further anguish for Jenny. Of Moss' documented radio efforts, *Folks from Dixie* appears to be a bit of an outlier with its more humorous content.

Folks from Dixie featured many of the cast members from *Careless Love* including **Eva Taylor**, **Edna Thomas**, Georgia Burke, **Frank Wilson**, and Moss himself. **William Edmondson**, a member of the **Southernaires** quartet, served double-duty as the series villain, Jasper, as well as singer for the group which provided music. Other participants were Willa Gottford and Allan Josyn, the lone white actor. The series was directed by Henry Stillman.

Critical response was tepid. Writing for *The New York Amsterdam News* Roi Ottley gave the series three stars, admitting he was "weary of this type of production" and that "it sound[ed] as if Mr. Moss dug it up from among the mothballs in his garret trunk." Ottley wondered "if [Moss] couldn't be persuaded to write something more adult." It appears that Moss himself was looking at projects further down the road even as he cranked out *Folks from Dixie*. When asked at the time why he chose to write a comedic series compared to the more sophisticated *Careless Love*, Moss replied matter-of-factly "the comic idea seemed to be the sort of Negro program NBC wanted at this time." But he quickly went on to say that his next series would focus on "a Negro town," modeled after all-black deep South towns with black local governments.

Just as Moss did not seem overly invested in the series, neither did the public latch on to it. *Folks from Dixie* ran weekly only until August 6, 1933, a mere fourteen weeks. An early Sunday afternoon timeslot (1:30–2:00) likely did not help. Interestingly, despite a significantly shorter run, it appears that *Folks from Dixie* achieved wider network distribution than the longer running *Careless Love*, airing on at least 50 stations, four to five times as many as *Careless Love* at points in its run. Additionally, the stations were even more diverse, encompassing the continental U.S.; Seattle to San Diego, New Orleans to Miami, Detroit to Fargo, ND, and all points in between. Significantly, it aired outside the U.S. on at least two stations, CFCF in Montreal and CKGW in Toronto.

Sources: *Baltimore Afro-American*, May 20, 1933, p. 10; *Herald-Star* (Steubenville, OH), April 20, 1933, p. 13; *New York Amsterdam News*, May 10, 1933, p. 10; *The Times* (Hammond, IN), May 6, 1933, p. 8; All broadcasting stations identified in various issues of the industry magazine *Radex*.

Forecast

In 1941 CBS broadcast a series called *Forecast*, the final program of which featured an entirely African American cast. Aired on August 25, 1941, the episode came about through the work of a group called the Negro Radio Workshop. The hour-long episode was split into two parts, the first of which aired from New York and was entitled "Jubilee." It featured impersonations of prominent black performers including Bert Williams, Butterbeans and Susie, and Florence Mills. Black actors such as **Maurice Ellis, Frank Wilson**, Bob Allen, Flourney Miller, **Georgette Harvey** and Hamtree Harrington were in the cast and music was written by Will Vodery and performed by the **Juanita Hall** Choir. The second half was broadcast from Hollywood and featured musical acts **Ethel Waters** and **Duke Ellington**. The script was based on one originally written by Langston Hughes and Arna Bontemps and subsequently revised by members of the Negro Radio Workshop.

Source: *New York Amsterdam News*, August 30, 1941, p. 21.

Foulks, N. B.

N. B. Foulks was not an entertainer and apparently had no ambition for a radio career. Nonetheless, he was intrigued enough by the technology that as a student at Columbia University he sang and read his own poetry over WJZ in 1925.

Source: *Baltimore Afro-American*, February 28, 1925, p. 4.

Four Bon-Bons

The Four Bon-Bons, a female quartet consisting of **Georgette Harvey**, Musa Williams, Lois Parker, and Ravella Hughes, had a twice-weekly program over the CBS network by June 1931, via WABC, New York. They formed in the fall of 1930 when Georgette Harvey joined the Ravella Hughes Trio and the newly formed quartet dubbed themselves the Bon Bons. Hughes continued to arrange songs for the quartet. In August 1931, they became some of the first African Americans to be broadcast on television when one of their radio programs was aired simultaneously. The Bon Bons left the air in February 1932, but continued to appear on stage in such productions as *Blackberries of 1932* and with such stars as Claude Hopkins and **Bessie Smith** through the end of the 1932. A trio billed as the Three Bon Bons was still performing on stage into 1934 but it is not

clear if the members were a continuation of the Four Bon Bons.

Sources: *Baltimore Afro-American*, June 13, 1931, p. 6B, July 25, 1931, p. 5, February 27, 1932, p. 8, April 16, 1932, p. 19, October 1, 1932 p. 4; *New York Amsterdam News*, July 14, 1934 p. 6, July 21, 1934 p. 6.

The Four Dusty Travelers

The Four Dusty Travelers were one of countless African American quartets that received airtime in the late 1920s and early 1930s. They were notable, however, for being members of the larger **Dixie Jubilee Singers** lead by **Eva Jessye** and for including two members, **Ray Yeates** and **Jester Hairston**, who would go on to have significant careers on radio. The foursome debuted on New York's WOR in August 1929, and broadcast until April of the following year. For at least two years thereafter they continued to perform live around the New York area. Critics found it pertinent to point out that the Four Dusty Travelers were the only black quartet on radio who were not restricted to singing spirituals, southern tunes, and using dialect. In addition to a weekly radio gig they also sang the theme song for the *Van Heusen Orchestra Hour* sponsored by Phillips-Jones and Company and recorded a number of sides for Columbia Records. Members were Yeates, first tenor, Hairston, baritone, James Waters, second tenor, and Viviande Carr, bass. Jessye directed and wrote all the continuity for the group.

Sources: Griffith and Savage p. 229; *Baltimore Afro-American*, November 30, 1929, p. 8, December 28, 1929, p. 12; *New York Amsterdam News*, November 27, 1929, p. 11, January 22, 1930, p. 11, March 16, 1932, p. 9, September 21, 1932, p. 16.

Franklin, William

As a young man growing up in Shaw, MS, during the first two decades of the 20th century William Franklin is not known to have displayed an unusual aptitude for singing. For a time he played trombone with **Earl Hines'** band then had the chance to appear on a WGN radio program featuring Harold Stokes. After winning a vocal contest on the show, he seems to have developed a real interest in singing and even won a scholarship to study at the Chicago Conservatory of Music. In 1937 Franklin received rave reviews for his appearance with the Chicago Civic Opera Company's 1937 staging of *Aida*, a role he would repeat on occasion. During the late 1930s sources indicate he appeared somewhat regularly on the air, presumably as a singer though details are scarce.

Though an accomplished classical singer, Franklin earned his living on stage, cast in such musicals and light operas as *The Hot Mikado* (1938), *The Swing Mikado* (1939), *The Chimes of Normandy* (in which he was featured in the stage version during 1940 as well as a radio adaptation over NBC on August 8, 1940), *Porgy and Bess* (1944), and *Carib Song* (1945). Individual radio performances include WGN's *Symphonic Hour* (May 19, 1940) and WGN's *Music That Endures* (December 29, 1941, and May 11, 1942). In late 1941 Franklin received his own weekly radio slot on WGN's experimental FM station W59C backed by the Studio Salon Orchestra; it's not clear how long the show lasted on the air. *New World A' Coming* (February 25, 1945 and April 15, 1945) and *This Is My Best* are two other series with which Franklin is credited.

In July 1948, Franklin was recruited by the Southernaires quartet, a successful group that formed in 1929 and had been steadily broadcasting since 1930. Baritone **Jay Stone Toney** died of a heart attack while on tour and Franklin stepped in almost immediately to replace him. As a Southernaire Franklin was performing on radio within three days and would participate in their weekly broadcasts until they disbanded in 1950. Franklin did not participate in the brief Southernaires revival two years later.

Sources: Grams, *Radio Drama*, p. 358; Southern p. 415; Woll pp. 38, 162; *Baltimore Afro-American*, July 24, 1948, p. 6; *Chicago Tribune*, December 27, 1937, p. 12, May 19, 1940, p. W7, July 27, 1940, p. 9, August 4, 1940, p. 5S, August 9, 1940, p. 7, December 21, 1941, p. S4, December 28, 1941, p. 4NW, May 10, 1942, p. S5; *Chicago Defender*, July 31, 1948, p. 7; *New York Amsterdam News*, July 3, 1948, p. 23.

Freedom's People

The roots of *Freedom's People* stretch back to August 1940, when Ambrose Caliver, an African American employee at the U. S. Office of Education, approached NBC about broadcasting a 13-week series of shows depicting notable incidents from black history. The program was to be called *We, Too, Are Americans*. NBC hemmed and hawed for nearly a year before finally approving the project, retitled *Freedom's People*, in the summer of 1941.

Freedom's People, which aired from New York's WEAF, was one of the first series in the wave of African American programs that were produced during the 1940s which dramatized the lives of notable black men and women and important events in black history. Roi Ottley's *New World A' Coming*, **Clifford Burdette's** *Those Who Made Good*, and **Richard Durham's** *Democracy—USA* and *Destination Freedom* were other prominent productions in this genre. *Freedom's People* was funded by the Rosenwald Fund and the Southern Education Foundation. In an unusual scheduling move it broadcast just once a month for eight months, from September 1941, to April 1942. Below is a month-by-month description of each episode in the series.

September 21, 1941—The premier episode featured **Paul Robeson** (because he would bring "gravity and social consciousness" to the broadcast), **W. C. Handy**, the Leonard DePaur Chorus, Noble Sissle's Orchestra, and Joshua White. The night's theme was the depiction of African American contributions to American music and included dramatizations of the origin of black spirituals and the blues and an interview with Handy who described how he came to write his famous tune "St. Louis Blues." Josh White demonstrated the spirituals and blues, Robeson sang, and the DePaur Chorus furnished some background music.

October 19, 1941—In the featured sketch Dick Campbell, then the director of the Rose Mclendon Players, portrayed Dr. George Washington Carver as a young man entering Iowa State College and then as a contemporary man. This was an interesting role for Campbell because Carver gave a speech from Tuskegee seconds after Campbell finished his on-air performance. One critic raved that "the studio audience gasped in amazement at the similarity of the two voices." Additionally, Matthew Henson of Robert Peary's North Pole expeditions made an appearance while **Count Basie** and his band provided the music.

November 23, 1941—Joe Louis, **Cab Calloway** and Jesse Owens were the evening's guest stars. Louis was interviewed by prominent announcer Ken Carpenter and Owens was questioned by Bill Stern, noted sports commentator. Calloway and his band performed along with the Golden Gate Quartet while an unidentified cast dramatized the careers of Louis and Owens.

December 21, 1941—African American heroism in wartime was the theme of this fourth episode. The featured performance was a story called "The Battle of Henry Johnson" about two wounded black soldiers in World War I, Henry Johnson and Needham Roberts, who fended off 24 German soldiers. Roberts himself appeared on the broadcast, Johnson having passed away by then. Colonel West Hamilton also spoke and men from Virginia's Fort Belvoir were interviewed. Fats Waller and his band provided the music and Edward Matthews sang.

January 18, 1942—The series' first broadcast of 1942 featured some of the era's most prominent African American radio artists including **Juano Hernandez, Frank Wilson,** and **Maurice Ellis**. Other guests included A. Philip Randolph, **Mercedes Gilbert,** the

Southernaires, the Leonard De Paur Chorus, John Marriott, Dick Campbell, and **Venzuela Jones**.

February 15, 1942—This month's theme was the history of African American education in the United States since the Civil War. To commemorate the advances in educational opportunities, John Studebaker, U. S. Commissioner of Education, spoke. Dorothy Maynor, soprano, sang for the nationwide audience.

March 15, 1942—The lives and work of black writers, artists and musicians were the focus of the March broadcast. Paul Laurence Dunbar, Henry Ossawa Tanner, Lawrence Whisonant, baritone, and Hazel Harrison all performed in honor of the arts theme.

April 19, 1942—The finale of *Freedom's People* was topped off by the reading of a letter from President Roosevelt praising the series. Nevertheless, this letter was a deep disappointment to Caliver because Roosevelt had earlier assured him of a personal appearance. The broadcast's title was "The Negro and Christian Democracy" and featured **Canada Lee** narrating an overview of the historical development of democracy. Lee also participated in a dramatic skit about the Emancipation Proclamation. The other featured presentation was the Rev. W. H. Jernagin, president of the Fraternal Council of Negro Churches, who described the place of religion in black life. Baritone Todd Duncan sang, J. Rosamond Johnson read "The Creation" by James Weldon Johnson, Juano Hernandez dramatized a scene from "The Green Pastures," and the De Paur chorus and NBC staff orchestra provided plenty of music.

Ambrose Caliver, U. S. Office of Education specialist, supervised the series, Cliff Engle served as the announcer, and Edward Dunham directed. The series' scripts were written by Irve Tunick and the music and arrangements were composed by Dr. Charles Cooke. Among the series' advisers were W. E. B. DuBois, Alain Locke, and Carter Woodson.

Sources: Blue pp. 278–279; Savage pp. 68–102; Sklaroff p. 174; *Baltimore Afro-American*, September 27, 1941, p. 14, October 18, 1941, p. 14, November 22, 1941, p. 14; *New York Amsterdam News*, September 20, 1941, pp. 20, 21, November 1, 1941, p. 22, November 22, 1941, p. 18, December 20, 1941, p. 18, January 24, 1942, p. 9, February 21, 1942, p. 16, March 14, 1942, p. 17, April 25, 1942, p. 7; *Pittsburgh Courier*, February 14, 1942, p. 1.

Freeman, Ann

Ann Freeman has so far only been linked to one radio program, the popular *Dinah and Dora* which aired twice a week over WEAF and WOR by the end of 1930. Paired with **Artie Bell McGinty**, the two starred as Dinah (McGinty) and Dora (Freeman), the girlfriends of Goldie and Dusty, the Gold Dust Twins (sponsored by the Gold Dust Corporation). Though little is known of her radio work, she was involved in the acting profession enough to be an active member of the Negro Actors Guild of America.

Sources: *Baltimore Afro-American*, October 24, 1931, p. 9; *New York Amsterdam News*, October 15, 1930, p. 12, October 22, 1930, p. 4, May 27, 1939, p. 24.

Friendship Baptist Church

Members of Friendship Baptist Church, Atlanta, GA, gave a concert over radio in February 1923. The church choir sang "Deep River," "Down by the Riverside," and "Great Day." Parishioners Myrtle King-Brown and Albert Dent sang "Mah Lindy Lou" and "Smilin' Through" respectively. George Maddox, 14, played "Martha" on the violin with Agnes Maddox, 12, on the piano. A quartet comprised of King-Brown, Jessie Homes, Johnnie Ford, and Susie Skinner sang "The Rosary."

Source: *New York Amsterdam News*, February 28, 1923, p. 9.

George, Maud

Maud George was on radio as early as October 27, 1922, when the soprano sang in celebration of "Negro Night," part of Chicago's "Hear America First" week. The evening's broadcast was sponsored by *The Daily News*' radio station. In the following weeks George sang over WMAQ with the Umbrian Glee Club accompanied by Theo Taylor and Nora Douglas.

Source: *Chicago Defender*, November 4, 1922, p. 5.

Gibson Family

The Gibson Family was an ambitious NBC aural production which attempted to bring the songs and music of Broadway to a weekly radio feature. The concept actually began as a series of newspaper advertisements in January 1934, for Proctor & Gamble's Ivory Soap. Then in September of that year the various family members who had appeared in the ads were brought to the air for a full hour musical dramatic production. White cast members included Adele Ronson, Jack Clemens, Warren Hull, Loretta Clemens, Jack Roseleigh and Anne Elstner. **Ernest Whitman**, who had previously appeared not only on the stage for fifteen years but radio series such as *Careless Love* and *The Townsend Murder Mystery* was cast as a butler named Awful.

Writing for the series was originally done by Courtney Ryley Cooper and the songs and music were written by the Tin Pan Alley team of Howard Dietz and Arthur Schwartz. Just three months into the run writing duties were given to the father and son team of Donald and Owen Davis. In January 1935, it was announced that a second African American actor would be joining the cast, newcomer **Gee Gee James**. James was a Philadelphia native who started on radio there before earning a spot on *The Gibson Family*, her first major radio credit. James played Mignonette, a servant, alongside Whitman's character who was by then known as Theopholis but still worked as a valet and handyman.

The pair proved to be popular, finding themselves twice voted the first (Whitman) and third (James) most popular members of *The Gibson Family* cast by a Proctor & Gamble survey. In the spring of 1935 as ratings continued to be mediocre and the sponsor debated the program's fate, Theopholis and Mignonette were married in a gala celebration that included guest stars the **Hall Johnson** Choir. The grand experiment of wedding a musical to radio drama fizzled and the series went off the air June 23, 1935. Similar shows *Music at the Haydns* and *The House by the Side of the Road* also failed to capture the public's attention.

Proctor and Gamble made one last attempt to save the show by bringing on board Charles Winninger who had previously appeared on the popular *Maxwell House Show Boat*. He played a character named Uncle Charlie and the series was rebranded *Uncle Charlie's Tent Show*. There's no evidence that James made the transition but Whitman did and found himself teamed with African American comedian **Eddie Green** as the pair Big Sam and Little Jerry. Uncle Charlie could not save the musical effort and Proctor and Gamble cancelled it after the September 8, 1935, broadcast. Sadly, Ernest Whitman's wife passed away just one week later.

Sources: Dunning pp. 282–283; Sies pp. 222, 601; *Baltimore Afro-American*, October 20, 1934, p. 7, January 19, 1935, p. 9, February 2, 1935, p. 8, May 11, 1935, p. 9, July 6, 1935, p. 5; *Chicago Defender*, March 23, 1935, p. 11; *New York Times*, January 14, 1934, p. RP7, November 11, 1934, p. X15, May 26, 1935, p. X11.

Gilbert, Mercedes

Mercedes Gilbert was born in Jacksonville, FL, and began writing very early. At age six she began composing poems and at ten she was putting on plays in neighborhood churches. Gilbert studied at Edward Waters College with the goal of becoming a nurse. When she found it difficult finding work in New York, she took a job as a manager with Arto Records and began writing her own songs and vaudeville scripts. On a

bet Gilbert auditioned for a part in 1920's *The Call of His People* and got it. Her debut on the vaudeville stage was in *Home Bound* written by Billy Pierce. Her acting breakthrough came when she got a starring role in Langston Hughes' *Mullato*. Other roles came in *Bamboola* (1929), *Green Pastures* (1930), *How Come, Lawd?* (1937), *Carib Song* (1945), and *Tobacco Road* (1950). Gilbert's first book, "Selected Gems of Poetry, Comedy and Drama," was published in 1932 and her most well-known work, "Aunt Sara's Wooden God," was published in 1938.

In 1931 Gilbert made her first documented radio broadcasts in a series of poetry readings over station WPCH in New York between May and September. However, she is credited with several radio parts which are undated but likely earlier than the WPCH spot including reciting monologs for the Whitewash Syncopators on WOR. These monologs led to poetry reading and additional monologs on WABC's *A Little Bit of Something for Everyone*. Gilbert also worked in some southern sketches on WRNY and another series of sketches and monologs over WMCA. Her only continuing dramatic radio scripting was *Ma Johnson's Rooming House* which aired over WINS and then WMCA between May 1938, and January 1939. As an actress Gilbert appeared in a handful of broadcasts including *The Cavalcade of America* (December 25, 1940), *The Mystery Man* (January 12, 1942–February 6, 1942), *New World A' Coming* (February 26, 1946), *The Ford Theatre* (February 1, 1948), and *Theatre Guild on the Air* (April 21, 1946, and January 22, 1950).

Gilbert also appeared on broadcasts not connected with the more prominent series highlighted above. She starred in at least two one-time radio plays: the first was over WMCA as a supporting actress to Charlotte Buchwald (August 7, 1936) and another was the WABC drama "Women for Freedom" (March 20, 1943), sponsored by the National Urban League, in which she played Sojourner

Truth. Mercedes Gilbert passed away March 1, 1952.

Sources: Cox, *Radio Crime Fighters*, p. 190; Grams, *Radio Drama*, p. 341; Peterson p. 93; Sampson, *Blacks in Black and White*, p. 521; Woll pp. 12, 38, 71, 83, 168–169; *New York Amsterdam News*, July 29, 1931, p. 7, October 1, 1938, p. 12, March 2, 1946, p. 14, April 13, 1946, p. 8; *New York Times*, May 11, 1931, p. 21, August 7, 1936, p. 15, March 20, 1943, p. 29, March 6, 1952, p. 31; *Pittsburgh Courier*, March 13, 1943, p. 20; www.radiogold index.com.

Gillespie, Robert

Robert Gillespie lays claim as one of the first, if not the first, African American radio men. He was noted by the press as being one of only three wireless black operators in the country in 1910. Like many radio experimenters of the era, Gillespie was young, only 18 at the time. He was a member of Popular Electrics, the Wireless Club of America, and the Wireless Association.

Source: *Chicago Defender*, January 22, 1910, p. 1.

Gilpin, Charles

Charles Gilpin, an actor playing in *The Emperor Jones* at the Selwyn Theater in Boston, broadcast over a station in Medford Hillside, MA, on April 3, 1922. He read some lines from the play over the air and added a song to top it off.

Source: Haskins pp. 57–62; Sampson, *Blacks in Black and White*, pp. 521–522; *Baltimore Afro-American*, April 28, 1922, p. 11.

Gist, Ada

Ada Gist, the so-called "Colored Radio Girl," made multiple broadcasts over New York's WDT in 1923.

Sources: *Chicago Defender*, June 30, 1923, p. 8, July 14, 1923, p. 8; *New York Amsterdam News*, July 18, 1923, p. 8.

Glenn, Roy

Roy Glenn, a native of Pittsburgh, KS, started his acting career in *John Henry* with the Federal Theatre in New York, a project of the Depression-era WPA. He claims to have started in radio in 1936 on *The Gilmore Gasoline Show*, a program with a bi-racial cast. Also featured on the show were the Red Devils of Radio, a black quartet made up of Carlyle Scott, D. A. Scott, Emerson Scott, and Windy Weldon. In one interview Glenn recalled playing on *Show Boat* along with three other African Americans. The four did a series of historical satires and acted in dialect.

Glenn then dropped out of radio for several years and earned parts in various stage works and motion pictures. In 1946 he was cast in *The Amos 'n' Andy Show* and a few years later received parts in *Beulah*, but over the next decade Glenn got roles in a wide variety of radio programs that went beyond these two series on which African Americans more regularly appeared. His resume of radio work includes some of old time radio's most fondly remembered programs: *The Jack Benny Program, Suspense* (March 17, 1952, April 14, 1952, March 15, 1954, May 10, 1954, December 9, 1956, February 3, 1957, March 16, 1958, July 19, 1959), *Yours Truly, Johnny Dollar* (June 16, 1953, August 11, 1953, June 4, 1956, June 5, 1956, June 6, 1956, June 7, 1956, June 8, 1956—the 5-part "The Indestructible Matter," December 16, 1956, April 17, 1960), *Broadway Is My Beat* (June 27, 1953, July 11, 1953), *Tales of the Texas Rangers* (March 18, 1951, April 1, 1951, August 24, 1952), and *Lux Radio Theatre* (April 5, 1954). Other shows in which Glenn was cast included *Richard Diamond, Private Detective, The Adventures of Ellery Queen* (February 12, 1948), *Rocky Jordan* (October 9, 1949), *Screen Director's Playhouse* (November 16, 1950), *Romance* (June 16, 1952), *Crime Classics* (December 9, 1953), *CBS Radio Workshop* (February 17, 1956, August 25, 1957), *Pete Kelly's Blues, Hallmark Hall of Fame* (September 13, 1953, January 17, 1953, December 26, 1954, January 16, 1955), and *Last Man Out* (October 11, 1953).

Beyond radio Roy Glenn made multiple

television appearances and is credited with dozens of motion pictures. He died in 1971 at the age of 56.

Sources: Abbott pp. 300, 315, 557–561, 566–568, 941–942; Berry and Berry p. 131; Billups and Pierce pp. 496, 600; Cox, *Great Radio Sitcoms*, p. 33; Cox, *Radio Crime Fighters*, pp. 86, 247; Edmerson pp. 34–35; Grams, *Radio Drama*, pp. 80, 116, 423, 469, 472, 475, 477, 484, 486 Grams *Suspense*; McLeod pp. 145, 147; Nevins and Grams p. 169; Sampson, *Blacks in Black and White*, p. 522; *Los Angeles Sentinel*, March 23, 1950, p. B2, May 18, 1950, p. B1, January 17, 1952, p. B3, October 8, 1953, p. B3, January 27, 1955, p. 10; *New York Amsterdam News*, August 6, 1938, p. 5, October 12, 1946, p. 21, March 20, 1971; www.radiogold index.com.

Glover, Gilbert G.

Gilbert Glover appeared with partner **J. L. "Bobby" Robinson** on radio and in live performances during the summer of 1930. The content of their routine is unknown but they were credited with writing their own material and being the "only Negro artists doing the kind of work they do." Sparse documentation indicates they were together only a very short time, but during their brief partnership they appeared on WWRL, New York.

Source: *New York Amsterdam News*, July 9, 1930, p. 10.

The Good Time Society

The Good Time Society was a Saturday night musical program which aired from 10:00 to 10:30 for at least two years over WJZ and the Blue network. The program is difficult to find in historic radio logs but references to the show exist in various contemporary sources. It appears that Ella Fitzgerald and Chick Webb frequently performed along with other African American musicians. During the spring of 1937 **Juano Hernandez** wrote scripts for the series and also served as the interlocutor. Taft Jordan, the **Juanita Hall** Choir, and the Four Ink Spots all made appearances on the show.

Sources: *New York Amsterdam News*, April 25, 1936, p. 8, May 9, 1936, p. 9, February 20, 1937, p. 9.

Gosden, Freeman

Freeman Gosden was a true son of the Old South, born in Richmond, VA, to a Confederate veteran of the Civil War. Like future partner **Charles Correll**, Gosden became enamored with the stage as a child while attending local vaudeville shows. His family faced tragedy after tragedy with the death of both parents, a brother, and a sister by the time he turned 18. One constant through his developmental years was an African American boy named Garrett Brown who numerous researchers have concluded was his closest companion. Gosden would later claim that his dialect patterns were heavily influenced by his childhood friend as well as the residents of the black neighborhood near which his family lived for many years.

Gosden discovered radio while serving in the navy during World War I. After his discharge he found his way onto the staff of Joe Bren's minstrel company based out of Chicago. In 1920 a forty-year partnership was initiated when Correll was assigned as trainer to the newly hired Gosden. The next several years the two worked side by side, frequently in black face minstrel acts, and also had their initiation to radio in Louisiana during 1920.

By 1925 they were appearing regularly on four Chicago-area stations, WKY, WLS, WEBH, and WQJ. WEBH became their primary source of air time until the end of 1925 when they were hired by powerful WGN, owned by the Chicago Tribune newspaper. After grueling weeks of song and patter, station brass asked them to created a radio version of the popular newspaper serial *The Gumps*. Demurring, Gosden and Correll instead proposed a serial that featured two black men and that was not, contrary to other programs featuring whites caricaturing blacks, filled with demeaning songs and jokes.

If WGN had reservations about the proposal the station didn't stop Correll and Gosden from hitting the airwaves on January 12, 1926, in the serial *Sam 'n' Henry*. This daily story of two black men traveling north to make a new life in Chicago could have been the story of countless African Americans during the Great Migration. When WMAQ offered better terms the pair jumped stations and, with only minor changes, continued on their new show *Amos 'n' Andy*. The program was nothing less than a smash and by 1931 it commanded the attention of 75 percent of radio listeners. Despite protests that *Amos 'n' Andy* was a disservice to African Americans, black listeners tended to be favorably inclined to it, if not as wholeheartedly as whites.

For 32 years Gosden played Amos Jones, a kind and honest husband and father who was frequently called upon to extricate his friend Andy Brown from predicaments. During the 1940s, as the show entered its third decade, Amos' prominence on the program slowly gave way to the Kingfish, a conniving huckster who habitually made a sucker of Andy. This third role, which in time became as major a character as either Amos or Andy, was also played by Gosden. While both Gosden and Correll wrote every script during the 1928–1943 serial run, Gosden is considered by historians to have been the primary developer of story lines and characters. When the ill-fated television program went into production in 1951, historian Melvin Ely indicates that Gosden was more closely involved than partner Correll.

Gosden's radio career consisted solely of his roles on *Amos 'n' Andy* and guest appearances in character on other programs. After *Amos 'n' Andy Music Hall* left the air in 1960 he made one last commercial effort, again with old partner Correll. The two teamed up and, using the familiar voices of Amos and Andy, provided voice-overs for a television cartoon called *Calvin and the Colonel*. The effort lasted from 1961 to 1962. Gosden

disappeared from public view after that, spending time with friends and family in Southern California. Though always proud of his work on *Amos 'n' Andy* he was disappointed in his later years about the diminished and increasingly controversial status the series held in the public eye. Gosden outlived Correll by a decade, passing away December 10, 1982.

Sources: Cox, *Great Radio Sitcoms*, pp. 36–37; Cox, *This Day in Network Radio*, p. 84; Ely pp. 14–15, 21–25, 36–39, 47–56, 205–206; McLeod pp. 150–151.

Green, Eddie

Eddie Green died in 1950 at the relatively young age of 49 but he managed to squeeze an entire career's worth of achievements in that short span. Born in Baltimore, Green grew up in Chicago where he began performing and got into vaudeville. His first notable accomplishment was penning the tune "A Good Man is Hard to Find" in 1918. Just a few years later in the early 1920s Green was appearing in various New York productions such as the famous *Shuffle Along* in 1923. By the end of the decade he was getting cast in various film shorts, some by the Vitaphone company.

Green's first radio work was in 1930 when he worked as an announcer for the short-lived Harlem Broadcasting Corporation along with **Geraldyn Dismond** and appeared on an episode of *The Negro Achievement Hour* (March 13, 1930), radio's second black series which had debuted in 1928. Throughout the mid–1930s Green was a guest on *Rudy Vallee's Fleischmann Hour* and other Vallee programs (January 18, 1934, March 5, 1936, March 26, 1936, April 9, 1936, April 16, 1936, July 16, 1936, July 23, 1936, August 27, 1936, September 3, 1936, September 10, 1936, January 28, 1937, April 8, 1937, August 5, 1937, November 25, 1937, and June 30, 1938). Other mid–1930s efforts include *The General Tire Revue* (August 3, 1934) and *Echoes of New York* (September

1936). Perhaps his first continuing role was on *Uncle Charlie's Tent Show*, the replacement for *The Gibson Family* in the summer of 1935. He teamed with **Ernest Whitman** to play Jerry and Sam, a comedic duo. Predating **Eddie Anderson**'s role on *The Jack Benny Program* by two years, promotional material claimed they were the only African American comics on a network series.

The Tent Show did not last long and once again Green was left to make scattered appearances across the radio dial. Some of these included: *The Royal Gelatin Hour* (January 28, 1937), *Harlem*, **Louis Armstrong**'s roundly booed series of April and May 1937, *The Royal Desserts Hour* (June 30, 1938), Kate Smith's program (June 4, 1939), and *The Magic Key Program* (June 4, 1939). Amongst the one-time appearances, Green was cast as **Hattie McDaniel**'s husband on *Maxwell House Show Boat* from August 19 to October 21, 1937. In early 1940 Green earned his third recurring role on *Quaker Party* starring Tommy Riggs and Betty Lou. The part lasted from January 28 to March 25, 1940. One critic claimed his comedy saved the show "from a slow death" and another described him as Rigg's Rochester. Like *Uncle Charlie's Tent Show*, this series was not overly successful and lasted just two months.

Perhaps frustrated with the inconsistent work in radio, Green founded Sepia Arts Pictures, a film production company in Harlem, in 1939. Though it never released any big name films it did steadily produce pictures featuring black casts for several years. Though an enduring role remained elusive, Green continued to get cast on a variety of radio series. Documented programs include the July 1940, premier episode of *Harlem Serenade*, a black variety show on WMCA sponsored by the Greater New York Coordinating Committee, *The Pursuit of Happiness* (January 31, 1940), *The Jack Benny Show* (April 28, 1940, December 15, 1940, October 12, 1941, possibly August 3, 1934), and

Forecast (August 25, 1941), a review of which said the African American cast was "more than impressive." Additionally, he returned to Rudy Vallee's program on July 4, and September 26, 1940, and was cast in *The Bishop and the Gargoyle* written for WJZ (September 20, 1940), *Star Spangled Theatre* (December 22, 1940) *The Columbia Workshop* (April 27, 1941, an episode which included **Juano Hernandez, Frank Wilson, Maurice Ellis** and **Amanda Randolph**, August 17, 1942), a War Department broadcast (August 12, 1941, with **Canada Lee**), *Rinso-Spry Vaudeville Theatre* (nearly a dozen episodes between July 19, 1941, and January 5, 1942), *Meet the Colonel* (July 6, 1943), *The Radio Hall of Fame* (January 30, 1944, February 18, 1945), *Mail Call* (April 26, 1944), *The Folks on Fourth Street* (May 14, 1946), *Beulah* (August 26, 1946), *Mirth and Melody* (December 2, 1948), and *Men Who Made Good* (June 21, 1941, hosted by **Clifford Burdette** over WNYC).

During these years Green received more recurring jobs including the part of Sweeney the jockey on Ben Bernie's weekly show beginning March 1941, and on Colonel Stoopnagle's Saturday afternoon broadcasts in 1944. From June 2 to September 22, 1946, he was a regular on *The Fabulous Dr. Tweedy*, then from October 2, 1945 to May 25, 1948, he played Mayor LaGuardia Stonewall on *The Amos 'n' Andy Show*. Between 1943 and 1945 Green appeared on approximately two dozen episodes of *Jubilee*, a few of which used repeated material: #8 (recorded January 28, 1943), #75 (recorded April 17, 1944), #77 (recorded May 1, 1944), #79 (recorded May 8, 1944), #82 (recorded June 5, 1944), #107 (recorded November 6, 1944), #110 (recorded November 27, 1944), #114 (recorded January 2, 1945), #119 (recorded February 5, 1945), #122 (broadcast June 30, 1945), #127 (recorded April 2, 1945), #130 (recorded April 23, 1945), #131 (recorded April 30, 1945), #136 (recorded June 4, 1945), #138 (recorded June 18, 1945), #139 (recorded June 25, 1945),

#141 (recorded July 9, 1945), #145 (recorded August 27, 1945), #154 (recorded October 29, 1945), #215 (used material from #119), #218 (used material from #122), #221 (used material from #130), #222 (broadcast January 16, 1947), special Christmas episode (recorded August 6, 1945). Finally, beginning September 15, 1944, Green was cast as Eddie, a wisecracking waiter, on *Duffy's Tavern*. This, his most memorable role to fans of old time radio, lasted until May 4, 1950.

Sources: LOC; Berry and Berry p. 139; Dunning pp. 212, 239, 283, 676; Grams pp. 112–113; Leff vol.1 pp. 158, 393, 411, 437; Lotz and Neuert; McLeod p. 184; Patterson p. 47; Woll pp. 210–211; *Chicago Defender*, August 24, 1929, p. 6, November 16, 1929, p. 7, August 8, 1930, p. 5, June 22, 1935, p. 6, June 10, 1939, p. 20, August 5, 1939, p. 4, February 17, 1940, p. 21, March 16, 1940, p. 21, September 21, 1940, p. 21, March 8, 1941, p. 21, April 8, 1944, p. 8; *New York Amsterdam News*, March 14, 1923, p. 5, March 19, 1930, p. 11, January 24, 1934, p. 14, March 14, 1936, p. 8, August 1, 1936, p. 9, October 3, 1936, p. 24, April 17, 1937, p. 16, March 30, 1940, p. 17, July 27, 1940, p. 13, September 7, 1940, p. 11, May 3, 1941, p. 20, June 21, 1941, p. 21, July 26, 1941, p. 15, August 9, 1941, pp. 20, 21, September 23, 1950, p. 1.

Griffin, Frank

Frank Griffin was one of the few African American writers working on a network show in 1943 when his *Labor for Victory* was aired over NBC's Red network under the sponsorship of the Congress of Industrial Organizations. Griffin had previously written for *Native Sons* over WNYC and *Freiheit*, described as a "German-American pageant" which was produced by the Hotel Capitol in June 1942. Before the *Labor for Victory* assignment he had served as publicity director for the Negro Freedom Rally and as co-producer for Langston Hughes' *For This We Fight* staged in New York's Madison Square Garden. In 1941 Griffin wrote a series of articles for *The Baltimore Afro-American* criticizing the radio industry for the lack of opportunities provided African American artists. *Labor for Victory* aired for three months and would be Griffin's final radio assign-

ment. Tragically, he died in 1945 at the age of 37.

Sources: *New York Amsterdam News*, May 3, 1941, p. 21, January 27, 1945, p. 5; *Pittsburgh Courier*, October 16, 1943, p. 19.

Hairston, Jester

Jester Hairston, born July 9, 1901, was a musician and actor whose radio work was just a tiny portion of a performing career that lasted nearly seven decades, from the time he got involved with New York City choirs in 1930 until his death January 18, 2000. Hairston always considered North Carolina home though he moved shortly after his birth to Homestead, PA, near Pittsburgh where he grew up.

With the financial backing of a white woman, Hairston finally graduated from Tufts University in Boston in 1929 with a B.A. in music. Soon afterward he moved to New York and began working various theatrical jobs, including a stint with **Eva Jessye's Dixie Jubilee Choir**. Singing with this choir may have been Hairston's first radio experience when NBC aired them on a Christmas Day broadcast in 1931. The same source noted the Choir also sang regularly on *The General Motors Hour*. Hairston's big break came in 1932 when he won a spot on the **Hall Johnson** Choir with which he appeared again on NBC, this time on their *Maxwell House Coffee Hour* for thirteen weeks. Within a year he was also selected to sing with one of Johnson's choral ensembles, the Hall Johnson Sextet, with whom he was first bass. The sextet performed folk songs and secular tunes in addition to their traditional spirituals. To polish his musical skills Hairston spent a year at Julliard from 1932 to 1933. In the meantime he continued his work with the Johnson Choir and was promoted to the post of assistant conductor.

Hall Johnson's signature show, *Run, Little Chillun*, (alternately called *Run, Little Children*) a production that owed much of its success to Hairston, was first staged in 1933.

Through the early months of that year Hairston, Richard Brown, and **Juanita Hall** kept the choir (now expanded to a massive 175 singers) fed and housed while rehearsing the program. In March the work paid off and *Run, Little Chillun* opened on Broadway and ran until June. In October of 1933 Hairston returned to radio on CBS as a member of the Hall Johnson Singers which may have included the entire choir or been a smaller selection of choir singers. At this time he may have made his solo debut on the air when he stepped in for co-singer William Bowers after Bowers forgot the words to a song in mid-broadcast.

In 1934 Hairston began expanding beyond pure singing. In March he was publicly identified as a leader in the Choir and also as a dramatic reader. Over the summer he performed with the H. P. Madison Choir, a "dramatic club" that presented some one-act plays. By the end of the year a boys choir of which Hairston had taken charge competed in the Boys' Club City-Wide Radio Contest over WNYC in New York. Hairston branched into comedy in 1935, earning "hilarious laughter" with a one-man comedic presentation he developed. He was also in charge of a women's choir for the Works Progress Administration by 1936.

The Hall Johnson Choir was hired to sing for a motion picture based on *Green Pastures* and relocated to Hollywood for six weeks of filming. Hairston ended up settling in Southern California despite the success he'd experienced in New York. The choice was a good one; his career hummed along and in 1939 he met and married his wife, Margaret Swanagan. Their union lasted nearly half a century until her death in 1986. In 1938 Hairston's leadership was developed to the point where he was hired to conduct a revival of Johnson's *Run, Little Children* in San Francisco as a project of the Federal Theatre program. It may have been around this time that Hairston departed the Hall Johnson Choir and started his own groups.

Hairston's main choir was formed in 1943 and went on to provide vocal music for several films including *We're Not Married, Somebody Loves Me, Sixth Convict, Four Posters*, and *Portrait of Jenny*. The earliest documented radio appearance for one of his groups was the fourth broadcast of *Jubilee*, recorded December 18, 1942. It was a multiracial effort, the fifty-member choir split evenly between black and white singers. The next year, 1944, Hairston was hired on *The Amos 'n' Andy Show*, a series with which he would be associated for many years. He portrayed Sapphire's brother, Leroy, a role he claimed lasted 16 years. If this is accurate (and his memories during a 1980 interview align very closely with historical sources) Hairston must have made appearances on *Amos 'n' Andy Music Hall*, a song-and-patter radio show that lasted until November 25, 1960. Radio historians Frank Buxton, Bill Owen, and Jim Cox also identify Hairston as Johnny the cleaner, a character on the *Beulah* radio show (1947–1954), a role confirmed by contemporary sources. Interestingly, he never mentioned the program when discussing his past radio work. His final long-term radio role was King Moses, a calypso singer on *Bold Venture*, a Ziv syndicated program starring Humphrey Bogart and Lauren Bacall and produced between 1951 and 1952.

While Hairston claimed to have done many radio shows, in an interview he could not recall their titles and the other broadcast efforts so far discovered have been on local radio. He recalled once working with Betty Davis and George Brent on an unidentified radio production. Other verified appearances include *Jubilee* (episode #4, recorded December 18, 1942 and aired 1943) with his Hallelujah Four quartet, *These Are Your Neighbors* (May 1947), an interview program on L. A.'s KRKD sponsored by the Los Angeles County Committee on Human Relations, *Cavalcade of America* (January 1, 1952), an episode featuring **Ethel Waters** and the Hairston Choir,

Man of Color (June 1953) on KECA, *Yours Truly, Johnny Dollar* (August 11, 1953) and *Confession* (September 1953), starring James Edwards on KFI. In the middle of these dramatic radio jobs Hairston made at least two broadcasts as a musician, leading the South Central Adult Civic Chorus in January 1950, over the Mutual network. He again led them on the air in February 1952, over NBC.

Hairston made steady television appearances throughout the rest of his life, notably as Henry Van Porter on *Amos 'n' Andy* (a part played by **Charles Correll** on radio) and *Amen* from 1986 to 1991. He also had acting and musical responsibilities with many films over four decades. As a good-will ambassador for the State Department and music teacher at various educational institutions Hairston had an impact on countless young men and women. He was always proud of his work and defiant in the face of younger African American generations who criticized his early acting roles: "We had a hard time back then fighting for dignity. We had no power. We had to take it, and because we took it the young people today have opportunities."

Sources: Abbott p. 315; Andrews and Julliard p. 54; Buxton and Owen p. 28; Cox, *Great Radio Sitcoms*, p. 71; Ely p. 241; Dunning p. 109; Grams, *Cavalcade*; Lotz and Neuert; McLeod pp. 142, 147, 151; Sampson, *Swingin' on the Ether Waves*, pp. 70–71, 803; *Baltimore African American*, March 22, 1929, p. 3, March 18, 1932, p. 3, April 8, 1933, p. 9, October 21, 1933, p. 18, March 10, 1934, p. 16, June 2, 1934, p. 14, June 6, 1936, p. 12, May 8, 1943, p. 8, January 13, 1945, p. 8, November 10, 1945, p. 8, December 30, 1950, p. 9, February 10, 1951, p. 8, January 12, 1952, p. 7, September 27, 1952, p. 6, August 1, 1953, p. 7; *Los Angeles Sentinel*, May 1, 1947, p. 21, June 25, 1953, p. B5, September 17, 1953, p. B2, January 27, 2000, p. A1; *New York Amsterdam News*, June 22, 1932, p. 9, July 14, 1934, p. 7, December 22, 1934, p. 11, August 3, 1935, p. 19, September 13, 1952, p. 12, July 24, 1965, p. 22; Interview http://www.umich.edu/~afroammu/standifer/hairston.html accessed July 22, 2010.

Hall, Juanita (also Juanita Hall Choir)

Juanita Hall was born in Keyport, NJ, on November 6, 1901. Her interest in performing developed early and she attended Julliard in New York after graduating from high school. Hall began to get some attention as a featured singer in the **Hall Johnson** Choir, a prominent African American performing group through much of the 1930s. Hall likely appeared numerous times on radio as part of Johnson's choir. As the Depression worsened Hall struck out on her own and formed the Juanita Hall Choir with funding by the Works Progress Administration. It was as a singer and choir leader that Hall began making regular radio appearances under her own name.

One of the first radio appearances by the Juanita Hall Choir was a broadcast called *Negro Achievement* on New York's WOR in 1935. Written by pioneering black radio dramatist **Carlton Moss**, it's not clear if this *Negro Achievement* is connected to the earlier *Negro Achievement Hour* which went on the air over WABC in January 1928. Other documented broadcasts by the Choir include a 1936 appearance over WEAF as part of an all-black show and performances in 1937 on WJZ as part of NBC's *Good Time Society*. The Choir was featured alongside Chick Webb, Ella Fitzgerald, and the Four Ink Spots. The next year they got a gig on WJZ when they provided music for the play *In Abraham's Bosom* which aired over the Blue Network and featured **Juano Hernandez, Frank Wilson**, and Southernaires' members **William Edmondson, Jay Stone Toney**, and **Homer Smith**.

Hall made at least one broadcast as leader of the Negro Melody Singers in 1939, a group she formed in 1935. Maude Simmons, contralto, and Ernest Show, baritone, were two of the original members. In late 1940 the Juanita Hall Choir provided music for an episode of *Cavalcade of America* (December 25, 1940) in a version of *Green Pastures* which starred Juano Hernandez and Frank Wilson. From May to July 1941, Hall's Choir sang on a WNYC program called *Native Sons* which for thirteen weekly installments dramatized the lives of famous African Americans. During World War II in 1944 the group appeared on NBC's *Words at War* in a story about George Washington Carver. Additionally, they provided music for the final episode of a CBS series called *Forecast*, an episode that featured an all-black cast, in August 1941.

In 1948 Juanita Hall appeared in one of her first non-musical roles on an end-of-the-year special with Juano Hernandez that reviewed the progress made by African Americans during the year. She is also credited with appearances on programs featuring Norman Corwin, Kate Smith, and Rudy Vallee, probably all with her choirs. After broadcasting on radio for nearly two decades, Hall finally received her own series in 1950 over New York's WNEW. Called *Juanita Hall Sings* it was primarily songs and entertainment commentary. The Roy Ross Trio served as the backing band on the quarter-hour program.

In 1954 she was cast as Ruby Valentine, the lead character of *The Story of Ruby Valentine*, an all-black radio soap opera broadcast over the National Negro Network. This role was likely her first lead dramatic part on the air. In addition to playing Valentine, Hall also wrote the program's theme song, "Ruby's Blues." The series premiered January 25, 1954, and ran until April 1955.

Hall continued to act throughout the 1950s on stage but she never equaled the success she had as Bloody Mary in the Broadway and film versions of *South Pacific*. In 1949 she signed with Victor Records but a recording career never panned out nor did television, though she made occasional appearances there as well. In 1963 Hall opened a night club in New York even as she continued performing. She passed away two years later on February 28, 1965.

Sources: Grams, *Cavalcade*; Sampson, *Blacks in Black and White*, pp. 524–525; Woll p. 212; *Balti-more Afro-American*, August 24, 1935, p. 9, May 3, 1941, p. 14, August 9, 1941, p. 14, April 8, 1950, p. 3; *Chicago Defender*, January 9, 1963, p. 16; *New York Amsterdam News*, October 12, 1935, p. 11, December 12, 1936, p. 11, February 20, 1937, p. 9, July 2, 1938, p. 7, June 24, 1939, p. 2, January 4, 1941, p. 17, August 30, 1941, p. 21, February 5, 1944, p. 11, January 31, 1948, p. 13, September 10, 1949, p. 5, April 29, 1950, p. 4, March 9, 1968, p. 34.

Hall, Maude

Maude Hall worked as a staff member of New York's Pictorial Review during the early 1920s. It's possible she can lay claim to being the first African American with a weekly radio series with her broadcasts over WOR during the fall of 1922. On her Saturday program she discussed clothing fashions and related topics. Reports indicated Hall was heard as far as Nebraska.

Source: *Chicago Defender*, November 11, 1922, p. 5.

Hall, Thomas

Thomas Hall broadcast over WJY, New York, in 1924. Hall was a concert singer who trained under Lottie Peterson, director of the Baltimore School of Music in 1910. Songs for this early broadcast included "Is Not His Word Like a Fire," "Ride on Moses," and some traditional black folks songs.

Source: *Baltimore Afro-American*, December 13, 1924, p. 9.

Hamilton, George, Jr.

George Hamilton, Jr. broadcast a daily children's hour over WCCO, St. Paul, MN in 1925, the title of which, unfortunately, has not been discovered. The program included stories, jokes, riddles, songs, and other entertainment. Born in Topeka, KS, Hamilton graduated from the nearby University of Kansas with a degree in law in 1922. Notably, he was the school's first African American student to make the debate team.

Source: *Baltimore Afro-American*, July 18, 1925, p. 1.

Hampton Institute

Musicians from the Hampton Institute, a historically black college in Hampton, VA, made multiple appearances on the radio dating back to the early twenties. One of the earliest appearances by representatives of the Institute was a May 1922, concert by the Hampton Institute Quartet. The foursome performed a number of songs over a Newark radio station including "I Want to Be Ready," "Go Down, Moses," The Gospel Train's a-Coming," and "Swing Low, Sweet Chariot." Robert Ogden Purves, the school's field secretary, also gave a talk on the Institute's history and mission.

Eighteen months later the Hampton Glee Club gave a concert over a Philadelphia radio station on November 7, 1924 after having completed a concert at the city's Traymore Hall Club. The Club, then under the direction of Dr. Nathaniel Dett, performed "Deep River," "Father Abraham," and "There Were Shepherds."

Not long after the Glee Club's concert the Quartet returned to the air for a series of five Sunday concerts in conjunction with the Tuskegee Institute Quartet. These five broadcasts ran through January 1925, and ended on February 10. General Electric, owners of WGY, Schenectady, which aired the quartets, picked up all costs associated with the broadcasts which also aired over Newark's WJZ. Reports indicate that an estimated one million listeners tuned in each week. The singers took some criticism from the black press and listeners for including "darky" songs in their repertoire, songs which many felt were below the dignity of these institutions.

In an unusual broadcast from New York in March of 1925 students from Hampton and Tuskegee aired a demonstration of brick-making, plastering, and blacksmithing. Additionally, Dr. R. R. Moton gave a lecture and Nathaniel Dett led the school glee clubs.

Sources: *Baltimore Afro-American*, January 10, 1925, p. 5, January 31, 1925, p. 4, February 7, 1925, p. B4, March 7, 1925, p. 1, March 28, 1925, p. 2; *Chicago Defender*, June 3, 1922, p. 11, November 8, 1924, p. 4, January 10, 1925, p. 2.

Handy, W. C.

William Christopher Handy, the so-called "Father of the Blues," was born in 1873 and became one of the premier publishers of popular black music in the 1920s. His prime performing days were long behind by the time he started appearing on radio. Two historians of black history claim that Handy was broadcast over a Memphis amateur station in 1914 or 1916. If such a broadcast was made it was not promoted years later when he began appearing on New York–area commercial stations. Handy's first confirmed radio work was an appearance on WGBS in January 1927, to discuss his role in the development of blues music. Two months later on March 6 he returned to WGBS and played a variety of songs.

Handy's children followed his lead into the music business and were singing tunes published by Handy regularly on radio by early 1928. January 26, 1928, Handy was a guest on *The Negro Achievement Hour* where he played "blues, jazz, spirituals and popular songs" with his daughters. A similar appearance followed on April 5, 1928, on *The Floyd Calvin Hour* with his daughters. Three months later on July 6, 1928, Handy performed his own tunes on WEVD's *Negro Art Hour*. He was a guest on radio shows at least twice in 1929, on the April 12 broadcast of WABC's *Littman Program* and the July 25 broadcast of WEVD's *Music Publisher's Hour* on which he conducted the Seminole Orchestra. Handy returned to *The Negro Art Group* on January 12, 1930, over WEVD and then to *The Negro Achievement Hour* on March 13, 1930. Subsequent aural spots include a performance on May 25, 1930, over WOR at which time he was playing with **LeRoy Smith Band**, and NBC's *Southland Sketches* on March 8, 1931, as a guest speaker.

Though Handy was never a regular radio performer, broadcasting royalties collected from his songs, especially "The St. Louis Blues," provided a comfortable income even during the darkest years of the Great Depression. It was reported in 1932 that he collected $4,000 from the American Society of Composers, Authors and Publishers the prior year. Later in the decade reports suggest his royalties approached $20,000 per year.

Other noted broadcasts include a February 11, 1933, relief broadcast over WRNY, a March 16, 1936, rendition of his classic "St. Louis Blues" over WABC, and a September 21, 1941, episode of *Freedom's People* with **Paul Robeson** and Noble Sissle. Handy appeared over the air as late as 1945 when he played "St. Louis Blues" as part of a tribute to **Canada Lee** on *New World 'A Coming*.

Sources: Halper; Sampson, *Swingin' on the Ether Waves*, pp. 7, 21; Southern pp. 338–339; Barlow p. 82; *Baltimore Afro-American*, October 22, 1932, p. 10; *Chicago Defender*, January 29, 1927, p. 9, February 25, 1928, p. 6, March 17, 1928, p. 7, May 31, 1930, p. 7; *New York Amsterdam News*, January 25, 1928, p. 4, July 4, 1928, p. 8, April 10, 1929, p. 11, July 24, 1929, p. 11, January 8, 1930, p. 11, March 19, 1930, p. 11, February 8, 1933, p. 16, March 21, 1936, p. 9; *Pittsburgh Courier*, April 14, 1928, p. 7, March 14, 1931, p. 8, September 11, 1937, p. 21, September 20, 1941, p. 21.

Harlem, USA

June 21, 1948, saw the debut of *Harlem, USA*, a half hour program on WMCA, with the stated goal to "tell the story of Harlem's life and needs" through the songs and words of Harlem musicians and residents. The series was created by Harlem's unofficial mayor Sherman Hibbitt and initially produced by Jack Caldwell of Don Productions. Caldwell also acted as one of the original master of ceremonies. St. Claire Bourne, publicity director for the New York State Department of Labor, conducted guest interviews while the American Youth Theatre Guild under the direction of Herman Baron sang and provided dramatizations.

The debut broadcast featured Manhattan Borough president Hugo Rogers who talked about two new planned housing projects in Harlem. Other guests included Dr. Channing Tobias, Grant Reynolds, a member of the New York State Board of Corrections, Dr. Weissman, director of Sydenham Hospital, Heber Maultsby Dawson, and Amy James Mallard, the wife of a lynched man. By 1949 production duties had been assumed by Frederick S. Weaver and Associates. Constance Curtis of *The Amsterdam News* was recruited to do interviews as well and Dorothy Chappell did some announcing. Other participants were Ed Bouey who took on producing and directing tasks and Phil Gordon who sang regularly. *Harlem, USA* was cancelled in June 1950, due to mounting costs.

Sources: *Baltimore Afro-American*, January 8, 1949, p. B4, January 29, 1949, p. 7; *New York Amsterdam News*, June 19, 1948, p. 14, June 26, 1948, p. 9, July 17, 1948, p. 6, August 14, 1948, p. 2, February 5, 1949, p. 25, March 19, 1949, p. 25, July 16, 1949, p. 20, April 22, 1950, p. 5, September 30, 1950, p. 15, November 22, 1958, p. 16.

A Harlem Family

Originally called *Muddy Waters*, writer **Venzuella Jones**' serial of black life in Harlem moved from WBNX to the larger WMCA beginning October 6, 1935, under the moniker *A Harlem Family*. The broadcasts continued to be sponsored by the Adult Education Bureau of the Emergency Relief Bureau. No notable African American performers appeared on the series, nor did it get much attention even by the black press. One (presumably Caucasian) writer disparaged that "the happiest part of the sketch is when the cast begins the spirituals when signing off." Further, "it fails to measure up to its dramatic possibilities and does not pique the interest of white listeners." With such a lukewarm reception perhaps it's no surprise the effort was off the air by December.

Sources: *Baltimore Afro-American*, October 26, 1935, p. 19; *New York Amsterdam News*, October 5, 1935, p. 15, December 14, 1935, p. 11.

Harlem Fantasies (also Harlem Fantasy)

The National Broadcasting Company aired *Harlem Fantasies* on Friday and later Saturday evenings in 1932 over WEAF and WJZ alternately. Presumably a musical program, it featured **Eva Taylor**, the **Southernaires**, and **Clarence Johnson**, all of whom were regulars on the air. Wilhemina Brown and **Joe Smothers** made frequent appearances on the program as well.

Sources: *Baltimore Afro-American*, May 28, 1932, p. 18, September 10, 1932, p. 10; *New York Amsterdam News*, July 6, 1932, p. 7, October 19, 1932, p. 16; *Pittsburgh Courier*, August 6, 1932, p. 7.

Harlem Headlines

The Victory Mutual Life Insurance Company sponsored the weekly *Harlem Headlines* on WMCA which featured **Joe Bostic** and Jack Caldwell. Every Wednesday night employees of *The Amsterdam News* conducted interviews and reported on stories of interest to its Harlem audience. Bostic and Caldwell worked on the show from its debut on July 13, 1938, until August when they left and were replaced by Theodore Hernandez. Every week nine-year-old Bobby Tunstall opened and closed each show with the catch phrase "Get your Amsterdam News." The program was short-lived, leaving the air in September 1938.

Sources: *New York Amsterdam News*, July 16, 1938, p. 9, August 20, 1938, p. 7, September 10, 1938, pp. B6, B9.

Harlem on Parade

Joe Bostic's first New York radio production was a series called *Harlem on Parade* which debuted Saturday June 29, 1935, over WHN. The broadcast was primarily musical in nature; the first episode featured Dick Porter with piano and songs, Jesse Cryor and his Rhythm Rascals, the Bronze Harmonizers under the direction of Nettie Olden Oliver, Edna Brevard with piano selections, a solo by Matthew Edward, and Rudy Smith

playing his composition "New York Sky Line." However, it also featured a routine by the comedy team of Bootsie Swann and Joe Lee. The series switched to Wednesday nights thereafter where it aired until October. At that time the program moved to Friday nights on station WEVD. Others who appeared over the weeks included The Palmer Brothers and Laura Duncan. Evidence suggests that *Harlem on Parade* had left the air by the end of 1935.

Sources: *New York Amsterdam News*, July 6, 1935, p. 5, October 5, 1935, p. 15.

Harlem Varieties

At least three distinct radio series aired under the moniker *Harlem Varieties*. The first lasted from July through October 1936, over WMCA. It was primarily a musical effort including guests such as Bob Gaillard, Bernice Crowder, and the Four Chords.

In 1938 the second incarnation debuted over WINS, a station in the Hearst chain. The weekly series was produced and written by Jimmy Christian and proved so popular that after one broadcast it was increased from thirty minutes to a full hour. This *Harlem Varieties*, described as a black *Make Believe Ballroom*, was sponsored by various local African American businesses. This series lasted just a few weeks.

The final version, named *The New Harlem Varieties* debuted in February 1939, over WHOM. The hour-long program was sponsored by *The New York Amsterdam News* and regularly featured Buddy Walker, Muriel Kahn, and Dick Campbell. The broadcasts included interviews, talks, and musical performances. This program lasted until April 1939.

Sources: *New York Amsterdam News*, July 11, 1936, p. 8, January 29, 1938, p. 4, 7, February 4, 1939, p. 16, February 11, 1939, p. 5, February 25, 1939, p. 20, March 4, 1939, p. 17.

Harris, Bass

Bass Harris spent the earliest years of his

radio career in Boston before moving Seattle, WA, where he had a two-hour afternoon spot jockeying music over station KING as early as 1936. During this time he also broadcast over Portland's KOL. In February 1952, Harris debuted a new hour-long program, *Bass Harris at Home*, over KMPC every Saturday night. Soon after he took on additional announcing duties at KFAC. Harris was still on the airwaves in 1956 with a program called *House of Cheer*.

Sources: Barlow p. 94; Sies p. 252; *Los Angeles Sentinel*, February 7, 1952, p. B3, May 8, 1952, p. B2, July 19, 1956, p. 10; *New York Amsterdam News*, February 7, 1948, p. 11.

Harrod's Jubilee Singers

Numerous "Jubilee" groups hit the airwaves in the 1920s but one of the first was Harrod's Jubilee Singers who were on the air by January 1925. Their program over WHN, New York, included plantation songs, comedy and "pot pouri" entertainment.

Source: *Baltimore Afro-American*, January 31, 1925, p. 4.

Harvey, Georgette

Born in St. Louis, Georgette Harvey was performing by age ten and spent sixteen years on the stage in Europe during the early 20th century, especially Russia. In 1917 she fled the turmoil engulfing Russia and made her way back to the United States. Harvey began making a name for herself in various productions, one of the earliest being 1923's *Running Wild*. She later was cast in the role of Maria in the original *Porgy* (later *Porgy and Bess*). Harvey's first known radio appearance came in 1925 when she appeared with members of the *Running Wild* company and sang "Log Cabin Days" from the production over Washington, D.C.'s WPC. Two years later she led the Runnin' Wild Quartet on the second episode (December 15, 1927) of the *Pittsburgh Courier Hour* (later the *Floyd Calvin Hour*) on WGBS with the Georgette Harvey Runnin' Wild Four. Composed of Lillian Cowan, first soprano, Clarissa Blue,

second soprano, Musa Williams, first contralto, and Harvey, second contralto, this is possibly the same foursome that earlier went by the Runnin' Wild Quartet moniker.

In 1931 Harvey was on the air with a different group, the **Four Bon-Bons**, made up of Musa Williams, Lois Parker (who was replaced by Katherine Parker), and Ravella Hughes. The Bon-Bons aired on CBS twice a week for six months. Most of the 1930s was spent on stage but she made occasional broadcasts including an appearance on Al Jolson's show sponsored by Kraft (February 8, 1934) and on WEVD (May 6, 1934) where she sang spirituals with **Ray Yeates**, future Southernaires tenor. During the late 1930s and early 1940s Harvey stayed busy with roles on numerous daytime serials such as *Betty and Bob* (on which she played a maid for 26 weeks), *Our Gal Sunday* (24 weeks), *The Perfect Crime* sponsored by Philip Morris, *Follow the Moon* (22 weeks) with Nick Dawson, and *I Love Linda Dale* (April 29, 1940, to February 7, 1941, as Savannah the maid). Harvey also earned spots on *Pretty Kitty Kelly*, and *The Man I Married*, a Ray Bloch program sponsored by Philip Morris.

Harvey had been passed over for the role of Mammy in *Gone With the Wind* due to her light skin tone, a role that ultimately went to **Hattie McDaniel**. However, when plans were made to turn the epic film into a radio serial in the fall of 1940 Harvey was the lead candidate for Mammy's part. There's little evidence to suggest that the adaptation was ever aired. She made at least three other radio broadcasts in 1940, all of which were with predominantly African American casts: *Great Plays* (March 10, 1940) on the Blue network, *Bishop and the Gargoyle* (Fall, 1940) with **Eddie Green** and **Juano Hernandez**, and *Cavalcade of America* (December 25, 1940) with Juano Hernandez and **Frank Wilson** in "Green Pastures." Harvey's status in the black community was such that in May 1941 she was elected vice-president of the Negro Radio Workshop.

After Harvey's spate of serial work before the war her radio career slowed down considerably. She made a handful of radio appearances during the decade including **Clifford Burdette's** *Those Who Made Good* which premiered in 1941, *The Free Company* (March 23, 1941, and April 13, 1941), *Forecast* (August 25, 1941) with other members of the Negro Radio Workshop, *Grand Central Station* (December 12, 1941), the first *American Opera Festival*'s rendition of *Porgy and Bess* (May 7, 1942), *New World A' Coming* (June 18, 1944, and April 30, 1946), *This Is My Best* (September 19, 1944), United States Steel's *Theatre Guild on the Air*'s "The Green Pastures" (April 21, 1946), and *The Ford Theater*'s "Green Pastures" (February 1, 1948). Her last known broadcast was a March 1948, appearance on ABC's "To Secure These Rights" which commemorated the contributions of the black press.

Sources: LOC; Sampson, *Swingin' on the Ether Waves*, p. 405; Southern 306, 450, 451; Woll p. 214; *Baltimore Afro-American*, October 3, 1925, p. 5, July 16, 1927, p. 12, May 12, 1934, p. 8, October 21, 1939, p. 14, May 17, 1941, p. 14, October 16, 1943, p. 8, January 31, 1948, p. 7, March 20, 1948, p. 6; *Chicago Defender*, September 8, 1923, p. 6, November 25, 1939, p. 20, April 20, 1946, p. 17; *New York Amsterdam News*, October 19, 1927, p. 20, July 15, 1931, p. 7, July 22, 1931, p. 7, July 29, 1931, p. 4, June 1, 1940, p. 17, August 31, 1940, p. 17, September 28, 1940, p. 13, December 28, 1940, p. 5, May 10, 1941, p. 16, May 31, 1941, p. 20, August 9, 1941, p. 21, August 30, 1941, p. 21, March 1, 1952, p. 22; *Pittsburgh Courier*, December 3, 1927, p. 3, February 2, 1934, p. 8; www.radiogoldindex.com.

Helvey's Symphonic Troubadours

Based out of Cincinnati, Helvey's Symphonic Troubadours broadcast regularly over WKRC in the Queen city during late 1925.

Source: *Chicago Defender*, November 14, 1925, p. 7.

Henderson, Fletcher

Though not nearly as well remembered today by the general public as contemporaries such as **Duke Ellington, Count Basie,** and **Louis Armstrong**, Fletcher Henderson was one of the premier jazz band leaders through the 1920s and 1930s. Born and raised in Georgia, Henderson moved to New York in 1920 with the goal of attending Columbia. Instead he found himself in the music business both as musician and song plugger. As an orchestra leader Henderson was on radio as early as 1923 on Chicago's WDT with an outfit called the Happy Harmonists. Soon after, records indicate a series of broadcasts over WBZ in Springfield, MA, between 1923 and 1924. After finishing in Massachusetts, Henderson received air slots on New York's WHN, a station over which he would appear with some regularity for the next three years.

In 1927 Henderson's orchestra returned to the Windy City and aired daily over station KYW beginning in September 1927. By 1929 he was back in New York and broadcasting over WPAP and WHN four times a week; within a month he was on an additional two stations, WAAM and WOR, for a total of six weekly shows. By June the band was off the air for the summer months but returned in November for a weekly spot on WPAP, a spot which was increased to twice weekly by the start of the new year. Despite nearly six years of radio experience by 1930, broadcast gigs were rare that year until an engagement on WABC netted Henderson two appearances a week during the fall. The following summer, 1931, Henderson's orchestra came roaring back for four weekly slots. However, 1932 proved to be fallow for Henderson's radio aspirations though he is known to have had a brief stint on WMCA, but the time period is unknown.

Network time slots, plum spots for any musician, came Henderson's way in 1933 when his orchestra was granted four broadcasts a week over CBS. The next year beginning June 16, 1934, Henderson took over Jimmie Lunceford's spot at the famed Cotton Club. Along with the spot came nightly appearances on WMCA and twice weekly spots on the NBC network. The band members found themselves back on WHN during the summer of 1935 where they had appeared on and off back to radio's early days eleven years before. NBC welcomed Henderson back early in 1936 while his orchestra was booked in Chicago's Terrace. Henderson had at least one other string of radio broadcasts on CBS in 1938 before joining Benny Goodman's orchestra in 1939. As part of one of the most popular swing bands of the era, Henderson racked up countless more radio appearances with Goodman beginning with regular broadcasts from July 8 to December 30, 1939, on the *Camel Caravan*. During the mid–1940s Henderson again went solo but there is no evidence that he fronted his own band on network radio. They did, however, perform on four *Jubilee* broadcasts: #76 (recorded April 24, 1944), #77 (recorded May 1, 1944), #79 (May 9, 1944), and #145 (recorded August 27, 1945).

Sources: LOC; Cox, *Music Radio*, pp. 16–51; Lotz and Neuert; Magee pp. 14–26; Sies pp. 260, 485; Balk pp. 58–59; *Baltimore Afro-American*, May 30, 1924, p. 4; *Chicago Defender*, September 10, 1927, p. 8, June 24, 1933, p. 5, April 4, 1936, p. 8; *New York Amsterdam News*, January 2, 1929, p. 8, February 20, 1929, p. 9, June 26, 1929, p. 11, November 13, 1929, p. 8, January 1, 1930, p. 11, December 24, 1930, p. 10, July 15, 1931, p. 7, August 12, 1931, p. 7, January 11, 1933, p. 16, June 2, 1934, p. 7, June 22, 1935, p. 5.

Henry Allen, American

Broadcast over WNYC from October 8 to November 12, *Henry Allen, American* was an early attempt to create an African American serial. The title played off the name recognition of the popular white comedy *The Aldrich Family* with the teen hero Henry Aldrich. This black program followed Henry Allen, a black youth, and "the pathos, humor, events ... that Henry and his family are confronted with." The series, like most dramatic black shows, could not find a sponsor, and aired only six times.

Source: WNYC files; *New York Amsterdam News*, November 25, 1944, p. 8B.

Here Comes Tomorrow

Before **Richard Durham** launched his ground-breaking black radio series *Destination Freedom*, he honed his radio writing skills on *Democracy—USA* and *Here Comes Tomorrow*. Largely forgotten today, *Here Comes Tomorrow* lays claim to being the first black soap opera on the air. The thrice-weekly quarter-hour feature was broadcast over Chicago's WJJD from 10:00 to 10:15 A.M. on Mondays, Wednesdays, and Fridays. Of Durham's three radio series, it was the only one to land a commercial sponsor, the Metropolitan Mutual Assurance Company of Chicago.

Its cast included actors who had appeared on Durham's first radio program, *Democracy—USA*, and would go on to appear in his final effort *Destination Freedom*. **Fred Pinkard** starred as Milton Redmond, a pilot in the 99th Pursuit Division who returns from Italy with amnesia, and **Janice Kingslow** played Sarah, Milton's girlfriend. Other actors from the DuBois Theater Guild included **Oscar Brown, Jr., Wezlynn Tildon**, Harris Gaines, Jr., and Jack Gibson. Frank Sweeny announced, Wilson Doty provided organ accompaniment, and Allen Harris directed. Durham was credited with writing, production, and some directing duties.

Here Comes Tomorrow was originally planned to premier March 17, 1947, as a daily serial from 3:15 to 3:30. When a coveted sponsor was found, *Here Comes Tomorrow* cost Metropolitan just $500 a week, "a steal for the advertiser" according to *Billboard*. The first ten weeks were told in a flashback format with Sarah reminding Milton of his prior life in the south and the injustices they faced. The series clearly stood out from the other serials that filled the network's daytime hours. One reviewer raved "If all 'soap operas' were as well written, produced and directed as this show, if they all had its intense dramatic content, its social significance and its potential as a weapon against intolerance, no one would ever again have to level an accusing finger at daytime dramatic serials." Further, it was awarded second prize in 1948 in the highly-competitive 50,000 watt class for the nation's key dramatic programs, a contest sponsored by *Billboard*. It left the air in early spring, 1948.

Sources: *Billboard*, March 15, 1947, p. 5, October 25, 1947, p. 13, 16; *Chicago Defender*, September 13, 1947, p. 8, December 18, 1948, p. 18, January 8, 1949, p. 9, February 19, 1949, p. 22; *Los Angeles Sentinel*, April 3, 1947, p. 20.

Hernandez, Juano

Juano Hernandez was born in Puerto Rico sometime between 1896 and 1901 (sources give conflicting dates) and moved to the United States in 1905. As a young man he earned a paycheck undertaking various jobs from working cattle ships in Europe and Africa to rolling cotton on a Mississippi levee. He spent several years wandering the South working for various medicine and minstrel shows. These experiences were enough to land Hernandez parts in such Broadway productions as *Constant Sinner*, *Savage Rhythm*, and *Show Boat*. His most famous radio role was that of John Henry on the self-titled *John Henry, Black River Giant* program which originated from CBS's New York affiliate WABC in 1933. Hernandez was credited with being the force that brought the program to the airwaves as well as being its primary writer and musical arranger.

Hernandez became so connected with the John Henry figure that after the show went off the air he went on tour with members of the radio cast and played John Henry on stage as part of a revue. The troupe played all around the Eastern seaboard before finishing off with a multi-week run at the Cotton Club in the spring of 1934. Later that year members of the cast reunited and performed an hour-long version of Eugene O'Neill's *The Emperor Jones* over NBC.

After the *John Henry* stage production

closed Hernandez worked regularly on the Harlem stage for the next decade. There was at least one unsuccessful radio effort soon after *John Henry*. It was reported in June of 1934 that **Carlton Moss** was working on an audition script for Lambert Pharmacal's Listerine, which was in the market to sponsor an hour-long program. The proposal featured Hernandez and his Choir along with other notable singers **Ethel Waters**, Eubie Blake's Orchestra, and **Hall Johnson**'s Choir. Listerine, apparently, looked elsewhere and passed on Moss' script.

Though Hernandez would stay busy in radio, the jobs were never lucrative enough for him to give up live theater. Between September 3, 1936, and August 9, 1937, he was featured in NBC's *Cabin in the Cotton*. During 1937 he also appeared on *The Good Time Society*, a Blue network broadcast which originated from WJZ from 10:00 to 10:30 P.M. Hernandez both wrote the scripts and starred as the Great Potentate, essentially an MC who "preside[ed] over the good time folks of all the lands. Also featured on the program were Chick Webb and his band, Ella Fitzgerald, Taft Jordan, the **Juanita Hall** Choir, and the Four Ink Spots. *The Good Time Society* aired through the spring of 1937. He starred in other broadcasts with a black focus including an August 12, 1941, tribute to black soldiers sponsored by the War Department. **Eddie Green** and Bill Robinson also starred while Noble Sissle served as the master of ceremonies. Four years later Hernandez played Booker T. Washington next to **Canada Lee**'s Dr. George Washington Carver in a dramatization of Carver's life. Between 1939 and 1944 Hernandez made multiple appearances on ABC's *African Trek*, a variety program which featured songs, music, and folk stories from Africa. Josef Marais, a singer from South Africa, served as the program's host. On December 10, 1946 Hernandez had a role on the prominent black series *New World A' Coming*.

In addition to these Afro-centric broadcasts Hernandez made appearances on *Pulitzer Prize Plays* (June 23, 1938, with **Frank Wilson**), *Radio Guild* (July 13, 1940), *Cavalcade of America* (April 2, 1940, April 16, 1940, May 14, 1940, November 6, 1940, December 11, 1940, December 25, 1940, February 5, 1951, February 19, 1941, May 19, 1941, June 9, 1941, June 23, 1941, July 7, 1941, November 24, 1941, December 22, 1941, November 16, 1942, February 22, 1943, May 27, 1946, November 10, 1947, February 9, 1948, June 7, 1948, November 15, 1948, March 13, 1951), the fondly remembered *Inner Sanctum Mystery* (July 6, 1941, December 7, 1941), *Dangerously Yours* (August 6, 1944), *The United States Steel Hour* (April 21, 1946), *The Ford Theater* (November 16, 1947 and February 1, 1948), *The Eternal Light* (More than twenty episodes between July 1, 1945, and December 6, 1953) on which he frequently played rabbis and even the Bible's Adam, *Creeps By Night*, *Green Valley, USA* (with Canada Lee, 1942), *Words at War* (March 7, 1944), *Tennessee Jed* (as a Native American chief), *Jungle Jim* (as Kolu), *Mr. Keen, Tracer of Lost Persons* (as a prosperous black attorney), *Mandrake the Magician* (as Lothar), *March of Time*, *Open Letter to the American People* (CBS, 1943), and *Library of Faith* (1948's "The Bookseller" over WNEW).

Hernandez received ongoing roles over the years, including a spot on the serial *Portia Faces Life* where he played Trouble beginning April 2, 1942, as well as on *Aunt Phyllis' Coffee* that same year. He played Mr. Bones on *We Love and We Learn* from April 3 to September 29, 1944 and Dewey on *The Jimmy Edmondson Show* from February 2 to February 23, 1946. Generally acknowledged as a premier actor, Hernandez came under criticism for taking an Uncle Tom role on a June 6, 1943 episode of *Radio Reader's Digest*. He insisted afterward he didn't see the harm in the role. As late as 1950 Hernandez still found radio parts, including a short stint as

Eddie on *Duffy's Tavern* on May 11, 1950 and from September 7 through September 21 of the same year. His last known radio part was on the December 21, 1955, broadcast of *Truth or Consequences*.

Hernandez would go on to do a few motion pictures and television episodes. In 1950 he was awarded the degree of Doctor of Fine Arts from University of Puerto Rico. He died of a heart attack in 1970.

Sources: LOC; Berry and Berry p. 158; Cox, *Radio Crime Fighters*, pp. 72, 148, 170, 250; Grams, *Cavalcade*; Grams, *Radio Drama*, pp. 63–64, 71, 73, 124, 170, 191, 359, 388, 401, 507; Patterson pp. 128–129; Sampson, *Blacks in Black and White*, p. 526; Segal p. 50; Swartz and Reinehr pp. 215, 575; Woll pp. 214–215; *Baltimore Afro-American*, January 14, 1933, p. 10, January 21, 1933, p. 10, January 28, 1933, p. 10, February 18, 1933, p. 19, April 15, 1933, p. 8, September 30, 1933, p. 18, October 14, 1933, p. 18, April 14, 1934, p. 21, June 23, 1934, p. 8, June 30, 1934, p. 8, January 16, 1937, p. 10, August 9, 1941, p. 14, August 29, 1942, p. 10, June 12, 1943, p. 10, November 3, 1945, p. 10, March 20, 1948, p. 6, November 13, 1948, p. 6, June 17, 1950, p. 8, July 16, 1955, p. 7; *New York Amsterdam News*, March 16, 1932, p. 7, January 11, 1933, p. 16, March 22, 1933, p. 1, April 19, 1933, p. 17, November 15, 1933, p. 7, November 10, 1934, p. 9, March 27, 1937, p. 10, December 18, 1937, p. 19, December 28, 1940, p. 5, May 3, 1941, p. 20, June 12, 1943, p. 17, August 29, 1942, p. 14, March 20, 1948, p. 14, November 13, 1948, p. 25, June 24 1950, p. 1, August 11, 1951, p. 26, June 22, 1957, p. 24, April 18, 1970, p. 4; *Pittsburgh Courier*, January 14, 1933, p. 6, February 11, 1933, p. 7, April 11, 1936, p. 18, March 6, 1937, p. 18, June 12, 1943, p. 20.

The High Brown Five Orchestra

The High Brown Five Orchestra performed over the air to a Portland, OR, listening audience on September 1, 1922. Octavia Doran, singer with the group, sang "The Sheik," "Doo Dah Blues," "I Wish I Knew," "Nobody Lied," and "Arkansas Blues." Pianist A. Thompson played "Four O'Clock Blues," his own arrangement. The Orchestra was made up of Sam Ketchul, drums and directing duties, A. Thompson, piano, D. Oliver, saxophone, F. Junion, banjo, and D. Smith, trombone. Orchestral numbers included "Lonesome Mama Blues,"

"Kicky Koo," "I've Got My Habits On," "School House Blues," "Don't Bring Me Posies," "She's a Mean Job," "Sneak," and "Home Again Blues." The broadcast was sponsored by the Oregonian and the Shipowners' Radio Service.

Source: *Chicago Defender*, September 2, 1922, p. 6.

Hill, Ruby

While a junior at Armstrong High School in Richmond, VA, Ruby Hill began singing over local station WRVA in 1930. Her fine soprano voice earned her the nickname the "Virginia Songbird" and kept her on the air until 1931.

Source: *Baltimore Afro-American*, August 8, 1931, p. 9.

Hines, Earl

Earl Hines claimed to be one of the first black performers on radio, recalling a 1921 broadcast he did over Pittsburgh's KDKA with partner **Lois Deppe**. The duo played "Isabel" and "For the Last Time Call Me Sweetheart." His regular series of broadcasts originated from Chicago's Grand Terrace Hotel in the mid–1920s over WEDC. His band was still broadcasting from the Grand Terrace in the early 1930s over WSBC. By 1932 Hines' outfit had received enough recognition to get a regular spot on NBC which turned into a nightly broadcast by 1933. Hines was featured on *The Chamber Music Society of Lower Basin Street* in the early 1940s, two decades after debuting on radio, and he also had a weekly broadcast on the Mutual chain at the time. As late as 1945 he was airing from Chicago's Club El Grotto on WIND. Hines was still regarded highly enough throughout the 1940s to be invited on *Jubilee* nearly a dozen times: #105 (broadcast March 4, 1945), #106 (broadcast March 10, 1945), #194 and #195 (both undated), #268 (broadcast April 1948), #294 (broadcast October 1948), #337 (broadcast August 6, 1949), #339 (broadcast August 20, 1949),

#344 (broadcast September 24, 1949), #347 (October 15, 1949), and #382 (broadcast January 10, 1953). Between 1947 and 1948 Hines made three guest appearances on *The Dave Garroway Show* and an additional appearance on the *King Cole Trio Time*.

Sources: LOC; Barlow pp. 22, 24; Dance, *Earl Hines*, p. 25; Dunning p. 147; Lotz and Neuert; Sampson, *Swingin' on the Ether Waves*, pp. 52–53, 394; Spaulding pp. 22–23; *Baltimore Afro-American*, February 27, 1932, p. 3, March 10, 1945, p. 8; *Chicago Defender*, April 1, 1933, p. 5.

Holley, Otis

Otis Holley was a soprano who was prominent in the New York area throughout the 1930s. Holley was born in Talladega, AL, and raised in rural towns in Alabama and Tennessee where she was responsible for two young children after her parents died when she was eight years old. What became of them is not known but Holley eventually moved to New York where she quickly found work as a cook in the home of one Pauline Gold. Ms Gold happened to be a voice and piano instructor and upon overhearing Otis singing at work offered to give her formal lessons.

The practice paid off and by the spring of 1932 Otis was engaged to sing for such groups as the James Weldon Johnson Literary Guild and the NAACP. The next year, 1933, Holley was performing over WOR on Tuesdays at 2:45 with a group called the Heywood Singers. Contemporary reviewers thought little of the Singers but were positive about Holley's voice and she soon earned her own broadcast slot on the station singing semi-classical numbers. By June 1934, she was appearing twice a week on WOR on Tuesdays and Thursdays. About that time she also began singing on the station's Sunday morning program *Deep River*.

The highlight of Holley's radio career came in 1935 when she competed on *Major Bowes Amateur Hour* and took first place. That fall several *Amateur Hour* winners were invited to go on a nationwide tour displaying their skills but Holley was not among them. While not questioning Bowes' racial attitude (he had numerous African American performers on his show), black groups protested that he was not willing to stand up to Jim Crow conditions that made it difficult for black performers on the road. Bowes denied such allegations but never explained the reason for Holley's omission from the *Amateur Hour* tours. There's no record that Otis Holley ever appeared again on the air but she continued to sing for private functions at least until the late 1940s.

Sources: Edmerson p. 26; *Baltimore Afro-American*, April 16, 1932, p. 8, June 4, 1932, p. 3, December 9, 1933, p. 19, June 9, 1934, p. 9, June 16, 1934, p. 8, June 23, 1934, p. 9, July 6, 1935, p. 8, November 2, 1935, p. 12, November 23, 1935, p. 8, May 9, 1936, p. 10, May 30, 1936, p. 20, January 30, 1937, p. 3, March 5, 1938, p. 16; *New York Amsterdam News*, June 6, 1936, p. 13, December 24, 1949, p. 8.

Honesty, Eddie

Eddie Honesty broke into radio after a formal education at Howard University and Fisk University. In 1925 he entered the industry as an engineer at Chicago's WIBO. A few years later he landed at WJOB in nearby Hammond, IN, where he worked as a disc jockey and program director into the 1950s. He is most prominently remembered for his long-running program *Rocking in Rhythm*.

Sources: Barlow p. 94; Spaulding p. 32; *Chicago Defender*, April 24, 1948, p. 7, June 9, 1951, p. 18.

Horne, Lena

Lena Horne sang regularly over radio through much of the 1940s beginning, it appears, on WOR's *Cats' n' Jammers* variety show in 1941. The Sunday morning program ran through the summer and before it went off the air she had earned a spot on NBC's *Strictly From Dixie*. Horne left that show in October 1941, and was replaced by Ella Fitzgerald. Her most widely remembered air work was on *The Chamber Music Society of Lower Basin Street*, an early 1940s series which spoofed classical music programs with down-home rhythm and blues music. Horne also made early appearances on Ralph Cooper's *Jumpin' Jive* on WMCA.

Other highlights of her radio work include the Blue Network's *What's New?* (1943-1944), *The Free World* (May 23, 1943), Norman Corwin's broadcast "Document A/777" which focused on the United Nations, and guest shots on *Jubilee*: #2 (recorded October 27, 1942), #9 (recorded January 31, 1943), #19 (recorded April 5, 1943), #30 (recorded June 21, 1943), #40 (broadcast December 23, 1944 and February 27, 1945), #45 (recorded October 10, 1943), #49 (recorded November 2, 1943), #59 (recorded January 3, 1944), #63 (recorded January 31, 1944), #73 (recorded April 3, 1944), #77 (recorded May 1, 1944), #84 (recorded June 19, 1944), #89 (recorded July 24, 1944), #90 (recorded July 31, 1944), #108 (recorded November 13, 1944), #111 (recorded December 5, 1944), #112 (December 11, 1944), #114 (recorded January 2, 1945), #117 (broadcast May 26, 1945), #119 (recorded February 5, 1945), #123 (broadcast July 13, 1945), #133 (broadcast August 1945, and September 1, 1945), #140 (recorded July 5, 1945), #150 (recorded October 1, 1945), #151 (recorded October 8, 1945), #157 (recorded November 18, 1945), #160 (recorded November 30, 1945), #164 and #166 (undated), #167 (broadcast April 26, 1946), #168, #170, #172, #210, #215, #224, and #230 (all undated), and the 1945 Christmas episode, *Command Performance* (April 1, 1944), and *Nothing But the Blues*.

Horne was invited to appear on several prominent network programs including the *Chase & Sanborn Hour* (November 24, 1943, December 12, 1943, December 19, 1943), *Suspense* (November 9, 1944), *Duffy's Tavern* (May 31, 1946), the *Chesterfield Supper Club* (January 5, 1948), and the *Eddie Cantor Show* (June 15, 1948).

Sources: LOC; Balk p. 215; Bannerman p. 213;

Cox, *Music Radio*, p. 81–89; Dunning p. 147, 168, 716–717; Grams, *Radio Drama*, pp. 198, 460; Grams, *Suspense*; Lotz and Neuert; Swartz and Reinehr p. 272; Sampson, *Swingin' on the Ether Waves*, pp. 348, 358, 376, 431–432, *Chicago Defender*, September 13, 1941, p. 21;

H. T. Ford and the Musical Mustangs

The Musical Mustangs, led by one H. T. Ford, made at least one appearance on a Cleveland radio station in July 1922.

Source: *Chicago Defender*, July 22, 1922, p. 6.

Hubert, Celia

Celia Hubert was one of the few African Americans on the air within the first couple years of the industry's birth. Hubert was a pianist who accompanied two white singers (John Berry and William Valiant) on a broadcast in late April 1922. A graduate of Chicago's Institute of Musical Arts, Hubert resided in Brooklyn and was organist for the Antioch Baptist Church.

Source: *Chicago Defender*, June 3, 1922, p. 9.

Huey, Richard

Born in Louisiana and raised in Los Angeles, Richard Huey discovered theater while studying at the University of California. In the mid–1920s he moved to New York and was receiving parts regularly by 1927. Huey was on radio early, making an appearance on *The Floyd Calvin Hour* on January 26, 1928. *The Calvin Hour* was successor to *The Pittsburgh Courier Hour* which debuted in 1927 and became the first regularly scheduled African American radio program. On the January broadcast he recited "Creation" from James Weldon Johnson's "God's Trombones." On March 1, 1929, Huey appeared on a broadcast sponsored by the Florence Mills Theatrical Association.

In addition to *The Floyd Calvin Hour* Huey was cast on another ground-breaking series, *Careless Love*. This program, penned by Carlton Moss, is identified as the first black dramatic program for radio and ran from 1930

to 1932. The next year, 1933, he was cast in the most famous early black program, *John Henry, Black River Giant* which starred **Juano Hernandez**. The series aired over CBS for most of the year. In the early to mid–1930s Huey was also cast on programs with the Marx Brothers, Will Rogers, and the *Good Gulf Gas Program* with Irvin Cobb and Al Goodman on WABC. In September 1934, he starred in a Moss-scripted mystery program on WMCA. Premier black performers Rose McClendon and **Frank Wilson** also starred and Alston Burleigh's Choir provided the music.

Money from radio was sporadic so Huey was constantly engaged in theater productions. His biggest role was that of Crown in *Porgy and Bess* but he also worked in such shows as *All God's Chillun Got Wings*, *Solid South*, *Five Star Final*, and *Wild Waves*. Huey also enjoyed working behind the scenes and formed the Harlem Players in 1930 with William Jackson, and the YMCA Players in 1933.

Interestingly, Huey was perhaps as famous in Harlem for his restaurant Dinah's Kitchen as for his acting. The business provided a steady income when Depression-era acting jobs were hard to come by. The place was described as being "decorated with periodicals, photographs, programs, and drawings, all with black themes." Dinah's Kitchen was acknowledged by many as a meeting place for Harlem's performing elite. Across the hallway from his restaurant Huey ran a black theater booking office.

Radio work dried up in the late 1930s but in 1940 Huey returned with a role on the oddly-titled all-black feature *Sheep and Goats Club* over WOR. Various black actors such as Frank Wilson appeared on the show during its run of a few months. *The Club* was described as "a humorous musical diverting contest between good and evil." The performances were also presented on the New York stage. In 1941 Huey dubbed himself the Lenox Avenue Record Man and earned a fifteen-minute disc jockey spot on WOR on which he played music that was "in the groove, never too hot and never too cold." He was cast in a number of early 1940s dramatic broadcasts which featured predominantly black casts including *Cavalcade of America* (December 25, 1940), *Columbia Workshop* (April 27, 1941), *Columbia Presents Corwin* (March 21, 1944 and May 16, 1944), *New World A' Coming* (April 2, 1944), *We, the People* (November 1944), and *The United States Steel Hour* (April 21, 1946). Huey, a large man of "Taftian proportions" died unexpectedly in 1948.

Sources: Grams, *Cavalcade*; Grams, *Radio Drama*, pp. 104, 507; Peterson pp. 90, 102; *Baltimore Afro-American*, April 7, 1934, p. 8, April 6, 1940, p. 14, June 15, 1940, p. 14, August 1, 1942, p. 11, November 27, 1948, p. 6; *New York Amsterdam News*, February 29, 1928, p. 5, 17, October 29, 1930, p. 11, April 27, 1932, p. 7, February 15, 1933, p. 8, March 15, 1933, p. 8, March 22, 1933, p. 1, January 26, 1933, p. 9, April 21, 1934, p. 9, August 25, 1934, p. 1, September 15, 1934, p. 9, June 22, 1935, p. 11, November 16, 1935, p. 12, March 9, 1940, p. 7, February 1, 1941, p. 17, May 3, 1941, p. 20, November 18, 1944, p. 10, January 1, 1949, p. 21; *Pittsburgh Courier*, February 4, 1928, p. 1, February 11, 1933, p. 7, July 13, 1940, p. 21, May 9, 1942, p. 20; www.radiogoldindex.com.

Hurt, Marlin

Born in DuQuoin, Il., on May 27, 1904, Marlin Hurt was a white actor who made his most memorable mark in radio impersonating African American men and women. He was the son of a show businessman and began working in vaudeville himself when he was old enough. An accomplished musician, Hurt played with the Jean Goldette Orchestra in Chicago and Detroit. From there he formed his own orchestra and played the saxophone. After Hurt broke up his band he returned to Chicago and appeared with Paul Ash at the city's Oriental Theater. There he began experimenting with various voices including the black caricature dialects for which he would become most famous. Around 1929 he went to work for Chicago

station WGN, both as part of the trio Tom (Bud Vandover), Dick (Hurt), and Harry (Gordon Vandover) and in the station's air minstrel acts. The trio played nearly every day, sometimes multiple times, through much of the 1930s and the WGN Minstrels broadcast at least until early 1933.

Beulah, Hurt's most famous character, was created in 1939 and featured on the NBC program *Home Town Unincorporated* from November 26, 1939, until April 28, 1940. The voice and mannerisms for Beulah were based on a cook named Mary who worked for Hurt's family when he was a boy. Shortly after the stint on *Home Town Unincorporated* he and Beulah moved to the popular *Show Boat* program, also on NBC, between May 1940, and April 1941. Two months later Beulah was back on the air in *The Fred Brady Show*, again over NBC, as a 1941 summer replacement for *The Bob Burns Show*. In addition to playing Beulah, Hurt also portrayed her bumbling boyfriend, Bill, and himself as well. Meanwhile, he continued to sing in Tom, Dick and Harry on such shows as *Uncle Walter's Doghouse* (1939–1940) and *Plantation Party* (1938–1943), though not necessarily on every broadcast. Around this time Hurt also appeared on some broadcasts of *The Red Skelton Show* as Madamoiselle Levy, described as "the Beulah voice without the blackface accent."

Fibber McGee & Molly writer Don Quinn overheard Hurt's Beulah and knew he had to write the character into a script for the top-rated program. She debuted on the McGees' show January 25, 1944, and became the family's maid soon after. Beulah proved so popular that she was given her own series, following in the footsteps of Hal Peary's *Great Gildersleeve* who was also spun off from *Fibber McGee & Molly* a few years before. *The Marlin Hurt and Beulah Show* (later called *The Beulah Show*, *The New Beulah Show*, and simply *Beulah*) premiered on NBC July 2, 1945. Hurt's solo run in the *Beulah* program was cut short, however, when he unexpectedly died of a heart attack on March 21, 1946. Another white man, Bob Corley, took over the role of Beulah for six months but failed to match Hurt's popularity. From 1947 until the show finally left the air in 1954 Beulah was played by a succession of African American actresses.

Sources: Dunning pp. 269, 548, 568, 613, 690; Cox, *The Great Radio Sitcoms*, pp. 74–75; Sies p. 464; Stumpf and Price p. 263; *Chicago Defender*, September 7, 1940, p. 16; *Chicago Tribune*, June 6, 1929, p. 18, May 24, 1931, p. G6, December 27, 1931, p. F4, February 19, 1933, p. SC4.

Ingram, Rex

Rex Ingram briefly pursued a career in medicine after graduating from Northwestern University and moving to Los Angeles. Shortly thereafter he began appearing in films as early as 1920, most notably an early Tarzan picture. Ingram worked consistently in motion pictures and on stage for over forty years before passing away in 1969. He never starred in a regular radio series but made a handful of appearances over the years. Ingram's earliest radio credit was a July 1934, appearance on *The Kraft Hour* with Paul Whiteman. Two years later in August 1936, he was cast on *Maxwell House Show Boat* and subsequently criticized for singing "That's Why Darkies Were Born." At the end of 1936 Ingram starred in a radio adaptation of *Green Pastures* on which he played De Lawd, the same role he played in the film, perhaps his most memorable screen part. The broadcast was aired over WOR on December 23, 1936, and co-starred **Frank Wilson**. At the end of the decade he earned a spot on the February 2, 1939, broadcast of *Good News of 1939*.

Ingram was the lead in a CBS radio play based on the life of Booker T. Washington called "Pursuit of Happiness" (April 7, 1940), and then in 1941 he was the subject of an episode of *Those Who Made Good*, an African American program aired over WNYC. Ingram appeared on the premier episode of *Jubilee*, a series that was broadcast only to overseas soldiers during World War II. He assisted on the premier episode recorded October 9, 1942. Ingram starred with **Lena Horne** on the May 23, 1943, episode of *The Free World*. The last known radio acting role of Ingram's career was in an American Negro Theatre presentation of "The History of Dr. John Fause" in early 1946 over WNEW on which he played the title character. Later that year on September 20 Ingram was a guest on Jim Young's *Broadway and Hollywood* program.

Sources: Bannerman p. 142; Berry and Berry p. 173; Grams, *Radio Drama*, p. 198; Lotz and Neuert; Patterson p. 259; Peterson p. 145; Sampson, *Blacks in Black and White*, p. 529; Woll p. 220; *Baltimore Afro-American*, July 28, 1934, p. 9, August 29, 1936, p. 20, May 17, 1941, p. 14, February 9, 1946, p. 10; *New York Amsterdam News*, December 26, 1936, p. 17, March 30, 1940, p. 16, September 21, 1946, p. 20, September 27, 1969, p. 26.

International Bible Students' Association

This religious organization had a weekly Sunday morning program in the fall and winter of 1930 which aired over WBBR and WMCA, New York, as well as a wider 300-station hook-up. Every month the producers aired one program entirely with African American talent.

Source: *Baltimore Afro-American*, December 24, 1930, p. 10.

Interracial Musical Hour

While not the first broadcast to feature an interracial cast, the *Interracial Musical Hour* may very well be the first to publicize itself as such. The program lasted just a few months over WGBS, New York, in the second half of 1930 before switching over to the city's municipal station WRNY in October.

Sources: *New York Amsterdam News*, August 27, 1930, p. 10, October 1, 1930, p. 10.

Jackson, Hal

Hal Jackson was a Charleston, SC, native

who started his decades-long radio career in 1937 at WINX then WOOK, both in Washington, D.C. His program, *The House That Jack Built* also aired on Arlington's WEAM and Baltimore's WSID in addition to its WOOK origination. Jackson was credited with being the first African American disc jockey on Washington, D.C.'s WOL. In 1949 he moved to New York where he started on WLIB. Jackson later appeared on WBMD. He moved around the radio dial during the 1950s, appearing on WMCA in 1952, nightly on WABC in 1953, and then again on WLIB by 1957. Jackson found himself caught up in the payola scandals of late 1950s but survived and continued to thrive on radio a decade into the 21st century.

Sources: Barlow pp. 95–96; Jaker, et al. p. 111–113; Sies p. 480; *Baltimore Afro-American*, April 14, 1951, p. 8, November 29, 1952, p. 7, August 8, 1953, p. 11, November 12, 1949, p. 13, January 19, 1957, p. 11, May 28, 1960, p. 1.

James, Regina "Gee Gee"

Born in 1902 or 1903, Regina James grew up and got into show business in Philadelphia. It's not known when she began going by the nickname Gee Gee but the earliest references so far uncovered refer to her by that moniker. In 1927 James started working on the Philadelphia stage as a chorus girl before building up to more prominent roles, some of which may have been with the Brooks-Burns-Wiltshire outfit with whom she was associated for quite a while. Her first radio work was on Philadelphia's WIP-WFAN in the late 1920s or early 1930s. Her earliest confirmed radio performances were in 1931 when she had a half-hour program on Sunday nights in which she frequently sang the popular tune "If You Don't Love Me Make Believe You Do." By October she was sharing a 45-minute broadcast block with Jim Winters' Roadside Unit, also on Sunday nights.

The next year, 1932, James migrated to New York City where she promptly found work in various theater productions. She labored in obscurity until 1935 when she was chosen from a group of 23 to play the part of Migonette on NBC's *The Gibson Family*. Co-star and fellow African American actor **Ernest Whitman** was credited by some sources as discovering James for the show. Her singing was such that one contemporary commentator noted "If you hear a singing voice on the Gibson Family program every Saturday that sounds like **Ethel Waters**, don't be disillusioned.... The voice is that of a young girl from Harlem by the name of Gee Gee James." NBC announced in January 1935, that she would soon be joining the show. Unfortunately, *The Gibson Family*, which was an experimental blend of Broadway musical tunes and stage drama, did not live up to the network's hype since its 1934 debut and was struggling to stay on the air. Her role lasted barely six months as the series left the air in June 1935, and she was not included in the program's successor, *Uncle Charlie's Tent Show*.

Undeterred, by autumn James found herself singing on Kate Smith's thrice-weekly program and working Smith's concert tours as well. Smith had been working on radio most of the 1930s and in 1938 her rendition of "God Bless America" would become a national sensation. During the 1935-1936 season which James worked, Smith's program was sponsored by the Great Atlantic and Pacific Tea Company, otherwise known as A&P. Dubbed *Kate Smith's A & P Coffee Time*, the show aired Tuesdays, Wednesdays, and Thursdays over the CBS network. Late in 1935 James' personal life changed drastically when she adopted her three-year-old niece, also named Regina.

Gee Gee James found new radio work in April 1937, on an NBC Blue hour-long program sponsored by Fleischmann Yeast called appropriately enough, *The Fleischmann Yeast Hour*. **Louis Armstrong** was the headline performer on the series but it also featured comedian **Eddie Green** and James. Green and James starred in a sketch continued week to week about an engaged Harlem couple who get into assorted predicaments when Green's character inherits three thousand dollars. The *Hour* was written by Octavus Roy Cohen, writer of detective and mystery stories, several of which prominently featured black characters. He had earlier written the radio serial *The Townsend Murder Mystery* which aired in 1933. The series got poor reviews and blame was heaped on Cohen for lousy scripts. It was rumored that Rudy Vallee had helped persuade NBC to go forward with *The Fleischmann Hour* but nobody could save it; Armstrong's series aired for the last time on June 25, 1937, after a run of less than three months.

In 1938 James took the radio role which would be her most well remembered, the maid Tulip on daily soap opera *Hilltop House*. Carolo DeAngelo, director of *The Gibson Family*, happened to be director of *Hilltop House* and likely had a say in hiring a known performer. James was a regular by August 1938, and lasted several months before leaving in the spring of 1939 to go on tour with Katherine Cornell's stage production of *No Time For Comedy* in which she also played a maid. One source indicates she also left a series called *Her Honor, Nancy James*, a daily program over CBS to do the tour. After the tour was over Tulip was written back into *Hilltop House* and James resumed her daily role. She left the serial a second time in November 1940, and did not return. During this same time period James was cast as Aunt Jemima on *Quaker Party* from October 1, 1938, to March 25, 1940. As with *Hilltop House*, she missed several weeks while on tour in the spring of 1939.

James made radio appearances throughout the early 1940s, the longest recurring part being that of Jennie on NBC's *The Nichols' Family of Five* (October 5, 1941, to March 29, 1942), sponsored by Vick Chemical. She performed on *The O'Neills*, a long-running series which ran from 1934 to 1943, but it is not known when. Between 1940 and 1941 James made three appearances on *The Jack Benny Program* (December 15, 1940, December 22, 1940, and October 12, 1941). She appeared on *The Rudy Vallee Show* in the 1930s, as Guinevere on *Gaslight Gayeties* from February to July 1945, and a 1945 article credits her with a role on *Mr. & Mrs. North*. At the same time she began working more regularly in live theater in such works as *The Wife Takes a Child* with Evelyn Davis (late 1942 and early 1943), *Three is a Family* (May 1943) and in Broadway's *A Streetcar Named Desire* which featured Marlon Brando and Jessica Tandy.

Sources: LOC; Cox, *The Great Radio Soap Operas*, p. 71; Edmerson p. 21; Hayes p. 47; Leff vol. 1 pp. 411, 412, 437; Sies p. 421; *Baltimore Afro-American*, January 19, 1935, p. 9, February 2, 1935, p. 8, February 9, 1935, p. 9, November 2, 1935, p. 9, December 14, 1935, p. 9, January 18, 1936, p. 10, April 10, 1937, p. 17, May 15, 1937, p. 11, January 1, 1938, p. 10, April 9, 1938, p. 11, May 13, 1939, p. 19, December 16, 1939, p. 13, November 30, 1940, p. 14, January 2, 1943, p. 10, May 22, 1943, p. 10, December 20, 1947, p. 6; *Chicago Defender*, June 1, 1935, p. 6; *New York Amsterdam News*, January 19, 1935, p. 10, October 12, 1935, p. 8, April 17, 1937, p. 16, August 6, 1938, p. 6, April 8, 1939, p. 21, March 24, 1945, p. 22; *Philadelphia Tribune*, September 17, 1931, p. 6; October 1, 1931, p. 6, December 3, 1931, p. 6, April 7, 1938, p. 15.

Jarrett, Vernon

From 1948 to 1951 Vernon Jarrett worked with **Oscar Brown, Jr.**, on *Negro Newsfront*, a daily fifteen-minute radio news program aired over Chicago's WJJD. In an 1996 interview Brown recalled airing the newscasts from 1947 to 1952 so its possible Jarrett was not involved with *Negro Newsfront* during its entire run on radio. A native of Tennessee, Jarrett made his career as a journalist in Chicago, first with *The Chicago Defender* beginning in 1946, then later with *The Chicago Tribune* and *The Chicago Sun-Times*. He provided news for Chicago-area television as well. Jarrett died May 24, 2004.

Sources: Porter and Wojcik; *New York Times*, May 25, 2004.

Jaxson, Frankie (Half Pint)

Nicknamed Half Pint because of his short stature, Frankie Jaxson cut his teeth as a band leader in Chicago where he started on WJJD in early 1932. After the station cancelled his daily concerts in May 1933, he was picked up by WBBM from 7:00 to 7:15 P.M. on Wednesdays and Fridays. The station was confident in the potential of Jaxson and his six-piece orchestra, the Original Hot Shots, signing them to a 26-week contract. The group stood out from their fellow African American musicians as one of the few performers who attracted a sponsor, cosmetic company Golden Peacock, Inc.

Sources: *Baltimore Afro-American*, July 1, 1933 p. 8; *New York Amsterdam News*, November 16, 1932, p. 8; Oxford Music Online.

Jessye, Eva

Eva Jessye, a native of Kansas, was one of the first renowned female choir directors and her singers were famous from stage, film, and radio appearances. Jessye's choirs performed under various names and participants changed over the years, but their popularity never waned. Their earliest known radio broadcast was October 29, 1925, on WEAF. They returned to the station soon after on October 31 and November 2. Jessye and her choir made at least on appearance away from WEAF in September 1927, when they sang on WABC. The next year on September 23, 1928, her **Dixie Jubilee Singers** sang on WOR. In the latter part of 1929 the Singers were featured on *Aunt Mandy's Children*, a weekly WOR series directed by Jessye. At the same time the **Four Dusty Travelers**, a male quartet under her direction, debuted on WOR.

The popularity of Jessye and her singers continued into the Depression years. On December 29, 1931, her choir was featured on NBC and then again on February 12, 1932, the Dixie Jubilee Choir and Dixie Jubilee Male Choir sang on a NBC Lincoln Day program. As part of the program they par-

ticipated in a sketch dramatizing the story of early blacks in Oklahoma. Later, in the fall 1932, one of Jessye's choirs performed Sunday evenings on WJZ. During this same period they starred in *Carolina Thanksgiving* on Thanksgiving Day, 1932, on NBC and then on Christmas Day, 1932, they broadcast the Nativity story over WJZ (NBC again) with **Frank Wilson**.

Jessye also found rare opportunities to perform on radio outside her role as choir director. In the spring of 1933 she was cast as Magnesia on NBC's *The Townsend Murder Mysteries* with Frank Wilson and **Ernest Whitman**. Nevertheless, her singers provided most of her aural exposure. Jessye's choir members were the featured performers on NBC's July 4, 1933, *Tribute to the Negro Soldier* and they even received their own weekly show of spirituals and philosophy on Sunday afternoons over NBC during the fall of 1933. At the same time the choir made an appearance on the immensely popular *Capitol Theatre Family Hour* on NBC (November 5, 1933). Records indicate that radio work began to decline for the outfit beginning in 1934. They earned spots on the *Terraplane Travelcade* (May 1934) sponsored by the Hudson Motor Car Company on NBC, a special NBC broadcast to Russia with the **Southernaires** and **Eva Taylor** (July 8, 1934), and a return engagement on WEAF's *Capitol Family Hour* with Etta Moten and Bob Hope. Four later radio spots include guest appearances on RCA's *Magic Key* (December 1, 1935), Rudy Vallee's show (August 19, 1937), a program sponsored by the American Can Company (August 31, 1937) with Ben Bernie, and then WABC's *Heroines in Bronze* (March 20, 1943) sponsored by the National Urban League on which the choir provided background music.

Sources: LOC; Southern p. 422–423; Spaulding p. 23–24; *Baltimore Afro-American*, November 7, 1925, p. 4, March 19, 1927, p. 9, April 16, 1927, p. 9, September 24, 1927, p. 14, August 10, 1929, p. 13, September 28, 1929, p. 9, April 22, 1933, p. 10, April 29, 1933, p. 10, July 15, 1933, p. 10, September 16, 1933, p. 19, November 4, 1933, p. 19, May 26, 1934, p. 8, June 30, 1934, p. 8, August 18, 1934, p. 8, September 4, 1937, p. 11, March 27, 1943, p. 10; *New York Amsterdam News*, September 26, 1928, p. 8, February 3, 1932, p. 9, February 10, 1932, p. 9, December 21, 1932, p. 7, May 17, 1933, p. 16, March 13, 1943, p. 8, March 20, 1943, p. 11, November 13, 1976, p. D16; *Pittsburgh Courier*, December 26, 1931, p. 1, February 27, 1932, p. 2, November 5, 1932, p. 7, November 26, 1932, p. 16; Kansas Historical Society, www.kshe.org accessed November 6, 2010.

John Henry, Black River Giant

John Henry, Black River Giant may have been the first bonafide hit black radio program. The program, based on the book of the same name written by Roark Bradford, debuted Sunday evening, January 15, 1933, at 8:00 over WABC. Its scheduling was unusual; one episode aired from 8:00 to 8:15 and then a second episode aired from 8:45 to 9:00. Contemporary accounts make clear the two broadcasts were stand-alone stories, rather than one half-hour program broken into two separate fifteen-minute broadcasts. Over the summer the episodes were split across the week, one on Sunday and one on Thursday, but station execs soon returned to the twice–Sunday format.

The program's path to the air was not an easy one. Bob Wachsman bought the rights to the book and immediately set about recruiting **Juano Hernandez** to handle the project. Excited about the idea, Hernandez worked for ten grueling months fashioning the script into something to which a sponsor or station would commit. That *John Henry* was markedly different from other African American programs on the air made it a tough sell. Eventually CBS's New York affiliate WABC accepted the show and the network aired it nationwide.

The cast of *John Henry* included several seasoned African American actors including Rose McClendon, **Richard Huey**, and **Georgia Burke**. Other players were Emmett Lampkin, Ralph Ransom, **Maurice Ellis** and Jack McDowell. The lead role was taken

by Hernandez, a West-Indies born actor. Hernandez's 15-year-old son Ivan played a role and the series was announced by Alston Stevens. Geraldine Garrick was the director and Hernandez handled the musical arrangements.

Critical acclaim was quick to come to these aural plays adapted from Bradford's book. *The New York Daily News'* radio reviewer gushed that the debut "made me forget all about [competitor] Eddie Cantor" and *The New York Sun* promptly declared it the "best program on the air." *Radio Guide* magazine proclaimed the series "thoroughly American, brilliantly performed." Even *Billboard* took notice and insisted "if there was such a thing as a Pulitzer Prize for the best radio dramatization of the season, this series of programs would have had a strangle hold on it from the first broadcast."

Hernandez would spend three days writing each script before handing them off to Garrick who would then get it ready for the air. Multiple sources indicate both Hernandez and Garrick co-wrote the scripts, at least initially. A contemporary profile of Hernandez's efforts stressed his desire for authenticity; *Black River Giant* was to present a true portrait of life in the Southern Black River region in Mississippi. He kept near at hand lists of local medicinal roots, colloquialisms, dishes, and ailments to use in the scripts.

The actual contents of *John Henry* are sketchy at best. The first audition script, dated August 1, 1932, relates the story of John Henry's birth. The program opened with the Hernandez-penned tune "Mississippi" before the announcer intoned "In all the glorious south, never was there a mightier man than the legendary John Henry. Through the generations that have their root in the early days of slavery, John Henry moves with his enormous strides, his flaying arms, his powerful body, his slow but sure mentality overcoming every obstacle; a veritable god among the patient black folk, whose world is the muddy shores of the Mississippi." An elderly Uncle Sim proceeds to tell his grandson Dink of how Henry weighed in at forty pounds at birth and his raw power broke the slats of his bed when he yawned. By the end of the fifteen-minute episodes Henry was out the door to make his way in the world.

The only other complete script so far uncovered is episode #35 from May 14, 1933. In it Henry stands up to the Reverend Culler who is haranguing Sister Belzona for being a sinner. He turns the table on Culler, bringing the parishioners to see their own wrongdoings and leading them in a rousing spiritual.

The accompanying music was primarily folk songs, including the aforementioned "Mississippi." Chants often interrupted dialogue. One episode's climactic scene involves Henry calling forth the spirits in the room of "the Conjure woman's cabin." In another episode an "organ-voiced braggart loaded sugar by thousand pound loads and led his men in lusty songs of the river."

Accounts indicate Hernandez invested himself deeply in his role. During rehearsals one observer recalled that he "divests himself of his coat, rolls up his sleeves, lets his rather unruly shock of hair do what it will, and goes to it. The rest of the cast watch his wildly gesturing arms for their cues and for the volume of their voices." Even outside the studio Hernandez sometimes assumed the persona of John Henry. While getting reprimanded by a theater usher for trying to move to a seat closer to the front, Hernandez roared in response, "Who do you think you're talking to? Don't you know I'm John Henry?"

Despite the positive reviews, John Henry never could attract a commercial sponsor. In fact, writers from The Sun and Baltimore Afro-American wondered aloud why the program could not get that elusive sponsor. Could it be that companies did not like the thought of their products being represented by black performers? Even without a sponsor John Henry ran for nine months, departing the airwaves September 17, 1933. The next year,

in a letter to **Eva Jessye**, Hernandez contended CBS intentionally chose not to find a sponsor and keep the program on a sustaining basis. This was not detrimental to the cast because they were paid a salary comparable to what they would have received if CBS had found a sponsor for the show.

Further, Hernandez insisted John Henry was not canceled but ended by mutual agreement between him and the network. The original contract was completed and Hernandez and his supporting cast wanted to take John Henry on the road in an unusual nightclub show which included a dramatic sketch. Soon after the series went off the air the CBS Artists' Bureau arranged a stage tour for the company around the Northeast. The tour included dates at the Harlem Opera House and Lafayette Theater in New York, the Howard Theater in Washington, D.C., and the Lincoln Theater in Philadelphia. Other performers on the tour included **Bessie Smith** and Tommy Miles and his Washingtonians. On March 11, 1934, the act settled in for a multi-week run at the Cotton Club. Though John Henry ran for only nine months, the program was remembered fondly by members of the African American press for years to come.

Sources: Scripts—August 1, 1932, and May 14, 1933 (John Henry scripts, Emory University); Baltimore Afro-American, January 14, 1933, p. 10, January 21, 1933, p. 10, January 28, 1933, p. 10, February 18, 1933, p. 19, April 15, 1933, p. 8, September 30, 1933, p. 18, October 14, 1933, p. 18, April 14, 1934, p. 21, June 23, 1934, p. 8; New York Amsterdam News, January 11, 1933, p. 16, March 22, 1933, p. 1, April 19, 1933, p. 17, November 15, 1933, p. 7, November 10, 1934, p. 9; Pittsburgh Courier, January 14, 1933, p. 6, February 11, 1933, p. 7.

Johnson, Hall

Hall Johnson made his radio debut on The General Motors Hour over WEAF during the spring of 1928. Around the same time he was a guest on the May 15, 1928, broadcast of The Eveready Hour, a recording of which still survives according to historian Elizabeth

McLeod. Weeks later, and after an engagement on WOR (June 24, 1932), Hall returned to WEAF's *Eveready Hour* (July 3) and then performed again on the station July 17 with the accompaniment of an orchestra. Nearly 18 months later, in December 1929, Hall Johnson and his Choir performed at the Roxy Theatre and many of their numbers were broadcast.

Johnson's choir had three air credits during the summer of 1933 on WOR (June 14 and July 17) and WJZ (August 1) before they became regularly featured on *The Show Boat Hour*, aka *Captain Henley's Show Boat* on NBC sponsored by Maxwell House. A payment sheet for their November 17, 1932, appearance indicated each singer received $12, the accompanist $20, and the conductor $25. The group appeared on the Maxwell program until January 1933. That fall, beginning September 1933, the Hall Johnson Singers co-starred with Claude Hopkins' Orchestra on a weekly CBS show called *Harlem Serenade*, a musical program which originated from New York's famed Roseland Ballroom. During that time they sang as guests for the first time on the October 26, 1933, episode of Rudy Vallee's *Fleishman Hour*.

Vallee invited the singers back for a second appearance on March 8, 1934 and then a third time on the March 15 broadcast where they accompanied the white singer Lee Wiley on "Sometimes I Feel Like a Motherless Child." Over the next few years the Hall Johnson Singers performed on a variety of radio programs, including the premier episode (April 1934) of *The Union Assembly* over WEVD, a series sponsored by the International Ladies' Garment Workers' Union. Further performances that year included the July 26, 1934, *Kraft Music Hall* on NBC, the August 2, 1934, *Paul Whiteman Hour* on which they performed a condensed version of *Run, Little Chillun* with Al Jolson, the October 7, 1934, *Hall of Fame* with **Ethel Waters**, a broadcast sponsored by Lehn and Fink Products Company, and WABC's *Cobina Wright Variety Hour* (December 17).

Radio work was plentiful during the last half of the 1930s. The Choir was signed to appear regularly on *America Sings* as well as on NBC's *Gibson Family* in May 1935. On WNEW's *The Great Camp Meeting* premier broadcast in July 1935 Johnson led them in spirituals and songs about the Biblical character of Samson. Network jobs continued with a broadcast sponsored by the New York City YMCA over WEAF with Ethel Waters, the **Southernaires**, and **Frank Wilson** in November 1935, and a radio version of *The Green Pastures* with Al Jolson again on WEAF in February 1936. Another semiregular gig came along in late 1936 on the *Irving Cobb Plantation Hour*, aka *Paducah Plantations*, with Chick Webb and **Clarence Muse** on NBC.

As the 1930s wound down and gave way to the 1940s, Hall Johnson's Choir was offered fewer radio opportunities. What radio work they did get included a performance on Mutual's *Golden State Hour* (July 10, 1938), which came on the heels of multiple appearances on a program sponsored by National Dairy, a concert on WABC (February 26, 1939) with Clyde Barrie and a 50-piece orchestra, and *Cavalcade of America*'s rendition of *The Green Pastures* over CBS on December 25, 1940. A guest spot on the popular *Kraft Music Hall* followed a year later (November 20, 1941). Sources indicate the choir made few broadcasts during the war years. Beginning July 2, 1944, however, they were granted a weekly series on Sunday afternoons over WMCA on which they covered classic spiritual tunes. Johnson's group is also credited with appearances on the *Command Performance* armed forces series and WMCA's *New World A' Coming* during the early 1940s. One of their last known radio works was an April 21, 1946, broadcast of *The Green Pastures* on ABC's *The Theatre Guild on the Air*, featuring **Juano Hernandez**, **Richard Huey**, **Maurice Ellis**, **Juanita Hall**, and **Mercedes**

Gilbert. Their singing was aired over NBC on December 22, 1946, December 24, 1947, and again on January 18, 1948. Hall Johnson himself is known to have made at least one radio appearance after this on November 24, 1950, as a guest on an interview show.

Sources: LOC; McLeod pp. 116–117; Simpson pp. 17–19; Southern pp. 420–422, 444–445; Spaulding p. 24; *Baltimore Afro-American*, December 28, 1929, p. 12, October 22, 1932, p. 10, October 29, 1932, p. 10, September 30, 1933, p. 19, November 18, 1933, p. 19, December 23, 1933, p. 18, March 17, 1934, p. 7, July 28, 1934, p. 9, September 15, 1934, p. 7, October 6, 1934, p. 7, October 31, 1936, p. 13; *Chicago Defender*, April 28, 1928, p. 6, May 18, 1935, p. 6, April 20, 1946, p. 17; *Los Angeles Sentinel*, July 7, 1938, p. 1; *New York Amsterdam News*, July 4, 1928, p. 8, July 18, 1928, p. 8, December 28, 1932, p. 16, April 7, 1934, p. 2, July 27, 1935, p. 20, November 23, 1935, p. 8, February 15, 1936, p. 9, February 25, 1939, p. 16, January 4, 1941, p. 17, July 8, 1944, p. 11; *New York Times*, June 24, 1932, p. 17, June 14, 1933, p. 22, July 17, 1933, p. 18, August 1, 1933, p. 22, March 8, 1934, p. 20, April 6, 1934, p. 25, December 17, 1934, p. 28, November 26, 1935, p. 23, February 15, 1936, p. 18, April 10, 1936, p. 33, August 6, 1936, p. 17, February 26, 1939, p. 133, July 21, 1940, p. 31, May 27, 1941, p. 30, November 20, 1941, p. 54, July 27, 1943, p. 35, February 12, 1944, p. 27, August 11, 1944, p. 27, August 26, 1946, p. 27, December 24, 1947, p. 32, November 24, 1950 p. 36; *Pittsburgh Courier*, October 8, 1932, p. 7, January 14, 1933, p. 6; www.radiogoldindex.com.

Johnson, Walter

Walter Johnson was a Boston-area jazz pianist and orchestra leader. After a stint as soloist with a Cleveland radio station, he signed to broadcast exclusively over Boston's WEEI in December 1925. The station was owned by the Edison Light Company.

Sources: *Baltimore Afro-American*, December 26, 1925, p. 1; *Chicago Defender*, September 26, 1925, p. 7.

Johns, Vere Everette

Vere Johns was a black reporter who originally hailed from Jamaica. In the early 1930s he worked for station WOV where he covered the Harlem beat. Johns had a Tuesday afternoon slot on which he reported the news every week, making him one of the first black radio journalists.

Source: *Baltimore Afro-American*, May 28, 1932, p. 18.

Jones, Clarence

Born in Wilmington, DE, Clarence Jones studied piano in Cincinnati before heading to Chicago where he led an orchestra for twelve years. The outfit featured some his own compositions including "One Wonderful Night" and "Down Among the Pyramids." He once claimed to have accompanied on thousands of records.

Jones was a radio mainstay, appearing as early as September 11, 1922, with the self-titled Clarence Jones Orchestra on a broadcast concert during which J. Wright Smith was featured on a violin solo. The "Sultan of Syncopation" spent the 1920s working the Chicago music scene, cutting records, performing concerts, and broadcasting whenever possible. In 1925 Jones began appearing regularly over WBCN owned by The Southtown Economist and by the end of the year he had been hired as the staff pianist for WBBM, both Chicago stations. Jones historian Alex van der Tuuk has compiled a detailed account of his two years of radio appearances over WBCN. He premiered on the station in April 1925, and began with a weekly program. He proved popular enough that by October he was playing up to five times a week. His spot with WBCN lasted until June 1927.

After moving to New York at the turn of the decade Jones first worked with the **Southernaires** on the NBC program *Slow River* from 1932 to 1933. In 1933 he officially joined the quartet as arranger and pianist, roles he carried out until April 1940, when he had a nervous breakdown. **Spencer Odom** stepped in temporarily and wound up replacing Jones when he was unable to return to his work with the quartet.

Sources: Kennedy p. 37–46; *Chicago Defender*, September 16, 1922, p. 5; *New York Amsterdam*

News, June 11, 1938, p. 6, April 27, 1940, p. 1; http://paramountshome.org.

Jones, Elizabeth Fields

Elizabeth Fields Jones organized the Tall Corn Jubilee Singers, a group which broadcast regularly over KFKF in Shenandoah, IA. Raised in Hannibal, MO, where she taught for many years, Jones later worked as a principal for twelve years at Dunbar School in Platte City, MO. By 1925 she had moved to Clarinda, IA, where she worked with the Tall Corn Jubilee Singers. Whether she continued as an educator at that time is unknown. Unlike many African American performers, the Singers attained sponsorship by the Henry Field Seed Company. Some of Jones' singers were Richard Fields, Allee Jones, Walter Sweet, Jessie Howe, Glen Oldham, Frances Ramey and Joe Cason.

Source: *Chicago Defender*, March 21, 1925, p. 5.

Jones, La Frantz

La Frantz Jones of Wilmington, DE, in a letter claimed he preceded Roland Carrington as the first black licensed amateur operator. Noting that amateurs were first licensed with the passage of the Radio Act of 1912, Jones received his first license—amateur 2nd grade—on November 8, 1913. He subsequently went on to hold amateur 1st grade and commercial 2nd grade licenses.

Source: *Baltimore Afro-American*, November 22, 1924, p. 3.

Jones, Venzuella

Venzuella (or Vanzella) Jones had a minor career in the performing arts, most prominently in the mid–1930s with government-funded projects. She was a graduate of Kings School of Dramatic Art in Pittsburgh, PA, after which she studied drama at the University of Pittsburgh and Emerson College in Boston. Before finding work in New York, Jones worked as the head of the drama department at Morgan College, Baltimore. In New York she was cast in Broadway's *Savage Rhythm* and then became an instructor of adult education dramatic classes. Among Jones' directorial efforts was a version of *A Mid-Summer Night's Dream*. In the fall of 1935 she wrote two radio series, *Muddy Waters* and *A Harlem Family*. They lasted a combined four months on the air and left little impression on the black radio scene. Soon after *A Harlem Family* left the air in December 1935, Jones was back at work on the stage as the founder and leader of the Youth Theatre Project which focused on modern works using younger black performers. Other radio work with which Jones has been credited are roles on the serial *Young Widder Brown* and with *Cavalcade of America* (June 20, 1950, March 13, 1951).

Sources: Grams *Cavalcade*; Peterson pp. 139–140; *New York Amsterdam News*, March 30, 1935, p. 10, October 5, 1935, p. 15, December 14, 1935, p. 11.

Jubilee

During World War II various programs were created by the military to boost the morale of troops around the world. Some of the most widely remembered today include *Mail Call* and *Command Performance*. While these featured primarily white entertainers, *Jubilee* was created to be aimed at African American soldiers and spotlighted many black entertainers, though whites were also featured, increasingly so as the program continued after the war.

Historians Rainer Lotz and Ulrich Neuert credit one Major Mann Holiner with coming up with the idea for *Jubilee*. Originally to be called *Freedom's People*, the final program title was based on a civilian show by Holiner also called *Jubilee*. The first five shows were produced in studio space rented from the major networks by the Radio Section of the Special Services Division beginning sometime between November and December 1942. AFRS historian Theodore DeLay claims production started November 2 while Lotz and Neuert claim December.

In January 1943, production moved to Los Angeles where it remained for the rest of its run. *Jubilee* was not intended for a civilian audience nor was it every intentionally broadcast to United States listeners. The program was beamed from shortwave stations on the East and West coasts to overseas stations and transcriptions were also sent straight to some overseas stations. The program proved very popular with servicemen; it was second only to *Mail Call* in the amount of fan mail received.

In subsequent years some of these transcriptions would become available to collectors, leaving an incomplete record of the vast array of performers who appeared on the show. Episode 67, recorded February 28, 1944, represents a typical line-up for the weekly program. The show opened with "One O'Clock Jump," the same song used for many years. This was followed by "Wednesday Night Bop" performed by Andy Kirk and His Orchestra, a band that appeared on nine episodes. The Armed Forces Radio Trio, led by Les Paul on guitar, then played "I Can't Believe That You're in Love with Me" and "I Found a New Baby." Andy Kirk's outfit returned for three numbers, "McGhee Special," "Knock Me a Kiss (If You Can't Smile and Say Yes)," and "47th Street Jive," followed by the Esquire All-American All-Stars (including Coleman Hawkins and Art Tatum) performing "Esquire Blues." Kirk's orchestra closed the program with "Peeping Through the Keyhole" and signed off with a reprise of "One O'Clock Jump." Tim Liemert is credited as the AFRS announcer and master of ceremonies duties went to **Ernie Whitman** (who appeared on over 200 episodes) and Leonard Feather. Some episodes, such as #138, featured comedy skits. This one starred **Lillian Randolph**, **Eddie Green**, and Ernest Whitman in a version of Romeo and Juliet.

Beginning in 1947 a good number of episodes began to reuse at least segments of prior episodes and some were cut together with

all recycled performances. Budget cuts finally led to the show's demise after the recording of #433 on February 14, 1953. *Jubilee* outlasted similar shows like *Jill's Jukebox* and *Command* Performance by four years. Those logging some of the most appearances on *Jubilee* included **Count Basie**, Benny Carter, George Dvorak, **Lena Horne**, Verne Smith, Lucky Thompson, and Ernest Whitman.

Sources: DeLay pp. 150–152; Dunning pp. 376–377; Lotz and Neuert; Sklaroff p. 178.

Kennedy, John B.

Kennedy was a white newscaster and announcer who made a long career in radio, debuting in the late 1920s and broadcasting well into the 1950s. He did at least one broadcast of special interest to African Americans over NBC's WJZ. From 10:00 to 11:00 on December 9, 1933, he took the radio audience on a "tour" of Harlem. Prominent black performers reenacted daily scenes from Harlem including a rent party, a con game, a historical Marcus Garvey meeting, and a swinging night club. Actors and musicians included **Eva Taylor**, **Ethel Waters**, **Georgia Burke**, Bill Robinson, Bert Williams, the **Southernaires**, and **W. C. Handy**. Continuity for the program was provided by Katherine Seymour and Elizabeth Todd, a white writer.

Source: Cox, *Radio Speakers*, p. 158–159; *New York Amsterdam News*, December 13, 1933, p. 7.

King, Lulu

Little is known of Lulu King outside of a minor acting career. She began appearing in black theater productions in the early 1930s, notably **Hall Johnson**'s *Run Little Children* in 1933. In 1934 King was identified as a founding member of the National Negro Theatre. King was cast in various plays over the decade including *The Trial of Dr. Beck* (1937) and *Haiti* (1938) before she made her first documented radio broadcast in 1941. The program was a special show called *Harlem Salutes the Greater New York Fund* aired over WMCA. It was a dramatic play about health, welfare, and social conditions of blacks in New York which also starred **Amanda Randolph** and **Artie Bell McGinty**. That same year King appeared on an all-black episode of *Forecast* over CBS. The first half of the show traced the history of black theater and the second half featured various black musicians. Nineteen forty-one also witnessed the formation of the Negro Radio Workshop, on whose board King sat. Her primary radio work was 1954 to 1955 as the era of dramatic radio began to wind down. She was cast in *The Story of Ruby Valentine*, the second known African American soap opera, as Mrs. Booker, wife to Earle Hyman's character Henry Booker. King experimented with television work, working on the programs *Lux Video Theatre* and *Harlem Detective* in 1953.

Sources: Billups and Pierce p. 559; Woll pp. 73, 170; *New York Amsterdam News*, November 15, 1933, p. 7, May 19, 1934, p. 7, June 14, 1941, p. 21, August 9, 1941, p. 21; *Pittsburgh Courier*, October 24, 1953, p. 18; February 20, 1954, p. 17.

King Biscuit Time

Debuting in 1941 over station KFFA, Helena, AR, *King Biscuit Time* featured a blues artist named Rice "Sonny Boy Williamson" Miller. In exchange for the opportunity to plug his live shows, Williamson and his backing band, the King Biscuit Boys or King Biscuit Entertainers, played every weekday at noon. Later the performers received a small payment, perhaps five or ten dollars per week. Legendary bluesman B. B. King recalled tuning into the King Biscuit program every day when he was still a boy working in the cotton fields. By the 1950s Williamson was finally getting his songs on record which led to increased touring. The blues program continued on as popular as ever even after Williamson's appearances became infrequent.

Sources: Barlow pp. 96–97; Cantor pp. 157–158; Newman pp. 95–101.

Kingslow, Janice

Janice Kingslow was a native of Williamson, WV, but spent most of her childhood in Chicago. Though she participated in various theater projects growing up, Kingslow did not get seriously into acting until her twenties. After graduating from Hyde Park High School she attended Wilson Junior College and Chicago Teachers' College where she prepared for a career in education. Multiple sources mention her performing in very minor radio roles as a young girl, including bit parts on WMAQ, WGN, WENR, and WCFL. Her break came in October 1945, when she won the role of understudy to the lead in the play *Anna Lucasta* before getting her break and taking over the part June 1, 1946.

Kingslow's first notable radio role came in **Richard Durham**'s second series *Here Comes Tomorrow*, an African American soap opera that ran from September 1947, into the Spring of 1948. She played Sarah, the girlfriend of Milton Redmond, a war veteran suffering from amnesia. Soon after *Here Comes Tomorrow* left the air she was cast in Durham's third and final radio series *Destination Freedom* where she appeared regularly over its two year run.

After *Destination Freedom* left the air in 1950 Kingslow continued to do stage work and served as a publicist for NBC for a time. Her latter years remain a mystery.

Sources: *Billboard*, October 25, 1947, pp. 13, 16; *Chicago Defender*, November 10, 1945, p. 16, May 11, 1946, p. 10, February 19, 1949, p. 22; *Jet* July 9, 1953, p. 62, August 27, 1953, p. 58.

Knoxville College Men's Quartet

The Men's Quartet of Knoxville College, Knoxville, TN, toured England during July and August of 1925. While there the four were featured on several broadcasts via the BBC.

Source: *Chicago Defender*, October 31, 1925, p. 1.

Lattimore, Harlan

Like the much more popular **Mills Brothers**, Harlan Lattimore called Pique, OH, home. After graduating from a Cincinnati-area high school he attended three years at Johnson C. Smith University in Charlotte, NC, where he sang baritone in a school quartet. Upon completing his studies Lattimore moved back to Cincinnati and earned a spot on WLW, the same station which had launched the Mills Brothers years before. Lattimore got his break by getting a gig at Harlem's Yeah, Man Club. Soon thereafter bandleader Don Redman heard him and invited him to audition for his band, a spot which Lattimore won in 1932.

Source: *Baltimore Afro-American*, September 3, 1932, p. 10; Oxford Music Online.

Layton and Johnstone

The American duo Turner Layton and Clarence Johnstone were aired over the BBC while playing some dates in London in January 1925. Little is known of the broadcasts other than they were said to receive "handsome fees" for their daily radio work.

Sources: *Baltimore Afro-American*, January 17, 1925, p. 4, December 11, 1948, p. B10.

Lee, Baron

Originally christened Jimmy Ferguson, Baron Lee performed with such stars as Sissle and Blake and Ada Brown. In the late 1920s and early 1930s Lee spent a good deal of time touring Europe before returning to the United States in early 1932. Back in the States he began working with Irving Mills' band. Lee proved so popular with audiences that the group was renamed from the Mills Blue Rhythm Band to Baron Lee and His Blue Rhythm Band. Soon after their formation the band had gigs over NBC and were radio regulars through the end of the year.

Sources: *Baltimore Afro-American*, February 27, 1932, p. 8, December 17, 1932, p. 8; *New York Amsterdam News*, July 20, 1932, p. 8; Oxford Music Online.

Lee, Canada

Canada Lee fought as a professional boxer for many years in the late 1920s before a detached retina forced him to exit the ring permanently. Within a few years Lee turned to acting and became involved in various WPA theater projects during the 1930s. However, it was not until the 1940s that he made his mark on radio. His earliest known work was that of narrator on *Flow Gently, Sweet Rhythm* (also known as *The John Kirby Show*) from 1940 to 1941. Lee appeared on NBC a number of times during 1941, often as a master of ceremonies or narrator. Additionally, Lee narrated a July 24, 1941, dramatization of the life of Pine Top Smith, episodes of *Freedom's People* (April 19, 1942) with **Frank Wilson** and **Juano Hernandez**, a November 1942, broadcast called "Judgment Day" produced by the Office of Military Intelligence, and a 1943 National Urban League episode called *Heroines in Bronze*.

The only series on which Lee seemed to have worked regularly was *New World 'A Coming*, a long-running program originally based on Roi Ottley's book. Each of these broadcasts was a self-contained story and Lee is known to have been featured in the first 23 episodes and then an additional ten in subsequent months. There are many documented individual broadcasts on which Lee appeared including *Your Hollywood News Girl* (June 1941, NBC), *Destination Freedom*, *Columbia Presents Corwin* (April 25, 1944), *Jubilee* (#8 recorded January 28, 1943), *Free Company* (April 13, 1941), a War Department program (September 9, 1941), "Beyond the Call of Duty" (February 14, 1943, WOR), "Women for Freedom" (March 20, 1943, CBS), "Two Men on a Raft" (ca. 1944), *Words at War* (February 8, 1944), *Columbia Presents Corwin* (April 25, 1944), a WOR program with Hazel Scott (December 24, 1944), *War Town* (ca. 1945), *The American School of the Air* (February 8, 1945), *The United States Steel Hour* (November 11, 1945), *American Portrait* (March 30, 1946), *Lest We Forget* (ca. 1946 and 1947), *They Shall Be Heard* (September 19, 1946), *This Is Jazz* (May 31, 1947), "A Christmas Carol" (May 31, 1947), *Molle Mystery Theater* (February 13, 1948), *Bill Stern Colgate Newsreel* (April 16, 1948), *You Are There* (May 30, 1948, December 5, 1948, January 2, 1949, January 23, 1949, April 10, 1949, May 1, 1949, June 12, 1949), *Turning Points* (February 21, 1949), *The Big Story* (June 8, 1949), and *The Barry Gray Show* (September 23, 1949). Lee was a guest on **Cliff Burdette**'s *All Men Are Created Equal* and *Lest We Forget—The American Dream* (circa 1949 over WLNA). In 1948 he also starred in the self-named *Canada Lee Show* over WNEW. The program featured "mood music, blues ... boogie-woogie ... spirituals" every Saturday night. Some undated performances include roles on *Green Valley, U.S.A.*, *Passport for Adams*, *Service Unlimited*, and *Hickory*.

Lee's health was poor during the last two years of his life and he died of a heart attack in 1952. Despite a healthy radio career he is largely forgotten among fans of old radio, likely because he was not regularly on big-name network programs. He was cast mainly in dramatic roles when most popular African American radio performers were comedians. In addition, his outspokenness on civil rights issues led to a certain diminishing of his reputation soon after his death.

Sources: LOC; Barlow pp. 78–81; Dunning p. 256; Grams, *Radio Drama*, pp. 27, 104, 197, 357–359, 506, 514, 519, 529; Lotz and Neuert; Sampson, *Blacks in Black and White*, p. 536; Savage pp. 74, 142, 170, 251, 263; Sies pp. 97, 125; Smith, *Becoming Something*, pp. 70–71, 111, 133, 170–171; *New York Amsterdam News*, July 5, 1941, p. 21, July 26, 1941, pp. 8, 15, March 20, 1943, p. 11, July 24, 1943, p. 20, December 23, 1944, p. 3, February 7, 1948, p. 12, May 29, 1948, p. 22, February 26, 1949, p. 24; *New York Times*, May 10, 1952, p. 21; Finding Aid for Canada Lee Papers, Schomburg Center for Research in Black Culture, The New York Public Library, http://www.nypl.org/ accessed December 8, 2010; www.radiogoldindex.com.

Lee, Johnny (also Johnnie Lee)

John Dotson Lee, Jr. spent much of his life performing but gained what little fame he has through his role as Lawyer Algonquin J. Calhoun on radio's *The Amos 'n' Andy Show* and, later, the television adaptation. His birthplace is not entirely clear but more print sources suggest Springfield, MO, than any other city (notably Springfield, IL, and Los Angeles, CA) and he was likely born July 4, 1898. One account claims he was raised in Pueblo, CO, and won first prize in a local amateur show. He subsequently joined a traveling troupe and journeyed west where he found steady work on the coast.

Records show for sure that by late 1929 Lee had arrived in New York where he earned a role in *Dream Girls* in August of that year. He was billed alongside Bootsy Swan (variously spelled *Bootsie* and *Swain*) as the team Lee and Swan. Coincidentally, the show also featured "Manda" Randolph, surely the same **Amanda Randolph** who would also appear on *Amos 'n' Andy* in years to come. Lee and Swan would appear together in several shows over the next two years including the aforementioned *Dream Girls*, *Adam and Eve in Harlem* (November 1929), on the bill with singer **Bessie Smith** (May 1930), and as a duo at the popular Connie's Inn nightclub. Confusingly, there was a Johnny Lee Long who worked many stage productions in and around New York all through the 1920s and up until 1934 when he passed away.

In an interview with Estelle Edmerson Lee recalled doing his first radio work during this time, a series featuring two characters named Slick and Slim which also featured Swan (or Swain), Billy Holiday, and Bob Howard. The sustaining WHN series had an all–African American cast and depicted "the everyday life of the Negro." No other references to the show have been uncovered, however. Presumably Lee continued to get regular theater work through the 1930s but print references to his career are rare during this period. He was cast in at least one film during this era, *Rufus Jones for*

President (1933). Jobs picked up in the 1940s with a role in Lew Leslie's 1940 effort *Rhapsody in Black*. The next year he was featured in *The Mikado* starring Bill "Bojangles" Robinson and in 1942's *Harlem Cavalcade* which also featured Tim Moore.

After World War II Lee earned a spot on a 1946 international tour playing in *Shuffle Along* in Italy, France, Germany and Austria. Over the course of 150 performances the cast played before an estimated 1.25 million soldiers. That same year Disney's *Song of the South* was released which featured Lee's voice as that of Br'er Rabbit. Other post-war efforts included *Meet Miss Jones* by Flournoy Miller and James Johnson in 1947 and *Sugar Hill*, also by Miller and Johnson, in 1949. Lee worked with Flournoy Miller on several occasions, at least one of which was on radio. In a 1950s interview he claimed to have co-starred with Miller on a series of five broadcasts over NBC called *Serving Time at the Savoy*. Other performers included Lucky Millinder, Noble Sissle, and comedian Jackie Mabley. As with *Slick and Slim*, no additional information has been discovered concerning the program.

Lee debuted on radio's *The Amos 'n' Andy Show* in 1949 as the lawyer Algonquin J. Calhoun. His character may have been intended to fill the void left when a lawyer played by **Eddie Green**, LaGuardia Stonewall, was written out with Green's departure. When the television version of *Amos 'n' Andy* was produced between 1951 and 1953 Lee reprised his role as Calhoun. This would be by far Lee's most famous role, one with which he would be connected for the rest of his life.

Lee stayed busy through the post *Amos 'n' Andy* years with stage work including *Three Men on a Horse* and *Pick It Up* (also with **Lilian Randolph**) and *What's New?* in 1955. He made brief forays into television and had occasional bit parts in various films. Perhaps his most notable television appearance outside of *Amos 'n' Andy* was a 1954 episode of NBC's *Fireside Theatre* which featured an all-black cast in a dramatic story. In 1956 Lee took on some directing duties with two one-act plays sponsored by the Holman Drama Guild. The next year Lee took one final bow as the lawyer Calhoun when four cast members of the *Amos 'n' Andy* television show (Spencer Williams, Jr., Tim Moore, Alvin Childress, and Lee) embarked on a tour of one-nighters through 45 cities around the country booked by Lil Cumber Attractions. Lee served as a pallbearer at Tim Moore's funeral in 1958 and he himself died in 1965 from complications resulting from a heart attack.

Sources: Dunning pp. 32, 35; Edmerson pp. 29–30; Sampson, *Blacks in Black and White*, p. 422; Woll pp. 76, 233; *Baltimore Afro-American*, September 21, 1940, p. 13, October 11, 1941, p. 14, May 4, 1946, p. 6, November 15, 1947, p. 6, June 25, 1949, p. 8; *Los Angeles Sentinel*, February 16, 1950, p. B7, January 21, 1954, p. B3, March 18, 1954, p. A10, September 30, 1954, p. A11, October 27, 1955, p. A11, August 9, 1956, p. A6, May 30, 1957, p. B8, December 18, 1958, p. A1, December 16, 1965, p. A1; *New York Amsterdam News*, September 4, 1929, p. 9, November 20, 1929, p. 8, May 7, 1930, p. 27, May 14, 1930, p. 8, May 30, 1942, p. 17, December 18, 1965, p. 34.

Leroy Smith Band

The Leroy Smith Band was an obscure 12-piece group led by Leroy Smith that made a few records between 1924 and 1928. One writer noted that while many white bands were accused of mimicking the style of black bands, the Leroy Smith band could be considered an imitator of the popular (and white) Paul Whiteman Orchestra. In 1925 the group had a weekly radio show in New York while also playing regularly at the prominent nightclub Connie's Inn, owned by George Immerman. Smith's outfit provided music for the 1929 musical *Hot Chocolates* which included contributions by Fats Waller and **Eddie Green**.

Sources: Woll p. 79; *Baltimore Afro-American*, January 31, 1925, p. 4, February 7, 1925, p. 5, February 28, 1925, p. 6; *Chicago Defender*, May 12, 1928, p. 6; Oxford Music Online.

Log Cabin Four

The Log Cabin Four, consisting of Ezrel Dorsay, Maurice Johnson, Robert Hamlet and James Lewis, formed in 1926 as high school students in Owensboro, KY. Gaining popularity with their own creative arrangements of spirituals and popular songs, they headed north to Cincinnati where they got a spot on WLW. From there they moved further north to Cleveland and hit the airwaves over WTAM.

Finally, in early 1932, the quartet arrived in New York under the management of one R. Vincent Ottley (very possibly Roi Ottley, writer of *New World A' Comin'*). By March 1932, the Log Cabin Four were airing over WABC, and by June had earned two ongoing slots over WMCA, Friday evenings at 10:30 and Sunday evenings at 6:15. They also were given a 5:45 P.M. spot on WINS. As with most musical groups, live performances were still their bread and butter and the Log Cabin Four were soon booked into Harlem's Lafayette Theatre. They were skilled enough to back up **Earl Hines** but talent couldn't overcome poor management and the foursome were disbanded by the end of 1932.

Sources: *New York Amsterdam News*, June 22, 1932, pp. 7, 9, January 11, 1933, p. 16.

Luke, William

William Luke started in radio in the early 1950s over stations KOWL and KPOL where he announced and wrote some scripts including an early version of *Man of Color* which would eventually be broadcast elsewhere. Unable to get steady radio work, he proposed a series to ABC based on stories of interest to African American listeners. Jack Meyers, production manager of ABC's Western Division, accepted the idea and *Man of Color* debuted June 6, 1954, over KECA, Los Angeles. Luke worked as announcer, writer, and producer before finally leaving in April 1954 to accept a job as a minister. Estelle Edmerson replaced Luke as producer of *Man of Color*.

Source: Edmerson pp. 46–48.

Ma Johnson's Harlem Rooming House (Also Ma Johnson's Harlem Boarding House)

Actress and author **Mercedes Gilbert** premiered her only radio writing on station WINS beginning May 17, 1938. Titled *Ma Johnson's Harlem Rooming House* (and sometimes referenced as *Boarding House*), Gilbert's series featured herself and a supporting cast of Henrietta Lovelace, the Chanticleers Quartet, and the Chauncey Northern Singers. Such guest stars as Langston Hughes and Noble Sissle were featured on a regular basis. The program moved around the broadcast schedule several times and even switched stations to WMCA by August. The content of the show is unknown beyond one source that described it simply as a serial. *Ma Johnson* remained unsponsored during her time on radio which lasted through January 1939.

Sources: *New York Amsterdam News*, May 14, 1938, p. 17, May 28, 1938, p. 21, June 11, 1938, p. 6, November 26, 1938, p. 20.

Man About Harlem

Joe Bostic got his start in radio in Baltimore in 1932 but was producing programs out of New York by 1935. His first was *Harlem on Parade*, which debuted in June 1935, but this effort was soon followed by his second series, *Man About Harlem*, which begins to show up in radio logs in October 1935, on station WBNX. Not much is known about the series at this point; one source describes it as a commentary. The broadcasts only seem to have lasted a few weeks.

Sources: *New York Amsterdam News*, October 5, 1935, p. 15, December 11, 1937, p. 1.

Man of Color

Man of Color, announced, written, and produced by **William Luke**, debuted June

6, 1953, on Los Angeles station KECA. The series covered black contributions to Los Angeles' cultural life and presented prominent blacks in the arts, sciences, and business. The premier episode featured Laura Slayton and Ruby Berkely Goodwin, both public relations writers who would continue to assist Luke with the show for some time. Additionally, Thurston Frazier, choral director of Victory Baptist Church, sang "Water Boy" with Robert Mosely on piano. In April 1954, Luke left the program and was replaced by Estelle Edmerson whose masters thesis at UCLA is one of the earliest scholarly works to document African Americans in early radio. Inexplicably, Edmerson is consistently referred to as "Edson" in the pages of *The Los Angeles Sentinel*. *Man of Color* went off the air in December 1954, and was scheduled to resume in January 1955, but there is no evidence to support that it went back on the air. Below is a summary of the program's weekly broadcasts.

June 13, 1954—Guest: Dr. Roy Peyton, physician and author of *In Quest of Dignity*.

June 20, 1954—Guest: The Honorable Thomas Griffith, Jr., L.A. Municipal Court.

June 27, 1954—Guest: **Jester Hairston**.

August 8, 1954—Guest: Dr. Leonard Stoval, tuberculosis specialist.

August 15, 1954—Guest: Marvin Hayes, singer, formerly of *Wings Over Jordan*.

August 22, 1954—Guest: composer William Grant Still.

August 29, 1954—Guest: George A. Beavers, Jr. chairman of the Board of Directors and Treasurer for the Golden State Mutual Life Insurance Company.

September 5, 1954—Guest: Benny Carter.

September 12, 1954—Guest: Herbert Duckett, L.A. City chemical engineer.

October 3, 1954—Guest: Madame Sul-Te-Wan, actress.

October 10, 1954—Guest: August Hawkins, California Assemblyman.

October 17, 1954—Guest: Christopher Scott, postal supervisor.

October 24, 1954—Guest: Ivan Harold Browning, actor and singer.

October 31, 1954—Guest: Edward Burch, manager of L. A. Industrial and Labor Office.

November 7, 1954—Guests: members of national nursing sorority Chi Eta Phi.

November 14, 1954—Guest: Floyd Covington, racial relations advisor with the Federal Housing Administration.

November 21, 1954—Guest: Arthur Lee Simpkins, singer.

November 28, 1954—Guest: Leon Simmons, musician and teacher.

December 5, 1954—Guest: Mildred Blount, hat designer.

December 12, 1954—Guest: Anne O'Ferrall, community volunteer.

December 19, 1954—Guest: West Adams Civic Chorus.

December 26, 1954—Guest: McNeil Choir.

January 2, 1955—Guest: Cathedral Choir of the People's Independent Church of Christ.

January 9, 1955—Guest: Sarah Flowers, metaphysician.

January 16, 1955—Guest: Emmett Ashford, athlete.

January 23, 1955—Guest: Bertrand Bratton, certified public accountant.

January 30, 1955—Guest: Florence Cole Talbert, opera singer.

February 6, 1955—Guest: Oden Browne, actor. This episode was recorded but never aired because the tape was lost.

February 13, 1955—Guest: Dr. James H. Kirk, chairman, department of Sociology, Loyola University.

KECA becomes KABC.

February 20, 1955—Guest: Naida McCullough, pianist.

February 27, 1955—Guest: the Rev. F. Douglass Ferrell.

March 6, 1955—Guest: Dr. Geraldine Woods interviewed by Mildred Blount.

March 13, 1955—Guest: McNeil Choir.

March 20, 1955—Guest: Ernest Bendy, AKA Dynamite Jackson, ring referee.

March 27, 1955—Guest: Ralph Billingslea, tenor.

April 3, 1955—Guest: Henry Talbert, Director of Group Work for the Church Federation of L. A.

April 10, 1955—Guest: Carnella Barnes, executive secretary of the Avalon Community Center.

April 24, 1955—Guest: Ralph Billingslea, tenor.

May 22, 1955—Guest: Brice Taylor, student.

May 29, 1955—Guest: Robert Le House, dancer, choreographer, and teacher.

June 5, 1955—Guest: **Earl Hines**.

June 12, 1955—Guests: Dr. Clarence Cook and his wife Bernice Lawson, pianist.

June 19, 1955—Guests: Constance Maxey, social worker, and Bertha Holmes, boarding home mother.

June 26, 1955—Guest: William Banks, Grand Master of the Masons St. Anthony Lodge.

July 10, 1955—Guest: Hazel Lamarre, theatrical editor of *The Los Angeles Sentinel*.

July 31, 1955—Guest: Archibald Carey, United Nations.

August 7, 1955—Guest: Suzette Harbin, actress, and Jeep Smith and his orchestra.

August 14, 1955—Guest: Archibald Carey.

August 28, 1955—Guest: Archibald Carey.

September 4, 1955—Guest: Archibald Carey.

September 25, 1955—Guests: Richard Yeaman, attorney, and George Herbert, executive assistant to the mayor.

October 9, 1955—Guest: George Meany, president AFL, and Lester Bailey, NAACP.

October 16, 1955—Guest: Roy Wilkins, NAACP.

November 6, 1955—Guests: Firefighters regarding the integration of fire services.

Sources: *Los Angeles Sentinel*, June 4, 1953, p. 2, June 11, 1953, p. B2, June 18, 1953, p. 3, June 25, 1953, p. B5, August 6, 1953, p. B3, August 13, 1953, p. B3, August 20, 1953, p. B2, August 27, 1953, p. B4, September 3, 1953, p. B4, September 10, 1953, p. B2, October 1, 1953, p. B2, October 8, 1953, p. B2, October 15, 1953, p. B2, October 22, 1953, p. B2, October 29, 1953, p. B3, November 5, 1953, p. A4, November 12, 1953, p. C8, November 19, 1953, p. B7, November 26, 1953, p. 6, December 3, 1953, p. C6, December 10, 1953, p. 6, December 17, 1953, p. C10, December 24, 1953, p. 6, December 31, 1953, p. 6, January 7, 1954, p. B2, January 14, 1954, p. B2, January 21, 1954, p. B2, January 28,1954, p. B3, February 4, 1954, p. C6,February 11, 1954, p. C6, February 18, 1954, p. 10, February 25, 1954, p. 10, March 4, 1954, p. 11, March 11, 1954, p. C6, March 18, 1954, p. 10, March 25, 1954, p. 11, April 1, 1954, p. C6, April 8, 1954, p. 11, April 22, 1954, p. 11, May 20, 1954, p. 10, May 27, 1954, p. 11, June 3, 1954, p. 10, June 10, 1954, p. 10, June 17, 1954, p. 11, June 24, 1954, p. 10, July 8, 1954, p. 1, July 29, 1954, p. 10, August 5, 1954, p. 10, August 12, 1954, p. C3, August 26, 1954, p. 10, September 2, 1954, p. 10, September 23, 1954, p. 10, October 7, 1954, p. 10, October 14, 1954, p. 10, November 4, 1954, p. 1, December 2, 1954, p. 10.

Martin, Sarah

Sarah Martin was primarily a blues recording artist for Okeh Records but in February 1924, she sang over WFAA, Dallas. Response was such that listeners sent telegrams from Ohio, Pennsylvania, Kentucky, Indiana, Wisconsin, Minnesota, Kansas, Arkansas, Missouri, and even Preston, England.

Source: Peterson p. 126; Southern p. 370; *Baltimore Afro-American*, February 1, 1924, p. 4.

Mason Jubilee Singers

The Mason Jubilee Singers, directed by Bertha Dickerson-Tyree, performed over KNX in Los Angeles during Christmas week, 1924.

Source: *Chicago Defender*, January 10, 1925, p. 11.

Maxwell, Sherman "Jocko"

Sherman "Jocko" Maxwell, the rapid-fire announcer who reputedly read ten sports papers a day, was widely acknowledged as the first African American sportscaster on radio.

If anyone beat him to that honor then that individual was overlooked by the major black press of the time. Maxwell, born in 1907, was a native of Newark, and played baseball while in high school. Though he made a career with the postal service, Maxwell's journalism interest may have come from his father who was an editor at *The Newark Star Ledger*. Accounts differ as to when exactly he first went on the air. Late in life (he lived to be 100) he claimed he began by reading sports scores for five minutes every Saturday over WNJR in 1929. At least one source claims he started at WNJ in 1930 before moving to a thrice-weekly spot at WRNY. During much of his career through the 1940s and 1950s he claimed that his first sports program was aired on March 19, 1932 over WNJ. Whether these three jobs were, in fact, the same is not clear but seems possible with faulty memories accounting for the difference in exact years and similarity in station call letters.

By 1934 Maxwell broadcast three times per week over WHOM on which he provided sports commentary and interviews. His Saturday night show was called *Sport Hi Lites* and covered clubs, high school, semi-pro, and professional games. In early 1935 he gained a new Sunday show, *The Sportsman's Melody Parade*. WLTH was Maxwell's next stop in 1936. While maintaining his WLTH spot he moved his Saturday show, *Five Star Sports Final*, to WWRL. Maxwell's new series premiering in July 1941, *The Sports Huddle*, was a primitive version of modern call-in sports shows with listeners writing in to explain why they were qualified to be guests on the show to dispute some of Maxwell's analysis and opinions. After at least a decade on the air he earned the title of Sports Director at WWRL.

Other sports programs hosted by Maxwell included the daily (except Sundays) *Sports with Maxwell* (inaugurated May 1942, WWRL), *Five Star Sports Final* (1947) sponsored by Donniford Pipe Tobacco, the twice-weekly *Sportscope* (1947) and *Sports Reviews and Previews* (1947). Sources indicate he was absent from the air for a 39-month span that concluded at the end of 1945 during which he was in the Army Special Services Department. Maxwell debuted at least two more shows in 1950, *Colored Sports Review* and *Negro Sports Digest*. Beginning in 1957 he signed with WNJR to do a daily program. Maxwell retired from broadcasting (though he claimed to have never been paid a dime for his radio work) in 1967.

Sources: *New York Amsterdam News*, April 21, 1934, p. 10, April 28, 1934, p. 10, June 16, 1934, p. 10, February 23, 1935, p. 11, December 5, 1936, p. 19, March 25, 1939, p. 20, March 8, 1941, p. 19, July 19, 1941, p. 18, August 30, 1941, p. 20, April 18, 1942, p. 13, May 23, 1942, p. 15, December 29, 1945, p. 28, June 7, 1947, p. 13, July 19, 1947, p. 10, February 18, 1950, p. 33, June 7, 1952, p. 29, April 6, 1957, p. 27, March 22, 1958, p. 27; www.nj.com (October 15, 1998, and July 16, 2008), accessed November 23, 2010.

McCray, James

Though not a radio performer, James McCray wrote a regular technical column about radio matters for the weekly *Philadelphia Tribune* during 1924 and 1925.

Sources: *Philadelphia Tribune*, August 23, 1924, p. 7, October 18, 1924, p. 15, November 8, 1924, p. 15, January 24, 1925, p. 15, March 14, 1925, p. 15, June 13, 1925, p. 16.

McDaniel, Hattie

Hattie McDaniel was born June 10, 1895, in Denver, CO, to Henry and Susan McDaniel, both of whom had been born into slavery. She performed informally as a child with her siblings but during her first year in high school McDaniel claimed to have won first prize in a drama contest sponsored by the Women's Christian Temperance Union, an event that inspired her on to greater performing success. Later that year in December 1908, she joined J. M. Johnson's Mighty Minstrels, her first professional gig. Soon after, her brother Otis formed a troupe that hit the road and he took sister Hattie with him, necessitating her dropping out of school.

McDaniel spent the next decade working whatever shows she could and by 1925 had her first opportunity at radio over KOA, Denver. Her touring partner George Morrison sang over the station in December 1925, and McDaniel biographer Jill Watts concludes it's very possible Hattie sang with him that night because she later claimed to have sung with Morrison "early in her career." McDaniel's first regular radio work came in 1931 when her brother Sam talked KNX in Los Angeles into adding her to the *Optimistic Donuts Hour* program on which she played three roles and acquired the nickname "Hi Hat." A second source pinpoints these roles with the Perfection Bakery program on station KHJ. She proved so popular that the station eventually gave McDaniel her own show called *Hi Hat Hattie and Her Boys*, the boys being Sam McVea's Band, a jazz outfit. Biographer Carlton Jackson identified one other radio job on a program identified simply as a NBC musical series from 1932 to 1933.

Film proved a much more lucrative career, however, and remained the focus of McDaniel's performing ambition. Nonetheless, she continued to take occasional radio work. In July 1937, she joined *Show Boat*, a musical variety program sponsored by Maxwell House. She played the role of Queenie, a part she'd played years before in *Show Boat*'s stage version, and frequently performed with **Eddie Green** who would become one of radio's most prominent African American actors. Despite winning a Best Supporting Actress Oscar in 1939 for her role in *Gone with the Wind*, film parts became harder to come by in the 1940s when she turned to freelancing and so McDaniel increased her radio workload.

McDaniel took parts on *It's Time to Smile* hosted by Eddie Cantor, *The Billie Burke Show*, and *The Amos 'n' Andy Show* (as Sadie Simpson from 1945–47), which employed a number of African American performers despite the lead characters being played by

Freeman Gosden and **Charles Correll**, both white. Individual broadcasts at the beginning of the decade included *Good News of 1940* (January 11, 1940, on NBC), *Wings Over Jordan* (July 7, 1940, over Cleveland's WGAR), *Gulf Screen Guild Theatre* (February 9, 1941, on CBS), and a *Salute to* **Canada Lee** (July 1941, over Mutual Broadcasting System). In 1943 McDaniel starred in *Blueberry Hill* with **Ernest Whitman** but the series didn't survive beyond the premier episode. She made a single appearance on *The Lady Esther Screen Guild Theatre* (January 15, 1945, on CBS) and four on the military's *Jubilee* series: #8 (recorded January 28, 1943), #23 (recorded May 10, 1943), #63 (recorded January 31, 1944), and #141 (recorded July 9, 1945). The high point of McDaniel's radio career came when she earned the role of **Beulah,** a black maid who had received her own program after proving extremely popular on *Fibber McGee & Molly*. Ironically, she was the first black actress to play the part; Beulah was created and portrayed by **Marlin Hurt,** a white man from Illinois, and then by another white male, Bob Corley, when Hurt died of a heart attack in 1946. McDaniel started in the role in November 1947. During the next two years she made appearances on Bing Crosby's *Philco Radio Time* as well.

Sponsor Proctor & Gamble moved *Beulah* to a daily fifteen-minute format to capitalize on her popularity with listeners. Subtly, McDaniel transformed the blackface mammy character into "an intelligent and mature woman who knew what she wanted" as described by Watts. McDaniel played Beulah for approximately four years before being replaced by **Lillian Randolph** in the fall of 1951 because of mounting health concerns which included diabetes and cancer. Hattie McDaniel died on October 29, 1952.

Sources: Cox, *Great Radio Sitcoms*, pp. 76–79; Cox, *This Day*, p. 108; Dunning pp. 220–221; Grams, *Radio Drama*, pp. 216, 283; Jackson p. 175; Lotz and Neuert; McLeod p. 184; Sampson,

Swingin' on the Ether Waves, p. 99; Watts; *Baltimore Afro-American*, January 26, 1935, p. 8, March 9, 1940, p. 14, March 8, 1941, p. 13; *Chicago Defender*, July 6, 1940, p. 20, June 21, 1941, p. 20, April 10, 1943, p. 19; www.radiogoldindex.com.

McGinty, Artie Bell

Artie Bell McGinty was an early black actress and one of the first to earn an acting role on a nation-wide program. She was born in Atlanta, GA, to a shoemaker and music teacher. While her father dreamed of a teaching career for her, after graduating from Spelman College she focused on show business. In 1916 she toured as a part of Tolliver's Circus and Musical Extravaganza then put her earlier music training to use as a part of the Legge and McGinty team which toured until 1921.

McGinty got her start on radio with a 32-week stint as Aunt Jemima on the *Aunt Jemima Pancake Flour Program* in 1929. Katherine Tift-Jones, a white actress, originated the role when the program went on the air in January but at the end of May she left for England for a series of concerts. It may be at this time that McGinty took the role. She continued with stage productions such as *Lily-White* to supplement her radio work. Besides Aunt Jemima she also played Dinah in the early short-lived series *Dinah and Dora* which aired on NBC in 1930.

Bell was earning five dollars a week as a tailor's seamstress before producer John Medbury re-discovered her. Medbury, it was claimed, remembered her performances as Aunt Jemima and designed some skits involving her and George Givot who played a Greek grocery boy that were incorporated into Fred Waring's *Old Gold Hour*. In the spring of 1933 McGinty became a staple on the program, playing a maid named Magnolia. Months later her character's name was altered to Mandy Lou (who was married to a character played by **Clarence Williams**) with no explanation given by any of the sources citing this change. In September 1933, McGinty's contract with the program expired and was not renewed. Taking her place were two white actors, including one with a bright future, Milton Berle.

Though Mandy Lou would be her most popular aural role, she also appeared on *The Rise of the Goldbergs* for eight years (at least part of that time as a maid), *Amanda of Honeymoon Hill* (where she played Luella), *The Aldrich Family*, and *Mystery Man*.

Sources: Abbott and Serroff p. 139; Ansbro p. 51; *Baltimore Afro-American*, October 24, 1931, p. 9, April 8, 1933, p. 9, April 22, 1933, p. 11, April 29, 1933, p. 11, June 10, 1933, p. 9, July 8, 1933, p. 9, September 30, 1933, p. 19, October 7, 1933, p. 18, October 28, 1933, p. 10, April 2, 1938, p. 10, March 27, 1943, p. 10; *New York Amsterdam News*, October 15, 1930, p. 12, October 22, 1930, p. 4, January 19, 1935, p. 10, May 27, 1939, p. 24.

McQueen, Butterfly

Butterfly McQueen had a relatively brief acting career but because of her role as Prissy in *Gone with the Wind* she's an actress who is widely remembered beyond what her short filmography might suggest. She was born Thelma MacQueen in Tampa, FL, in 1911 but ended up graduating from high school in Babylon, Long Island.

With little vocational direction she took a friend's suggestion in 1934 and joined some drama groups in New York City. At this time McQueen started using the name Butterfly professionally and in 1937 began appearing in local productions. In 1938 she signed with David O'Selznick for a part in *Gone with the Wind*. While by far McQueen's biggest film role, she made an additional seven pictures through 1948. Because big screen roles were few and far between McQueen did some radio work roughly between 1943 and 1947.

Biographer Stephen Bourne identifies *The Goldbergs* as McQueen's introduction to radio though no time-frame is offered for this work. The most popular show on which she appeared was *The Jack Benny Show* where she was cast occasionally as Rochester's (**Eddie**

Anderson) niece between November 28, 1943, and June 4, 1944. When the writers wanted to switch her role to that of Mary Livingston's (Benny's real-life wife) maid, McQueen declined and departed the program. Interestingly, in a personal reflection reprinted by Bourne, McQueen revealed that her main reason for leaving the show was because "Mr. Benny in a temper over Rochester's lateness, said he hated *all* Africans" (an event related in Irving Fein's biography of Benny).

Other radio work included roles on *Birds Eye Open House* (sometimes called *The Dinah Shore Show*) from October 5, 1944, to May 31, 1945, *The Danny Kaye Show* in 1945 and 1946 (as "president of his one-woman fan club"), and at least 18 *Jubilee* broadcasts: #30 (recorded June 21, 1943), #33 (recorded July 12, 1943), #34 (recorded July 19, 1943), #35 (recorded July 26, 1943), #37 (recorded August 9, 1943), #38 recorded (August 16, 1943), #39 (recorded August 23, 1943), #40 aired (December 23, 1944 and February 27, 1945), #41 (recorded September 6, 1943), #76 (recorded April 24, 1944), #80 (recorded May 15, 1944), #83 (recorded June 12, 1944), #85 (recorded June 26, 1944), #87 (recorded July 11, 1944), #91 (aired November 25, 1944), #96 (aired December 30, 1944), #97 (aired January 4 or 6, 1945), and #98 (recorded September 25, 1944).

McQueen had just a very few other known radio appearances in the latter half of the 1940s: *Here's to Veterans* (June 16, 1946), *Harlem Hospitality* (September 27, 1947), and *The Amos 'n' Andy Show* (October 16, 1949). She is also credited with supporting roles on *Beulah*.

After a decade of struggling in Hollywood McQueen turned to more mundane jobs and ground out a living folding underwear in a factory, running a restaurant, and working as a maid. She didn't give up completely on acting and managed to snag some television work, most notably as Oriole the maid in the small screen version of *Beulah*,

the role played by **Ruby Dandridge** on radio. Occasional stage roles continued to come her way but money was always tight. In 1975, at the age of 64 and thirty years after starting college, McQueen graduated from City College of New York with a degree in political science. She engaged in neighborhood work in Harlem and performed sporadically through the 1970s and 1980s including three more films, most notably Harrison Ford's *Mosquito Coast* (1986). In 1989 her apartment caught fire and Butterfly died from severe injuries.

Sources: LOC; Berry and Berry pp. 223–224; Bourne; Cox, *Great Radio Sitcoms*, p. 71; Fein pp. 105–106; Lotz and Neuert; Patterson p. 269; Sies p. 59; Sampson, *Blacks in Black and White*, pp. 542–543; www.radiogoldindex.com.

Meetin' House

Carlton Moss' third and final radio series—and his second with dramatic content—was *Meetin' House*, a half-hour program that premiered December 24, 1934, at 11 pm on WJZ (the audition was only fifteen minutes). NBC's files indicate a sporadic broadcasting schedule over its seventeen-month life. *Meetin' House* aired two one-time broadcasts (April 9, 1935, and October 18, 1935), the first of which was picked up by the Blue Network while the second was only heard in New York. Between December 3, 1935, and February 25, 1936, *Meetin' House* was broadcast at 3:15 in the afternoon over the Blue Network. From March 10 to June 16 the series was moved to 5:00 where it finished its coast-to-coast run. The program had two more New York–only broadcasts on August 25 and September 1. Like *Careless Love*, *Meetin' House* was the victim of numerous schedule changes, ranging in time from mid-afternoon to late night and on various days of the week. Records also indicate lapses of sometimes multiple weeks between episodes.

While September 1, 1936, appears to be the final regular episode, radio schedules suggest the series was reprised for a five-week run in March 1937, over WEAF. Network files, however, don't confirm this. Whether these broadcasts used new scripts, re-aired old scripts, or were transcription re-runs cannot be ascertained from the available records. If they were re-runs, this is the only clue so far to hint that at least some of Moss' work was recorded, thus preserving the unlikely possibility that samples of his radio work could be discovered in the future. Old-time radio scholar Martin Grams finds it very unlikely that WEAF would have re-broadcast a program originally run on competitor WJZ; first, WJZ probably would not have allowed WEAF's use of their own recordings and second, WEAF would have run the risk of earning a "copy cat" label by re-running another network's programming.

Performers on this third production included veterans **Frank Wilson, Georgia Burke,** Laura Bowman, **Eva Taylor** and the **Southernaires** along with Isabelle Washington Powell. Like Moss' prior works, the story was located in the South, this time featuring weekly installments of the adventures of a circuit preacher. It also followed the example of *Folks from Dixie* and featured at least one recurring character as opposed to using an anthology format similar to Moss' debut effort, *Careless Love. The New York Amsterdam News* critic Roi Ottley's reviews were ambiguous at best, hostile at worst. Across two of his "Hectic Harlem" columns he claimed Moss "deserve[d] ... sustained and sincere applause for his outstanding work in the field of radio drama" and that he was "the outstanding author of radio scripts of the race." Not long after, however, he goes on to blast *Meetin' House* as "dull and uninteresting entertainment" with a weak lead character (the preacher). That the series was dramatic in nature is confirmed by various references which describe *Meetin' House* as a drama.

Sources: NBC files; *New York Amsterdam News,* April 20, 1935, p. 9, June 1, 1935, p. 11, and June 8, 1935, p. 11.

Men o' War

During World War II the Navy produced an all-black series called *Men o' War* which was broadcast from the Naval Training Center in Great Lakes, IL. It was claimed to be the only such weekly series produced by the armed forces at the time. Each episode featured a variety of performers such as Willie Smith, **Southland Singers,** and other well known performers who had enlisted, as well as a black recruit who would share his experiences in the navy. The program was aired over upper-midwest stations on the CBS network in 1944.

Sources: Spaulding p. 27; *Chicago Defender,* August 12, 1944, p. 14.

Metropolitan Solo Choir

The Metropolitan Solo Choir was an African American organization which broadcast over WLS in Chicago's Hotel Sherman July 10, 1924. The Choir was directed by Prof. J. Wesley Jones while Jessie Harris, Jane Majors, Bernice Coleman, Dora Porter, Katherine Davis, Hattie Parker, and Magnolia Lewis offered solos. A quartet consisting of Marion Daily, Isabel Chriswell, Lucia Pitts, and Ruth Taylor also performed on the program.

Source: *Chicago Defender,* July 5, 1924, p. 5.

Midnight Scamper

The Midnight Scamper was not a radio series but rather the name given to a star-laden one-time broadcast on September 27, 1924, over WGN. From half past midnight until 2 A.M. Florence Mills, Hamtree Harrington, John Dunn, Nelson Kincaid, George Dickson, Juan Harrison, Brown & Dermont, Danny Small, Cora Green, Allie Ross, and William Tyler entertained listeners. Noted performances were Mills, Billie Cain, and Alma Smith singing "Jazz Time Comes from the South" and Harrison singing "Why Live a Lie."

Source: *Pittsburgh Courier,* September 27, 1924, p. 9.

Miller, Ted

Ted Miller started in radio as a teenager around the age of 18 in Philadelphia. He joined the staff of WCAU, the city's CBS outlet where he held the position of "manager of floors" which put him in charge of electrical transcriptions. It's not clear if Miller ever went on the air at WCAU but he did broadcast over WDAS where he served as a staff announcer for five years while continuing in the employ of WCAU. One writer labeled him the "colored Graham McNamee of the radio" and he is connected with a handful of WDAS programs including a Philadelphia version of *Negro Achievement* programs as early as 1930, weekly broadcasts from the Standard Theatre (ca. 1932), a Sunday morning children's show (ca. 1932), and *Ted Miller's Harlem Revue* on Saturday nights in 1934. In September 1935, Miller hosted a weekly fifteen-minute news program dubbed *The Negro News of the Week* over New York's WMCA. Sponsored by the city's Howard Radio stores, he shared stories culled from the latest *New York Amsterdam News*. The series only lasted a few weeks that fall. Miller is known to have been on the air at least until 1938 when he was announcing from Philadelphia's Parrish Cafe.

Sources: *Baltimore Afro-American*, July 28, 1934, p. 12; *New York Amsterdam News*, September 21, 1935, pp. 3–5, 14, 17, September 28, 1935, p. 6, October 12, 1935, p. 6; *Philadelphia Tribune*, March 20, 1930, p. 15, November 3, 1932, p. 11, April 12, 1934, p. 11, March 10, 1938, p. 15.

Mills Brothers

The Mills Brothers must be mentioned in any discussion of the most popular black radio artists. The four brothers, John, Jr., guitar and bass, Herbert, tenor, Harry, baritone, and Donald, lead tenor, were all born in Piqua, OH, between 1910 and 1915. In 1927 they moved to Bellefontaine, OH, and at the same time left school to hone their singing skills.

In 1928 Grace Rain, an employee at Cin-cinnati's WLW, encouraged the brothers to come to Cincinnati along with the Harold Greenemeyer Band and audition for an air-slot on the station. In 1931 Tommy Rockwell of Okeh Records heard about the quartet and sent a representative named Joe Stevens, who had just terminated his managerial contract with **Fletcher Henderson,** to hear them while Okeh recording artist **Duke Ellington** was on tour in the Midwest.

Stevens liked what he heard and Rockwell hired the four to come record in New York. At about the same time they came to the attention of William Paley, head of the CBS radio network and in November 1931, they debuted on the network's flagship station WABC in New York City. Their popularity was instantaneous and they became entertainment fixtures for the next thirty years. Along with the fame came big money, an estimated $4,000–$5,000 per week by the end of 1931 between their concerts and radio work. This compared to a more modest $40 per week while working for WLW and an initial $300 contract with CBS.

Their CBS series quickly found a sponsor, Vapex, a cold medicine. The company recognized the value of their advertising dollars and received $750 from CBS when the network allowed the Mills Brothers to perform over WOR. Vapex had signed an exclusive contract for their talent and wasn't about to overlook this transgression. In April 1932, the popular kitchen products manufacturer Crisco took over sponsorship of the brothers' twice-weekly program. Crisco's sponsorship would later be replaced by that of Chipso. During the summer of that year the Mills Brothers took their act on the road for a sixteen-week tour. This didn't affect their radio work; CBS simply broadcast their concerts over the network via remote. Victor Young and his orchestra, based in New York, also appeared on these programs which had to cut back and forth between New York and the Mills Brothers' concert city. Even while on tour they managed to squeeze in a guest appearance on *The Jack Benny Program* (June 29, 1932), then broadcasting from New York City. During the summer of 1932 their take at various Paramount stages was comparable to that of such white stars as Morton Downey, Bing Crosby, and Guy Lombardo. The year ended as successfully as it began and the quartet admitted publicly to earning in the range of $150,000 for the year.

The Brothers were never associated with any dramatic programming but were featured on their own program for years. During the early 1930s CBS aired them twice a week and they were a featured quartet on the 1933-1934 season of Bing Crosby's program. By the mid–1930s NBC featured them on a weekly program called the *Elgin Campus Revue* and in 1936 they starred in a transcribed program sponsored by Dodge. In January 1936, tragedy struck when 25-year-old John passed away. He was subsequently replaced by their father, John, Sr.

While the Mills Brothers were a radio-created sensation during the early 1930s, their popularity endured and they continued to find broadcasting opportunities during the length of radio's Golden Age. The group sold tens of millions of records over a performing career that lasted half a century into the early 1980s. Even today John Mills performs under the Mills Brothers banner, carrying on the legacy of his father, grandfather, and uncle.

Sources: Dunning pp. 90, 460; Leff vol. 1, p. 37; Lotz and Neuert; McClure p. 189; *New York Amsterdam News*, October 28, 1931, p. 7, December 2, 1931, p. 10, December 9, 1931, p. 7, March 30, 1932, p. 9, May 4, 1932, p. 9, January 11, 1933, p. 16, October 5, 1935, p. 15, January 11, 1936, p. 15, February 1, 1936, p. 4; *Baltimore Afro-American*, November 7, 1931, p. 8, December 26, 1931, p. 9, January 16, 1932, p. 9, April 9, 1932, p. 19.

Mitchell, Abriea "Abbie"

Abbie Mitchell was a New York–born soprano singer who had a long career on stage which culminated with the role of "Clara" in George Gershwin's *Porgy and Bess* in 1935.

Her radio work is not widely known but she appeared regularly on WGN and WMAQ, Chicago, in the last half of 1930 on programs sponsored by the Studebaker Champions (WGN), Williams' Oil-o-Matics (WGN), and Hydrox (WMAQ). In 1931 she made further appearances on a Blue Valley Homestead–sponsored program on WENR. As late as 1936 she was singing on chain programs such as the *Hammerstein Music Hall of the Air* on CBS.

Sources: Haskins pp. 77–78; Southern pp. 417–418, 450, 451; *Chicago Defender*, December 20, 1930, p. 3, February 14, 1931, p. 11; *New York Amsterdam News*, December 31, 1930, p. 10, October 31, 1936, p. 10.

Mitchell, James

James Mitchell was one of the very few black child actors during this era. A student at Chicago's Dunbar Junior High School, he used his radio paycheck to support his family. He made his broadcast debut on *Uncle Quin's Day Dreamers* in January 1933, as the character Wishbone. The group of children (all white except Mitchell) would make a wish on Wishbone's magic wishbone and were then whisked anywhere they wanted to go. The program was aimed at children and featured historical stories while being aired from Chicago on station WGN.

Source: *Chicago Defender*, January 21, 1933, p. 16.

Moe Levy and Son's Colored Review

The musical program *Moe Levy and Son's Colored Review* was aired over New York's WOR from May 2 to July 7, 1930. Allie Ross' orchestra provided the music and Aida Ward and Rollin Smith regularly provided vocals. The source of the program's name, which is unrelated to any known cast members, is unclear.

Sources: NBC archival material; *New York Amsterdam News*, May 28, 1930, p. 10, July 9, 1930 p. 10.

Moreland, Mantan

A popular black actor during the 1930s and 1940s, Mantan Moreland did have a handful of radio credits to his name. Perhaps his earliest appearance on the air was an April 8, 1932, benefit program for a Harlem hospital on WMCA. Other guests included **Cab Calloway**, the **Mills Brothers**, and **Eddie Green**. This is his only known broadcast until 1943 when he was cast in an audition episode of *Blueberry Hill*, a musical program pitched to CBS with **Ernest Whitman** and **Hattie McDaniel**. In 1944 Moreland was a guest on *The Rudy Vallee Show* (October 14, 1944) and the AFRS' *Jubilee* (#106). He was cast in *The Radio Hall of Fame* (January 28, 1945) with partner Ben Carter and soon after the two appeared on *The Bob Burns Show* (February 8, 1945). Moreland's most notable radio gig *Duffy's Tavern* on which he took over Eddie Green's role when Green became ill and later passed away.

Sources: Dunning, *On the Air*, p. 102; Price pp. 88–89; Sies p. 489; *Los Angeles Sentinel*, September 21, 1950, p. 1; *New York Amsterdam News*, April 6, 1932, p. 7; www.radiogoldindex.com.

Morgan College Glee Club

While not as prolific on the air as other college groups, the Morgan College Glee Club lays claim to at least one early radio broadcast, an hour-long performance over WGBA in February 1925. In addition to the Club's program of spirituals, President J. O. Spencer spoke on the history, growth, and work of Morgan College. Dean J. Haywood served as announcer.

Source: *Baltimore Afro-American*, February 7, 1925, p. 5.

Morris, Charles Satchell, Jr.

Charles Satchell Morris, Jr. of Norfolk, VA, did not yearn for a radio career but his nationally recognized oratorical skills were worthy of at least one radio broadcast. In August 1924, Morris delivered a speech entitled "The Bright Side of a Dark Subject" to a packed house at Los Angeles' First Methodist Church and to listeners at home. Morris, the only black student at the time to attend Wilson Memorial Academy, Nyack-on-Hudson, NY, later attended Wheaton College and the University of Chicago. He made a career as a college professor.

Source: *Chicago Defender*, August 9, 1924, p. 8.

Morris, Clifton

Clifton Morris was a vocalist who sang with Robert Hicks's orchestra over Baltimore's WCBM in 1932. He also had a solo show at the city's Cotton Club.

Source: *Baltimore Afro-American*, May 7, 1932, p. 18.

Moss, Carlton

Born in Newark, NJ, Carlton Moss later attended Morgan College in Baltimore (now Morgan State University). There he became involved in the theater organization then under the guidance of Randolph Edmunds. Moving from producing responsibilities to acting, Moss appeared in *The Goose Hangs High* and *Nothing But Truth* in the Spring of 1928. In the fall of the same year he appeared as the namesake of *Aaron Boggs, Freshman* as well as taking over vice-presidential responsibilities for the club. In spring, 1929, Moss and company traveled to New York City where they performed in a series of fundraisers. Plays included *The Man Who Died at 12 O'clock*, *The House of Shame*, and *Shirlock Bones*. By the fall of 1929 Moss relocated to New York where he got work with a performing company based out of the Alhambra Theatre.

Less than a year later he was on radio, appearing on *The Negro Art Group Hour* over WEVD discussing intercollegiate dramatics. This was the beginning of what would be a nearly decade-long run on various radio programs. Moss got his own series beginning in November 1930. Entitled *Careless Love*, the program was based on "themes ... suggested by **W. C. Handy**'s 'blues' and Negro plantation life." *Careless Love* represents the first known dramatic series written by an African American as well as the first drama to feature an African American cast. This anthology ran until May 15, 1932.

In the course of preparing this show for the air Moss discovered **Georgia Burke** who would go on to be one of radio's most prolific African American actresses. The story is related in multiple sources that while calling on **Edna Thomas**, Moss found Burke visiting her friend Edna. Her voice sufficiently impressed Moss that he persuaded her to tryout for a part on *Careless Love*. She received the part and went on to act in many of his future productions.

At the same time *Careless Love* was winding down Moss was making regular appearances on *Beale Street Nightlife*, a daily program over WEAF that dramatized black life in a boarding house on Memphis' Beale Street. Coincidentally it went off the air May 15, 1932, the same day as *Careless Love*. These cancellations did not dampen his enthusiasm toward radio, however. Later in 1932 Moss announced a series of broadcasts sponsored by the University Scholarship Foundation over station WEVD. A few months later in February 1933, Moss and actor **Frank Wilson** appeared on *We, the People*, written by Elmer Rice.

Moss wrote two more series focusing on black characters and featuring African American casts, *Folks from Dixie* (1933) and *Meetin' House* (1934–1936). The first revolved around a black woman who inherits a small fortune and the second focused on a circuit riding preacher. Other series with which Moss was involved include *Slow River*, *The Negro Forum* (possibly also known as *Community Forum*), and *Carlton Moss Reports* (1945-46).

Besides these ongoing series, Moss also wrote numerous one-time broadcasts which included what may have been radio's first black mystery (1934, title unknown), a his-

tory of the Alpha Kappa Alpha sorority (1934), and some scripts that commemorated the YMCA entitled "Negro Achievement" (1935) and "Into the Light" (1938). At least one of his projects during this time did not come to fruition. In late spring of 1934 Listerine (marketed by Lambert Pharmacal) was fishing around for a series to sponsor. Hoping to put what they thought would be the first hour-long all-black show on the air (apparently unaware of **Jack Cooper**'s *All-Negro Hour* from years before), Moss wrote an audition script that would include performances by **Ethel Waters**, Eubie Blake's Orchestra, **Hall Johnson**'s Choir, **Juano Hernandez** and his Choir, Dick Campbell, and others. There's no evidence to suggest that Listerine bought the script.

While pursuing these radio projects Moss kept himself involved in various New York City theater efforts. In the mid–1930s he worked for the Works Progress Administration's Negro Theater Unit; Orson Welles also briefly worked with this group and would go on to his own famous radio career. Later in the decade he worked on the Federal Writers Project's New York Project. Co-writers included Ralph Ellison, Claude McKay, and Roi Ottley. Other writing commissions included a play to celebrate the unveiling of a painting by Aaron Douglas and a libretto for black composer William Grant Still. In 1933 Moss appeared in *Phantom of Kenwood*, a film produced by pioneering black film-maker Oscar Micheaux. He took part in an unusual project in April 1938, a revue sponsored by the Negro Cultural Committee. With Dorothy Hailparn he composed a satiric ballet called *Filibuster* based on a recent anti-lynching law filibuster in Washington, D.C. Choreography was by Anna Sokolow and music was written by Alex North. The revue also featured Frank Wilson, **Rex Ingram**, and Georgia Burke along with an original composition by **Duke Ellington**.

Around 1940 Moss relocated to Los Angeles where he became involved in the film industry. Most famous for writing *The Negro Soldier* for Frank Capra, Moss spent several decades creating industrial and educational films, an area in which he felt he had the most control over his work. In the latter years of his life Moss taught at Fisk University and the University of California-Irvine. Carlton Moss passed away in 1997.

Sources: Berry and Berry p. 236; Edmerson p. 203; Sampson, *Blacks in Black and White*, pp. 469–470, 548–549; Peterson pp. 70, 90, 93, 150; *Baltimore Afro-American*, January 28, 1928, p. 9, April 26, 1929, p. 8, October 6, 1928, p. 21, January 26, 1929, p. 7, October 26, 1929, p. 17, November 21, 1931, p. 23, January 6, 1934, p. 18, April 7, 1934, p. 3, June 30, 1934, p. 8; *New York Amsterdam News*, May 7, 1930, p. 12, November 19, 1930, p. 10, November 2, 1932, p. 16, February 1, 1933, p. 16, September 15, 1934, p. 9, October 12, 1935, p. 11; *New York Times*, August 15, 1997, p. D20; *Delta Democrat-Times* (Greenville, MS), October 31, 1938, p. 1.

Moulin Rouge Orchestra

The Moulin Rouge Orchestra, made up of Edward Smith, Theodore Weatherford, Arnette Nelson, Vernon Roulette, J. F. Wade, William Dover, and William Louis Gross, was credited as being the first band to play over KYW, Chicago, in 1924. Formed in 1920 the orchestra recorded for Paramount company and played regularly around Chicago in such places as the Drake Hotel, Sheridan Plaza, The House That Jack Built, and Claremont Cafe.

Source: *Baltimore Afro-American*, February 1, 1924, p. 10.

Muddy Waters

Venzuella Jones' first radio series was *Muddy Waters*, an exploration of the lives of "uneducated people in Harlem and the South." It aired on WBNX, a small station in New York City beginning August 15, 1935. The broadcasts were sponsored by the adult education bureau of the State Board of Education with the stated purpose of revealing the daily problems and struggles of the black

underclass. A quartet provided musical background. The premier episode was called "Fulfillment" and focused on the religion of poor blacks on the plantations. The subsequent episodes were "Child of the King" (August 22), "Harlem" (August 29), and "Depression" (September 5). Billed as "experimental theatre of the air" it was hardly a success. The program was renamed *A Harlem Family* in October and then left the ether permanently in December 1935.

Source: *Baltimore Afro-American*, September 24, 1935, p. 9.

Mundy, James

James Mundy was a regular on Chicago-area radio during the 1920s and 1930s. As early as March 12, 1922, his **Chicago South Side Opera Company** broadcast over Westinghouse's station. In 1923 Mundy is credited with leading the Mundy Choirsters again on Westinghouse's KYW and on many other occasions across the radio dial during subsequent years.

Sources: Spaulding p. 33–34; *Chicago Defender*, May 27, 1922, p. 4.

Muse, Clarence

Clarence Muse claimed to have started in show business in 1909 after studying at Dickinson College, Carlisle, PA, and he's documented to have been performing on stage with New York's Lafayette Theatre Company by 1915. He worked steadily in New York and on tours through the 1920s before beginning a prodigious film career that by one account totaled 219 motion pictures. Though Muse's radio work pales in comparison to his filmography, he was a regular feature on radio for much of the 1930s.

Muse is credited with regular appearances on CBS' Los Angeles outlet KNX in 1931 and 1932 on which he sang a variety of songs, including his own compositions "When It's Sleepy Time Down South" and "Alley-Way of My Dreams." The names of the programs are unknown. In 1932 he had a daily slot with the Bill Sharpeles troupe and during the next year, 1933, began producing a series that would run for over four years called *The Evelyn Preer Memorial Program* over KRKD. Created as a tribute to Evelyn Preer, an African American actress who died in 1932, the *Memorial Program* was on the air under Muse's leadership four years before he passed on the reins in 1937.

During Muse's time on the *Memorial Program* he made appearances on other local Los Angeles programs, some of which were transcribed and are still available in collecting circles. One (which is not known to exist) was a series over KRKD in 1934 that dramatized Walter White's "Flight," the story of a black girl who passes in white society. Muse played the role of Uncle Jean. That same year he was cast in several episodes of *The Laff Parade*, a 1934 production of the Radio Transcription Company of America. He appeared on other occasional broadcasts during these years including *California Melodies* (December 14, 1935), *The Jack Benny Program* (January 19, 1936, February 2, 1936), the syndicated program *Hollywood Spotlight* (1935), and an August 1935, tribute to Will Rogers over CBS.

Beginning October 17, 1936, Muse was cast on *Irvin and His Paducah Plantation*. The role required so much work that he had to step away from *The Evelyn Preer Memorial Program* which continued to air under another producer. Sponsored by Oldsmobile, the premier episode of *Paducah Plantation* featured Muse singing "River Stay Away From My Door" and acting in various skits. Other performers were the Four Blackbirds, the **Hall Johnson** Choir, and Dorothy Page. The program ran until 1937. During 1936 he had a weekly Friday night hour but the content and station is unknown. After 1937 Muse's documented radio work drops off and film seems to predominate his output. He is known to have made a handful of broadcasts over the succeeding years including *Thirty Minutes in Hollywood* (January 30, 1938), *Good News of 1939* (December 1, 1938), *The Campbell Playhouse* (March 17, 1940), *Cavalcade of America* (May 25, 1942), and *Lux Radio Theatre* (October 2, 1944).

Sources: Berry and Berry pp. 238–239; Billups and Pierce p. 317; Grams *Cavalcade*; Leff vol. 1 pp. 223, 225; Patterson pp. 124–125; Sampson, *Blacks in Black and White*, p. 18, 549–551; *Chicago Defender*, July 29, 1916, p. 4, March 6, 1932, p. 5, August 25, 1934, p. 8, March 14, 1936, p. 8, November 21, 1936, p. 20, March 20, 1937, p. 20, March 27, 1937, p. 20; *Los Angeles Sentinel*, June 14, 1934, p. 6, October 15, 1936, p. 7; *New York Amsterdam News*, January 27, 1932, p. 10, March 2, 1932, p. 7, September 1, 1934, p. 7, August 24, 1935, p. 17, October 10, 1936, p. 24, October 24, 1936, p. 12, November 14, 1936, p. 10, August 14, 1943, p. 17, October 27, 1979, p. 28; www.radiogoldindex.com.

N.A.A.C.P. (National Association for the Advancement of Colored People)

The NAACP recognized early in the development of radio the possibilities the technology offered in their work for African American civil rights. One of their earliest uses of the airwaves involved Robert Bagnall, Director of Branches for the organization, who broadcast a message entitled "How to Preserve the Spirit of Lincoln" over WJAR as part of a Lincoln Day recognition, 1924, Providence, RI. Just two months later in April he spoke over the air in Minneapolis, about the Dyer Anti-Lynching bill being debated in Congress. Not content with individual talks, on June 29, 1924, the NAACP broadcast one of their mass meetings over WIP, Philadelphia. The entire proceedings were aired from the Philadelphia Metropolitan Opera House. Listeners noted that the broadcast went suddenly silent whenever anti–Klan speeches were made.

Source: *Philadelphia Tribune*, June 21, 1924 p. 1.

National Negro Forum

The University Scholarship Foundation, an organization of young college graduates whose aim was to assist other students, sponsored the *National Negro Forum*. The *Forum* was a current events series focused on issues of importance to African Americans which premiered Thursday, November 10, 1932, and offered a place where speakers could "discuss problems and strides of advancement of blacks" every Thursday from 8:30–9:00 P.M. on WEVD.

Hosted by noted black radio writer **Carlton Moss**, the first episode featured Dr. George Hayes who gave a lecture entitled "The Story of the Negro Migration in New York." Other individuals who appeared were E. K. Jones, executive secretary of the National Urban League, George Schuyler, author and director of the Young Negro Consumer Co-operative League, H. C. Craft, secretary of the 135th St. YMCA, Albon Holsey, secretary of the National Negro Business League, and Channing Tobias, field secretary of the YMCA. LeNard Baker, national director of the University Scholarship Foundation, conducted interviews with such artists as **Cab Calloway, Paul Robeson**, the **Mills Brothers**, Bill Robinson, and the **Three Keys**.

Source: *Pittsburgh Courier*, November 5, 1932, p. 7.

National Negro Hour

The *National Negro Hour* was a Sunday night program which started on WGAR in Cleveland during July 1937. Six months later in January 1938, the broadcast was picked up on CBS' nationwide hookup. For the special network inauguration episode the Rev. Joseph Gomez was invited to be the guest speaker. Past notable speakers included Dr. Henry Allen Boyd, Nashville, the Rev. David Sims, Philadelphia, and Attorney Theophilus Mann, Chicago. The program was created by the Rev. Glenn Settle, Cleveland. A 45-voice choir under the direction of James Tate provided musical accompaniment.

Sources: *New York Amsterdam News*, January 7,

1938, p. 16; *Cleveland Call and Post*, September 30, 1937, p. 6.

National Negro Network

The National Negro Network was the creation of Leonard Evans, a native Kentuckian who got into advertising in Chicago before moving to New York to focus on selling the African American market. When exactly Evans teamed with Jack Wyatt and Reggie Schuebel to begin planning their radio network is not clear but by the fall of 1953 they had plans for a serial called *The Story of Ruby Valentine*. The program went on the air in January 1954, and thus the National Negro Network was born.

The men behind the network did not consider themselves social activists. It was a pure business venture on their part, an effort to tap into the estimated market of 13–15 million black radio listeners. They initially planned four programs but only one, *The Story of Ruby Valentine*, ever made it to the air. *Ruby Valentine* starred **Juanita Hall** in the title role and ran daily for over a year under the sponsorship of the Pet Milk Company and Philip Morris. Other proposed series were *The Cathy Stewart Show* (sometimes referred to as *The Life of Anna Lewis*), *It's a Mystery, Man*, and an unnamed feature with **Ethel Waters**. *The Cathy Stewart Show* was to star Hilda Simms and *It's a Mystery, Man* was slated to feature **Cab Calloway**. Calloway had optioned old *Inner Sanctum* scripts and planned to rework them with him as host and to cater the content to better appeal to a black audience. An audition program was recorded but no further broadcasts are indicated by any sources. The Waters program does not seem to have gotten far beyond the basic conception stage.

While Evans served as president of the new company, Reggie Schuebel worked as vice-president and treasurer and Calloway was assigned duties as a talent evaluator as well as sitting on the company's board. The performers were reported to have earned

$170 per week minimum. At least one source mentions sponsors beyond Philip Morris and Pet Milk including Wrigley, A&P Supermarkets, Coca-Cola, Firestone, Buick, GE, and Westinghouse. Since none of them sponsored *Ruby Valentine* their advertising deals may have fallen through, thus the Networks' lack of features beyond the single daily serial.

Sources indicate anywhere from 35 to 42 stations signed up with the National Negro Network. Those that have been identified are: WERD, Atlanta, WSID, Baltimore, WBCO, Bessemer, AL, WPAL, Charleston, SC, WGIV, Charlotte, NC, WMFS, Chattanooga, TN, WGES, Chicago, WCIN, Cincinnati, WJMO, Cleveland, WOCS, Columbia, SC, WPNX, Columbus, GA, WJLB, Detroit, WKBC, Fort Worth, TX, WESC, Greenville, SC, KCOH, Houston, WRBC, Jackson, MS, WOBS, Jacksonville, FL, KPRS, Kansas City, WLOU, Louisville, WDIA, Memphis, WMBM, Miami Beach, WMOZ, Mobile, AL, WRMA, Montgomery, AL, WSOK, Nashville, WMRY, New Orleans, WOV, New York, WHAT, Philadelphia, WHOD, Pittsburgh, WANT, Richmond, VA, KWBR, San Francisco, KENT, Shreveport, LA, WEBK, Tampa, FL, WOOK, Washington, D.C., KSTL, St. Louis, and WBMS, Boston.

Network planners hoped eventually to have programming of all sorts, such as news, sports, drama, panel, quiz, variety, music, and commentary. However, the only broadcasts beyond *Ruby Valentine* which are attributed to the company are coverage of the National Association of Real Estate Brokers conference in October 1954, and a salute to Liberia later that month. Lack of capital caused the young network to close its doors in April 1955.

Sources: Barlow pp. 130–131; Browne and Browne p. 97; Cox, *American Radio Networks*, p. 197; Cox, *Great Radio Sitcoms*, p. 80; *Pittsburgh Courier*, December 26, 1953, p. 22, January 9, 1954, p. 15, January 30, 1954, pp. 15, 30, February 6, 1954, p. 20, February 13, 1954, p. 18, October 2, 1954, p. 16,

October 30, 1954, p. 1; www.targetmarketnews.com accessed July 30, 2010.

Native Sons

Broadcast over WNYC for thirteen weeks in 1941, *Native Sons* was one of several series cast with African Americans that dramatized the lives of prominent blacks. Actors included Eric Burroughs, **Canada Lee**, P. J. Sidney, Jessie Zackerey, Jimmy Wright, and Rose Poindexter. The **Juanita Hall** Choir provided music while Mitchell Grayson directed. Writing credits were ascribed to John Griffin and one other unidentified writer. Author Richard Wright gave some commentary after the final broadcast. The program topics were:

> May 3, 1941—Frederick Douglass
> May 10, 1941—Harriet Tubman
> May 17, 1941—Estevanico, explorer
> May 24, 1941—Nat Turner
> May 31, 1941—Dr. Carver
> June 7, 1941—Madame Greenfield, singer
> June 14, 1941—Crispus Attucks
> June 21, 1941—Ira Aldridge, actor
> June 28, 1941—Robert Smalls, sea raider
> July 5, 1941—Benjamin Banneker
> July 12, 1941—Toussaint-Louverture
> July 19, 1941—Denmark Vesey
> July 26, 1941—**Paul Robeson, Marian Anderson,** and Roland Hayes.

Sources: *Baltimore Afro-American*, May 3, 1941, p. 14, August 9, 1941, p. 14.

Negro Achievement Hour (Harrisburg, PA)

On August 14, 1930, WHP in Harrisburg, PA, debuted a program dubbed the *Negro Achievement Hour*. Whether this is related to the long-running series of the same name out of New York is not clear. Several men and women connected with the *Hour* have been identified including Lillian Ball, Dr. Leonard Oxley, Allen Carter, Dr. Leslie Marshall, Dewey Trigg, Henrietta Robinson, and Reuben Parker and Helen Vass who performed weekly. None of these individuals were associated with the New York *Achievement Hour.*

Source: *Baltimore Afro-American*, September 13, 1930, p. 8.

Negro Achievement Hour (New York)

Following closely on the heels of *The Pittsburgh Courier Hour* which debuted in late 1927 and became *The Floyd Calvin Hour* in early 1928, WABC announced on January 26, 1928, a new program entitled *The Negro Achievement Hour.* WABC was a New York station owned by the Atlantic Broadcasting Company, Steinway Building, 113 W. 57th St. The *Achievement Hour* was created by Joseph J. Boris, editor and publisher of Who's Who in Colored America. Arthur Clark, WABC's station manager, played an important role in getting the new program off the ground.

Initially on Thursday evenings from 10:30 to 11:30, then on Friday evenings, this weekly feature's format was nearly identical to the *Calvin Hour*, consisting of numerous musical numbers and a featured talk by a notable speaker on some timely subject. Each week's program was the responsibility of a different sponsoring organization, frequently African American fraternities, university groups, and community and business organizations.

The show celebrated its first anniversary on January 11, 1929, with a special two-hour program which featured a multitude of guest speakers from prior broadcasts. *The Achievement Hour* ran on WABC for nearly two years. In September 1929, the series was shifted to WAAT after eighty-five consecutive weeks on WABC, possibly a record for black programming at the time. WAAT's managing director was Rudy Horst, Jr., a one-time sales director and announcer at WABC. H. Hampton, another WAAT staff member, also formerly worked at WABC. Likely these two had a significant impact on the station's decision to pick up *The Achieve-*

ment Hour. Joseph Boris, long-time director of the *Hour*, made the move with his production which moved from a Friday evening time slot to Sunday afternoons at 1:45.

The Negro Achievement Hour disappears from radio logs in December 1929, only to reappear in March 1930, on station WRNY, New York City. Horst, formerly of WABC and WAAT, now moved to WRNY with the program. The format remained unchanged, featuring a guest speaker and various musical interludes. The *Hour's* run on WRNY lasted into June of that year before switching stations again, this time to WWRL, a small station on Long Island (now Queens). Here the record of *The Negro Achievement Hour* ends because the station's schedule was not carried in local newspapers. Although not the first black radio series, it was a pioneering effort that aired for at least two-and-a-half years, focusing on African American intellectual, civic, and musical accomplishments.

Episode guide available in appendix.

Sources: Jaker, et al. p. 25; *Pittsburgh Courier*, January 5, 1929, p. 2; *Baltimore Afro-American*, January 5, 1929, p. 9, October 19, 1929, p. 8; *New York Amsterdam News*, September 4, 1929, p. 11.

Negro Art Group Hour

The Negro Art Group Hour was an early ongoing African American series that started soon after *The Negro Achievement Hour.* The earliest known broadcast dates to February 10, 1928. The show was a full hour every week and featured primarily black artists, both musical and literary, but featured some speakers later in its run. While weekly radio listings have left a good overview of artists and speakers who appeared on the show, little is known about its production.

In May 1928, producers of *The Negro Art Group* published a short letter in *The New York Amsterdam News.* It read: "A special feature on [WEVD] is the Negro Art Group from 3 to 4 each Friday. Well-known performers have taken part in this hour, giving pleasure to our listeners and helping to build up this feature. "Station WEVD wishes to reach further, however, and asks all talented and ambitious musicians, readers and speakers who feel concern for social justice and peace to help in the cause and to further their own development by taking part in this hour." The program had a long run and didn't leave the air until the summer of 1930.

Episode guide available in appendix.

Sources: *New York Amsterdam News*, February 8, 1928 p. 17, May 30, 1928, p. 8, July 9, 1930, p. 10.

Negro Business Hour (Baltimore)

In early 1932 WCBM, Baltimore, debuted a unique program with a focus on the black business community. The weekly show was hosted by **Joe Bostic**, a native of Mt. Holly, NJ, and graduate of Morgan College. The *Business Hour* was Bostic's brainchild, an outgrowth of his realization while in college that radio might be used to further business opportunities, whereupon he wrote "The Economic Emancipation of the Negro" for his graduation paper in 1929. In 1940 a program called the *Negro Business Hour* was aired in Cleveland, but the two series had no relation to each other.

April 3, 1932—Speaker: The Metropolitan Finance Corporation's Herbert Frisby.

April 10, 1932—Speaker: Josiah Diggs, owner and operator of East Baltimore's Dunbar Theatre. He told the audience of the motion picture house's growth over recent years. Music: Minnie Smith, backed up by Johnny Christian's Orchestra.

April 17, 1932—Speaker: Blanche Dixon shared about her business, the Dixon Beauty Parlor.

July 10, 1932—Speaker: Edward Gaskin, manager of the Harlem Hot Shots jazz group.

September 4, 1932—Baltimore singer Evelyn Westcott sang a variety of songs.

September 11, 1932–September 25, 1932—

Off the air so host Joe Bostic could enjoy a vacation.

October 16, 1932—Music provided by the Paradise Choir who were starring in the stage show *Adam and Eva*. The Choir sang songs from the show written by **River Chambers** and Ralph Matthews.

Sources: *Baltimore Afro-American*, March 26, 1932, p. 8; *Cleveland Call and Post*, June 22, 1940, p. 1.

Negro Business Hour (Cleveland)

Cleveland's *Negro Business Hour* began November 19, 1939, over WHK sponsored by the Progressive Business Alliance and aired before the famous *Wings Over Jordan* series. The half-hour program featured two Negro Business Hour Choirs which made performances around the city in addition to the Sunday morning broadcasts. Ralph Finley and John Morning regularly narrated the weekly broadcasts which were a mix of musical performances and informational presentations. In 1949 the radio series celebrated its tenth anniversary, a considerable achievement for an African American production at the time. Records indicate *The Negro Business Hour* left the air shortly after the milestone.

Sources: *Cleveland Call and Post*, November 16, 1940, p. 3, April 19, 1941, p. 2, November 27, 1943, p. 9, December 6, 1947, p. 6B, December 4, 1948, p. 13A, December 3, 1949, p. 4.

Negro Forum Hour

Little so far has been uncovered about WEVD's *Negro Forum Hour*, not to be confused with the *National Negro Forum* hosted by **Carlton Moss**. Like other contemporary African American programs it weighed in on such meaty topics as "The Olympics and Race Relations," a talk given by James Egert Allen, president of the New York branch of the NAACP, during an August 1932, broadcast.

Source: *Baltimore Afro-American*, August 6, 1932, p. 16.

Negro Musical Hour

The *Negro Musical Hour* was instituted over WMCA, New York, February 17, 1930, with the express purpose of providing an outlet for African American tunes performed by black musicians. It was presented in two separate nightly half-hour installments. The regular orchestra was dubbed the ACO Entertainers. Within a couple months the program was simply referred to as *The ACO Entertainers*. They proved so popular with listeners that by mid–1930 the group had acquired a slot on station WPCH as well and were appearing up to six times a week between the two stations.

Sources: *New York Amsterdam News*, February 12, 1930, p. 11, March 12, 1930, p. 11, May 14, 1930, p. 10.

Negro Newsfront

The first known black news program in Chicago, *Negro Newsfront* was one of the first African American radio newscasts in the country. **Oscar Brown, Jr.,** claimed to have started the show in 1947 over WJJD, and subsequently took it to WVON then WHFC. **Vernon Jarrett** is credited with working with Brown on the program from 1948 to 1951 leaving unclear the exact time frame the series aired. Brown recalled ending the broadcasts in 1952.

Sources: Porter and Wojcik; *Chicago Defender*, February 19, 1949, p. 22.

The Negro Progress Hour

Created to feed off the popularity of *Wings Over Jordan*, *The Negro Progress Hour* originated from Cleveland's WGAR and was produced by the same men who handled *Wings*. The premier episode, November 6, 1938, featured Tuskegee Institute president Dr. F. D. Patterson and the Wings Over Jordan Choir. Over 300 people crammed into St. Mark's Presbyterian Church from which the broadcast originated. Various local singers provided subsequent musical numbers. The Rev. W. L. Ransom, Richmond, VA, spoke at the second broadcast about the "interracial question" and urged his listeners to patronize black-owned businesses. Subsequent broadcasts featured a variety of speakers and singers:

November 20, 1938—Speaker: Edward Henderson of the D. C. public schools. Music: Boys Choir of the Rutherford B. Hayes School.

November 27, 1938—Speaker: Dr. James Shepard, Durham, NC, president of North Caroline College. Music: A'Cappella Choir of Central High School.

December 4, 1938—Speaker: John Holly of the Future Outlook League.

December 11, 1938—Speaker: the Rev. A. L. James, president of Lott Carey Baptist Missionary Convention in Roanoke, VA.

December 18, 1938—Speaker: Augustus Griggs, Augusta, GA, president of Haines Institute. Music: Revelation Chorus of Triedstone Baptist Church, Cleveland.

January 1, 1939—Speaker: John Wesley Dobbs, Grand Master of Masons of Georgia.

January 8, 1939—Special celebration of *Wings Over Jordan*'s first anniversary as a network feature.

January 15, 1939—Speaker: the Reverend Bradby, 2nd Baptist Church, Detroit.

January 22, 1939—Speaker: James Gayle, president of The National Baptist Laymen's Association. Music: Junior Choir of Mt. Haven Baptist Church.

January 29, 1939—Speaker: the Rev. Albert Jackson, Mt. Zion Baptist Church, Knoxville, TN. Music: Phillis Wheatley's Madrigal Chorus.

February 5, 1939—Speaker: Dr. Charles Garvin. Music: Junior Choir of Gethsemane Baptist Church.

February 12, 1939—Speaker: Richard Westbrooks, attorney and resident Consul of the Republic of Liberia. Music: Senior Choir of Lane Metropolitan C. M. E. Church.

February 19, 1939—Speaker: the Reverend Henderson, Greater Bethel AME Church, Indianapolis. Music: Senior Choir of St. John's AME Church.

February 26, 1939—Speaker: the Rev. J. Timothy Boddie, Union Baptist Church, Baltimore. Music: Emmanuel Baptist Church choir.

March 5, 1939—Speaker: Jennie Moton, president of the National Association of Colored Women, Capahosic, VA. Music: Phillis Wheatley Madrigal Chorus.

March 12, 1939—Speaker: Lafayette Ford, president of the National Alliance of Postal Employees.

March 19, 1939—Speaker: Channing Tobias, International Secretary of the YMCA.

March 26, 1939—Speaker: Prof. C. S. Woodard president of Agricultural, Mechanical and Normal College, Pine Bluff, AR.

April 9, 1939—Speaker: Pastor Holman Evans, Lane CME Church. Music: Lane senior choir.

April 16, 1939—Speaker: Attorney William Hueston, Commissioner General of Education of the Elks. Music: Acme Octette.

April 23, 1939—Speaker: the Rev. Robert Williams, Asbury ME Church, Washington, D.C. Music: Mt. Pleasant ME Church Gospel Choir.

April 30, 1939—Speaker: Dr. J. Hale of the George W. Hubbard Hospital, Nashville, TN. Music: Gospel Chorus of Gethsemane Baptist Church.

May 7, 1939—Speaker: the Rev. David McDodana, 1st Baptist Church McDonald, PA.

May 14, 1939—Speaker: Hazel Walker.

May 21, 1939—Speaker: the Rev. E. C. McLeod, Warren Memorial Church, Atlanta.

May 28, 1939—Speaker: Dr. Allen Jackson, Hartford, CT. Music: Gethsemane Junior Chorus.

June 4, 1939—Speaker: Dr. Theodore Spelgner, president of Martin Luther Institute of Tuscaloosa, AL. Music: Paramount Quartette.

June 11, 1939—Speaker: Lucy Hughes, president of the Woman's Home and Foreign Missionary Society of the AME Church. Music: St. James Choir.

June 18, 1939—Speaker: the Rev. Carlyle Stewart, St. Peter AME Church, South Minneapolis. Final broadcast before summer break.

September 17, 1939—Speaker: the Rev. William Peck, Detroit.

September 24, 1939—Speaker: Dr. Robert Daniel, president of Shaw University, Raleigh, NC. Music: Mt. Haven Baptist Church choir.

October 1, 1939—Speaker: M. C. Clarke, president Dunbar Mutual Insurance Society. Music: Avery AME Church choir.

October 8, 1939—Speaker: the Rev. W. A. Jennings, Mt. Vernon AME Church of Tulsa, OK. Music: Boys' Choir of Rutherford B. Hayes School.

October 15, 1939—Speaker: Ralph Finley, district manager of Fireside Mutual Insurance Co. Music: Harmony Four Quartet.

October 22, 1939—Speaker: Dr. Nathaniel Dett, Director of Music at Bennett College, Greensboro, NC. Music: St. John's AME Church choir.

November 5, 1939—Speaker: the Rev. T. J. King, Ebenezer Baptist Church, Pittsburgh, PA. Music: True Vine Baptist Church choir.

November 12, 1939—Speaker: Major Campbell Johnson, Executive secretary of the YMCA, Washington, D.C.

November 19, 1939—Speaker: the Rev. Grant Reynolds, president of Cleveland's NAACP,

November 26, 1939—Speaker: Lewis Downing, Dean of Howard University's School of Engineering and Architecture.

December 3, 1939—Speaker: William Walker, Cleveland councilman. Music: Senior Choir of Antioch Baptist Church.

December 17, 1939—Speaker: the Rev.

Adam Powell, Jr., Abyssinia Baptist Church, NYC.

December 31, 1939—Speaker: the Rev. Richard Bowling, 1st Baptist Church Norfolk, VA. Music: Metropolitan Baptist Church.

January 7, 1940—Speaker: Judge Armond Scott, Washington, D.C. Music: Junior Choir of 2nd Mt. Sinai Church.

January 14, 1940—Speaker: Eddie Tolan, runner. Music: Madrigal Chorus of Phillis Wheatley Association.

January 21, 1940—Speaker: William Walker, councilman. Music: Gospel Choir of St. John's AME Church.

January 28, 1940—Speaker: the Rev. P. Wilkinson, New Light Baptist Church, San Antonio. Music: Senior Choir of 1st Mt. Olive Baptist Church.

February 4, 1940—Speaker: Harry Parker Director of Recreation for Negroes, Greensboro, NC. Music: 2nd Mt. Sinai Baptist Church.

February 11, 1940—Speaker: Major R. Wright, Philadelphia. Music: Gospel Choir of Metropolitan Baptist Church.

February 25, 1940—Speaker: the Rev. F. Davis, Dean of the Religious Institute of the United Baptist Convention of Massachusetts and Rhode Island. Music: Triedstone Baptist Church choir.

March 3, 1940—Speaker: Dr. Charles Garvin, Cleveland physician. Music: Junior Choir of the Open Door Baptist Church.

March 10, 1940—Speaker: Dr. Charlotte Brown, president of Palmer Institute, SC.

March 17, 1940—Speaker: Prof. Merl Eppse, Tennessee State College, Nashville, TN. Music: Silver Leaf Chorus.

March 24, 1940—Speaker: Dr. T. W. Turner, Department of Biology, Hampton Institute. Music: Lee's Memorial Church.

March 31, 1940—Speaker: Dr. Eugene Clarke, Toledo physician.

April 7, 1940—Speaker: S. B. Simmons, founder and executive secretary of the New Farmers of America.

May 12, 1940—Speaker: Fannie Peck, president of the National Housewives League, Detroit.

May 19, 1940—Speaker: Dr. Henry Dickerson, president of Bluefield State Teachers College, WV.

June 2, 1940—Speaker: the Rev. Levi Terrill, 1st Bryan Baptist Church, Savannah, GA. Music: Bethel Baptist Church choir.

June 9, 1940—Speaker: Mamie Hoffman, Nashville, TN. Music: Wilson Jubilee Chorus.

June 16, 1940—Speaker: Ernest Attwell, Field Director Bureau of Colored Work National Recreation Association.

Sources: *Cleveland Call and Post*, November 10, 1938, p. 1, 31, November 17, 1938, p. 1, November 24, 1938, p. 1, December 8, 1938, p. 1, December 15, 1938, p. 1, December 22, 1938, p. 1, January 5, 1939, p. 1, January 12, 1939, p. 1, January 19, 1939, p. 1, January 26, 1939, p. 1, February 2, 1939, p. 1, February 9, 1939, p. 1, February 23, 1939, p. 1, March 2, 1939, p. 1, March 9, 1939, p. 1, March 16, 1939, p. 1, March 30, 1939, p. 1, April 6, 1939, p. 1, April 13, 1939, p. 1, April 20, 1939, p. 1, April 27, 1939, p. 1, May 4, 1939, p. 1, May 11, 1939, p. 1, May 18, 1939, p. 1, May 25, 1939, p. 1, June 1, 1939, p. 1, June 8, 1939, p. 1, June 15, 1939, p. 1, September 14, 1939, p. 1, September 21, 1939, p. 1, September 28, 1939, p. 1, October 5, 1939, p. 1, October 12, 1939, p. 2, October 19, 1939, p. 2, November 2, 1939, p. 11, November 9, 1939, p. 2, November 16, 1939, p. 1, November 23, 1939, p. 3, November 30, 1939, p. 1, 2, December 14, 1939, p. 1, December 28, 1939, p. 1, January 4, 1940, p. 1, January 11, 1940, p. 3, January 18, 1940, p. 1, January 25, 1940, p. 1, February 1, 1940, p. 1, February 8, 1940, p. 1, February 22, 1940, p. 1, February 29, 1940, p.1, March 7, 1940, p. 1, March 14, 1940, p. 1, March 21, 1940, p. 1, March 28, 1940, p. 1, April 4, 1940, p. 1, May 9, 1940, p. 1, May 16, 1940, p. 2, June 1, 1940, p. 1, June 7, 1940, p. 1, June 15, 1940, p. 1.

Negro Radio Stories, Inc.

In 1953 a commercial outfit called Negro Radio Stories, Inc., attempted to market four new African American soap operas as an hour-long block to stations. The first serial was *The Romance of Julie Davis*, the story of "a young girl ... thrown into the turbulent, pulsating life of New York, now knowing who she is or from where she came." The second, *Ada Grant's Neighbors*, concerned "one woman's firm belief that it is possible to live by the Golden Rule." *My Man* was "the poignant story of a young married couple and one woman's soul-stirring fight for the man she loves. The last new series was *Rebecca Turner's Front Porch Stories*.

Negro Radio Stories, Inc., lined up soap opera veterans to ensure a quality product. Blair Wallister (*Just Plain Bill, Front Page Farrell, Bachelor's Children*), Ruth Lieban (*The Romance of Helen Trent, Stella Dallas, Backstage Wife*), Steve Price (*Our Gal Sunday, Perry Mason, Bright Horizon*), and Henry Howard (*Lorenzo Jones, Young Widder Brown*) were engaged for directorial duties.

Actors engaged to work on the series included **Maurice Ellis**, **Emory Richardson**, Rai Tasco, William Dillard, John Marriott, Maude Russell, Evelyn Ellis, Pauline Meyer, Terry Carter, and Wardell Saunders. Though the company's vice-president Douglas Chandler announced that the four transcribed soaps would begin on March 15, 1954 over fifty stations, there's no indication they were ever broadcast.

Sources: Cox, *Historical Dictionary*, pp. 23–24; Cox, *Say Goodnight*, p. 78; *Billboard*, November 28, 1953, p. 6; *New York Amsterdam News*, December 26, 1953, p. 9; *Pittsburgh Courier*, February 13, 1954, p. 19.

Negro Youth Movement

The Negro Youth Movement did not have a regular radio effort but the organization took to the air at least once in its history. On January 8, 1925, the organization broadcast its national solo contest over KDKA, Pittsburgh. The contests winners were Naomi Dickerson, soprano, Inez Washington, contralto, Ruby Blakey, first tenor, and Benjamin Coles, first baritone. Other performers making an appearance were pianist Charlotte Enty, Pittsburgh singer **Lois Deppe**, and violinist Leon Wisdom. Amidst the musical talent I. J. K. Wells, head of the Negro Youth Movement, gave a short address outlining the group's mission.

Source: *Pittsburgh Courier*, January 3, 1925, p. 16.

New World A' Coming

Aired on WMCA from 1944 to 1957, *New World A' Coming* was one of the longest running series with a focus on African American themes. The series was inspired by Roi Ottley's book *New World A-Coming: Inside Black America* published by Houghton Mifflin in 1943 in which he recounted the history of blacks in New York. The weekly broadcasts were a pet project of Nathan and Helen Straus, WMCA's wealthy white owners who wanted a quality black series on radio. Since their station was unaffiliated with a network they didn't feel the need to bow to public pressure as others did when presenting controversial material. The City-Wide Citizens Committee on Harlem helped WMCA sponsor the broadcasts.

New World A' Coming premiered March 5, 1944, with the words "With the sweeping fury of a resurrection—a new world is coming!" Dorothy Norman spoke for the Citizens Committee on that first broadcast as did Roi Ottley. The first two years' scripts were primarily based on Ottley's book and covered such topics as black attitudes toward war, ghettos, and the history of black churches. **Canada Lee** narrated many of the early episodes and a mixed-race cast including Leigh Whipper, Josh White, Mary Lou Williams, Alexander Scourby, and Mercedes McCambridge performed scripts which were initially written by Ottley and later by Michael Sklar. Michael Grayson worked as producer and director and **Duke Ellington** wrote the theme song which was performed by the Jerry Sears Orchestra. The program's significance was recognized from its beginning; It won the 1944 Edward L. Bernays Radio Award sponsored by the Institute for Education by Radio of Ohio State University. The judges were noted radio men H. V.

Kaltenborn, Raymond Swing, and Norman Corwin. Said Corwin of the series: "It is an excellent demonstration of the principles that democracy begins at home. The series is fighting a fearless and socially responsible program based on the profoundest truth ever postulated to wit, that all men are created equal." Additionally, in March 1945, WMCA was awarded the Honor Roll of Race Relations by the Schomburg Collection of Negro Literature of the New York Library for its undertaking of the series.

Over the years episodes included documentaries, historical vignettes, fictionalized dramas, tributes to prominent African Americans, and music. Several historians have described *New World A' Coming* as a black version of the dramatized current events program *March of Time* which ran from 1931 to 1945. In 1948 the program won the distinguished Peabody Award for broadcasting excellence. Originally planned for a mere 26 weeks, the program ended up running at least fourteen years.

Sources: Barlow pp. 78–82; Blue pp. 286–289; MacDonald, *Don't Touch That Dial!*, p. 354–355; Savage pp. 247–260; Simpson p. 18; *New York Amsterdam News*, March 11, 1944, p. 1, October 7, 1944, p. B7, March 10, 1945, p. 1, June 6, 1945, p. B7.

New York Urban League

Founded in 1919, the New York Urban League went on the air with a regular weekly broadcast in the summer of 1929 on New York's WNYC. Supposedly created at the request of the station, the organization's series was originally intended to be a two month string of topical broadcasts with the goal of highlighting various areas of "racial progress." Interest proved high enough that they continued well into 1930.

Premiering July 1, 1929, the series kicked off with presentations by Elmer Carter, editor of *Opportunity*, Arthur Schomburg and Arthur Holden, chairmen of the New York Urban League, and George Harris, editor of

The New York News, who discussed "The Negro in Politics." All of this was packed into a fifteen-minute offering just before noon. The original slate of lectures gives an idea of the program's tone.

July 29, 1929—the Rev. William Lloyd Imes, "The Negro's Contribution to Religion."

August 5, 1929—Vernal Williams, attorney, "The Negro Lawyer."

August 12, 1929—Samuel Allen, New York Urban League, "The Negro Worker."

August 19, 1929—Carrie Bullock, president of the National Association of Colored Nurses, "The Negro Woman in the Field of Health."

August 26, 1929—Dr. Peter Murray, National Negro Medical Association, "The Negro Physician."

The format did not change after the original two months were up, as evidenced by some sample broadcasts from later in the year.

November 11, 1929—Dr. Lucien Brown, "Quacks and Quackery."

November 27, 1929—A. Philip Randolph, "The Negro Worker."

By the summer of 1930 the series was still on the air but was now appearing every other week, alternating with broadcasts of the National Association for the Advancement of Colored People.

Source: *New York Amsterdam News*, July 24, 1929, p. 11.

Oberndorfer, Mrs. Max

Little is known of Mrs. Max Oberndorfer, not even her first name. Nevertheless she has been identified as one of the first black women to appear on radio when she gave a lecture called "Negro Musicians" over Chicago's WMAQ in July 1923. The broadcast included various musical interludes by Maude Roberts-George, soprano, Lloyd Hickman (Columbus, OH), baritone, Clarence Cameron White (Oberlin, OH), violin,

Estella Bonds (Chicago), accompanist, and Carl Diton (Philadelphia), accompanist.

Source: *Chicago Defender*, August 4, 1923, p. 5.

Odom, Spencer

Spencer Odom was raised in Chicago and educated at the Chicago Piano College. Over the years he arranged songs for Dave Peyton, Lionel Hampton, and Vincent Lopez among others. Odom's primary radio work came during his years arranging and accompanying the **Southernaires** and the Mariners. Odom took over as pianist and arranger for the Southernaires quartet in 1940 when **Clarence Jones** fell ill from a nervous breakdown. The band left the air in 1950 then resumed touring in 1951 though **William Edmondson** remained the only original member; the others were Joseph Crawford, first tenor, John Taylor, Jr., second tenor, and Mulford Lee, baritone. Odom again accompanied the quartet during this brief revival. In the mid–1950s Odom appeared on Arthur Godfrey's program with the Mariners, a quartet which, interestingly, claimed **Homer Smith**—an original member of the Southernaires—as a founding singer. It's not clear when Odom joined the Mariners but it seems unlikely that he and Smith were members at the same time. Odom died of a heart attack on December 24, 1963. At the time he was engaged in some concert dates with **Juanita Hall**.

Sources: *Baltimore Afro-American*, May 4, 1940, p. 14, January 12, 1963, p. 11; *Chicago Defender*, January 2, 1954, p.7; *New York Amsterdam News*, August 4, 1951, p. 4, January 5, 1963, pp. 16, 35.

Oriole Glee Club

The Oriole Glee Club, led by Prof. R. A. Walker, aired over Baltimore's municipal station WPG in January 1925.

Source: *Baltimore Afro-American*, January 24, 1925, p. 12.

Palmer, Garland Clifford

Garland Palmer was primarily a play-

wright and dramatist for the New York stage but he appeared regularly on the Finkenberg Furniture Store Hour on WGBS, New York, in 1930. He was simply known as "the 'Impersonator' of the air."

Source: *Baltimore Afro-American*, September 6, 1930, p. 8.

Peters, Lowell

Originally from Cleveland, TN, Lowell Peters was a founding member of the long-running quartet the **Southernaires** and sang second tenor with the group. Before joining the famed foursome, Peters studied at Knoxville College where he took an A.B. Degree and sang in a school-sponsored quartet. It was on the collegiate circuit that he met **Homer Smith**, future Southernaires band mate. Peters graduated from Knoxville in 1927 and moved to New York in 1928 where he spent time with the **Hall Johnson** Singers, a prominent black choir. The Southernaires were one of the most popular black performing groups of the 1930s, appearing multiple times a week over NBC's chains and regularly touring the nation. The band was a Sunday morning radio staple, performing at that time for nearly twenty years most popularly in a program called *The Little Weatherbeaten Whitewashed Church*. In April 1948, Lowell fell ill and had to take a leave of absence from the quartet; John Taylor replaced him temporarily. By 1950 the Southernaires had disbanded, possibly due to the loss of most of its original members, thus ending their nearly uninterrupted run of radio performances dating back to 1930. When the quartet was briefly revived in 1951 Lowell did not sing with them.

Sources: *Baltimore Afro-American*, February 13, 1932, p. 9, January 13, 1951, p. 8; *New York Amsterdam News*, February 12, 1938, p. 6, June 11, 1938, p. 6, July 3, 1948, p. 23, August 12, 1950, p. 17; *New York Times*, November 3, 1929, p. 27.

Pinkard, Fred

Fred Pinkard spend most of his acting career working in one-man shows and numerous motion pictures and television shows through the 1990s. As a young man Pinkard studied at Chicago's Columbia College and served in World War II. Some of his first acting roles were on radio where he appeared on all three series written by **Richard Durham**, *Democracy—USA* (1946–1948), *Here Comes Tomorrow* (1947–1948) on which he played the lead character, amnesia-stricken Milton Redmond, and *Destination Freedom* (1948–1950). In 1967, well past radio's golden age, Pinkard starred in a series of ten broadcasts called *The Great Ones* that were produced by Group W and dramatized the lives of notable black Americans. The series was carried by a handful of stations including WINS, WBZ, KYW, KDKA, WOWO, WIND, and KFWB. The episodes were released on record in 1968.

During much of the 1960s Pinkard performed on stage, notably the Broadway play *Someone Else's Sandals* (1968) and the off–Broadway productions *The Blacks* (1963) and *In White America* (1963–1965). Beginning in the 1970s he began to make regular film and television appearances before passing away in 2004.

Sources: Woll pp. 88–89; *Chicago Defender*, February 19, 1949, p. 22, February 8, 1965, p. 17; *New York Amsterdam News*, March 2, 1968, p. 18, September 14, 1968, p. 20; http://www.einsiders.com/august-2004/hollywood-obituaries/august-2004-hollywood-obituaries.html accessed July 24, 2010.

Pullman Porters' Hour

The Brotherhood of Sleeping Car Porters received time on New York's WEVD every Friday afternoon beginning September 1928. The program was organized by A. Philip Randolph and presented singers, musicians, and various speakers.

Source: *New York Amsterdam News*, September 5, 1928, p. 8.

Rameses Rhythm Boys

This Baltimore-based quartet was one of many groups to imitate the popular **Mills Brothers** sound. The Rameses Rhythm Boys were George Douglass, William Hawkins, Harry Robinson, and Kermit Payne on guitar. Sponsored by Baltimore's Oriole Store over WCBM, the Rhythm Boys went on the air during the summer of 1931 and by 1933 still had a Sunday evening airtime.

Sources: *Baltimore Afro-American*, January 30, 1932, p. 15, March 26, 1932, p. 8, July 16, 1932, p. 16, December 17, 1932, p. 22, April 8, 1933, p. 9.

Randolph, Amanda

Amanda Randolph was born September 2, 1896, in Louisville, KY, but like her sister Lillian, was raised in Cleveland. A life in show business lay ahead which would take her far from the cities of her childhood. By the early 1920s Randolph had relocated to New York and in 1924 she had earned a spot with Sissle and Blake's touring company. She was an accomplished actress and found steady employment on the New York stage, notably at the Alhambra Theater. Some of Randolph's earliest credits include *Lucky Sambo* (1926) which also featured future radio co-worker **Ernest Whitman**, *Troubadors* (1927), and *Hot Dog* (1927) with Tim Moore, who would be cast with Randolph on the *Amos 'n' Andy* television program 25 years down the road. During this period Randolph appears to have made her radio debut on WGBS' *Pittsburgh Courier Hour* playing piano for the Runnin' Wild Four in December 1927.

That single performance is her only known radio work for a decade. In the meantime she toured England with a stage company in 1930 and began to get parts in various motion pictures. Over her career she would be credited for work in more than two dozen films. In the latter half of the 1930s Randolph began to acquire more radio roles, the earliest being parts on Al Jolson's *Shell Chateau* between 1935 and 1937. **Louis Armstrong** received his own series in 1937 and Randolph earned a spot on the debut broadcast on April 9. The program did not go over well due to poor writing and was off the air in a few weeks.

Like many African American women in radio, Randolph played her share of maids; sister **Lillian Randolph**'s most prominent role, in fact, was Birdie Lee Coggins on *The Great Gildersleeve*, a part Amanda took over from October 1956 until March 1958. Amanda also played a maid on *Love of Julie Borel* (1940), *Abie's Irish Rose* (1943–1944), *Meet Miss Julia* (ca. 1940), and *Miss Hattie*, a show starring Ethel Barrymore which aired over WJZ in 1941 on which she played Venus. Years later she would play the maid Aunt Martha on television's *The Laytons* (1948). Most famously she was the maid **Beulah** on the radio series of the same name. Randolph assumed the role for the final two seasons, 1952–1954, after her sister played Beulah during the 1951-1952 season.

Randolph's most famous radio role was arguably that of Ramona "Mama" Smith, mother-in-law of the Kingfish on *The Amos 'n' Andy Show*. She appeared as early as 1943 but was written into the program regularly from 1951 until 1955. Other dated broadcasts for which Randolph was cast are *Jubilee* (#303 and #304, both aired December 1948), *Forecast* (August 25, 1941), *Arthur Hopkins Presents* (October 18, 1944), *Joyce Jordan, Girl Intern* (later *Joyce Jordan, M.D.*) where she played Celia from November 29, 1945, until October 8, 1948, *When a Girl Marries* (starting September 15, 1947, in the part of Mary), *Cavalcade of America* (November 15, 1948 and May 23, 1949), *You Are There* (June 18, 1950), *CBS Radio Workshop* (January 13, 1957), *Columbia Workshop* (April 27, 1941, "Jason Was a Man"), *Harlem Salutes the Greater New York Funds*, WMCA (June 8, 1941), *Harlem Hospitality Club* (#11 1947, AFRS), and *Suspense* (February 3, 1957). Randolph also played roles on *Aunt Jemima*, *Kitty Foyle* (as Ellen), and *Young Dr. Malone* (as Ruby) but it's not known when any of these assignments came. She stayed busy enough on the air that by 1945 Randolph

claimed to be doing no acting outside of radio. Amanda preceded her sister in death, passing away August 24, 1967.

Sources: LOC; Buxton and Owen pp. 128, 261; Cox, *Great Radio Sitcoms*, pp. 33, 45, 71, 73, 83; Cox, *Great Radio Soap Operas*, p. 278; Dunning pp. 4, 31–32, 50, 83–84; Grams *Cavalcade*; Grams, *Radio Drama*, pp. 32, 79; Lotz and Neuert; MacDonald p. 337; Peterson p. 90; Sampson, *Blacks in Black and White*, pp. 558–559; *Baltimore Afro-American*, May 23, 1924, p. 5, December 24, 1927, p. 9, July 14, 1945, p. 10; *Chicago Defender*, April 8, 1944, p. 8; *New York Amsterdam News*, July 28, 1926, p. 10, May 18, 1927, p. 12, August 22, 1927, p. 7, November 16, 1927, p. 8, December 21, 1927, p. 10, May 7, 1930, p. 11, April 17, 1937, p. 16, September 7, 1940, p. 11, May 3, 1941, p. 20, June 14, 1941, p. 21, September 11, 1948, p. 23, October 22, 1949, p. 15; www.radiogoldindex.com.

Randolph, Lillian

Lillian Randolph was born December 14, 1898, in Louisville, KY, but she spent most of her childhood in Cleveland, OH, where she got her first vaudeville experience at age 17 in a revue called *Lucky Sambo*. Cleveland is also where she made her first radio appearances over station WTAM. Randolph's quarter-century radio career began in earnest in 1930 when she moved to Detroit and began working over station WXYZ. After auditioning with a choral group for a spot on WJR and being the only one called back, she went on to audition with the same group at WXYZ. After some basic training in, ironically, black dialect with James Jewell, she was hired as Lulu for a new show called *Lulu and Leander* along with Billy Mitchell. The show ran for 2½ years between 1930 and 1933.

Randolph moved to Los Angeles around 1935 where she appeared in various programs through the 1930s including *Shell Chateau* with Al Jolson (on which she played Mammy), thirty weeks on Joe Penner's program, and fifteen weeks with Al Pearce. In 1937 she spent some time on Rudy Vallee's program with **Eddie Green** and **Ernest Whitman**. Randolph's also credited with roles on CBS' *Big Town* program before landing her most famous role as Birdie Lee Coggins on *The Great Gildersleeve* in 1941. *Great Gildersleeve* historians Charles Stumpf and Ben Ohmart describe Randolph's initial try-out for the series: "During a lunch break she slipped away from the recording session, hopped in her car, rushed to the NBC studios, flew into the building, tripped, and literally slid up to the microphone. She laughed, excused herself, and proceeded to read the script that was handed to her." The producers obviously liked what they heard because Randolph received the part and would go on to appear in every *Gildersleeve* radio broadcast from 1941 to 1956 (at which point sister Amanda assumed the role), all 39 episodes of the television series, and the four *Gildersleeve* motion pictures. Randolph also played Birdie on *Summerfield Bandstand*, the 1947 summer replacement show for Gildersleeve. Though cast as the family's housekeeper, she was an integral part of many weekly adventures and became a defacto family member as the years rolled by.

Her two other most prominent radio jobs were on *The Amos 'n' Andy Show* on which she played Madame Queen between 1943 and 1955 (a part she transitioned to television), and *Beulah* on which she starred as the title character from November 12, 1951, when **Hattie McDaniel** became ill and had to leave, to June 27, 1952. She claimed in an interview that she left *Beulah* "because of the difficult schedule which kept her away from her family." Sister **Amanda Randolph** took over the role the following season.

Other less familiar programs on which Randolph was cast included *The Baby Snooks Show*, *The Billie Burke Show* (as Daisy the housekeeper), and *The Remarkable Miss Tuttle* (later *The Remarkable Miss Crandall*), a 1942 summer replacement for *The Jack Benny Program* on which she played Ramona, a maid. In addition to steady parts she received her share of one-time roles in a variety of classic radio programs: *My Mother's Husband*

(July 2 and 9, 1950, NBC) where she played Ella Mae, *Lux Radio Theatre* (February 16, 1942, January 18, 1943, March 1, 1943, March 8, 1943, May 28, 1945, December 9, 1946, September 8, 1947, April 26, 1948, September 13, 1948, September 27, 1948, October 10, 1949, October 17, 1949, December 5, 1949, September 25, 1950, January 8, 1951, February 19, 1951, April 23, 1951, October 22, 1951, February 25, 1952, November 10, 1952, September 28, 1953, October 19, 1953, May 10, 1955), *Command Performance* (July 21, 1942), *Dr. Christian* (September 30, 1942), *Jubilee* #11 (recorded February 3, 1943), #138 (recorded June 18, 1945), and #139 (recorded June 25, 1945), *The Star and the Story* (July 16, 1944), *Cavalcade of America* (September 18, 1944, February 25, 1946), "The Grand March of the United States of America," a recording for the Armed Forces Radio Service (May 1948), *Sweet Adeline* (April 30, 1949, possibly an audition recording according to noted old time radio collector David Goldin), *The Hour of St. Francis* (June 10, 1951), *First Nighter* (July 21, 1953), *Nightbeat* (November 23, 1951), *The Cascade of Stars* (September 26, 1952), *Last Man Out* (November 29, 1953) a series which documented the workings of the Communist Party in the U.S, *The Hallmark Hall of Fame* (February 14, 1954), and *Fibber McGee & Molly* (April 13, 1954, May 4, 1954, May 17, 1954).

A show called *The Lillian Randolph Show* was aired in April 1948, over ABC. The effort was primarily a musical one with the Jubilaires (Ted Brooks, Bill Johnson, John Jennings, George McFadden), Buzz Adlam and his 19-piece orchestra, and Lillian herself singing "T'ain't Necessarily So," "Can't Help Lovin' That Man," "Confessin'," and "Great Day." Evidence indicates the trial broadcast did not lead to an ongoing series.

Six years later Randolph did finally receive her own show beginning October 18, 1954, over KOWL entitled again *The Lillian Randolph Show*. Broadcast from 11:30 to noon (later expanded to a full hour), the daily show was aimed at homemakers and featured "home hints, music, and a potpourri of interesting chatter and interviews." The series later changed its name to *At Home with Lillian Randolph* and later still to *Cavalcade of Spirituals* in 1956. Randolph left KDAY (formerly KOWL) in the spring of 1956 to focus on a gospel choir she'd formed called the Lillian Randolph Choir, a project which lasted about a year.

As radio gave way to television Randolph made the transition smoothly and is credited with roles on such series as *The Jeffersons*, *Sanford & Son*, *Six Million Dollar Man*, *That's My Mama*, and *Room 222*. Over her decades in show business Randolph appeared in many motion pictures, the last of which was released in 1979, a year before she died. She passed away September 12, 1980, from cancer.

Sources: LOC; Billups and Pierce pp. 266–267, 284, 287, 331, 380, 393, 397, 398, 417, 421, 436, 442, 443, 448, 454, 462, 469, 487, 488, 511; Cox, *Great Radio Sitcoms*, pp. 33, 45, 80, 152, 156, 258; Cox, *This Day*, p. 167; Dunning pp. 54, 83–84, 89, 293, 574; Edmerson pp. 27–28; Grams *Cavalcade*; Lotz and Neuert; MacDonald pp. 331, 358; Sampson, *Blacks in Black and White*, p. 559; Stumpf and Ohmart pp. 104–6; *Chicago Defender*, December 13, 1941 p. 20; *Los Angeles Sentinel*, October 3, 1935, p. 4, May 6, 1948, p. 23, May 27, 1948, p. 22, December 23, 1948, p. 18, February 19, 1953, p. 1, November 19, 1953, p. B6, October 7, 1954, p. 10, January 6, 1955, p. 11, April 14, 1955, p. 10, July 28, 1955, p. 10, October 13, 1955, p. B2, March 15, 1956, p. 7, May 24, 1956, p. B7, October 17, 1957, p. B11, February 20, 1964, p. D5, September 18, 1980, p. 1; *Los Angeles Times*, November 25, 1937, p. 22, September 15, 1980, p. B17; www.radiogoldindex.com.

Ray, Wallace

In May 1952, Wallace "Wally" Ray was hired by KNBC, San Francisco, as announcer, thus becoming the first African American to be hired in such a capacity by any station in the Bay area. Ray was in charge of the station's overnight broadcast period during which he announced a program of classical and semi-classical music from midnight to 6 A.M. every weekday. Before moving to KNBC Ray worked as assistant station manager at KBLF, Red Bluff, CA, where he did announcing, sportscasting, reporting and wrote continuity and scripts.

Sources: Altschuler pp. 16–17; Edmerson p. 49; *Los Angeles Sentinel*, March 27, 1952, p. 5.

Reliable Quartet

This foursome was made up of McKinley Wiggins, first tenor, J. D. Howze, second tenor and manager, Charles Lewis, baritone, and J. W. Dix, bass. They were regulars on the *Truths About Harlem Hour* on WGBS, New York, during the spring of 1930.

Source: *New York Amsterdam News*, April 30, 1930, p. 13.

Reynolds, Ellis

Ellis Reynolds was a piano player and songwriter for the Southernaires, a group under the direction of George (Doc) Hyder. This was not the more famous **Southernaires** quartet which broadcast over network radio for the better part of twenty years. Curiously, no evidence has surfaced that either musical outfit was concerned about the dual use of the Southernaires name. In August 1932, one source reported that Reynolds was the only black member of ASCAP. His compositions included "Confessin' That I Love You," "Because I'm Yours Sincerely," "Stealing," and "In Tune."

Source: *Baltimore Afro-American*, August 6, 1932, p. 16.

Rhetts, Caswell

Caswell Rhetts was a baritone singer who appeared regularly on the *Negro Art Group Hour* from 1928 to 1930 over WEVD, New York. He also made occasional solo appearances on the station, primarily in latter 1930 after the *Art Group* had left the air.

See *Negro Art Group* Appendix.

Sources: *New York Amsterdam News*, August 27, 1930, p. 10.

Richardson, Chuck

Baltimorean Chuck Richardson was perhaps one of the youngest black performers to gain sponsorship on radio when, at the age of eighteen, the baritone sang over WCAO under the auspices of Bittles' Bakery in 1932 where he was known as the "Pieoneer." Richardson's path to radio was happenstance; while working as an elevator boy at a Baltimore department store he struck up a song with a store department manager. The unknown manager happened to have a brother, Morton Blum, who was a theatrical agent and subsequently got the young Richardson booked into various local venues.

Richardson soon came to the attention of Joseph Imbroglio, the musical director at WCAO, and was offered an audition. The station liked what they heard and called him back a few weeks later for a spot under the sponsorship of a local bakery called the *Bittles' Pie Hour*. When the *Pie Hour* was cancelled Amoco gasoline latched on to Richardson and continued his broadcasts. Later in the 1930s Richardson hooked up with **Fletcher Henderson** and his orchestra as a vocalist.

Sources: *Baltimore Afro-American*, March 26, 1932, p. 8, May 28, 1932, p. 18, October 1, 1932, p. 9, June 4, 1938, p. 11.

Richardson, Emory

Emory Richardson spent most of his acting career on stage, most notably in *Green Pastures*, a play in which he was working as early as 1930. In 1934 he assumed the role of Moses when Alonzo Fenderson died. With steady work in theater through the 1930s and 1940s including *Anna Lucasta* (1944) and *Our Lan'* (1947), Richardson began appearing on television as early as 1951 over some CBS series. Richardson's radio career is not well documented but he made at least two dramatic appearances on NBC radio; the first on *The Ford Theater*'s adaptation of "The Green Pastures" (February 1, 1948) and the

second on U. S. Steel's *Theatre Guild on the Air* (September 14, 1952).

Richardson's most prominent radio work was on *The Story of Ruby Valentine*, a black soap opera which ran from 1954 to 1955 on which he played the role of the Reverend Rockwell. Other aural credits were *Valiant Lady*, *Crime Fighters*, *Cavalcade of America* (December 25, 1940, March 13, 1951) and *Freedom's People*.

Sources: LOC; Grams, *Cavalcade*; Woll pp. 9, 71, 120; *Baltimore Afro-American*, September 29, 1951, p. 11; *New York Amsterdam News*, December 14, 1932, p. 1, October 20, 1934, p. 1; *Pittsburgh Courier*, July 24, 1954, p. 18.

Richardson, John

John Richardson was neither the first nor youngest African American to experiment with wireless but he deserves mention among black radio pioneers. A native of Yonkers, NY, he was working the airwaves as a sixteen-year-old in 1919 after being granted a first grade amateur radio operator's license. When interviewed by *The Chicago Defender* Richardson claimed to have heard messages from as far as Germany. He enjoyed listening to the U. S. Weather Bureau's nightly weather reports.

Source: *Chicago Defender*, September 20, 1919, p. 4.

The Riff Brothers (also The Four Riff Brothers)

The Riff Brothers were one of innumerable quartets that hoped to follow in the tracks of the renowned **Mills Brothers**. The Cincinnati-based quartet originally formed in Indianapolis before gaining a Tuesday evening timeslot on WLW in 1933. Soon they were playing four days a week at different times. The station's musical director, who was credited by one source as having developed the Mills Brothers and **Southern Singers**, had a strong influence on the Riff Brothers' style. The members played multiple instruments.

Source: *Baltimore Afro-American*, April 15, 1933, p. 8.

Robeson, Orlando

Orlando Robeson was a Kansas City native who attended the University of Kansas with the intention of practicing medicine. Instead, Robeson ended up performing on radio in Kansas City beginning in 1927. Finding success on the air, he moved on to Chicago where he worked as a soloist for **Sammy Stewart**'s Orchestra. Subsequent work included a stint with Ben Silvin's Orchestra with whom he sang vocal refrains and then Claude Hopkins' band which appeared regularly on New York radio in the early 1930s.

Source: *Baltimore Afro-American*, May 21, 1932, p. 18.

Robeson, Paul

Paul Robeson is best remembered by radio historians for his performance of "Ballad for Americans" in 1939 and his patriotic broadcasts during World War II. However, Robeson's broadcasting career began fifteen years before when he made a handful of radio appearances during the 1920s, radio's first commercial decade. June 1924, represents the earliest documented performance by Robeson over the airwaves. At the time he participated in a NAACP broadcast over WIP, Philadelphia, on which he sang some numbers. Later that year he broadcast a scene from Eugene O'Neill's play *The Emperor Jones* over New York radio which was reported to be the first time an excerpt from an O'Neill play went over the airwaves. In response to the popularity of this broadcast Robeson performed a concert of spirituals over WGBS on April 12, 1925. In October 1925, he was invited to sing on the BBC after *The Emperor Jones* closed in London. June 1927, found Robeson singing on WRNY's *Edison Hour* and in September on the *Maxwell Hour* accompanied by Lawrence Brown.

By 1930 Robeson was working on the English stage as were several other African American performers during that era. In June of that year he was heard over CBS from London discussing his role in *Othello*. In 1931 Robeson sang over NBC from London. Two years later in May 1932, Robeson made a guest appearance on *The Eastman Hour* and then, a few days later, *The Ziegfeld Radio Hour* where he participated in a condensed version of the *Show Boat* musical with Helen Morgan and Eddie Dowling which was running concurrently on Broadway. The next month the cast repeated the *Show Boat* presentation over WABC. On June 5 of that year Robeson was a guest on General Electric's *Twilight Hour*.

As 1933 dawned Robeson opened the new year with some songs on *The Kodak Hour* in January. While touring Europe early in the year he sang over a Dutch radio program. During the summer he sang on NBC's G.E.-sponsored *Circle* and Rudy Vallee's popular program (July 20) on which he sang "Water Boy" and "Old Man River." He returned to the BBC for a New Year's concert. Then, in 1935, Robeson was featured on the General Motors Concert Series, a coast-to-coast series of broadcasts on NBC in October, and in December on the *Shell Chateau Hour* (December 7) out of Hollywood. Robeson made another broadcast (RCA's *Magic Key*) from London on September 27, 1936, which was picked up by the Blue network. Robeson appeared on Soviet radio at least once, in January 1937, where he implored black people around the world to involve themselves more in international affairs. Six months later he recorded a message and some songs for the National Joint Committee for Spanish Refugee Children which, after much controversy, was aired as intended.

In 1939 Robeson made a second guest appearance on Rudy Vallee's show (June 1) then performed on Norman Corwin's "Pursuit of Happiness" on November 5 and sang

Earl Robinson's "The Ballad of Uncle Sam," retitled "Ballad for Americans" for the broadcast. The performance was an instant hit; the six hundred-person studio audience roared their approval for fifteen minutes after the show went off the air, the CBS switchboard was allegedly swamped with calls, and letters poured in. "Ballad for Americans" took its place in the lore of American radio history.

Robeson was part of the August 25, 1941, episode of *Forecast* which adapted Eugene O'Neill's *All God's Chillun Got Wings* for the airwaves (script by John Whedon and John Tucker Battle). **Eva Jessye** and her choir accompanied Robeson on the CBS broadcast. Robeson rarely appeared on popular commercial broadcasts but during 1941 and 1942 he was a guest on Bing Crosby's *Kraft Music Hall* at least three times (February 6, 1941, December 11, 1941, February 26, 1942). On June 7 Robeson participated in a salute to **Canada Lee** aired over the Mutual network. That same month he was a guest on a fund raising program over New York's WMCA alongside **Nick Stewart** (Nicodemus) and the Four Saints in Three Acts Choir.

Robeson was featured in the debut broadcast of *Freedom's People* over NBC September 21, 1941. The musical and dramatic program also featured **W. C. Handy, Frank Wilson**, and Noble Sissle. Singer Joshua White and the DePaur Chorus provided further musical entertainment. The next day Robeson co-starred with prominent boxer Joe Louis on an hour-long radio hook-up called *Salute of Champions*. On June 27, 1943, he starred in a program sponsored by the Congress of Industrial Organizations alongside Langston Hughes and Earl Robinson. The broadcast was carried by NBC's popular Red Network. That fall on September 9 he starred in a radio version of *Stage Door Canteen* on which he sang signature tunes "Water Boy" and "Ballad for Americans."

Robeson appeared on Mutual's *Saturday Night Bandwagon* on January 28, 1944, and

then, a few months later participated in a CBS salute to the black press. Black radio stalwarts **Duke Ellington, Carlton Moss,** and **Juano Hernandez** were heard as well. He concluded 1944 with an appearance on *Answering You* on Mutual in December. In April 1945, he spoke over a six-continent hook-up via CBS concerning the performer's role in the world war. On April 24 Robeson was part of a broadcast commemorating the beginning of the United Nations Conference in San Francisco.

Robeson made another appearance honoring Negro Newspaper Week on March 2, 1946. NBC featured him along with Ralph Cooper, Ella Fitzgerald, Joe Louis and **Jackie Robinson**. Never bashful about his political views, Robeson was one of several who spoke out forcefully at a 1949 gathering deploring the limited opportunities African Americans had received on radio over the years. That summer the House UnAmerican Activities Committee reviewed Robeson's seemingly pro–Soviet statements that black Americans should not participate in aggression toward the communist country. While long a popular radio singer, Robeson never had his own series nor was he ever a regular on any programs. The networks tolerated his left-wing political views during the war years but afterward his radio appearances dwindled as the Cold War heated up.

Sources: LOC; Bannerman pp. 48–49; Barlow pp. 59–66; Barnouw, *The Golden Web*, pp. 120–121; Boyle and Bunie pp. 162, 258, 287, 366, 375–6; Duberman p. 236; Grams, *Radio Drama*, p. 194; Robeson, Jr. pp. 139, 231; *Atlanta Daily World*, June 12, 1932, p. 6, August 21, 1940, p. 1, September 22, 1941, p. 1, February 15, 1946, p. 1; *Baltimore Afro-American*, September 24, 1927, p. 14, December 21, 1935, p. 8, September 27, 1941, p. 14, March 2, 1946, p. 8, July 16, 1949, p. 1; *New York Amsterdam News*, April 8, 1925, p. 2, June 11, 1930, p. 4, June 15, 1932, p. 9, January 4, 1933, p. 4, October 19, 1935, p. 5, October 3, 1936, p. 24, December 5, 1936, p. 27, June 7, 1941, p. 20, February 26, 1944, p. 1, April 28, 1945, p. 8B; *Chicago Defender*, June 21, 1924, p. 10, April 11, 1925, p. 2, April 18, 1925, p. 8, May 4, 1932, p. 5, July 29, 1933, p. 5, October 19, 1935, p. 8, December 2, 1939, p. 4,

February 26, 1944, p. 1; *Philadelphia Tribune*, September 22, 1927, p. 15, June 5, 1930, p. 6, September 3, 1931, p. 6; *Pittsburgh Courier*, June 21, 1924, p. 3, February 11, 1933, p. 7, August 5, 1933, p. 6, November 11, 1939, p. 21, September 20, 1941, p. 21, October 11, 1941, p. 20, June 26, 1943, p. 8, September 11, 1943, p. 21; www.radiogoldindex. com.

Robinson, J. L.

J. L. "Bobby" Robinson was one half of an obscure African American twosome along with **Gilbert Glover**. References to Robinson and Glover are few, indicating a short-lived radio series in July 1930, on New York's WWRL and live appearances in the New York metropolitan area. A writer for *The New York Amsterdam News* considered their material unique and took pains to point out that they penned it themselves.

Source: *New York Amsterdam News*, July 9, 1930, p. 10.

Robinson, Jackie

Jackie Robinson is legendary for becoming the first African American baseball player of the modern era when he took the field for the Brooklyn Dodgers during the 1947 season. However, he made various forays into radio in the late 1940s and early 1950s. Robinson's first radio appearance outside of baseball-related interviews may have been a salute to National Negro Newspaper Week broadcast during February 1946, on CBS. The following year, soon after debuting with the Dodgers, Robinson was a guest on CBS' *Information Please* (April 23, 1947) along with Rufus Clement, president of Atlanta University.

Robinson's first radio series premiered in November 1948, over New York's WMCA. It was intended to run daily during the off-season until March 1949. Initially it was moved around the broadcast schedule but by December was appearing during an evening time slot. Officially christened *The Jackie Robinson Sports Show* it was sometimes referred to as *The Jackie Robinson All-Sports*

Broadcast and simply *The Jackie Robinson Show*. The daily program frequently featured a mystery voice singing some popular tunes; the listener who could first identify the voice won various prizes. Guests who appeared on Robinson's first series included Buddy Hassett, Eddie Yostof, and Allie Clark. The *Sports Show* left the air in March 1949, before Spring training started. That summer Robinson testified before the House UnAmerican Activities Committee regarding singer **Paul Robeson**'s comments that African Americans would not fight in a war against the Soviet Union. On July 24, 1949, some of Robinson's testimony was broadcast as a part of *Voices and Events* over NBC.

During the 1949 World Series Robinson joined sportscaster Bill Corum after each game on WJZ and WJZ-TV to discuss game highlights. Just a few months later on January 22, 1950, Robinson hosted his second radio series, *The Jackie Robinson Show*, which was his first to be aired over a national network, ABC. Robinson was credited with writing the script for weekly series with Harold Parrott who was a former sports writer. While broadcasts primarily were concerned with sports issues Robinson also had a passion for "combating juvenile delinquency" and hoped his radio work would address that issue. Robinson appeared in a special broadcast April 29, 1950, celebrating the inauguration of a new Harlem radio station, WLIB.

The Jackie Robinson Show left the air December 31, 1950, after nearly one full year on the air. Just two weeks before Robinson had premiered a television program called *Jackie Robinson's Sports Classroom* over WPIX, a project that may have hastened the demise of his radio show. Robinson didn't give up on radio; between July and August 1951 he had a disc jockey program called *Jackie Robinson's Platter Up Club* which originated from WNBC. Robinson was a guest four times in 1953 on *For Better Living* (October 4, October 11, November 8, November 29 and then the next year in 1954 he was featured in yet another on-going series, this one called *The Jackie Robinson Club* which aired on WNBC each weekday morning for most of the year. He was a guest on at least one further non-sports broadcast on December 14, 1954, when *America's Town Meeting* addressed the issue "How Can We Break Down Prejudices?" Robinson is only known to have acted in one dramatic radio play, an episode of *Adventures of the Abbotts* on March 6, 1955, over NBC.

Sources: LOC; Barlow p. 76; Edmerson pp. 44–45; Hickerson (2nd ed.) p. 234; MacDonald p. 359; *Time*, February 6, 1950 p. 71; *New York Amsterdam News*, April 19, 1947, p. 21, November 27, 1948, p. 23, December 4, 1948, p. 25, December 25, 1948, p. 15, February 12, 1949, p. 24, July 23, 1949, p. 27, April 22, 1950, p. 27, April 29, 1950, p. 4; *New York Times*, September 28, 1948, p. 54, October 6, 1949, p. 62, December 13, 1950, p. 50, January 26, 1952, p. 19, April 5, 1952, p. 13, December 14, 1954, p. 50.

Robinson, Louise

Louise Robinson, soprano, teamed with Jewel Knott, pianist, to perform on an August 1923, broadcast over KDKA, Pittsburgh.

Source: *Pittsburgh Courier*, August 25, 1923, p. 5.

Rocking Chair Memories

The **Southernaires** had various programs across the dial in the early 1930s and *Rocking Chair Memories* was the name of their 1933 Wednesday evening feature which went out over the NBC chain.

Source: *Baltimore Afro-American*, May 27, 1933, p. 10.

Roy Johnson and His Happy Pals

Drummer Roy Johnson led the little-remembered Happy Pals in the late 1920s and early 1930s. The ensemble was made up of Leroy Wyche, piano, cornetists Slim Harris, Edwin Hume, and Chester Millingran, trombonists Noisy Richardson and Fleming (Beans) Edwards, sax men Emmett Johnson,

Harold Griffin, and Buster McPherson, Edward (Skinny) Trent on banjo and guitar, and William Allen, bass violin and tuba. The band was a favorite on Virginia airwaves in 1928 and by 1931 they were appearing weekly on stations WAPC (Long Island), WOR (New York), and WRVA (Richmond, VA). "Happy Pal Stomp," recorded on Okeh Records, was their signature song.

Sources: *Baltimore Afro-American*, December 24, 1927, p. 19, July 21, 1928, p. 10, October 12, 1929, p. 9, May 16, 1931, p. 18.

Rudd, Wayland

Wayland Rudd had a very minor radio career, appearing only in *Careless Love*, **Carlton Moss'** first program and the first black radio drama. The series ran from November 1930, to May 1932, but it's not clear how often Rudd was featured. Like most of Moss' players, Rudd was a theater performer who gave up a career in journalism. Originally with *The Chicago Defender* in the early 1920s, by 1927 he was cast in regional productions in Washington, D.C., and Philadelphia. In New York Rudd played alongside **Frank Wilson, Ernest Whitman,** and **Juano Hernandez,** black actors who would go on to do substantial radio work. In 1932 after *Careless Love* went off the air Rudd emigrated to the Soviet Union to pursue acting opportunities there. Believing he would always be limited by racial attitudes in the United States, Rudd ended up spending the rest of his life overseas where he worked steadily in Soviet stage and film productions.

Sources: Baldwin p. 15; *Baltimore African American,* November 19, 1927 p. 9, March 22, 1930 p. 8, February 11, 1933 p. 17, November 21, 1931 p. 23; *New York Amsterdam News,* February 3, 1932, p. 10, March 9, 1932, p. 7, July 7, 1934, p. 15, April 17, 1937, p. 16, August 16, 1945, p. 13.

Sam and Jenny (Later Sam and Liza)

This duo, inspired by *Amos 'n' Andy*, consisted of Larry Drenard (who was supposedly an old acquaintance of **Freeman Gosden** and **Charles Correll**) and Charlie Schear.

They started on WMCA then moved to WAAT where they weekly depicted an African American man and woman from the deep South. Their show ran through the spring and summer of 1930.

Sources: *New York Amsterdam News*, January 15, 1930, p. 11, May 14, 1930, p. 10.

Sam 'n' Henry

Widely unknown outside the small circle of old time radio enthusiasts, *Sam 'n' Henry* was a series featuring **Charles Correll** and **Freeman Gosden** who are better known as the creators of *Amos 'n' Andy*. After hooking up around 1920 via their employment with the Joe Bren theater company, Gosden and Correll settled in Chicago about 1925 and began making regular radio appearances.

In April of that year the duo appeared on Chicago's WQJ, owned by Calumet Baking Powder Company, as a harmony team. Other than some earlier radio work the two had done promoting the Bren Company, this was their first radio experience and it seemed to go over quite well. Later in the week Gosden and Correll auditioned for staff of WEBH, owned by the Edgewater Beach Hotel. Impressed by their act, WEBH granted them a twice-weekly slot through the spring and summer. The broadcast was advertised as *Correll and Gosden, the Life of the Party* and featured other obscure performers as well.

Over a series of broadcasts the team began building a comedic routine around the song "The Kinky Kids Parade," a popular tune of the time. They successfully sold a stage act to local performer Paul Ash and he eventually requested a follow-up act. In October 1925, they were offered employment by WGN, the Chicago Tribune's radio station. While their prior work on the air had been unpaid, the positions with WGN allowed them to focus full-time on radio. There they continued their harmony act which they had originated on WEBH and were also hooked up with announcer Bill Hay who would end up staying with them until 1942.

As they began to build up their reputation as a song duo WGN asked them to create a broadcast version of *The Gumps*, the Tribune's popular comic strip serial which debuted in 1919. Reluctant to potentially harm their growing popularity if the show was a dud and hesitant about the domestic nature of the strip (both men being single), Gosden and Correll responded with an outline of a story about two black men relocating from rural Alabama to Chicago. The proposal got no traction until January 1926, when they were told with little notice to prepare the program for broadcasting. Sam Smith and Henry Johnson debuted on January 12 and changed the face of radio. For the first time on the air characters were presented in dramatic stories which were continued day after day.

Sam 'n' Henry was not an immediate hit. Gosden (Sam) and Correll (Henry) were disappointed in the lukewarm reception of their new creation and for several weeks attempted to keep secret their roles in the show. Listenership increased throughout 1926 and by the end of the year they could boast a respectable following. The success of recordings they made for the Victor Talking Machine Company convinced them they could get even more listeners by recording their programs and selling them to stations around the country. WGN would have none of it, however, fearing they would be creating competition for themselves by letting others stations broadcast *Sam 'n' Henry*. By the end of 1927 their fame had spread beyond the Midwest with two appearances on the embryonic National Broadcasting Company network.

On December 18, 1927, Gosden and Correll played Sam and Henry for the last time and the series temporarily left the air after 586 episodes. With some minor changes the pair reemerged on the air playing Amos Jones and Andy Brown over WMAQ. WGN was convinced that they didn't need Gosden or Correll to continue the *Sam 'n' Henry* show.

Two men on the WGN staff, Henry Moeller and Hal Gilles, were handed the roles of Sam and Henry. Having worked with Correll and Gosden on the Joe Bren circuit and experienced in minstrel dialect work on other WGN broadcasts, Moeller and Gilles were natural replacements.

Moeller grew up in Davenport, IA, while Gilles hailed from Evansville, IN. It's not clear when the two ended up working for WGN but the station had enough confidence in them to put them on the air as Sam and Henry beginning January 10, 1928. Listeners were not impressed; *Sam 'n' Henry* was off the air permanently a few weeks later. The failure didn't hurt Moeller's or Gilles' career. On March 5th they debuted their new effort, a German-dialect act that eventually settled on the name *Louie's Hungry Five*. Like *Sam 'n' Henry, Louie's Hungry Five* aired six days a week and appears to have used continuing story lines. Louie and his little band of German musicians lasted on WGN until 1932 and then played live engagements around Chicago until 1946 when Moeller died of a heart attack.

Sources: Andrews and Julliard pp. 10–14; Cox, *Great Radio Sitcoms*, pp. 37–38; Ely pp. 52–57; Hopkinson and Ellett p. 12; McLeod pp. 25–35.

Sam Woodling's Orchestra

Sam Woodling's Orchestra broadcast over the AT&T station (WEAF) in New York in early March 1924. The year before the outfit appeared in James Johnson's musical review *Plantation Days*.

Source: *Chicago Defender*, March 15, 1924, p. 9.

Sammy Stewart's Knights of Syncopation

The Knights of Syncopation was an eleven-piece outfit which debuted on Chicago radio March 8, 1924, over KYW after radio dates in numerous smaller markets. What was to be a 15-minute broadcast turned out to last two hours because of all the positive calls that came in to the station.

The orchestra was led by Sammy Stewart on the piano. Other players were Douglass Speaks, piano, Harley Washington, saxophone and clarinet, David Smallwood, drums, Lawrence Dixon, cello, banjo, and clarinet, Paul Jordan, violin and saxophone, Roy Butler, saxophone and oboe, Millard Robbins, bass saxophone, tuba, flute, and piccolo, William Stewart, saxophone and clarinet, Rennan Robbins, bassoon, rothophone, cornet, saxophone, and Mance Worley, trombone, euphonia, French horn. All members provided vocals. Contemporary sources claim Stewart put his band together in Columbus, OH, and immediately got booked for long engagements in Cleveland, Columbus, Springfield (OH), Dayton, Toledo, and Detroit. They played Midwestern cities for twelve years before moving to Chicago in 1923.

Sources: *Chicago Defender*, March 3, 1923, p. 5, February 23, 1924, p. 6; *Philadelphia Tribune*, March 22, 1924, p. 15.

Sarah Butler's Old-Time Southern Singers

This California-based group, which numbered up to 50 members, debuted on L.A.'s KEGF in August 1931, and was soon being heard on KFI and KECA. Sarah Butler, head of the group, made various motion picture appearances, including *Arrowsmith, Lena Rivers*, and various shorts. They provided music for *Cabin in the Cotton* along with the Cotton Club orchestra. The huge ensemble was still singing in 1933.

Sources: *Baltimore Afro-American*, August 29, 1931, p. 9, July 2, 1932, p. 10; *Chicago Defender*, June 18, 1932, p. 5, September 8, 1934, p. 9.

Saunders, Dainty Gertrude

Dainty Gertrude Saunders starred in numerous Broadway and nightclub shows through the 1920s and into the early 1930s including *Liza* (1922) and *Blackberries of 1932* (1932). Her first air appearance may have been as a cast member of *Shuffle Along,* broadcast over WDBH in 1924. In the spring of 1925 she broadcast over WHN, New York, from the Everglade Club. Her signature song was "Double Crossin' Papa" written by Perry Bradford.

Sources: Woll pp. 24, 98, 147; *Chicago Defender*, October 11, 1924, p. 8, March 7, 1925, p. 7.

Scribner, Jimmy

Jimmy Scribner was a white radio actor who began doing blackface on radio in the early 1930s. He started on WLW with Bob Drake on a dialect series called *Sputter and Whine*. The program aired a reported 469 episodes before they moved on to the short-lived *Monkey Hollow* show. In October 1934, the duo started a new sketch called *The Jacksons*, perhaps the beginning of the famed *Johnson Family* series.

Drake apparently departed the show early because within a few years Scribner was credited with single-handedly bringing the African American town of Chickazola to life on *The Johnson Family*. This series, which ran from 1934 to 1950, was written by Scribner who also performed all the characters using dozens of voices and "distinct characterizations." Historian John Dunning described it as "a poor-man's *Amos 'n' Andy*," which was notably popular among Southern and black audiences. Scribner started his effort on WLW before moving to the Mutual network. Building on the popularity of *The Johnson Family*, he created a series in 1948 called *Sleepy Joe* in which he used black-dialect to narrate children's stories.

Sources: Dunning p. 375; MacDonald, *Don't Touch That Dial!*, p. 345; *Baltimore Afro-American*, October 27, 1934, p. 6.

Sharp, Louis

Louis Sharp was primarily a stage actor appearing in such works as *Black No More* (1936) written by **Carlton Moss** and featuring **Canada Lee**, *Conjur Man Dies* (1936), *Turpentine* (1936), *The Case of Philip Lawrence* (1937), *Haiti* (1938), *Mamba's Daughters*

(1939), *Pursuit of Happiness* (1939), *Cabin in the Sky* (1940) and *Fleetfoot* (1940). Sharp had two distinct radio runs, the first in 1931 when he had a program singing spirituals over WPCH for several months. Two decades later he was cast on *The Story of Ruby Valentine*, an African American soap opera produced by the **National Negro Network**. Sharp was engaged as Duke Valentine, Ruby's husband, described as a "shiftless and conniving husband who deserted her years ago and now returns to the scene when she is successful and well-to-do." Sharp died June 3, 1976, after a long illness.

Sources: Woll pp. 37, 40, 47, 72, 102, 173; *New York Amsterdam News*, July 22, 1931, p. 7, November 17, 1936, p. 10, December 31, 1938, p. 16, April 29, 1939, p. 20, September 9, 1939, p. 17, December 28, 1940, p. 15, August 21, 1954, p. 18, December 12, 1977, p. B4.

Shuffle Along

Shuffle Along, written by Flournoy Miller and Aubrey Lyles, with music and lyrics by Noble Sissle and Eubie Blake, is considered the first successful African American stage musical. Numbers from the show were aired regularly through the 1920s by various black performers. It may also have been the first stage show that was broadcast over radio in its entirety. *The Pittsburgh Post* made such a claim after a September 1, 1923, airing on KDKA. At the time *Shuffle Along* was touring on the road after a two-year Off-Broadway run and extended dates in Boston and Chicago. In a similar event, a stage production of the musical was aired simultaneous with its live presentation in Worcester, MA, over WDBH. This October 1924, event featured Charles Downz, Joseph Loomis, Walter Hilliard, and George Glasco among its cast members. Miller and Lyles were still milking the success of the play in 1931 when they signed a two year deal with CBS to broadcast two skits a week that borrowed liberally from *Shuffle Along*.

Sources: Barlow p. 23; Haskins pp. 63–68; Sampson, *Swingin' on the Ether Waves*, p. 7; Southern pp. 435–440; *Baltimore Afro-American*, August 15, 1931, p. 9; *Chicago Defender*, October 11, 1924, p. 8; *New York Amsterdam News*, July 22, 1931, p. 7.

Simms, Hilda

Hilda Simms was a Minnesota native who enjoyed moderate theater success during the 1940s and 1950s, primarily in New York. Before taking up acting she studied English and education at the University of Minnesota and then finished college at the Hampton Institute. In the mid–1940s she was credited with some unspecified announcing and dramatic readings on the air but roles with American Negro Theatre productions were her primary performance outlets. Simms continued to work full time as a secretary during the 1940s, unable to make a living on stage. Her career was highlighted by a starring role in *Anna Lucasta* which had a considerable run.

Simms first known radio work came on *New World A' Coming*, a black series based on Roi Ottley's book. She appeared on at least four episodes: November 12, 1944, December 10, 1944, January 14, 1945, and January 21, 1945. Simms is not known to have done further radio work until the 1950s when she had her own half-hour show on WOV from June 1954, until January 1957, which consisted of music and interviews. She had a shot before this spot at dramatic radio acting when she was considered for a role in *The Cathy Stewart Show*, to be produced by the **National Negro Network** in 1954. Due to money woes the network never produced the series.

Sources: Grams, *Radio Drama*, p. 358; Haskins p. 117; Patterson p. 164; *New York Amsterdam News*, June 10, 1944, p. 8, July 8, 1944, p. 9, December 30, 1944, p. 5B, January 23, 1954, p. 22, December 4, 1954, p. 28, January 5, 1957, p. 26; *Pittsburgh Courier*, June 5, 1954, p. 22.

Skanks, Earl

Earl Skanks, a tenor in **Eva Jessye's Dixie Jubilee Singers**, was credited in February 1927, with being the first African American to play the part of a white on radio. He portrayed a "poor white" who took part in Jessye's Lincoln Day broadcast over NBC which originated from station WJZ.

Source: *Pittsburgh Courier*, February 27, 1932, p. 3.

Skurlock, Arthur

After finishing high school at Chicago's Lane Tech High School in 1915, Arthur Skurlock got a job on a British ship as a wireless operator. Tragically, he died at the age of 19 in a Texas military hospital. It is possible this is the Arthur Sarenlock who was identified as a member of the **Woodlawn Radio Association**, a Chicago-area radio club in existence at the same time.

Source: *Chicago Defender*, February 9, 1918, p. 6.

Slow River

Radio stalwarts **Eva Taylor** and the **Southernaires**, along with **Clarence Jones** on piano, were featured in a weekly feature, *Slow River*, which aired over NBC for nearly eighteen months, from March 1932, to August 1933. The quarter-hour show was described as "southern ballads and plantation songs." At the beginning of 1933 descriptions suggest the show had expanded both in length and in cast, adding actors **Carlton Moss, Frank Wilson**, and **Georgia Burke** as well as the Levee Band, also of *Southland Sketches*. In February, Taylor even appeared on a separate program with an outfit called the Slow River Trio.

Sources: *Baltimore Afro-American*, April 8, 1933, p. 9, July 1, 1933, p. 8; *New York Amsterdam News*, March 23, 1932, p. 9, April 12, 1933, p. 17; *Pittsburgh Courier*, December 24, 1932, p. 8, January 7, 1933, p. 7, February 11, 1933, p. 7, August 19, 1933, p. 6.

Smith, Bessie

Bessie Smith, perhaps the most legendary female blues singer of all time, was born into a poverty-stricken family in Chattanooga,

TN. Her most prominent biographer, Chris Albertson, admits her birth date will likely never be known for sure, but her 1923 marriage application claims 1894 as the year and the 1900 Chattanooga census records indicate 1892. As a child Smith sang on Chattanooga street corners and earned her first professional spot in 1912 as part of a show financed by Moses Stokes. Also among the cast was no other than Gertrude "Ma" Rainey, the future "Mother of the Blues."

Smith kept busy through the war years and into the 1920s on the Theatre Owners Booking Association, an African American vaudeville circuit. She toured constantly, building up a following in the South and along the East coast. When Mamie Smith's "Crazy Blues," the first vocal blues record was released in 1920 it sold 100,000 copies in its first month, setting off a hunt by recording companies to find similar talent. Smith's first confirmed recordings date to 1923 with Columbia though rumors persist of earlier recordings. One of her first recordings for Columbia sold a whopping 780,000 copies in six months.

Riding the wave of popularity for the song "Down Hearted Blues," Smith made what is believed to be her first radio broadcast. On June 26, 1923, she appeared at 81 Theater in Atlanta, a venue she had played many times over the years. Unlike any prior known concert, however, this one was aired by the city's WSB. The program included Bessie Smith's Revue, her touring troupe. Highlighted performers were Charles Anderson, a yodeler, and Bob White and his Syncopated Orchestra. Others included the Melody Three (George Allen, Mary Jackson, and J. C. Davis), and pianists Eddie Hayward and Irving Thomas. Accounts suggest the Revue's audience was white.

A few months later on October 5 she made a second radio appearance, this time in Memphis, TN, over station WMC from the rooftop of the Commercial Appeal Building at 11:00 P.M. Smith herself sang two solos,

"Tain't Nobody's Business But My Own" and "Beale Street Momma," and then "Outside of That He's All Right with Me" accompanied by Irvin Johns on piano. So many phone calls and wires came in to the studio after she sang the last tune that she sang it again. Others on the bill included Baby Cox who opened the show singing "Way Down Yonder in New Orleans" and later joined her sister Dickey Cox to sing as the Cox Sisters. Henrietta Loveless and pianist James Alston were also credited with performances that night. The broadcast was arranged by A. Barrasso, manager of the Beale St. Palace Theater.

With 29 sides released, at least two successful radio appearances, and a new, improved contract with Columbia, 1923 proved to be a very good year for Smith. The next year, 1924, picked up where the previous year left off: more recording and more radio. In February 1924, she made a return engagement on WMC, again at 11:00 at night. Backing her up were Yancey and Booker's Orchestra and the Beale St. Palace Theater Orchestra. Songs that night included "Sam Jones Blues," "Chicago Bound," "St. Louis Gal," and "Mistreatin' Papa." Just a month later on March 28 she was on the airwaves again singing over WCAE, Pittsburgh. Her noted accompanists were Irvin Johns on piano and John Snow on violin. The half-hour broadcast was arranged by the Goldman & Wolf Music company. Evidence points to at least one other radio date that March in Cincinnati where she sang "Sinful Blues," written by Perry Bradford, over an unidentified station. Craig Havighurst, in his history of Nashville's WSM, notes a Smith broadcast over WDAD in 1925 which was "a rare instance of mainstream Nashville celebrating black blues."

Interestingly, though Albertson claims Smith "became a veteran broadcaster," no radio broadcasts beyond these few have been documented. While it's very likely that more of her countless concerts were broadcast over a career that would last fourteen years, they have yet to be identified. Further, despite all the press she got from the African American newspapers, rarely, if ever, was Smith referred to as a radio star, an appellation given to most any singer who had at least a nominal aural reputation. Despite the great number of black musicians and bands that received regular airtime in the late 1920s and 1930s, it's not clear why Smith never had her own show or even regular remote broadcasts from Chicago or Philadelphia, both cities in which she had a sizable fan base, or New York, where her fame was not insignificant. Thus, William Barlow's assessment that, in fact, Smith was "rarely heard on radio" seems to be more accurate than Albertson's claim.

Though Smith continued to record and tour up until her death, the peak of her popularity was during the mid-to-late 1920s. In 1929 she appeared in her only film, a 17-minute short called *St. Louis Blues*. She attempted to reinvent herself during the Depression and shed her reputation as an old-fashioned blues singer and Smith did have mild success adding pop tunes to her repertoire. Nevertheless, it is her early blues cuts that have cemented her place in music lore. Smith was killed in a car crash September 26, 1937.

Sources: Albertson pp. 24–69; Barlow pp. 22–23; Havighurst p. 27; Scott p. 139; Spaulding p. 23; *Baltimore Afro-American*, July 13, 1923, p. 5, March 14, 1925, p. 6, June 29, 1929, p. 8; *Chicago Defender*, July 7, 1923, p. 6, October 6, 1923, p. 8 February 23, 1924, p. 6; *Pittsburgh Courier*, March 22, 1924, p. 10.

Smith, Elwood

Elwood Smith was born in the early 1920s and studied at Xavier University before launching into a performing career. He was trained as a classical singer and found steady employment in the early 1940s with singing gigs in various night clubs. In 1942 Smith made his first known radio appearance when he competed on *Major Bowes' Amateur Hour* on which he won first prize. Smith added

dramatic acting to his resume when he was cast in the American Negro Theater's *Home Is the Hunter* in 1945, a play that was panned by critics despite approval of his performances. The following year, 1946, he appeared in another dramatic piece called *Peacemaker*, also sponsored by the Negro Theater. He returned to radio that year when WNEW broadcast a series of operas cast with black singers.

The next few years Smith stayed busy with night club engagements and stage roles in *St. Louis Woman*, *City of Kings*, and *Four Saints in Three Acts*. Smith was cast in an all-black film, *Boy! What a Girl!*, produced by Herald Pictures in 1949. In 1948 Smith performed on *The Ford Theater* on February 1, 1948, in an all-black episode that dramatized *The Green Pastures* stage play. Soon after in the late 1940s or early 1950s he appeared on another talent show, *Arthur Godfrey's Talent Scouts*. From 1954 to 1955 Smith was featured in his only known dramatic radio role as attorney Walter Williams on the African American soap opera *The Story of Ruby Valentine*. Television beckoned in 1958 when Smith appeared on an episode of *Frontiers of Faith* called "Light in the Southern Sky." His career beyond this point is vague and did not receive much media attention.

Sources: LOC; Woll pp. 78–79, 142; *Baltimore Afro-American*, April 12, 1952, p. 6, February 15, 1958, p.7; *Chicago Defender*, January 30, 1954, p. 19; *New York Amsterdam News*, December 29, 1945, p. 21, July 13, 1946, p. 19, July 27, 1946, p. 19, November 9, 1946, p. 26, January 25, 1947, p. 21, April 5, 1947, p. 19, October 4, 1947, p. 25, February 26, 1949, p. 24; *Pittsburgh Courier*, October 24, 1953, p. 19, April 16, 1955, p. 18.

Smith, Homer

Homer Smith, reportedly a relative of bluesman **W. C. Handy**, was a native of Florence, AL, before attending college at Ohio's Wilberforce University. While a student, Smith performed with the Wilberforce Quartet and met **Lowell Peters**, a singer with the Knoxville College Quartet. The two would later sing together as half of the famous radio quartet the **Southernaires**. Smith had relocated to New York by 1929 where he was singing and known as the "melody man of the radio." He appeared in the stage's musical comedy *Sugar and Spice* with Dusty Fletcher and Apus Brooks before forming the Southernaires in December 1929. The Southernaires were staples on NBC's Red and Blue networks through the 1930s appearing on multiple days and at various times. Their signature slot was Sunday mornings with a program called *The Weatherbeaten Whitewashed Church* which was broadcast into the late 1940s.

Smith's work was focused on the Southernaires until the late 1930s when he began striking out with independent projects. In 1937 and 1938 he led the Epsilon Glee Club in various concerts, though there's no record of radio appearances. Smith was cast in at least one dramatic role in the summer of 1938 on NBC's presentation of *In Abraham's Bosom*. He played Puny Avery alongside such dramatic stars as **Frank Wilson** and **Juano Hernandez**. Other members of the Southernaires had dramatic roles, too. In 1942 Smith joined the Coast Guard to do his part for the war effort. He was subsequently replaced in the Southernaires by **Ray Yeates**. Smith would not sing with the quartet again.

In the service Smith organized and directed a choral society at the Coast Guard's Manhattan Beach Training Station. His outfit was officially renamed the Quartet of the United States Coast Guard by hierarchy brass and consisted of Thomas Lockard, James Lewis, and Martin Boughan. They were perhaps the most prominent mixed-race group in the country and the Coast Guard scheduled them to perform at bond rallies, recruiting drives, and on CBS' *The Coast Guard on Parade*. The Coast Guard Quartet also appeared on *We Believe* (August 9, 1942, October 11, 1942), a U.S. Coast Guard memorial broadcast (June 3, 1943), NBC's

United Negro College Fund drive (May 26, 1944), and on WOR (December 24, 1944).

After the war ended the quartet remained intact and renamed themselves The Mariners. The foursome was highly regarded in entertainment circles and were invited on to Eddie Cantor's popular show. They also broadcast on the shows of Fred Allen, Paul Whiteman, Henry Morgan, and Jack Benny. Their most prominent assignment was on the daily morning show *Arthur Godfrey Time*. Beginning in 1946 the Mariners had a weekly show called *Songs for a Sunday Morning*. At some point during the quartet's run on Godfrey's show Smith left to pursue other opportunities. Upon departing the Mariners, Smith formed the Harmonaires at the end of 1947. In 1948 he is recorded as leading the Homer Smith Melodaires, possibly the same line-up as the Harmonaires. The original Melodaires were Glenn Bryant, Jasper Jackson, Robert Alexander, and Maurice Hill, with Julian Parrish on accompaniment. By 1951 the roster included Charles Riley, Wansa King, Leon Wisdom, and Smith himself with Parrish still accompanying. The Melodaires performed well into 1952 though not on radio. It's possible that Smith found many doors to radio shut by the late 1940s. One report indicated that he fell out with NBC in the mid–1940s when he sued the network for sending out Southernaires publicity photographs which included Smith though he'd already left the quartet. Evidence suggests that Smith retired from music in the early 1950s then passed away in 1974.

Sources: LOC; Peterson; Singer p. 98; *Baltimore Afro-American*, May 27, 1944, p. 17, February 9, 1946, p. 11, October 19, 1946, p. 3, February 8, 1947, p. 3, December 20, 1947, p. 6; *Jet*, May 30, 1974, p. 18; *New York Amsterdam News*, November 27, 1929, p. 8, 9, July 29, 1931, p. 7, December 14, 1932, p. 16, January 22, 1938, p. 13, June 11, 1938, p. 6, July 2, 1938, p. 7, October 17, 1942, p. 8, February 27, 1943, p. 14, June 12, 1943, p. 8, May 13, 1944, p. 4B, May 27, 1944, p. 4, December 16, 1944, p. 16, May 24, 1945, p. 1B, November 17, 1945, p. 27, February 16, 1946, p. 23, June 12, 1948, p. 18, October 2, 1948, p. 6, March 24, 1951, p. 14;

Pittsburgh Courier, January 16, 1943, p. 20, June 5, 1943, p. 21.

Smith, Trixie

Trixie Smith was a blues artist who appeared over WDT, NY, in 1923 while appearing at Connie's Inn. Her signature tune was "Trifling Blues."

Source: Peterson p. 126; Southern p. 371; *Pittsburgh Courier,* August 18, 1923, p. 16.

Smith, Wilford

Wilford Smith belongs to the group of early black amateur radio operators who came of age after World War I, a time during which many African Americans learned radio skills for the war. Smith had his license by 1921 at the age of 20. He graduated from the YMCA (86th & Lexington, Harlem) Wireless School and subsequently built a radio phone which transmitted voice signals 250 miles. His goal was to open his own radio school; whether this ever happened is unknown.

Source: *Chicago Defender,* September 17, 1921, p. 9.

Smith, Wonderful

Wonderful Smith (his given name) jumped quickly to radio after an appearance in **Duke Ellington's** stage revue *Jump for Joy.* He was noticed by Red Skelton and signed to a two-year deal on *The Raleigh Cigarette Program* from October 7, 1941, to June 3, 1943. During his run Smith appeared as a bank robber, game hunter, and gasoline attendant and performed a one-sided telephone monolog with President Roosevelt that was his trademark gag. With six months left on his contract Smith was drafted into the Army where he served for three years, much of that overseas. Smith was responsible for various entertainment projects while assigned to a trucking battalion on the Burma Road. He also had his own radio show aired from Calcutta for three months.

Smith returned to *The Red Skelton Show* on December 18, 1945, where he appeared intermittently for two years before being dropped with no explanation on June 3, 1947. Years later Smith confessed "I have a feeling I wasn't as Negroid as they expected ... I had difficulty sounding as Negroid as they expected, or as Negroid as the other characters sounded." Other documented radio appearances include *Jubilee #2* (recorded October 27, 1942), *Forecast* (August 25, 1941), and some episodes of *The Amos 'n' Andy Show.* Smith died in 2008.

Sources: LOC; Edmerson pp. 36–40; Dunning p. 568; Lotz and Neuert; McLeod p. 184; *New York Amsterdam News,* July 19, 1941, p. 21, June 6, 1942, p. 17, October 25 1947, p. 21; *Pittsburgh Courier,* January 12, 1946, p. 22; www.radiogoldindex.com.

Smothers, Joe

Joe Smothers had a weekly Sunday night gig during the early 1930s over WCBM, Baltimore, where he always sang his trademark "Underneath the Harlem Moon." He was accompanied by Marian Gibson, partner of four years. The duo proved popular enough to provide weekly songs on the *Negro Business Hour* late in 1932. After a short radio career Smothers worked the next several years on night club stages.

Sources: *Baltimore Afro-American,* September 10, 1932, p. 10, November 12, 1932, p. 10, December 3, 1932, p. 8, May 30, 1936, p. 11.

Southern Singers (later the Four Southern Singers)

The Southern Singers were a quartet which got its break on Cincinnati's WLW in 1931. By 1932 they were also appearing on WSAI, another station out of Cincinnati. They made their debut on NBC March 1, 1933, and a few months later changed their name to the Four Southern Singers to clear up listener confusion over the number of singers in the group. The Singers stood out from the countless other quartets because they included one female in their ranks, Annie Laurie Ward, wife of fellow band mate James Ward (also called Hornsby), tenor. James' brothers Robert, baritone, and Owen, second tenor, filled out the foursome. Moe Gale served as their manager. By the time they left Cincinnati for New York they were performing 19 shows a week on the air.

Their broadcast schedule slowed down on the East Coast but the Southern Singers still had three programs over WJZ, Mondays from 11 to 11:15 P.M., Wednesday's from 7:15 to 7:30, and Thursdays from 11 to 11:15. Not too much later they had added a Tuesday (8:45 P.M., WJZ) and Saturday (6:45 P.M., WEAF) broadcast to their busy schedule. However, by the end of the year they had been cut back to twice-weekly broadcasts. Beyond typical quartet music their act included comedy skits written by member James Ward which were generally set on a plantation. Their choice of instruments included a washboard and jug, more reminiscent of a hillbilly act than an urban black group. A skillet attached to the washboard (played by Annie Ward) served as a cymbal. By August 1934, the Southern Singers had left New York City for WGY in Schenectady.

Sources: *Baltimore Afro-American*, July 16, 1932, p. 16, March 18, 1933, p. 8, May 27, 1933, p. 10, August 12, 1933, p. 18, October 14, 1933, p. 19, August 18, 1934, p. 8; *New York Amsterdam News*, April 12, 1933, p. 17, April 26, 1933, p. 10.

The Southernaires

The Southernaires were one of many African American quartets that hit the airwaves in the late 1920s and early 1930s. The group became a staple on Sunday morning radio and was on the air into the early 1950s. The original line-up consisted of **William Edmondson**, bass, **Homer Smith**, tenor, **Jay Stone Toney**, baritone, and **Lowell Peters**, tenor. The four hooked up in late 1929 in New York City and officially formed the Southernaires in December 1929.

After a few live church performances the quartet hit the radio on February 1, 1930. From 6:00 to 7:00 they sang on *Goodwin's*

Goodtimers, a local program on WMCA sponsored by a clothing store. A month later in March they started a twenty-week engagement on WRNY during which they came to the attention of NBC. Two months after debuting on WRNY they signed with NBC and were soon heard on *RKO Theatre of the Air* on a segment entitled "Harlem on the Air." Other stars on this WEAF broadcast included Adelaide Hall, Bill "Bojangles" Robinson, and **Cab Calloway** and his Missourians. NBC also soon booked them on *Major Bowe's Capitol Family*, a Sunday night feature (7:30 to 8:30) that went out over an international hook-up. During this same time-frame the quartet also appeared on WGBS' *Visits with Uncle Ben in His Cabin*, a Saturday night (10:30) series of sketches.

Members of the Southernaires made small forays on radio beyond their musical gigs and into the broader world of radio drama. William Edmondson joined *The New Molle Show* as master of ceremonies in November 1933, and the quartet sang as the Molle Merry Minstrels from September 25, 1933, to July 11, 1935. The program was aired over WEAF every Monday, Wednesday, and Thursday at 7 P.M. In addition to MC duties, Edmondson also presented a segment called "The Comic Side of the News."

The first documented dramatic work by quartet members was an episode of NBC's *Magic Key*, relayed to over 100 stations. The particular episode was "David the Giant Killer," aired in late June 1938, and was based on the biblical story of David and Goliath. The broadcast featured Homer Smith as David and William Edmondson as Jonathan. Just a few days later Smith and Edmondson, along with Jay Toney, appeared in a June 23, 1938, broadcast called *In Abraham's Bosom* broadcast over the Blue network. The program was directed by James Church and featured music by the Southernaires and the **Juanita Hall** choir. The script was based on a Pulitzer Prize–winning play from the mid–1920s.

In Abraham's Bosom is the story of Abe McCranie, an African American man bent on providing educations to black boys in the oppressive environment of the Reconstruction-era South. The radio play was cast entirely by members of the Negro Actors' Guild of America, three of whom were also members of the Southernaires. Homer Smith was cast as Puny Avery, William Edmonson as Bud Gaskins, and J. Stone Toney as Douglass McCranie. Their parts were minor and critics called their performances "creditable." Such an underwhelming response perhaps explains why they were not featured in more dramatic productions.

On May 25, 1930, the Southernaires debuted on WEAF's *Southland Sketches*, a program of musical and dramatic fare. Originally contracted to air for five weeks, the quartet proved popular enough to earn a three year stint on the show, until early 1933. In August 1930, the foursome received yet more air time with their own half hour on WOR, a Monday evening timeslot (10:30). Within a year of forming, the Southernaires were broadcasting veterans appearing on at least five New York stations and seven series. While the quartet struggled to find sponsors for much of their existence, for a short time in late 1933 they had a thrice-weekly (Monday, Wednesday, Friday) program which was sponsored by Emmole Shaving Crème.

As with many radio acts of the time, live performances were still an important part of the job. In addition to gigs at prominent churches, including the Calvary Baptist Church and the Riverside Church, they played for society functions at the Hotel Astor, the Waldorf Hotel, and the Commodore Hotel. They even played for NBC president Merlin Hall Aylesworth at the Lotus Club in the fall of 1930 in celebration of the premier of Amos 'n' Andy's *Check and Double Check* motion picture. The Southernaires were so prominent that at least one account relates that the quartet was the only

African American singing group on NBC's payroll.

While the talent and popularity of the Southernaires is verified by their multiple aural engagements, the quartet also had a strong social conscience that surfaced once they received their own Sunday morning program. As was common with several African American radio series of the time, the Southernaires had various individuals give brief talks on topics of interest to the African American listening audience. Topics ranged from science and industry to entertainment to the armed forces.

Military themes were regular topics of presentations. These included a talk by Capt. DeLincoln Reid, reported as the first African American to serve in France during World War I, who spoke on black contributions to the war effort. Similarly, Col. Charles W. Filmore told the stories of black servicemen who served in the Spanish-American War and World War I. Filmore himself was a World War I veteran who had helped win the Croix de Guerre after helping to organize the New York National Guard's black regiment. On a separate program the role of black soldiers from Crispus Attucks' part in the 1770 Boston Massacre to the then-recent World War was chronicled.

Other educational topics included black efforts in entertainment, including a piece by **William Christopher Handy**, "daddy of the blues," (and uncle to Southernaire Homer Smith) on the origins of black music. Another episode honored James Bland, most famous for writing "Carry Me Back to Ol' Virginny."

The Southernaires also brought in notable African American figures to enlighten listeners about their own experiences or the experiences of other black men and women. One such guest was Moses Allen, a 107-year-old former slave who spoke on hearing the Emancipation Proclamation being read and who still possessed his own emancipation papers granted to him in Texas. Allen proved so popular that he was invited back to the show two months later. Another time Albon W. Holsey, former secretary to Dr. Booker T. Washington and then-head of the National Negro Business League, spoke on Washington's legacy. On another occasion Bishop J. A. Gregg, former president of Smith's alma mater, Wilberforce University, spoke to the nation. Channing Tobias, representative of the International YMCA, spoke one week. The original editor and publisher of the influential black newspaper *The Chicago Defender* was honored on the March 22, 1940, program a month after his death.

The quartet's Sunday morning program would occasionally focus on a non–African American individual who made significant contributions to black causes. One such individual was Julius Rosenwald, part-owner of Sears Roebuck and contributor to African American education efforts in the South, who received a tribute after his death in 1932.

These discussions went on for several years before trouble erupted in 1938. That year Major Arthur Springarn, president of the NAACP, refused to abide by the heavy editing his proposed talk received from the customary editing of NBC staffers. Ignoring the attempts to water down his comments on racial segregation, Springarn went on to give a "blistering attack" on the country's racial situation using such sensitive words as "lynching," "race riot," discrimination," and "segregation." Such impertinence resulted in the immediate cancellation of the program's guest-speaker segment for a while. They confronted Jim Crow off the air as well. As early as 1931 they refused to wear blackface during live performances and a year later they refused to use the freight elevator to reach an audition as requested by the New York hotel management. In 1942 the quartet initiated a lawsuit against a Rochester hotel that denied them service in the dining room despite their status as paying patrons. They were awarded $800. During the war the Southernaires added patriotic songs by black lyricist Andy Razaf to their songlist.

One interesting exception to their anti–Jim Crow broadcast work was the Southernaire's participation in *The Star Spangled Theater*'s presentation of *Uncle Tom's Cabin* on August 10, 1941 over the Blue network. Al Jolson starred as Uncle Tom and the quartet sang with the famous entertainer.

Despite their appearances across the radio dial during the quartet's first couple years, Sunday mornings became the Southernaires' staple broadcast. First guest-appearing on *Southland Sketches*, the program eventually became theirs and was renamed after them. The broadcast was also known to listeners as the *Little Weatherbeaten Whitewashed Church*. Later in their career as their radio work slowed, the Southernaires lent their talents to at least one episode of *Freedom's People* on which they provided music on the January 18, 1942 episode entitled "The Negro Worker." In 1950, exactly two decades after their radio debut, WJZ dropped the program with no explanation.

The membership of the Southernaires was remarkably consistent over this time. While the original four united in 1929, **Clarence Jones** joined in 1932 as arranger and accompanist. This lineup remained in tact until 1940 when Jones fell ill and was replaced by **Spencer Odom**. What was intended as a temporary assignment turned into a full-time job with the quartet when Jones' illness lingered on. Odom stayed with the Southernaires until 1950 when they disbanded.

The first founding member to leave was Homer Smith, who was drafted into the Coast Guard in 1942. **Ray Yates**, who had connections with fellow member William Edmondson from the late 1920s, replaced Smith. Edmondson, Toney, Peters and new band mates Yates and Odom soldiered on, keeping busy with their Sunday morning gig and live performances. Tragedy struck in 1948 when Jay Stone Toney died of a heart attack while the Southernaires were playing in Iowa. He was soon replaced by **William Franklin**, another Southerner. The revised lineup lasted two years before being dropped by WJZ in 1950.

The circumstances that led to the cancellation remain unclear, though the fact that the quartet never attracted a sponsor over their twenty year radio run surely played a part. The Southernaires reappeared briefly in 1951, replacing their traditional spiritual repertoire with modern pop tunes. Of the original members only William Edmondson was involved in this incarnation.

Sources: LOC; Allen pp. 26–29; Cox, *Say Goodnight, Gracie*, p. 63; Sampson, *Swingin' on the Ether Waves*, pp. 53, 66, 127; Sies p. 238; *Chicago Defender*, August 30, 1930 p. 5, December 19, 1931, p. 13, January 9, 1932, p. 13, February 6, 1932, p. 1, March 26, 1932 p. 1, June 18, 1932 p. 5, November 19, 1932 p. 5, July 8, 1933, p. 5, November 17, 1933, p. 5, February 16, 1938, p. 15, June 25, 1938, p. 18, July 2, 1938, p. 19; *New York Times*, August 10, 1941, p. X10; *Pittsburgh Courier*, November 15, 1930, p. 8, December 20, 1930, p. 6, June 27, 1931, p. 1, January 17, 1942, p. 3.

Southland Singers

The Southland Singers program was an NBC Sunday afternoon series in early 1930 with musical and dramatic productions authored by Ford Bond. The broadcasts featured stories set in the Old South with plenty of traditional Southern tunes. Music was provided by an unidentified black sextet and a banjo player. Bond, who first appeared in radio in 1922, played an old colonel who related the stories to the listening audience. At the same time Bond was announcing *Cities Service Band of America* and *The Collier Hour*. He retired in 1953 after three decades on the air.

Sources: Cox, *Radio Speakers*, pp. 36–37; *Baltimore Afro-American*, October 11, 1930, p. 9; *New York Amsterdam News*, May 21, 1930, p. 10.

Standard Theatre's Kiddies' Radio Revue

This Saturday morning musical revue sponsored by *The Philadelphia Tribune* newspaper over WDAS featured children and even toddlers displaying amazing musical prowess. The second episode, broadcast May 21, 1932, gives an example of the show's dazzling talent. Francis Steward, a one-year-old, was the returning winner from the premier broadcast where he "romped" through a melody in F. To defend his crown he banged out the "Bugle Call Rag" with the "ease ... of a jazz master." His main competition was Gertrude Banks who gave a song-and-dance routine with the tune "At the End of the Road."

Other stars in the making included six-year-old Harry Brown who performed a song-and-dance routine, three-year-old Jeanette Brown who sang "River, Stay Away From My Door" (after being placed on a chair to reach the microphone), and Baby Edwards who already had several radio credits to her name. About twenty other youngsters aired their talent for area listeners.

Sources: *Philadelphia Tribune*, May 12, 1932, p. 1, June 16, 1932, p. 7, June 30, 1932, p. 7, July 7, 1932, p. 7, July 21, 1932, p. 7, August 4, 1932, p. 11.

Star Quest

In an effort to promote local black talent, *The Chicago Defender* and station WBBM teamed up to sponsor *Star Quest*, a contest for amateur performers. The show seems to have run just a few weeks from March to May of 1947 on Tuesdays and Thursdays. Finalists were chosen from each broadcast who then competed for the grand prize, a thirteen-week contract on WBBM which paid $100 a week. Over 450 men and women auditioned for *Star Quest* and some of the finalists included Harriet Clemons, Delores Baker, James Hampton, Gladys Beaman and Ira Burton. The winner is unknown. The program is referred to as *Star-Questers* on at least one occasion.

Sources: *Chicago Defender*, February 22, 1947, p. 14, March 3, 1947, p. 20, May 10, 1947, p. 19.

Steel, Edward

Edward Steel, 19-year-old student at the Baltimore School for the Deaf and Blind, made multiple broadcasts over WEAR in February and March of 1924.

Source: *Baltimore Afro-American*, May 30, 1924, p. 8.

Stewart, Horace (Nick)

Horace Stewart, who commonly went by the name Nicodemus and is also referred to as Nick Stewart, had a prolific stage, television and film career. Stewart had a minor radio career, the highlight being guest appearances for several weeks early in 1938 on Eddie Cantor's *Texaco Town* on CBS. Stewart was credited with helping Hattie Noels land a role on the Cantor program at the same time. He was invited to do benefit performances, at least two of which were broadcast. Stewart was part of an all-star benefit program October 27, 1940, which was broadcast on WMCA and WINS. The next year he participated in a June 8, 1941, WMCA show sponsored by the Greater New York Fund with **Paul Robeson, Artie Bell McGinty,** and **Amanda Randolph**. In a turn from his usual comedic roles, the dramatic script portrayed harsh conditions faced by many New York–area African Americans. Stewart also starred in episodes of the black *Jubilee* series aired to overseas soldiers during the war.

Stewart was cast in at least two recurring roles. The first was that of Nicodemus on *The Fabulous Dr. Tweedy* from October 1946, to March 1947. Two years later he played an elevator boy on *The Alan Young Show* from February to July 1949. Stewart also played Eddie twice on *Duffy's Tavern* (May 18 and June 1, 1950), a role made famous by **Eddie Green**. Though not associated with the *Amos 'n' Andy* radio show, Stewart was cast as Lighting for the television version of the program which became, perhaps, his most famous role.

Sources: LOC; Berry and Berry p. 314–315; *New York Amsterdam News*, February 19, 1938, p. 17, June 7, 1941, p. 20, June 14, 1941, p. 21; *Pittsburgh Courier*, March 12, 1938, p. 20, May 28, 1938, p. 20.

The Story of Ruby Valentine

In January 1954, the **National Negro Network** finally hit the air with forty participating stations. The Network's first program was *The Story of Ruby Valentine*, a daily quarter-hour soap opera featuring an all African American cast. Noted old time radio historian John Dunning claims that this serial evolved from earlier white soap operas *As the Twig Is Bent* and *We Love and Learn* but contemporary accounts of Ruby Valentine made no mention of these other serials. Frequently cited as the first black soap opera, it was beaten in that honor by seven years when **Richard Durham's** *Here Comes Tomorrow* claimed that title in 1947. *Valentine* can, however, lay claim to being one of only two black serials and also to being one of the last soaps to go on the air.

Originally scheduled to hit the airwaves December 1, 1953, the debut of *The Story of Ruby Valentine* was pushed back to January 25, 1954. Pet Milk and Philip Morris undertook sponsorship. The series starred stage actress **Juanita Hall** as heroine Ruby Valentine, "once a famous singer and entertainer ... [and now] wealthy owner of a chain of New York beauty parlors." In the first story arc a young, innocent girl named Clara Johnson (played by Sara Lou Harris) moves from an unidentified small town to New York. There she seeks her proverbial fortune with only a letter to attorney Walter Williams (played by **Elwood Smith**) to get her started. When she meets Ruby typical soap opera adventures ensue.

In addition to Hill, Harris, and Smith, the cast included **Viola Dean** as Dinah Davis, **Wezlynn Tildon** as Louise Evans, Earle

Hyman as Henry Booker, **Lulu King** as Mrs. Booker, and Chauncey Reynolds in an unidentified role. **Frank Wilson**, veteran actor, joined the cast in May 1954, as Dr. Cade. His participation is notable because he acted in **Carlton Moss'** dramatic programming in the early 1930s making him the only actor who can boast of playing on the first dramatic African American programs (*Careless Love*, 1930–1932) and what may have been the last (*Ruby Valentine*). In June 1954, Terry Carter took the role of George Robinson, an amnesia victim. Radio veteran **Emory Richardson** (*Valiant Lady*, *Crime Fighters*, and *Freedom's People*) joined in July as the Reverend Rockwell and in September **Ruby Dee** came aboard as Rockwell's "vivacious" daughter. Ruby's husband Duke Valentine (played by Louis Sharp) was written into the story in August of 1954. He was described as a "shiftless and conniving husband who deserted [Ruby] years ago and now returns to the scene when she is successful and well-to-do." Others with supporting roles were Helen Marsh, Marie Young, Abbie Shuford, Ed Harding, and **Maurice Ellis**. **Georgia Burke** was originally announced as accepting a role in *Ruby Valentine* but there is no evidence that she ever broadcast on the series.

Former **Southernaires** singer **William (Bill) Edmondson** was the original announcer, possibly replaced by Pat Connell. Chet Gierlach directed the show, Luther Henderson was the music director, and Leonard Evans and Gwen Durham received writing credit. Evans also served as the show's producer. One source claimed Sidney Poitier appeared on the serial but that is not confirmed by any other accounts of the program. *The Story of Ruby Valentine*, which opened with the Juanita Hall–penned theme "Ruby's Blues," originated over WOV, New York, but was recorded and sent to National Negro Network stations who then replayed the daily installments at a time of their choosing. Despite enthusiasm for the project, Ruby and

her cast of characters left the air in late April or early May of 1955 after a fifteen-month run.

Sources: Cox, *Radio Soap Operas*, pp. 302, 305; Dunning p. 714; *Baltimore Afro-American*, January 23, 1954, p. 17, April 10, 1954, p. 6, September 26, 1987, p. 13; *Chicago Defender*, January 30, 1954, p. 19, February 6, 1954, p. 3, May 29, 1954, p. 18, June 5, 1954, p. 19, September 18, 1954, p. 6, November 20, 1954, p. 7, May 7, 1955, p. 6; *Cleveland Call and Post*, January 30, 1954, p. 2D; *New York Amsterdam News*, September 12, 1953, p. 23, August 21, 1954, p. 20, December 15, 1962, p. 19, May 8, 1965, p. 16; *Pittsburgh Courier*, October 24, 1953, p. 19, February 6, 1954, p. 20, February 20, 1954, p. 17, April 24, 1954, p. 18, July 24, 1954, p. 18.

Strongs, Alice

Four-year-old Alice Strongs made the news in 1931 when she earned a spot on Detroit's WMBC regularly singing and playing piano and violin.

Source: *Baltimore Afro-American*, May 16, 1931, pp. 1, 13.

Sumner High School

Sumner High School, Kansas City, KS, was recognized as the only school in the country training African Americans in wireless technology in 1913.

Source: *Baltimore Afro-American*, March 29, 1913, p. 7.

Tales of Harlem

Director **Joe Bostic** returned to the airwaves with yet another aural production, *Tales of Harlem*, on December 18, 1937. The series aired Saturday evenings over WMCA. The format resembled that of a variety show with musical performances, interviews with African Americans in the news, a review of news items of interest to black listeners, and sports and entertainment commentary. From the beginning Bostic was insistent that *Tales from Harlem* would "refrain from burlesque of the Negro and Harlem." Jack Caldwell served as business manager and announcer.

The initial episode featured the Five Budds, a novelty harmony group which provided music, an interview with Heshla Tamanyn, concert singer, and interludes sung by baritone Dan Jones, "The Lonesome Troubador." Following weeks featured Matt Henson, assistant to Commander Peary on his North Pole voyage, and the Palmer Brothers, a harmony trio who would make many repeat performances. In January 1938, Laura Bowman, dramatic actress, and **Harlan Lattimore**, singer with the Don Redman orchestra, appeared on the show. Lattimore proved so popular that he was booked on several subsequent episodes. Monette Moore and Buddy Bowser began making regular appearances in March 1938.

Other guests during 1938 included sports writer Jimmy Powers of *The New York Daily News* who appealed for black inclusion in the major leagues, featherweight boxer Henry Armstrong, actor **Rex Ingram, Louis Beavers**, and **Duke Ellington**. Joe Gordon and his orchestra were added as a permanent feature that summer as was Nina Mae McKinney. Louise Taylor, a popular singer, made multiple appearances on *Tales of Harlem* and prominent actor **Frank Wilson** and singer Rose Poindexter were guests. On October 28, 1938, after 45 weeks on WMCA, *Tales of Harlem* switched stations to WNEW and changed its broadcast day from Saturday to Friday night where it ran until sometime in 1939. Guests after the station change included Rodney Sturges, Louise Taylor, and the team of Swan and Lee.

Sources: Jaker, et al. p. 120; *New York Amsterdam News*, December 11, 1937, p. 1, December 25, 1937, p. 19, January 8, 1938, p. 16, January 29, 1938, p. 18, February 5, 1938, p. 16, March 26, 1938, p. 17, April 2, 1938, p. 17, 19, April 16, 1938, p. 21, May 7, 1938, p. 17, May 28, 1938, p. 21, June 18, 1938, p. 21, June 25, 1938, p. 9, July 9, 1938, p. 7, October 22, 1938, p. 21.

Taylor, Eva

Born Irene Gibbons Williams, Eva Taylor could rightly be considered one of—if not the—premier African American radio performer of the late 1920s and early 1930s. She claimed to have been discovered at the age of two by a promoter named Josephine Gassman. Though Taylor did not immediately get into show business, she ended up touring with Gassman for 18 years before striking out on her own. In the years before the first World War Taylor played on stages across Europe then spent two years in Australia before returning to the United States in 1916.

In 1922 Taylor was cast in Miller and Lyles' black musical *Shuffle Along* in New York. After *Shuffle Along*, Taylor moved on to *Queen of Hearts* where she met Vaughn de Leath, the manager of a small unidentified New York station who asked her to perform. Years later, accounts indicated that 1922 was also the first year in which she broadcast on radio, and it seems likely these broadcasts for de Leath represent her radio initiation. Taylor also began cutting records in 1922, the beginning of a recording career which would take her to Okeh, Black Swan, and Victor. Documentation indicates that her first regular radio broadcasts were with husband **Clarence Williams**, a prominent New York music publisher, and his trio on station WHN in 1924.

The next year Taylor was singing with William's new outfit the Blue Five on WGBS in March 1925. The Palisades Amusement Park in New Jersey was the origination of a June 16, 1927, two-hour musicale over WPAP, then in February 1928, Taylor was one of several stars to appear on the *Florence Mills Memorial Hour*. Documented radio appearances became more common in 1929 and include two broadcasts on *Major Bowes' Capitol Family* on WEAF (June 9, 1929, and June 23, 1929), NBC's *Morning Glories*, a morning musical program with The Wanderers (June 25, 1929), a Saturday night series of Broadway hits on WJZ with the Knickerbockers Orchestra, and a Christmas morning broadcast to London which was also heard on a nationwide hook-up. This holiday special was aired to Germany and

Holland the next day. During that winter season she also participated in a special short wave broadcast via a GE transmitter to Rear Admiral Richard Byrd's Antarctic expedition. Though Taylor frequently appeared with husband Williams and one of his bands, she was not dependent upon his talents and regularly performed solo and with other groups.

After eight years of musical work on the air, 1930 witnessed her debut on comedic and dramatic programs. The first was the *Alpha and Omega Opera Company Deluxe, Inc.*, a weekly opera spoof on WEAF in the spring of 1930. In November she was a member of the players on **Carlton Moss'** weekly *Careless Love*, a dramatic anthology series over NBC, the first cast with African Americans. Still, Taylor continued with her radio singing during this period with the Blue Streaks Dance Orchestra (a white band), a gig that aired three times a week. The *Opera Company Deluxe* series lasted just a few weeks but *Careless Love* aired until 1932 and her run with the Blue Streaks lasted until 1931 at which point they were on four times a week.

Upon separating from the Blue Streaks Dance Orchestra she immediately joined with Hugo Mariana's Marionettes, another orchestra broadcasting on WEAF. This was a daily spot that lasted nearly a year, late into 1932. The year proved to be another banner year for Taylor's radio career. After the popularity of her debut on the *Valspar Hour* (or *Club Valspar*) hosted by Andy Sannelia on WEAF, she returned on January 16, 1932, and several times afterward. In the spring of 1932 *Slow River*, an African American spirituals program, debuted and Taylor was a regular along with the **Southernaires** during much of its run. A third program, a weekly broadcast of songs, premiered in April 1932, and later in the year she was a regular on WFBR's weekly *Harlem Fantasy*. In late 1932 she teamed with Clarence Todd, Clarence Williams, and Lillian Armstrong to broad-

cast over NBC, possibly on one of the aforementioned series.

Taylor's radio work continued at a healthy clip in 1933. On February 11 she participated in a WRNY broadcast sponsored by the Abyssnia Relief Bureau which appealed for contributions for Harlem's unemployed. Included on the show were the Southernaires, Clarence Williams, and **W. C. Handy**. That spring she performed with the Lowland Singers (Clarence Williams, Lil Armstrong, Buster Bailey, Clarence Todd) over WOR three times a week then on Carlton Moss' *Folks from Dixie* during the summer of 1933. Later in the year she served as vocalist on Paul Whiteman's Kraft program (July 30, 1933), performed on *Hands Across the Border* (September 21, 1933), a special aired on a Canadian network and NBC, and as a guest on a sketch called "Harlem" on WJZ written by Katherine Seymour and featuring the Southernaires and **Cab Calloway** (December 9, 1933). During the early years of the 1930s Taylor performed frequently on WOR with Clarence Williams' Washboard Orchestra and Lillian Armstrong. While under contract with NBC she is reputed to have been on air ten to twelve times a week at some points.

The next three years, from 1934 to 1936, represent the apex of Taylor's radio career and were dominated by her trademark musical performances. She was part of a special broadcast to Russia (July 8, 1934) with the Southernaires and the **Eva Jessye** Choir over WJZ. Soon after she was on another coast to coast broadcast with the Southernaires and Chick Webb's orchestra (September 27, 1934) over NBC's Red network. By December Taylor was appearing on WEAF three times a week and also on WJZ once a week under sponsorship of Rye Crisp. Taylor was a featured singer on WJZ's *Harlem Musicale* in March 1935, along side the Southernaires and **Willie Bryant**. She was also credited with a weekly (Tuesdays) show on WEAF through the year called *Morning Glories* on

NBC, possibly the same series on which she appeared years before. Her songs were backed by a white band. On August 19 Taylor debuted a daily series on WEAF and soon after was hosting WJZ's *Soft Lights and Sweet Music*, directed by Austen Croom Johnson.

On October 2, 1935, Taylor began appearing on *The Log Cabin Show* with **Georgia Burke**. She performed under the moniker Aunt Jemima for a short time before Tess Gardella, the original Aunt Jemima, filed suit claiming exclusive rights to the designation. Gardella's 1936 suit against not only Taylor but NBC and General Mills was decided in Gardella's favor that spring and she was awarded $115,000. After a short respite from radio Taylor was back on May 1, 1936, with a Friday night series dubbed *Drowsy Rhythm* on WJZ.

After 1936 Taylor's radio work dropped off considerably; according to black critics this was due to network reluctance to air black performers. She made an appearance with Williams on a *Youth on Parade* episode (October 29, 1939) sponsored by Famous Furriers. The next year she was heard as Sister Clorinda Billup on **Richard Huey**'s *Sheep and Goats Club* over WOR in August 28, 1940. Her last known radio assignment was a 1950 transcribed series with her daughter Irene Williams, the title of which remains elusive.

Over the years Eva Taylor was credited with appearances on *Rise of the Goldbergs*, an Eveready program with Nat Shilkret, a General Motors–sponsored series with Erno Rapee, and programs sponsored by Gem Razor and Socony. She also made appearances on *Ladies' Radio Review* and *Plantation Days* but no further information is known about these roles.

Sources: Southern p. 445; *Baltimore Afro-American*, June 25, 1927, p. 7, November 8, 1924, p. 6, March 1, 1930, p. 9, September 12, 1931, p. 10, January 16, 1932, p. 9, March 26, 1932, p. 2, September 17, 1932, p. 10, September 30, 1933, pp. 18, 19, February 10, 1934, p. 6, March 31, 1934, p. 9, October 6, 1934, p. 6, August 24, 1935, p. 8, October 5, 1935, pp. 8, 9, May 2, 1936, p. 10, October 12, 1940, p. 14, September 30, 1950, p. 15; *Chicago Defender*, March 14, 1925, p. 6; *New York Amsterdam News*, February 15, 1928, p. 10, June 12, 1929, p. 11, June 19, 1929, p. 11, June 26, 1929, p. 11, December 11, 1929, p. 11, December 18, 1929, p. 13, December 25, 1929, p. 8, January 15, 1930, p. 11, April 30, 1930, p. 13, May 14, 1930, p. 10, June 4, 1930, p. 12, November 19, 1930, p. 10, July 22, 1931, p. 7, August 26, 1931, p. 7, December 16, 1931, p. 10, December 23, 1931, p. 7, January 20, 1932, p. 9, March 16, 1932, p. 9, April 27, 1932, p. 9, August 10, 1932, p. 7, October 12, 1932, p. 15, December 14, 1932, p. 16, February 8, 1933, p. 16, March 29, 1933, p. 16, August 2, 1933, p. 9, December 13, 1933, p. 7, July 14, 1934, p. 7, December 29, 1934, p. 10, March 9, 1935, p. 10, August 31, 1935, p. 11, April 11, 1936, p. 8, May 9, 1936, p. 9, May 16, 1936, p. 10, November 4, 1939, p. 20; *Pittsburgh Courier*, May 20, 1933, p. 16, September 21, 1940, p. 20.

Thomas, Edna

Edna Thomas appeared on the New York stage as early as 1925 as a member of the Lafayette Theatre's legendary Lafayette Players in *Puddin' Jones*. Her Broadway debut came the next year in 1926 in *Lulu Belle*. Thomas was one of several stage actors recruited by writer **Carlton Moss** to appear in the first African American dramatic series on radio, *Careless Love*, which premiered in November 1930. The anthology series lasted eighteen months to May 1932. In 1935 she was cast as Mattie in Moss' second program, *Folks From Dixie*, a weekly comedy series focusing on a black woman who inherits a sizable amount of money. The series did not win over audiences and ran only during the summer months before leaving the air. Thomas' only other known radio work was an episode of *Cavalcade of America* which dramatized the play *The Green Pastures* on December 25, 1940.

Thomas is credited with indirectly launching the radio career of **Georgia Burke**, one of the medium's most prominent black actresses. In 1931 Burke was visiting Thomas' home when Moss happened to stop by. Impressed by Burke's signing, he quickly offered her a try-out for *Careless Love* and she subsequently won roles on the show which was broadcast over NBC.

In between radio work with Carlton Moss, Thomas starred in **Hall Johnson**'s *Run, Little Chillun* while it went on tour. She made one of her lasting marks on the stage when she appeared in the classic *Voodoo* version of Macbeth staged by Orson Welles in 1936. The WPA production, set in Haiti, featured Thomas as Lady Macbeth. Reflecting her stature in the black acting community, Thomas was elected to the Negro Actors Guild of America board of trustees in 1937 and then served as supervisor of the Federal Theatre Project's negro unit in the late 1930s. Later she played in both the stage and big screen versions of *A Streetcar Named Desire*.

Confusingly, there was a second Edna Thomas in the 1920s and 1930s who was known for her singing of spirituals and Creole tunes. A white performer, she was disparaged by the black press. Although the black Edna Thomas was described as being light-skinned (which some claimed actually hurt her career in black theater), evidence strongly suggests they were two separate performers.

Sources: Grams *Cavalcade*; Patterson pp. 103, 106–107; 125; *Baltimore Afro-American*, May 16, 1925, p. 4, May 29, 1926, p. 5, January 6, 1934, p. 18; *New York Amsterdam News*, May 10, 1933, p. 10, May 17, 1933, p. 16, November 15, 1933, p. 7, April 21, 1934, p. 1, November 30, 1935, p. 12, April 4, 1936, p. 8, December 11, 1937, p. 19, June 10, 1939, p. 17, August 31, 1940, p. 11, January 4, 1941, p. 17, August 10, 1974, p. 9; *New York Times*, January 8, 1923, p. 23, July 24, 1974, p. 44; *Pittsburgh Courier*, April 30, 1932, p. 7; www.radiogoldindex.com.

Those Who Made Good (also referred to as Negroes Who Made Good and Men Who Made Good)

Those Who Made Good premiered May 11, 1941, as a quarter-hour series over New York City's municipal station WNYC. Originally scheduled to run for ten weeks it ended up running for 59. Conceived by **Clifford Burdette**, a recent Atlanta transplant, the shows was "designed to show the contribution Negroes have made in the entertainment field." *Those Who Made Good* was written and directed by Kirk Quinn while the Philharmonic Glee Club of the Abyssinian Baptist Church under the direction of Elfrieda Sandifer supplied the music. The NAACP sponsored the program during its entire run. Guests included:

May 11, 1941—**Canada Lee**
May 18—**Georgette Harvey**
May 25—James Peck, combat pilot in Spanish Civil War
June 1—Anne Wiggins Brown, soprano
June 8—Walter White, NAACP executive director
June 22—**Eddie Green**
June 29—**W. C. Handy**
July 13—Announced as the last episode, the Philharmonic Glee Club sang Earl Robinson's "Ballad for Americans." Likely due to positive listener responses, *Those Who Made Good* continued its run past the original ten weeks.
September 14—James Hubert (Executive Secretary for New York Urban League), Hazel Scott, and W. C. Handy
September 21—Lieutenant Samuel Battle.

In December 1941, Burdette began negotiations with the Mutual Broadcasting System to move his show. Nothing became of the talks and *Those Who Made Good* continued on WNYC.

January 4, 1942—Selma Burke, sculptor, and Snub Mosely and his band.
April 26—Paul Muni and Max Yergan.

Burdette's first radio effort ended up running for 59 weeks. He went on to create a follow-up program called *All Men Are Created Equal*.

Sources: *Baltimore Afro-American*, August 9, 1941, p. 14; *New York Amsterdam News*, May 10, 1941, p. 16, May 24, 1941, p. 4, May 31, 1941, p. 21, June 14, 1941, p. 6, June 21, 1941, p. 21, June 28, 1941,

p. 6, July 12, 1941, p. 9, September 20, 1941, p. 20, December 27, 1941, p. 16, January 10, 1942, p. 16, April 25, 1942, p. 16, May 2, 1942, p. 23, July 24, 1943, p. 20.

The Three Keys

Discovered singing in a Chester, PA club, NBC hoped the Three Keys trio would be the surprise smash of 1932 that the **Mills Brothers** proved to be for CBS in 1931. Unfortunately, the network's $25,000 investment didn't quite pan out. The group started on NBC August 12, 1932, with four times per week. In addition to their NBC work the trio had multi-week bookings on Broadway's Capitol Theater and Loew's theaters. They appeared over both NBC chains, the Red and Blue. While touring Chicago the threesome, Slim (piano), Bob (guitar), and Bon-Bon (voice), continued broadcasting over NBC by using the network's Windy City studios. While certainly a talented bunch, the popularity of the trio was attributed as much to NBC's marketing machine as to their performing. By March 1933, the group was fizzling and their addition to the comedy program of Jack McLallen, Sara, and Sassafras failed to reinvigorate them in the public's eye. They were effectively gone from the network scene by the end of 1933.

Sources: *Baltimore Afro-American*, August 20, 1932, p. 7, September 17, 1932, p. 10, October 15, 1932, p. 10, November 26, 1932, p. 15, March 25, 1933, p. 8, April 8, 1933, p. 9, December 30, 1933, p. 18; *New York Amsterdam News*, August 24, 1932, p. 7, April 19, 1933, p. 17.

Three Sharps and One Flat
(also Three Sharps and A Flat)

The Three Sharps and One Flat are a little-remembered quartet that had quite a long career together, performing from the early 1930s possibly into the 1950s. Consisting of Charles Ridgeley, Henry Larkins, Bobby Smith, and Edgar Dawson, the foursome emerged from Baltimore's Douglass High School in the early 1930s. They had a regular program over WCBM in 1932 and 1933 and appeared on local programs such as the *Negro Business Hour*.

During the late 1930s a quartet named Three Sharps and A Flat were regulars on the NBC network and in 1939 they cut their first records, some sides for Decca. Whether this was the same foursome that emerged from Baltimore is not clear.

Sources: Carr, et al. pp. 183–184; *Baltimore Afro-American*, September 10, 1932, p. 10, September 24, 1932, p. 7, February 25, 1933, p. 10; *Chicago Defender*, June 3, 1939, p. 21; *Pittsburgh Courier*, November 14, 1936, p. 10.

Tibbs, Lillian Evans

Lillian Evans Tibbs, soprano, was a classically trained singer heard over Washington, D.C.'s WRC in 1924.

Source: *Baltimore Afro-American*, May 30, 1924, p. 4.

Tilden, Wezlynn Develle (also Weslynne and Wezlyn Tildon)

Wezlynn Tilden was born in Fort Worth, TX, into a prominent African American family of doctors but primarily raised in Chicago. Once she reached high school her family moved to New York where Tilden could focus her studies on dramatics and the fine arts. Upon graduation Tilden attended New York University in the late 1930s where she excelled. Sources indicate she appeared first on radio over WMRO in 1945 when she starred in a play called *The Paccini Is Hungry* which she was credited with writing as well. One source identifies additional early radio appearances on WJOL, WJOB, and WCRW. While getting her feet wet in radio Tilden worked as a clerk for the Treasury Department.

Tilden's primary radio work came in the late 1940s when she was cast in all three of **Richard Durham's** series, *Democracy—USA* (1946–1948), *Here Comes Tomorrow* (1947–1948) on which she played both the Redmond family's daughter and mother, and *Destination Freedom* (1948–1950). She briefly served as master of ceremonies, along with Louise Pruitt and Helen Spaulding, on *The Pepsi-Cola Amateur Hour* which was broadcast over Chicago's WGES during the summer of 1948. In 1954 she was cast in her last known radio role, a supporting cast member on the African American soap opera *The Story of Ruby Valentine* which aired over the new **Negro Broadcasting Network**. Regarding her radio work Tilden claimed that even though she may have been the busiest black radio actress in Chicago, "If I tried to live on my art—I'd starve." Tilden appeared in various Broadway (*Kiss Me, Kate*) and Off-Broadway shows (*Dream About Tomorrow*, *Land Beyond the River*) through the 1950s and even wrote a three-act tragi-comedy in 1954 before disappearing from public view.

Sources: *Baltimore Afro-American*, December 6, 1952, p. 6; *Chicago Defender*, December 25, 1937, p. 14, November 24, 1945, p. 10, July 3, 1948, p. 9, February 19, 1949, p. 22, May 24, 1952, p. 23, January 30, 1954, p. 19, October 15, 1957, p. 19; *New York Amsterdam News*, May 8, 1954, p. 22; *Pittsburgh Courier*, July 20, 1957, p. 18.

Toney, Jay Stone

Jay Stone Toney sang baritone for the **Southernaires**, a quartet which played steadily on radio for nearly two decades. Originally from Columbia, TN, Toney is not known to have had any formal musical training and did not sing seriously until moving to New York in 1929 where he promptly began singing with the other soon-to-be members of the Southernaires. Unlike his band mates Toney never ventured into dramatic radio productions or experimented with side projects. Content with his role with the Southernaires Toney may have approached two thousand radio performances. The quartet's Sunday morning program aired weekly from 1930 to 1950 and they could be found on the radio an additional three or four times a week during the early and mid-1930s. While on tour in Marshalltown, IA, Toney

had a heart attack during a show intermission and died June 23, 1948, at the age of 53.

Sources: *Baltimore Afro-American*, November 23, 1935, p. 9, July 10, 1948, p. 6; *Pittsburgh Courier*, November 3, 1934, p. 7, July 3, 1948, p. 22.

Townsend, Vince

Vince Townsend claimed to have been involved with radio as far back as 1930 working as the manager of the Dixie Symphony Quartet over KFI, Los Angeles. The quartet was comprised of Elihu Sloane, George Jones, Townsend, and Kenneth Spencer. He also recalled heading the Dixie Vocal Symphony on a sustaining program over KNX in 1932. Townsend's quartet further appeared in a series of programs over a San Francisco station sponsored by J. E. French, Dodge Motor Distributors. Townsend wasn't an actor; rather, he made his career in law and as an assistant minister. The high point of his radio career was broadcasting on several episodes of *The Amos 'n' Andy Show* between 1948 and 1954 where he played various small roles.

Sources: Edmerson p. 31–32; *Los Angeles Sentinel*, December 8, 1955, p. 7.

The Townsend Murder Mystery

While some contemporary accounts of *The Townsend Murder Mystery* suggest it was an African American radio production, it was primarily a vehicle for white performers written by Octavus Roy Cohen, a Jewish author who wrote many mystery and detective novels featuring black characters. *The Townsend Murder Mystery* did feature two prominent African American characters, Quintus Jones and Jasper DeVoid, who were played by noted black thespians **Frank Wilson** and **Ernest Whitman**. Sources disagree as to which actor played which character but do indicate the roles provided comedy relief.

This mystery serial debuted in February 1933, and aired three times a week, Tuesdays, Thursdays, and Saturdays, (later Mondays, Wednesdays, and Saturdays) for fifteen minutes in the evening over NBC's WJZ (later WEAF). Based on a 600,000 word serial penned by Cohen, *The Townsend Murder Mystery* was scheduled to appear in 54 segments over 18 weeks between February and May of 1933. The story revolved around bumbling detective Jim Hanvey (a Cohen creation) who attempts to solve the murder of one John Prosser, a guest at a party held by the Townsends. Hanvey, the lead, was played by Thurston Hall, a white actor with a long stage history. Other cast members included Jonathan Hole, Cecil Secrest, Charles Slattery, Lois Campbell, Joyce Meredith, and the aforementioned black actors Frank Wilson and Ernest Whitman.

In April, **Eva Jessye**, who had gained some radio prominence with her **Dixie Jubilee Singers**, debuted on the show in the role of Magnesia, adding a third black performer to the cast. Tim Moore, a fourth black actor, was added at some point. Writer Octavus Cohen personally introduced the series during the premier broadcast and boasted of a 35-member cast. Production responsibilities were handled by Frank McCormack and sponsorship was assumed by Westinghouse. To accommodate different time zones the cast performed the show live over WJZ then reassembled four hours later to offer another live broadcast to stations west of Chicago.

Sources: *Baltimore Afro-American*, March 18, 1933, p. 9, April 22, 1933, p. 10, April 29, 1933, p. 10; *Chicago Defender*, March 4, 1933, p. 5; *New York Amsterdam News*, May 17, 1933, p. 16; *New York Times*, February 12, 1933, p. 147.

Trent's Adolphus Hotel Orchestra

Alphonso Trent's Orchestra was one of the premier jazz bands in the Southwest during the 1920s. Between 1923 and 1925 they were booked at the Adolphus Hotel in Dallas, TX, from which they were broadcast night over the city's station WFAA.

Sources: Dance, *Count Basie*, p. 112; Sies p. 10; *Chicago Defender*, November 14, 1925 p. 7.

Tribute to Unsung Americans

W. C. Handy's book *Tribute to Unsung Americans* was turned into a series of weekly broadcasts by that same name over New York's WMCA Sunday mornings from 10:15 to 10:30. The installments were dramatized vignettes from black history which aired from June 1941, through autumn of that year.

Sources: *Baltimore Afro-American*, August 9, 1941, p. 14; *New York Amsterdam News*, June 14, 1941, p. 20, October 25, 1941, p. 22.

Truths About Harlem

In December 1929, the YMCA began sponsoring a half-hour weekly series over New York's WGBS entitled *Truths About Harlem*. Like many radio features of the time it was focused on a topical lecture with perhaps some musical interludes. The creators had an ambitious agenda as indicated by the summary of initial broadcast topics: "Harlem: The Negro Mecca of the World," "The Negro in Art," "Present Trends in Education of the Negro," "The Negro in Music," "Child Welfare Work," "Tendencies in Population," "Wages and the Present Standard of Living," "Home Life in an Expanding Community," "Situation of Employment and the Unemployed," "The Religious Life of the People," "Negro Periodicals and Their Scope," "The Truth About Crime in Harlem," "Young Women and Their Problems," "Young Men and Their Problems," "The Negro in the Field of Law," "A New Day in Politics," "Harlem's Health," "The Negro in Literature," "The Negro in Business," "The Negro in the Theatre," and "The Outlook of Harlem."

Many of the speakers were familiar from appearances on other radio broadcasts and included Dr. Rudolph Fisher, Aaron Douglas, Ira De A. Reid, Philip Randolph, W. D. Simmons, Noah Thompson, Charles Allison, Dr. Channing Tobias, Francis Rivers, Hubert Delany, Benjamin Curley, Romeo L. Dougherty, Carl Diton, Dr. Peter Murray, the Rev. William Lloyd Imes, Vernon Ayer, Albert Reed, and Cecilia Cabiniss Saunders. *Truths About Harlem* ran for approximately seven months, leaving the air in June 1930.

Source: *New York Amsterdam News*, December 4, 1929, p. 11.

Tufts College

The Tufts College (Medford/Sommerville, MA) radio station broadcast the Vespers Quartet February 17, 1923. Members of the Quartet were Ethel Hardy Smith, soprano, Catherine Pipes, contralto, Harry Delmore, tenor, and Edward Boatner, baritone. Ernest Hays accompanied the four.

Source: *Baltimore Afro-American*, February 16, 1923, p. 4.

Twenty Harlem Fingers

This uniquely named musical outfit was a novelty piano duo made up of River Chambers and **Ambrose Smith**. They began airing over WFBR, Baltimore, Saturday nights in early 1932. By July they had moved to two slots a week, Wednesday and Friday afternoons. Chambers hailed from a musical family; his father was a musician in the Civil War and his mother was one of the first music teacher's in Baltimore. His brother, Ulysses, was organist at the Regal Theatre in Chicago. Chambers cut his chops at Harlem's Lafayette Theatre before moving down to Baltimore where he teamed up with Smith. Smith was an experienced orchestra leader, arranger, and composer when he partnered with Chambers.

The duo also appeared over Baltimore's WCBM. Smith was an established orchestra leader dating back to the early 1920s and in 1932 he formed Ambrose Smith's Orchestra on the side while continuing to perform with Chambers. Leon Nelson, guitar and tenor, and Buck Barnes, baritone, accompanied Chambers and Smith at times on their broadcasts as did George Hardy,

vocals. By the end of 1932 Chambers' stage musical *Adam and Eva, Inc.* was in production and its tunes were getting airtime across the city.

Sources: *Baltimore Afro-American*, March 26, 1932, p. 8, April 30, 1932, p. 18, May 14, 1932, p. 11, October 29, 1932, p. 10.

Two Black Crows

George Moran (George Searchy) and Charlie Mack (Charles Sellers) were featured as the Two Black Crows on *The Eveready Hour* from 1929–1930 and headlined CBS' *The Majestic Hour* between 1928 and 1930. They were popular recordings artists whose sketches are readily available to modern listeners.

Sources: Dunning pp. 236, 424; MacDonald, *Don't Touch That Dial!*, p. 112; *Baltimore Afro-American*, December 22, 1928, p. 8.

Vernon Hutchins and the Cinderella Inn Orchestra

Vernon Hutchins and the Cinderella Inn Orchestra broadcast over Baltimore's WGBA in 1925. Hutchins' eight-piece band included Sammy Lewis, soloist, Bernard Robinson, piano and banjo, Carlos Sanks, piano, James Thomas, violin, Sammy Davis, piano, Swayzo, cornet, and "Turk" Kerr, guitar.

Source: *Baltimore Afro-American*, March 7, 1925, p. 5.

Victory Life Insurance Company Quintet

The Victory Life Insurance Company Quintet was an obscure group which didn't leave many traces of its radio work. They made multiple appearances on New York's WGBS in late 1930 and early 1931 before making headlines by refusing to use the freight elevator as requested by staff of the Lincoln Hotel, home of WGBS.

Source: *Baltimore Afro-American*, January 24, 1931, p. 8; *New York Amsterdam News*, December 31, 1930, p. 10.

Wabash YMCA, Chicago, IL

The YMCA on Wabash Avenue in Chicago was associated with radio as early as 1917 when a Phillips High School student named Walter Hughes gave a presentation on the young technology. The facility sponsored radio telegraphy lessons beginning January 1920, in which they had 26 individuals enrolled. Two months later they were the home of the Wabash Radio Club which received its own operating license in May. Frank Waver and P. R. Piper served as club instructors. Piper's skills were acknowledged by the American Radio Relay League with a letter from the Executive Council awarding him a prize (a new vacuum tube) for "perfect hook ups." In June 1922, the branch began hosting radio concerts every Monday evening. Frank Waver, by then with the Mid-West Radio Service, was responsible for setting up and operating the receiving equipment.

Sources: *Chicago Defender*, January 24, 1920, p. 13, January 31, 1920, p. 16, May 15, 1920, p. 13, May 22, 1920, p. 13, June 10, 1922, p. 5.

Wade, Ernestine

Ernestine Wade made a name for herself around Los Angeles as a singer and even appeared on radio over *The Gold Hour* on KGPJ June 27, 1939. Her most famous radio work came that same year when she was cast as the first African American on *Amos 'n' Andy* as Valada Green, Andy's girlfriend. Wade also played Clara Van Porter and Sara Fletcher on the program but the role for which she would always be remembered was Sapphire Stevens, domineering wife of the Kingfish. From 1939 to 1955 she played Sapphire on the daily *Amos 'n' Andy* serial, the weekly *Amos 'n' Andy Show* and assumed the role on *Amos 'n' Andy*'s single season on television. Other parts would come her way on the big and small screen but all were overshadowed by the character of Sapphire.

Wade played on a variety of other broadcasts, though none as consistently as *Amos 'n' Andy*. Some of them include *Doctor Christian* (September 30, 1942) and *Lux Radio Theatre* (June 28, 1943, and December 17, 1945).

Sources: Billups and Pierce pp. 295, 343; McLeod pp. 84, 181,184; Sampson, *Blacks in Black and White*, p. 534; *Chicago Defender*, November 13, 1948, p. 16; *Los Angeles Sentinel*, June 22, 1939, p. 1; www.radiogoldindex.com.

Washington, Jerome

Jerome Washington, nicknamed "The Prince of Harmony," was a Baltimore-area pianist who broadcast over WCBM on Tuesdays at 8:00 in early 1932. By August of the same year he'd been granted three slots throughout the week. Clarence Bowman was known to join him occasionally on the air.

Sources: *Baltimore Afro-American*, February 6, 1932, p. 9, April 30, 1932, p. 18.

Waters, Ethel

From humble beginnings which included a first job as a chambermaid, Ethel Waters rose to become one of the most revered female blues singers of all time. Her performing career can be traced to a Philadelphia amateur contest in which she won first prize. Waters moved on to the Theatre Owners Booking Association, a black vaudeville circuit and, eventually, began cutting records with Cardinal and Black Swan during the 1920s. Success came slowly but steadily and by the end of the decade she was pulling down $1,250 per week, eight times what she earned as the 1920s began. In addition to her records and concerts, Waters began getting cast on the New York stage in such plays as *Blackbirds* (1930) and *Rhapsodies in Black* (1931).

Never a major radio star, Waters was nevertheless not a stranger to the airwaves. She was on the air as early as April 25, 1922, when she performed over a station owned by the New Orleans Daily Item. On the broadcast she was accompanied by the Black Swan

Jazz Masters directed by F. B. Henderson, Jr. with another broadcast in December 1927, when she was featured along with other prominent performers on NBC. The program was sponsored by Frigidaire and starred Graham McNamee as announcer. After two appearance on Rudy Vallee's program in the early 1930s (August 13, 1931, and May 11, 1933), Waters' received what is now her most well-known series in 1933. That spring Waters and **Duke Ellington** were broadcast from Harlem's famed Cotton Club multiple times per week on NBC. At the end of the year, beginning in October, she was a regular on a CBS (one source claims NBC) series called *The American Revue* sponsored by gas producers. Pearl Wimberly Wright accompanied Waters on the piano. Accounts vary as to why the program left the air in February 1934. Some say Waters was forced off due to continued complaints from Southern listeners while others claim her contract was cancelled due to strain from overworking her voice.

The stage, and film to a lesser extent, would be Waters' primary venue throughout her career but she continued to make radio appearances over the next two decades. She was a guest on the October 7, 1934, *Hall of Fame* program with **Hall Johnson** and his Choir. In the mid–1930s Waters is credited with hosting a variety show on NBC but details remain elusive. Between 1936 and 1937 she was a favored guest performer on Ben Bernie's network program which was sponsored by the American Can Company. She earned spots on Orson Welles' *Radio Almanac* which aired from 1943 to 1944, on the AFRS' *Command Performance* series which was produced through the 1940s, as well as *Kraft Music Hall* (June 12, 1941), and *Amos 'n' Andy* (January 28, 1944). The AFRS also invited her on to the black entertainment series *Jubilee* on four different occasions: #1 (recorded October 9, 1942), #49 (recorded November 2, 1943), #88 (recorded July 17, 1944), and #115 (recorded January 8, 1945).

Waters was still finding radio gigs into the 1950s, even as the medium's Golden Age was coming to an end. These included guest spots on *The Big Show* (March 18, 1951), the *Harlem Amateur Hour* in 1952 over WJZ, an episode of *Cavalcade of America* (January 1, 1952), and *Strike It Rich* (October 12, 1955). Ethel Waters was scheduled to host a variety show on the newly created **National Negro Network** (1954–1955) but the enterprise went bust before any broadcasts featuring Waters were made.

Sources: LOC; Balk p. 57; Barlow pp. 131, 147; Berry and Berry p. 347; Dunning pp. 28, 173, 376, 657; Gourse pp. 33–42; Grams *Cavalcade*; Lotz and Neuert; MacDonald, *Don't Touch That Dial!*, p. 335; Sies pp. 202, 251, 457; *Baltimore Afro-American*, December 24, 1927, p. 7, May 6, 1933, p. 10, November 11, 1933 p. 19, November 18, 1933 p. 19, March 3, 1934, p. 1, September 15, 1934, p. 7, October 6, 1934, p. 7, January 12, 1952 p. 7; *Chicago Defender*, September 30, 1933 p. 5, February 17, 1934, p. 5, March 3, 1934, p. 4, January 23, 1937 p. 11; *New York Amsterdam News*, December 14, 1927, p. 10, July 25, 1936, p. 8; *Savannah Tribune*, April 27, 1922, p. 1.

Whitman, Ernest

Born in Oklahoma City, OK, in 1892 or 1893, Ernest Whitman graduated from high school at the age of sixteen then studied at and graduated from the Tuskegee Institute. He started his stage career around 1916. Before turning to the theater full time he held a variety of jobs including those of bootblack, night club owner, amateur boxer, ball player, and producer/manager/owner of Ernie Whitman's Serenaders. During World War I he served as the assistant chaplain to the 805th Pioneer Division.

It's not clear when Whitman arrived in New York but by 1921 he began appearing in local productions. One of his earliest publicized appearances was in 1921 when he had a one-man act which incorporated the popular song *Better Days Will Come Again* by Tom Lemonier and Karl Rickman. His talent was recognized and he earned steady work in the black theater circuit. In 1922 he starred in the black musical comedy *Follow Me* and also a show called *Keep It Up*. *Follow Me* was so well received that it was reprised in 1923 and Whitman was again cast. An early critic described him as "the smiling and unctuous 'straight man' with the voice of an opera singer." He would gain a reputation for straight, dramatic roles.

Success on the stage continued throughout the 1920s and into the 1930s. In 1924 Whitman was featured in *Steppin' Out* which used much of the cast from the earlier *Follow Me* and ran through at least October of that year. Whitman's next role was as another straight man in the hit *Lucky Sambo* in 1925. The show played the black vaudeville circuit, the Theater Owner's Booking Association, through June of 1927. Other stage work over the next few years included *Aces High* (1928), *Dixie Vagabond* (1928), *Black Belt* (1928), *Fancy Trimmings* (1928), *Harlem* (1929), *The Last Mile* (1930), *Savage Rhythm* (which also featured radio co-workers **Inez Clough** and **Georgia Burke**, 1932) and *Bloodstream* (1932).

Whitman's first confirmed radio work seems to have been *Careless Love*, the first all-black dramatic series which was created by **Carlton Moss**. While one source indicates he was on the air in 1929 singing on NBC's *General Electric Show and* playing a comedic character in the soap opera *Blue Coal*, these roles remain unsubstantiated with other sources. It's not clear how frequently he was cast on the weekly *Careless Love* program which ran from November 1930, to May 1932. Other players included Georgia Burke, **Edna Thomas**, **Eva Taylor**, **Frank Wilson**, **Wayland Rudd**, **Richey Huey**, Inez Clough, **Georgette Harvey**, and **Clarence Williams**, all of whom were regulars on New York radio in the early 1930s.

His next radio assignment was *The Townsend Murder Mystery* which ran from February to May of 1933. The two black characters were Quintus Jones and Jasper DeVoid; both provided comedy relief and sources disagree as to which was played by Whitman and which was played by co-star Frank Wilson. The mystery program was written by Octavus Roy Cohen and also featured Tim Moore and **Eva Jessye** later in its run. Whitman is also credited with appearances on a series called *Circus Days* with Frank Wilson over NBC but no further details have been uncovered about this effort which aired from October 1933, to February 1934.

In 1934 Whitman got what is frequently cited as his first major network exposure (*The Townsend Murder Mystery* and *Circus Days* were both aired on a network but neither appears to have been an important series) on *The Gibson Family*, where he played a butler named Theopholis who may have gone by the nickname Awful. The program was described by a contemporary source as an hour-long "musical comedy" written by Donald and Owen Davis. Whitman was paired with **Gee Gee James**, an African American women who played the part of Mignonette, also a servant. Twice in 1935 Whitman was voted most popular character on the program by listeners. Soon after his role on *The Gibson Family* ended he was paired with black comedian **Eddie Green** in *Uncle Charlie's Tent Show*. The two played characters named Big Sam and Little Jerry and were described as the first African American blackface team on a network broadcast. Whitman's time on this show was brief, ending on September 15, 1935. Tragedy struck shortly before his departure (and possibly contributed to it) when wife Lena Whitman passed away.

Whitman had minor radio work in the mid–1930s after which he spent much of the rest of the decade focusing on films. In late 1935 he was cast in at least one episode of *Echoes of New York Town* and then gained a following on the Rudy Vallee program in early 1936. When he asked for a raise over his $50 dollar salary he was replaced. Around this time Whitman relocated to California seeking other acting opportunities and prompting **Joe Bostic**, host of *The Negro*

Business Hour in the early 1930s, to complain about the lack of quality roles that were available to African American radio performers.

In 1936 Whitman appeared in two of his first films, *Green Pastures* and *The Prisoner of Shark Island*. Whitman was featured in the May 2, 1938, *Lux Radio Theatre* broadcast of *Prisoner of Shark Island*. He was then cast in a steady stream of films into the 1940s. Pictures that attracted notable attention in the black press included several in 1939 such as *Jesse James* (with Tyrone Power and Henry Fonda), *Safari*, and *Pacific Liner*. Others were *The Return of Jesse James* (1940), *Maryland* (1940), *The Pittsburgh Kid* (1941), *Cabin in the Sky* (1943), and *Wilson* (1944).

The April 24, 1939, *Lux Radio Theatre* featured Whitman and he also was cast on the September 29, 1941, episode called "Third Finger, Left Hand." He reprised his role as a pullman porter, the film version of which he'd played the year before. In 1943 Whitman again returned to radio both on the revamped weekly *Amos 'n' Andy Show* and a little known program called *Blueberry Hill* which replaced *The George Burns and Gracie Allen Show* in June 1943, and also featured Ben Carter and Mantan Moreland. To the surprise of all involved the musical show was cancelled by CBS after only one broadcast. While *Blueberry Hill* was a failure, the new series *Jubilee* was much more successful. From 1943 to 1953 the program, which featured African American musicians (notably jazz artists) and, as years went by, more white musicians, was beamed to U.S. troops overseas. It was not, however, made available to domestic listeners. Whitman served as the master of ceremonies for much of the show's run and was described by one source as "a jive-talking bundle of energy." *Jubilee* #5, likely recorded in New York on January 17, 1943, is believed to be the first episode featuring Whitman in the role of MC. His last confirmed appearance was #205, recorded February 7, 1947, a total of 179 episodes over

four years. He is found on more than two dozen subsequent episodes but *Jubilee* researchers Rainer Lotz and Ulrich Neuert note that portions of these episodes—if not their entirety—were reused from earlier broadcasts. They credit him on 205 of 433 *Jubilee* recordings. Though frequently now referred to as Ernest "Bubbles" Whitman, it is only in connection with *Jubilee* that the nickname Bubbles is found. Not once was the nicknamed used by the black press over the many years the papers covered his career.

Radio jobs would prove to be more regular in the 1940s than they had been in the previous decade. Whitman was cast in an episode of *Cavalcade of America* (October 9, 1944) and then with Heddy Lamar and Alan Ladd in a 1944 broadcast of *Lux Radio Theatre*'s "Casablanca." In 1945 he is known to have played a West Indian alongside Orson Welles in a 1945 episode of *This Is My Best* and then a handyman on *The Billie Burke Show*. The following year, 1946, Whitman reprised another of his onscreen personas when he assumed the role of the servant Pinky on a radio version of *The Return of Jesse James* which was broadcast over NBC affiliate KFI.

In 1947 Whitman earned another ongoing radio role when he was hired for *The Beulah Show* to play Bill Jackson, the boyfriend of **Beulah**. Originally Bill was played by white actor Marlin Hurt who also played Beulah when the program debuted as *The Marlin Hurt and Beulah Show* in 1945. When Hurt died suddenly of a heart attack in March 1946, another white man, Bob Corley, became Beulah after the series returned to the airwaves nearly a year later. This second version was short-lived, lasting six months. Beginning in 1947 Whitman played Bill and would do so until *Beulah* left the air for good in 1954. Guest appearances also kept Whitman busy, including roles on *Mr. President* and *Sherlock Holmes* (1947), *The Eddie Cantor Show* and *Hollywood Story* (1948), and *The Bing Crosby Show* (1949).

During the late 1940s Whitman also appeared as the endman of a minstrel troupe on *The Mirth and Melody Show*, a sustaining program on ABC which may have been radio's last minstrel show. Another black actor, **Horace "Nicodemus" Stewart**, also appeared on the show. Whitman was featured in one episode of *Tales of the Texas Rangers* (with **Roy Glenn**) broadcast April 1, 1951.

Whitman's undated radio credits also include various Armed Forces Radio roles during World War II, *The George Burns and Gracie Allen Show*, *The Adventures of Maisie* (which also featured African American **Roy Glenn**), *Philco Radio Hall of Fame*, and a few unidentified Los Angeles–originated serials.

In addition to his highly praised acting skills, Ernest Whitman was an ordained Methodist minister and speaker of seven languages. He died August 1954, at the age of 61.

Sources: Billups and Pierce pp. 174, 210, 256, 306; Cox, *Radio Crime Fighters*, p. 247; Cox, *Great Radio Sitcoms*, pp. 71, 134, 267; Dunning pp. 83, 282–283, 376–377; Edmerson pp. 20, 22–25; Grams *Cavalcade*; Grams, *Radio Drama*, p. 484; Lotz and Neuert; McLeod p. 184; Peterson p. 90; Sies pp. 11, 117, 380, 458; *Baltimore Afro-American*, June 6, 1921, p. 4, September 29, 1922, p. 6, October 5, 1923, p. 4, March 28, 1924, p. 5, October 31, 1924, p. 6, August 8, 1925, p. 15, November 7, 1925, p. 4, January 23, 1926, p. 6, March 18, 1927, p. 9, January 14, 1928, p. 7, February 25, 1928, p. 7, May 19, 1928, p. 8, January 5, 1929, p. 9, August 31, 1929, p. 9, March 8, 1930, p. 9, January 9, 1932, p. 9, February 25, 1933, p. 16, March 18, 1933, p. 9, April 29, 1933, p. 10, February 16, 1935, p. 8, March 16, 1935, p. 9, May 25, 1935, p. 8, August 31, 1935, p. 9, April 25, 1936, p. 11, June 5, 1937, p. 11, June 12, 1943, p. 10, May 11, 1946, p. 6, December 13, 1947, p. 6; *Chicago Defender*, March 4, 1933 p. 5, March 23, 1935 p. 11, May 18, 1935 p. 6; *New York Amsterdam News*, November 26, 1922, p. 5, November 7, 1928, p. 6, March 30, 1932, p. 7, March 29, 1933, p. 16, September 21, 1935, p. 7, November 2, 1935, p. 13, February 8, 1936, p. 8, December 26, 1936, p. 8, October 29, 1938, p. 20, March 2, 1940, p. 20, August 30, 1941, p. 21, March 6, 1943, p. 17, August 12, 1944, p. 10, January 8, 1949, p. 23, August 14, 1954, p. 22; *New York Times*, January 24, 1944, p. 33, August 10, 1954, p. 19.

Wickliffe, John

John Wickliffe was a pioneering jazz musician who began performing in the teens. In the early 1920s he moved to the Chicago area where he had at least two different orchestras which were making regular radio appearances through 1922 and 1923.

Sources: *Chicago Defender*, October 28, 1922, p. 4, May 19, 1923, p. 4.

Williams, Clarence

Clarence Williams was a well-known African American musician from approximately 1915 to the 1950s when he sold his business interests to Decca. He began his performing career in New Orleans and later claimed his musical education consisted of eight piano lessons. During the teens Williams started his first music publishing venture with Armond Piron then spent a few years touring. Around 1920 he moved north to Chicago along with a great number of African Americans. Three years later he relocated to New York where he spent the rest of his life.

Williams was known as one of the most prominent African American music publishers in the country but was a competent performer as well. He was a regular recording artist with Okeh and Columbia Records as well as other smaller labels. In addition, Williams was a regular on the air during the heyday of black radio from the mid–1920s to around 1934. He's credited with appearing on New York's WHN as early as 1922 but the earliest first-hand account of one of his broadcasts dates from October 1924. After a November 6, 1924, broadcast the Clarence Williams Trio was offered a spot on the Keith circuit. Over the next two years Williams made occasional broadcasts with various groups but most often with the Blue Five and his trio. On February 13, 1925, he and the Blue Five performed on WGBS with Clarence Todd and Williams' wife Eva Taylor who provided vocals. A singer named Ted

Brown had to back out at the last moment so the group filled in on short notice. The group opened with "Santa Clause Blues" and also played "Pickin' on Your Baby," "Everybody Loves My Baby," and "All the Wrongs You've Done to Me." That same month the Blue Five were on WEBJ and WHN as well. A few months later in September the Clarence Williams Trio (Williams, Taylor, and Todd) was heard over WHN on the 18th.

By 1927 Williams became a semi-regular on the air and would star intermittently on music programs for several years. That year Ralph Brown was added to the Trio lineup at least temporarily and in June they began making irregular appearances on WPAP. Publicists also claimed that by this time Williams had appeared on most of the nation's major stations though there's no solid evidence he ever broadcast outside New York. Since his bands frequently toured, however, such out-of-town broadcasts are very likely. By the fall of 1927 the Clarence Williams Trio's WPAP efforts had turned into a weekly gig which was later switched over to WPCH and lasted into 1928. During this same period Williams also had a self-titled program on WHN.

Outside of his musical series on WHN and WPCH Williams made his only known appearance on WABC's *Negro Achievement Hour*, radio's second black series and one that ran at least until the early 1930s. On the February 9, 1928, episode he sang alongside frequent performing partner Eva Taylor. He returned to WABC on July 21 with more songs. By March 1929 he was back with a weekly effort entitled *Clarence Williams' Pals* on WOV, a show that aired until June. Williams and Taylor made what may have been their biggest broadcast to date on June 9, 1929, when they were featured in the sketch "In Our Cottage of Love" on *Major Bowes' Capitol Family* on WEAF. They were popular enough to make a return engagement June 23rd. Around the same time the pair premiered a new morning show on NBC

called *Morning Glories*; a group called The Wanderers also entertained.

During the spring of 1930 Williams worked on his first show that was more than just music, an opera-spoof series called *The Alpha and Omega Opera Company DeLuxe, Inc.* on WEAF. Later in the year he appeared with Taylor on WEAF's *Blue Streak Hour*. Taylor sang on the program until 1931 but it's not clear if Williams provided accompaniment during that entire span or not. June 1930 found Williams playing Southern songs on WABC. A few months later the Clarence Trio reunited and was booked weekly starting in October on WHN and WOR, dates that lasted into 1931. He showed up on yet another program in 1930, NBC's Sunday afternoon show *Southland Sketches*, on which he played a vinegar jug as a member of the Levee Band. Little remembered now, *Southland Sketches* became the launching pad for the long-running radio quartet the **Southernaires**.

The next year Williams departed *Southland Sketches* and inaugurated a competing Sunday program, *Clarence Williams' Spiritual Quartet*. It was broadcast over WPCH beginning September 1931 and lasted until at least the summer of 1932. While doing his Sunday show he also made some appearances on NBC's WEAF with Taylor and the Southernaires on a weekday afternoon show. The radio work continued in late 1932 with a modified outfit that added **Louis Armstrong**'s ex-wife Lillian Armstrong, to the trio lineup of Williams, Taylor, and Todd. Williams had one more busy year in radio, 1933, before he turned most of his attention to his music publishing business. WRNY held an Abyssinian Relief Bureau benefit program on February 11, 1933, and Williams and Taylor contributed performances along with numerous other black New York musicians. The next month, March, he tried his hand at directing a radio group, the Lowland Singers, who received three weekly slots on WOR. During the summer months Williams took what is believed to be his only acting role on radio, as the husband of **Artie Bell McGinty**'s "Mandy Lou" on WABC's *Old Gold Program* featuring Fred Waring. Williams' last known ongoing radio effort was an NBC show that ran from the fall of 1933 to May 1934 and featured songs by Eva Taylor.

Williams effectively retired from broadcasting but made at least two more appearances at the end of the decade. On October 29, 1939, Williams and Taylor made an appearance on *Youth on Parade*, a show sponsored by Famous Furriers. The next year he made some guest appearances in August 1940, on **Richard Huey**'s *Sheep and Goats Club* over WOR.

It's very likely this overview underestimates Clarence Williams' radio work. His wife Eva Taylor was a staple on NBC during the late 1920s and early 1930s and Williams is known to have been a frequent accompanist. Though he was only occasionally given credit on their dual radio performances, it's reasonable to think that a significant number of her broadcasts would have included Williams.

Sources: Southern pp. 309, 350, 370, 445; *Baltimore Afro-American*, October 10, 1924, p. 10, November 8, 1924, p. 6, February 14, 1925, p. 5, June 11, 1927, p. 8, November 19, 1927, p. 7, June 30, 1928, p. 8, September 17, 1932, p. 10, June 10, 1933, p. 9, July 8, 1933, p. 9; *Chicago Defender*, September 26, 1925, p. 6, September 24, 1927, p. 7; *New York Amsterdam News*, September 21, 1927, p. 12, November 30, 1927, p. 10, January 18, 1928, p. 8, February 8, 1928, p. 9, July 18, 1928, p. 8, March 20, 1929, p. 9, June 12, 1929, p. 11, June 19, 1929, p. 11, June 26, 1929, p. 11, February 26, 1930, p. 11, March 26, 1930, p. 9, October 15, 1930, p. 12, November 12, 1930, p. 12, September 23, 1931, p. 7, December 14, 1932, p. 16, February 8, 1933, p. 16, March 15, 1933, p. 16, May 3, 1933, p. 10, November 4, 1939, p. 20, August 31, 1940, p. 11.

Williams, Nat D.

On October 25, 1948, Nat D. Williams went on the air over Memphis' WDIA and became the first recognized African American disc jockey in the South. But Williams was much more than a trail-blazing radio announcer. He had earned two degrees from Nashville's Tennessee Agriculture and Industrial School and over the years took courses at countless other institutions. For decades he penned columns for black newspapers, notably *The Pittsburgh Courier* and *The Chicago Defender*.

During the 1930s Williams laid the groundwork for his future radio work through his involvement in Amateur Night on Beale Street (which may have been broadcast), the Cotton Makers' Jubilee talent contest, and Booker T. Washington's Ballet. He not only honed his keen eye for talent but made contacts with the biggest names in African American entertainment.

Racial tensions were high in the city and across the South when Williams' *Tan Town Jubilee* went out over the Memphis airwaves in 1948. Station employees were on edge, not knowing what the public's response would be. However, after receiving just a few calls of displeasure from white listeners, staff knew they had struck gold. Whites were not overly concerned with Williams and nearly every black radio listener was sure to tune him in. Williams' success spawned *Tan Town Coffee Club*, *Nat D.'s Supper Club*, and *Brown America Speaks*.

Sources: Barlow pp. 111–124; Cantor pp. 25–55, 158–160; Ward p. 85.

Williams, Samuel

Sixteen-year-old Williams played piano over KYW in Chicago April 20, 1923, as part of a Midnight Follies program. He also broadcast from the Drake Hotel's WDAP.

Source: *Chicago Defender*, April 28, 1923 p. 4.

Wilson, Frank

Frank Wilson was one of the most highly acclaimed African American actors from his early stage work in the 1920s until his death in 1956. Although his radio career was not as extensive as other black actors such as **Juano Hernandez** or **Georgia Burke**, it spanned three decades and included the first and last all-black drama programs.

Born in 1885 in New York City, as a youngster Wilson worked in Eddie Leonard's minstrel show before starting his own vaudeville act called "The Carolina Four." Sometime around the start of World War I he went to work for the United States Post Office, a position he kept until the late 1920s when his acting career took off. In 1921 Wilson began studying with Butler Davenport, a theater director. About this time he also took night classes at the American Academy of Dramatic Art in New York while continuing to work for the post office during the day. It's possible his studies with Davenport took place at the Academy.

Wilson got his theater start in 1923 as a writer, not an actor, when two of his plays, *The Heart Breaker* and *A Train North* were staged at a YWCA. These were not the first works he'd written, however. Some of his earlier plays included *Race Pride*, *Friendship*, and *Colored Americans*. In the fall of 1923 Wilson had his first play, *Pa Williams' Gal*, staged at a legitimate theater, the Lafayette. His acting skills by then were honed enough to earn him a role as James Thomas in the 1923 production *Justice*. Asked at the time why he didn't write plays for both whites and blacks and expand his popularity, Wilson responded, "I shall write for one race, and that race is my own. I sincerely feel that when the great American play is written it will come from the heart of my own people."

In 1925 Wilson organized and directed the Aldrich Players, a troupe in Corona, NY, his home on Long Island. Later that year he led a group of twelve African Americans in a ballet called *Skyscrapers* by American John Alden Carpenter at New York's Metropolitan Opera House. The next year Wilson got his first big break with a role in Paul Green's Pulitzer Prize–winning play *In Abraham's Bosom*. The production also featured Rose McClendon with whom he would work frequently both on stage and in radio up until her death in 1936. Just prior to receiving a role in Green's play, Wilson had played in Eugene O'Neill's *All God's Chillun Got Wings* and between the two productions he began getting considerable attention in the African American press.

Wilson's role in the show *In Abraham's Bosom* lasted a year and would have run longer but the show went on tour in the fall of 1927 and he was by then scheduled to play the male lead (with McClendon as the female lead) in *Porgy and Bess*. His Aldrich Players were still around and earned background work in the production. Writing continued to be a successful endeavor for Wilson and his play *Sugar Cane* was published in a 1927 volume called *Plays of Negro Life*. At the same time as *Porgy and Bess* was taking off and *Sugar Cane* appeared in print, his work *Meek Mose* was being produced in New York.

The role of Porgy was perhaps the highlight of Wilson's career, a role with which he would be identified the rest of his life. He played Porgy from autumn 1927 until the summer of 1929 when the cast left for London. In England his troupe performed *Porgy and Bess* for about two months and then *All God's Children Got Wings* for a few weeks. In the meantime his play *Sugar Cane* was produced in November 1928. Wilson returned from England in late summer of 1929 long enough to cast and begin rehearsals for his new play *The Wall Between* before returning to London for a role in *In Abraham's Bosom*.

By October 1929, Wilson was back in the States and touring with the established cast of *Porgy and Bess*. A few months later, on March 12, 1930, he made his first documented radio appearance on a program sponsored by the NAACP. His participation on the WNYC broadcast consisted of giving a talk called "The Negro on the Stage." In 1930 Wilson's prominence in the African American theater community was demonstrated by his election to the Board of Directors of The Florence Mills Theatrical Association. The fall of 1930 found Wilson cast in *Sweet Chariot*, a story of the life of Marcus Garvey. More notably, however, he took parts on **Carlton Moss'** radio program *Careless Love*, an anthology series of dramatic stories focused on black life and utilizing an all-black cast. It should be recognized as the first African American drama program on the air. Though he did not play any recurring roles, Wilson was credited with playing the lead roles week in and week out. In the midst of his stage and radio work yet another of his compositions, *Confidence*, played in Harlem during the fall of 1931.

Weekly appearances on *Careless Love* and stage productions kept Wilson busy through 1931 and in 1932 he added film to his resume when he starred in an Oscar Micheaux picture called *The Girl from Chicago*. For a few weeks in the spring Wilson appeared with several of his *Careless Love* co-stars on a series called **Beale Street Nightlife** on WEAF, a quarter-hour show about life on the famous Memphis street. *Careless Love* left the air in May 1932, but Wilson made at least two other broadcasts that year. In November he recited James Weldon Johnson's "Go Down Death" over WEVD and then on Christmas Day he played the Black Magi on a Nativity special over WJZ with the **Eva Jessye** Choir.

The next year, 1933, proved to be one his busiest in radio up to that point. He started off the year appearing on Rudy Vallee's popular show in January where he was featured in a skit based on *Emperor Jones*. A few weeks later he participated in a relief broadcast over WRNY in February for jobs, clothing, and food for Harlem residents. On it he gave a dramatic reading of Johnson's "God's Trombones." In April 1933, he was cast as Jasper DeVoid, one of two black characters (the other played by **Ernest Whitman**) in *The Townsend Murder Mystery*, a thrice-weekly serial written by Octavus Roy Cohen. The

series left the air in May and Wilson went directly to a role in Carlton Moss' second series, *Folks from Dixie*. A contemporary reviewer insisted that Wilson was "better cast in [*Folks from Dixie*] than in *The Townsend Murder*" and that he gave "a robust and believable interpretation of Booker, and was easily the outstanding artist." *Folks from Dixie* was a short-lived effort lasting only through the summer. In November Wilson was cast in an obscure program called *Shoestring Charlie's Circus* over NBC, a comedy spot with Ernest Whitman. By the end of the year he had taken on some directing duties with the YMCA Players in Harlem which put on several of his plays. Wilson closed out the year with a role in another Micheaux film, *The Phantom of Kenwood*, also starring Carlton Moss.

Radio work was slow in 1934, thus Wilson kept busy with stage work. In October he was cast in a broadcast called *Dismal Swamp* over WMCA. Described as a mystery thriller set in the Deep South, it's not clear if the show was a one-time production or an ongoing series. Also featured in that work were **Richard Huey** and **Georgia Burke** with whom he worked regularly on Moss broadcasts. In December he was cast in Moss' final regular series, *Meetin' House*, the weekly story of a circuit riding preacher (played by Wilson).

While Wilson continued to star in *Meetin' House* over NBC Blue through 1935, he made only a handful of other known radio broadcasts that year. In October he worked a special program called *Negro Achievement* (unlikely related to the *Negro Achievement Hour* of earlier years) over WOR. The broadcast was written by Carlton Moss and dramatized the lives of five notable African Americans. November found Wilson in two features over WEAF, *Echoes of New York* and a separate broadcast sponsored by the YMCA on which he gave a dramatic interpretation of "God's Creation" by James Weldon Johnson.

Meetin' House left the air in August 1936. Earlier that year Wilson narrated the Harlem Easter Parade over WEAF and then worked in the film version of *The Green Pastures* and on various Federal Theater Projects. In October, WMCA broadcast three of his plays and in December he participated in an aural version of *The Green Pastures* with **Rex Ingram** over WOR. That month he also had a role on an episode of an obscure NBC program called *Dreams of Long Ago*. In addition to the series' December 13 broadcast he would return on August 1, 1937, and January 9, 1938.

The members of the Negro Actor's Guild of America elected Wilson as one of the organization's vice-presidents December of 1937. After his January 1938, appearance on *Dreams of Long Ago*, Wilson was featured on **Joe Bostic's** *Tales of Harlem* over WMCA later in the year. He was cast once again in a version of *In Abraham's Bosom* on *Pulitzer Prize Plays* broadcast June 23, 1938, over NBC. Wilson made his first appearance on *Cavalcade of America* on December 25, 1940, and then made a return appearance November 15, 1948. A notable radio credit in 1941 was on *The Columbia Workshop* over CBS in an episode entitled "Jason Was a Man." It featured black stars Juano Hernandez, **Eddie Green**, and **Amanda Randolph** and was also penned by Jack Caldwell. Nineteen forty-one also saw Wilson earn a short-term role on *Young Dr. Malone* on CBS. His character was a native of a Caribbean island where Dr. Malone was visiting. That same year Wilson served as narrator of *Freedom's People*, a program focused on stories of interest to black audiences, and acted with members of the Negro Radio Workshop in an all-black episode of *Forecast* on CBS in August.

In 1943 Frank Wilson acted in at least one broadcast, a National Urban League–sponsored piece over CBS about African American patriotism called "Heroines in Bronze." From 1944 to 1945 he made appearances on several episodes of WMCA's *New World A' Coming*, stories based on Roi Ottley's book of the same name. Wilson's wife passed away during this period and he subsequently seemed to virtually disappear from the airwaves for the next several years. Wilson did play Eddie on *Duffy's Tavern* (a role made famous by Eddie Green and played by several other African American actors) from November 24, 1950, to January 12, 1951. He also earned roles on *Best Plays* (May 1, 1953) and *Eternal Light* (February 15, 1953). Wilson was to land one last radio gig, a role on *The Story of Ruby Valentine*, a daily serial produced by the **National Negro Network** beginning in 1954. It seems appropriate that Wilson would act on this series as it was possibly the last all-black drama to air on radio. With roles on *Careless Love*, the first black dramatic program, and *Ruby Valentine*, the last, Wilson participated in African American dramatized radio from its beginning to its end. Wilson made a few appearances on early 1950s television including roles on *The United States Steel Hour*, *General Electric Theater*, *Ethel and Albert*, and *Studio One*. However, he died in 1956 while the medium was still young.

One note of interest concerns a writer named Frank Wilson who wrote for a number of NBC programs in the 1940s and early 1950s. While so far no evidence has been discovered to prove this was a different Frank Wilson, it seems very likely they were two separate men. Despite some early playwright credits, not once does the black press mention the black Frank Wilson writing for shows such as *Academy Award Theater*, *The Frank Sinatra Show*, or *The Big Show*, all of which had a writer named Frank Wilson. Also, this second Frank Wilson was assigned to the NBC show *Mystery in the Air* in 1947 by J. Walter Thompson, a major advertising company. It seems unlikely that such a business would risk the controversy that could possibly result from assigning a black writer to a mainstream program.

Sources: LOC; Dunning, "Poe on the Radio," p. 7; Grams *Cavalcade*; Grams, *Radio Drama*, pp. 358, 388; Patterson pp. 45–46, 60, 66, 71, 104; Peterson pp. 123–124; Sampson, *Blacks in Black and White*, p. 571; Sampson, *Swingin' on the Ether Waves*, p. 155; Woll pp. 262–263; *Baltimore Afro-American*, December 1, 1928, p. 8, February 6, 1932, p. 22, November 12, 1932, p. 10, January 28, 1933, p. 22, February 25, 1933, p. 17, May 20, 1933, p. 10, June 14, 1941, p. 13, September 27, 1941, p. 14, March 27, 1943, p. 10; *Jet*, May 21, 1953 p. 66; *New York Amsterdam News*, May 23, 1923, p. 5, September 5, 1923, p. 5, September 23, 1925, p. 8, February 17, 1926, p. 5, December 22, 1926, p. 22, September 14, 1927, p. 22, September 28, 1927, p. 8, October 12, 1927, p. 18, December 7, 1927, p. 20, February 1, 1928, p. 20, February 8, 1928, p. 11, November 7, 1928, p. 9, May 1, 1929, p. 13, June 26, 1929, p. 13, August 14, 1929, p. 9, September 11, 1929, p. 9, March 12, 1930, p. 11, August 6, 1930, p. 8, September 3, 1930, p. 9, December 3, 1930, p. 18, November 30, 1932, p. 16, December 21, 1932, p. 7, January 11, 1933, p. 16, February 8, 1933, p. 16, February 22, 1933, p. 16, May 10, 1933, p. 10, December 6, 1933, p. 7, October 12, 1935, p. 11, November 23, 1935, p. 8, January 18, 1936, p. 1, March 14, 1936, p. 8, April 11, 1936, p. 8, October 24, 1936 p. 12, December 26, 1936, p. 17, February 27, 1937, p. 10, December 11, 1937, p. 19, June 25, 1938, p. 9, January 7, 1939, p. 16, May 3, 1941, p. 20, August 9, 1941, p. 21, May 6, 1944, p. 3, June 19, 1954, p. 51, February 25, 1956, p. 3; *Pittsburgh Courier*, November 11, 1933, p. 6, October 11, 1941, p. 20, May 29, 1954, p. 18; http://www.hillbillyheart-throbs.com accessed July 29, 2010.

Wings Over Jordan

The Negro Hour, a Cleveland production started on WGAR July 11, 1937, was broadcast as *Wings Over Jordan* over a 107-station CBS hook-up November 11, 1937. The fifteen-minute program contained five selections sung by the Negro Choir. The Rev. Glenn T. Settle served as the announcer and James Tate directed the choir. The show proved popular enough to warrant a follow-up on December 14 again under the name *Wings Over Jordan*. The series was officially picked up for regular broadcast by CBS beginning January 9, 1938.

Wings Over Jordan followed the same basic format as *The Negro Hour* with the addition of national speakers from major urban centers. The Rev. Joseph Gomez, Cleveland, gave the talk on the debut episode. He was followed by Dr. Charles Hubert, Morehouse College, Atlanta, the Rev. L. K. Williams, Chicago, and Dr. Mordecai Johnson, Howard University president, Washington, D.C. A mini-drama erupted one month into the nation-wide run. Worth Kramer (white), WGAR's program manager, had been brought in initially to prepare the choir for the higher standards expected by CBS. When it became apparent that he would not be stepping aside any time soon, Tate, who had directed the choir since its inception, left the post. Rather than taking the spot himself, Kramer hired Williett Firmbanks for the directorship. When letters of protest poured into the station Firmbanks was promptly put back in her position as pianist and Tate was rehired as director. Kramer ultimately ended up replacing Tate by year's end. Wayne Mack served as announcer from the beginning.

After ten months on the air a second series, *Negro Progress Hour,* was created and broadcast directly after *Wings Over Jordan*. The *Jordan* guest speaker also appeared on the *Progress Hour*. The *Hour* was sponsored by *The Cleveland Call and Post* newspaper.

The Reverend Settle found himself embroiled in controversy in the spring of 1939 when the Baptist Minsters' Conference attempted to have him barred for allowing Pauline Coffee to preach from his pulpit. Allowing a woman such a platform was unacceptable. On February 27, 1939, the Baptist Ministers' Conference "withdrew the right hand of fellowship from the Rev. Glen T. Settle." At the same time Settle was honored by Cleveland's Civic Progressive League for his work on *Wings Over Jordan* and *Negro Progress Hour*. Later in 1939 Settle was listed as an American Negro of Distinguished Achievement for 1939 in a poll sponsored by the Schomburg Collection of Negro Literature of the New York Public Library.

Wings Over Jordan was known not only for its music but for bringing to the air black messages by such speakers as Mary McLeod Bethune and the Rev. Adam Powell, Jr. who were rarely heard on mainstream white media. *Wings Over Jordan* occasionally ran into trouble with its speakers. In April 1939, New Orleans station WWL intermittently interrupted the speaker's message with pre-recorded material. They denied the disruptions were due to race "but said that lately the speakers had been 'straying from the program's original purpose.'" The station ended up dropping the program.

In late 1939 the producers of *Wings Over Jordan* signed an exclusive contract with WGAR for the station to act as the group's promoter and booking agent, the first such contract for WGAR. Six months later in June Settle announced that the contract was being terminated amiably and the station would continue to broadcast the network show. At the same time Worth Kramer left the station and was hired full-time as the choir's director.

After 3½ years on CBS *Wings Over Jordan* was awarded a daily network slot beginning July 28, 1941, which was to last through the summer. Kramer continued to direct and Settle continued as narrator. Just a few months later the weekly Sunday spot was moved later in the morning to better accommodate listeners on the West Coast, demonstrating the popularity of *Wings Over Jordan* nationwide. Soon after, Ohio governor John Bricker proclaimed September 29, 1941, Wings Over Jordan Day in Columbus, OH. Still, sponsorship continued to elude the choir.

Worth Kramer, *Wings* director, stepped down from his post in early 1942 for a management position with a West Virginia station. He was subsequently replaced by 27-year-old Gladys Olga Jones, a graduate of Dillard University, Joseph Powe, and Hattye Easley. The directorial turn-over ended when Maurice Goldman (who was white) was hired

at the end of 1943. Statements indicate the organization felt the hiring was crucial to "revitalizing the work of this famed ... organization looking toward the post-war world."

During the war the Wings choir did their part to bolster morale on the home front by participating in bond drives and offering the speaker's microphone to the Office of War Information. Known for touring extensively around the country, during the early 1940s the choir increased its presence at military facilities. Beginning in May 1945, the *Wings Over Jordan* choir left the air for a ten-month tour of Europe to entertain troops. They returned to CBS March 3, 1946.

On August 10, 1947, the Wings choir celebrated its 500th broadcast over CBS. The milestone was tarnished soon after when members of the choir went public with deep grievances against Settle and his management of the organization. Claiming poor working conditions and morale, the entire choir refused to perform by the end of the month as long as Settle was in charge. In response, many original members were brought in to take over singing duties. While internal dissension continued, CBS decided the choir no longer had a place on their network and terminated its Sunday morning broadcasts in October 1947. Ultimately *Wings Over Jordan* returned to the air in January 1949, on the Mutual radio network but its popularity never again reached the heights of earlier years which included records and film appearances in addition to sold-out concert tours and weekly network radio.

Sources: Barnett; Balk p. 204; Barlow p. 34; Dunning p. 574; Ward pp. 26–28; *Cleveland Call and Post*, November 4, 1937, p. 1, November 25, 1937, p. 2, January 6, 1938, p. 2, January 13, 1938, p. 1, February 10, 1938, p. 1, February 17, 1938, p. 7, February 24, 1938, p. 3, November 10, 1938, p. 3, December 29, 1938, p. 8, January 5, 1939, p. 3, 12, March 2, 1939, p. 1, 3, March 16, 1939, p. 1, May 4, 1939, p. 2, October 26, 1939, p. 1, January 4, 1940, p. 3, February 15, 1939, p. 12, June 29, 1940 p. 1, July 19, 1941, p. 1, August 2, 1941, p. 2, September 20, 1941, p. 9, September 27, 1941, p. 3,

March 7, 1942, p. 1, June 27, 1942, p. 12, October 31, 1942, p. 20, March 6, 1943, p. 5B, December 11, 1943, p. 8, February 23, 1946, p. 5B, August 2, 1947, p. 6B, August 30, 1947, p. 1, September 13, 1947, p. 7B, October 18, 1947, p. 1, January 8, 1949, p. 3.

Woodlawn Radio Association

The Woodlawn Radio Association was an early Chicago-area organization of radio enthusiasts. A 1915 report indicates Sumner Webster served as president, Arthur Turnbull as vice-president, Arthur Sarenlock as chief operator, Robert Martin as secretary, and Theodore Teves as treasurer.

Sources: *Chicago Defender*, October 2, 1915, p. 4, October 9, 1915, p. 6, October 16, 1915, p. 6.

Yeates, Ray

Ray Yeates hailed from Winston, NC, and was educated at Hampton Institute before beginning his professional singing career in New York. His first known gig was a role in *Blackbirds of 1928*. In the early 1930s Yeates received perhaps his first radio exposure when he began singing tenor with **Eva Jessye's Dixie Jubilee Singers**. He continued with them at least until 1941 by which time he was one of the group's longest-running members. Not long after starting with the Jubilee Singers Yeates began singing with the **Four Dusty Travelers**, Columbia recording artists and regular radio singers. That quartet also included James Waters, 2nd tenor, **Jester Hairston**, baritone, and Viviande Carr, bass. Along the way Yeates was cast in **Hall Johnson's** *Run, Little Chillun* and served as director of music at the Waters Institute. Other theater credits include *Stevedore* (1934), *Porgy and Bess* (1935), and *John Henry* (1940).

During the early 1940s Yeates was credited with writing ABC's Sunday morning show *Good Will Hour*. In 1942 he was invited to join the **Southernaires** when first tenor **Homer Smith** left to join the Coast Guard.

The Southernaires, a radio staple on NBC since 1930, became the third musical outfit with which Yeates performed on radio. His place with the Southernaires lasted eight years until 1950 when he either quit or was fired depending upon the source.

Sources: Woll pp. 93, 127, 140, 158; *Baltimore African American*, April 7, 1934, p. 7, July 19, 1941, p. 8, January 14, 1950, p. 8, April 22, 1950, p. 8, January 22, 1966, p. 11; *New York Amsterdam News*, October 14, 1931, p. 7, March 16, 1932, p. 9, May 24, 1933, p. 16; *Pittsburgh Courier*, January 16, 1943, p. 20.

YMCA Quartet

The YMCA Quartet consisted of James Woodruff, first tenor, Jefferson Howge, second tenor, L. Brown, baritone, and Care Taylor, bass. They appeared on the short-lived *YMCA Hour* over WOR, New York, during the summer of 1929 as well as on self-titled slots on WRNY and WGBS.

Source: *New York Amsterdam News*, July 10, 1929, p. 11.

Zora Hurston's Choral Group

Zora Hurston's Choral Group was an artistic endeavor by the famed Harlem Renaissance writer Zora Neale Hurston which had as its goal the presentation of all-black music to listeners. Primarily a stage show, the act made at least three radio performances in February and March 1932, over WOR. The Group's singers were Percy Potter, **Georgia Burke**, Rosetta Crawford, Viola Anderson, Dora Bacote, Bruce Howard, Sarah Evans, Reginald Allday, Red Davis, William Winters, Alfred Strouchan, Joseph Neely, Leonard Sturrup, John Dawson, Nehemiah Cash. Actress **Georgette Harvey** served as the production's master of ceremonies.

Source: *New York Amsterdam News*, March 2, 1932, p. 9.

Appendix 1: Debuts and Notable Events

This brief chronology places the series' debuts and selected notable events discussed in this book in their proper historical sequence. It also includes such milestones as the beginning and ending of radio's golden age and the formation of the major networks. This gives the reader an overview of developments in African American radio in relation to the wider broadcasting industry.

1920

Pittsburgh's KDKA goes on the air, generally considered the beginning of commercial radio.

1921

Lois Deppe and Earl Hines sing over KDKA, widely credited as first black performances on radio.

Bernice Ellis sings over unknown Fort Smith, AR, station. Considered by some to be the first black performer on radio.

1922

Maude Hall discusses fashion on weekly broadcasts.

1923

Duke Ellington on air.

Shuffle Along musical broadcast on KDKA.

1924

Jack Cooper, possibly the first African American announcer, begins on WCAP.

Louis Armstrong likely on radio with Fletcher Henderson's Orchestra over unknown New York station.

1926

National Broadcasting Company forms.

Sam 'n' Henry (serial-comedy, WGN) ends 1927.

1927

The Pittsburgh Courier Hour, later *Floyd Calvin Hour* (music and speakers, WGBS) ends 1928.

1928

Amos 'n' Andy (serial-comedy, WMAQ) ends 1943.

Black Cameos (drama and comedy sketches, WOR) ends after three months.

Cabin Door (dialect comedy, WEAF) ends 1929.

Columbia Broadcasting System forms.

Cellar Knights (comedy, WABC) ends 1929.

169

Negro Achievement Hour (music and speakers, WABC, New York) ends 1930.

Pullman Porters' Hour (music and speakers, WEVD) end date unknown.

1929

All-Negro Hour (variety, WSBC) ends 1935.

Aunt Mandy's Chillun (drama and comedy sketches and music, WOR) ends 1930.

Cabin Nights (comedy sketches and music, WJZ) ends 1929.

Truths About Harlem (music and speakers, WGBS).

1930

Alpha and Omega Opera Company de Luxe (comedy, WEAF) ends 1930.

Aunt Mandy's Kitchen (unknown content, WPAP) ends 1930.

Baltimore Achievement Hour (music and speakers, WFBR) end date unknown.

Cab Calloway debuts on radio.

Careless Love (drama, WEAF) ends 1932.

Dinah and Dora (comedy, WEAF) ends 1930.

Interracial Musical Hour (music, WGBS) end date unknown.

Moe Levy & Son's Colored Review (music, WOR) ends 1930.

Negro Achievement Hour (music and talks, WHP, Harrisburg, PA) end date unknown.

Negro Musical Hour (music, WMCA) ends 1930.

Sam and Jenny (dialect comedy, WAAT) ends 1930.

Southernaires debut on radio and air, broadcast weekly until 1950.

1932

Beale Street Nightlife (comedy-drama sketch, WEAF) ends 1932.

Colored Kiddies' Radio Hour (children's, WPEN) ends 1933.

Evelyn Preer Memorial Program (variety, KRKD) ends 1937.

Harlem Fantasies (music, WEAF) ends 1932.

National Negro Forum (current events, WEVD) end date unknown.

Negro Business Hour (business speakers and music, WCBM) ends 1932.

Negro Forum Hour (current events, WEVD) end date unknown.

Slow River (music, NBC) ends 1933.

Standard Theatre's Kiddies Radio Review (children's talent show, WDAS) ends 1932.

1933

Folks from Dixie (comedy, NBC) ends 1933.

John Henry, Black River Giant (drama, CBS) ends 1933.

Rocking Chair Memories (music, NBC) ends 1933.

Townsend Murder Mystery (drama, NBC) ends 1933.

1934

Count Basie on radio.

Gibson Family (musical, NBC) ends 1935.

Jimmy Scribner's *The Johnson Family* debuts (dialect comedy, WLW) ends 1950.

Meetin' House (drama, NBC) ends 1936.

Mutual Broadcasting Company forms.

1935

A Harlem Family (serial, WMCA) ends 1935.

Harlem on Parade (music, WHN) ends 1935.

Man About Harlem (current events, WBNX) ends 1935.

Muddy Waters (drama, WBNX) ends 1935.

1936

Good Time Society (music, WJZ) ends 1937.

Harlem Varieties (music, WMCA) ends 1936.

1937

Eddie Anderson joins *The Jack Benny Show* (comedy, NBC).

National Negro Hour (speakers and music, WGAR) ends 1938.

Tales of Harlem (variety, WMCA) ends 1939.

Wings Over Jordan (speakers and music, WGAR) ends 1947.

1938

Echoes of Harlem (human interest, WBNX) ends 1938.

Harlem Headlines (interviews and news, WMCA) ends 1938.

Ma Johnson's Harlem Rooming House (serial, WINS) ends 1939.

Negro Progress Hour (speakers and music, WGAR) ends 1940.

1939

Marian Anderson sings from the Lincoln Memorial.

Negro Business Hour (speakers and music, WHK) ends 1949.

1940

Sheep and Goats Club (comedy sketches, WOR) ends 1940.

1941

Forecast (variety, CBS) one episode.

Freedom's People (drama, NBC) ends 1942.

King Biscuit Time (music, KFFA) still on the air.

Native Sons (drama, WNYC) ends 1941.

Those Who Made Good (drama, WNYC) ends 1942.

Tribute to Unsung Americans (drama, WMCA) ends 1941.

1943

American Broadcasting Company forms.

Jubilee (variety, AFRS) ends 1953.

1944

Henry Allen, American (serial, WNYC) ends 1944.

Men O' War (speakers and music, CBS).

New World A' Coming (drama and current events, WMCA) ends 1944.

1945

Al Benson debuts on radio (disc jockey, WGES).

Beulah (comedy, NBC) ends 1954.

1946

Democracy—USA (drama, WBBM) ends 1948.

Nat King Cole receives network show (music, NBC) ends 1948.

1947

Here Comes Tomorrow (serial, WJJD) ends 1948.

Negro Newsfront (news, WJJD) ends 1952.

Star Quest (talent show, WBBM) ends 1947.

1948

Destination Freedom (drama, WMAQ) ends 1950.

Harlem, USA (variety, WMCA) ends 1950.

1949

Brown Women in White (current events, NBC) ends 1949.

1953

Man of Color (interviews and current events, KECA) ends 1954.

National Negro Network forms.

Negro Radio Stories, Inc. forms.

1954

Amos 'n' Andy Music Hall (music, CBS) ends 1960.

Story of Ruby Valentine (serial, syndicated) ends 1955.

1962

Considered the end of radio's golden age when *Suspense* and *Yours Truly, Johnny Dollar* go off the air.

Appendix 2: Episode Guides to Two Early Series

The detailed contents of most of the radio series profiled in this book remain elusive to current researchers. However, *The New York Amsterdam News* and *The Baltimore Afro-American* newspapers frequently provided weekly descriptions of *The Negro Achievement Hour* and *The Negro Art Group Hour*, two of the earliest African American radio series. The following episode guides for these two series are included to shed light on speakers and entertainers who were of interest to black radio listeners between 1928 and 1930, the early years of commercial radio.

The Negro Achievement Hour

JANUARY 26, 1928—This premier broadcast featured W.C. Handy, Father of the Blues, with his daughters Catherine, Lucille, and Elizabeth and son William.

FEBRUARY 2, 1928—Talk by Romeo L. Dougherty, sport and theatrical editor for the *New York Amsterdam News*, on African American achievement in various sports. Also, a short history of the growth of *The Amsterdam News*.

FEBRUARY 9, 1928—Produced by Florence Mills Theatrical Association. Performers included: Chappell and Stinnette, Tom Fletcher, Abbie Mitchell, Eva Taylor and Clarence Williams, W. C. Elkins and his Dexter Chorus. Talk: Jesse Shipp, president of the Theatrical Association.

FEBRUARY 16, 1928—Talk: Matthew Henson and his 1903 trip to the North Pole with Robert Peary. Also, J. LeCount Chestnut,

New York manager of *The Baltimore Afro-American*. The evening's program was supervised by A. D. Clark of WABC and the announcer was H. P. Sampson. Deacon Johnson, president and directing manager of the Clef Club from 1915 to 1919, arranged the musical entertainment which included vocal solos by Mitchell Lewis ("Blue Heaven"), F. Addison ("Broken Hearted"), and Arthur "Strut" Payne ("Loves Old Sweet Song"). Wayne Talbert played piano while William Jordan sang "Here Comes Miss Clementine." J. Arthur Gaines sang "Go Down Moses" while W. P. Tiller and Ernest Elliott accompanied on saxophones with William Cole on piano.

MARCH 1, 1928—Speaker: John M. Royall, president of the Upper Harlem Board of Real Estate Brokers, on problems in Harlem's real estate market.

MARCH 8, 1928—Speaker: Eugene Kinckle Jones, executive secretary of the National Urban League. Music: George Webb, teacher and organist from Newark. Performers included Arthur Foster, Dr. L. Rolorfort, Dr. L. Davenport, Joseph Woodie, John O'Fake, Albert Tillary, the Bach Quartet, and the Syncopated Five.

MARCH 15, 1928—Speakers: Lemuel Foster, New York representative of the Victory Life Insurance Company, Anthony B. Overton, and Dr. P. Savory. Music: Edward Margetson, director of the Schubert Music Club, and Church of Crucifixion choir.

MARCH 22, 1928—Master of Ceremonies: Charles Johnson, editor of *Opportunity* magazine. Speaker: Dr. Albert Barnes, founder and president of the Barnes Foundation, on African art. Artists: Countee Cullen, Arna Bontemps, Helene Johnson, Gwendolyn Bennett and Aaron Douglas. Music: Violinist David Auld, tenor Alexander Gatewood, pianist Jessie Covington, and soloist Lyndon Hoffman-Caldwell.

MARCH 29, 1928—Special two-hour program. The first hour featured Wilson Lamb, concert singer and voice instructor, accompanied by Cora Wynn Alexander and choir. The second hour focused on Lincoln University. Dr. E. Roberts, president of the Alumni Association and board of trustees member spoke as did Dr. W. Alexander, a former member of the Assembly of New Jersey who was then working for the Lincoln Endowment Fund. The Lincoln University Quartet, glee club, orchestra, and violin trio all provided musical selections under the direction of James Dorsey.

APRIL 5, 1928—Master of Ceremonies: Dr. Peter Murray. Speaker: Harry Pace, president of Northeastern Life Insurance Co., on "the Business of Life Insurance Among Colored People." Music: Charlotte Murray, Raymond Claymes, Gertrude Martin, S. B. Moss, and Florence Jones.

APRIL 12, 1928—Speaker: Philadelphia representative and sports critic for *The Pittsburgh Courier*, W. Rollo Wilson, on "Sport Shoes, Past and Present." Profiled many black athletes including Bill Richmond, Peter Jackson, George Dixon, and the Negro National League. Music: Olyve Jeter directed the choir of the Grace Congregational Church and Hugo Bornn performed.

APRIL 19, 1928—Speaker: E. Washington Rhodes, editor of *The Philadelphia Tribune* and Assistant U.S. Attorney for Eastern Pennsylvania. Music: The Imperial Elks No. 127 band played popular tunes.

APRIL 26, 1928—This hour was sponsored by the National Health Circle for Colored People, Inc. Master of ceremonies and speaker: Dr. Louis Wright, executive committee chairman, on "The Objects of the Organization." Also, Belle Davis, executive secretary of the Health Circle, and H. Hunt, principal of the Fort Valley High and Industrial School of Fort Valley, GA. Music: Rebecca DeGreer Norcom, Minnie Brown, soprano, Lydia Mason, David Johnson, Jr., violin, and Beatrice Henderson. Also, Countee Cullen read some of his poetry.

MAY 3, 1928—The Intercollegiate Association was responsible for this week's broadcast. Master of Ceremonies: Aston Sewell, vice-president of the association. Speaker: Lucille Spence. Music: Elanorist Young, pianist, Leslie Coles, tenor, Ethel Clark, Raymond Claymes, baritone, and a 20-voice choir from the New York Choral Art School.

MAY 17, 1928—Master of Ceremonies: Binga Dismond, then the world record holder in quarter mile. Speaker: J. Finley Wilson, grand exalted ruler of the Elks. Music: Edward Errington Steel, piano, Florence Jordan, Francis Ceciton, Gertrude Martin, *Keep Shufflin'* Glee Club, and Gilbert Holland, cast member of *Keep Shufflin'*. Andrew Mitchell, exalted ruler of the Manhattan lodge, recited the Elks' Code.

JUNE 7, 1928—Speaker: A. M. Wendell Malliett, secretary of the sponsoring West Indian Committee, on "West Indies, Its Men and their Achievement." Director: Dr. P. Savory. Music: Mrs. Domingo, arranger, J. Dewitt Spencer, Loretta Anthony, Mrs. Jackson, and Domingo.

JUNE 15, 1928—Sponsor: The Harlem Life Insurance Company. Speaker: Pope Billups.

Music: Arthur Nixon of the Nixon School of Music.

JUNE 22, 1928—Sponsor: *Africa* magazine, published by Continental African Publishing. Speaker: Duse Mohammed Ali, *Africa* editor, spoke on "African Origins." Music: Edet Effong of Nigeria led a West African drum group. Also, Mudge Paris, West African baritone.

JUNE 29, 1928—Speaker: Robert Nelson, managing editor of *The Washington Eagle*.

JULY 13, 1928—Sponsor: Gossip publication *The Interstate Tattler*. Master of Ceremonies: Floyd Nelson, Jr., theatrical editor. Speaker: Geraldyne Dismond, managing editor of the *Tattler*, on "Newspaper women of the Negro Press." Music: Jazzmania Negrotesques, a musical company formed by producer Clarence Robinson. Performers included in the troupe were Maude Russell, Honey Brown, Margaret Lee, Four Pepper Shakers, and Johnny Vigal, all of whom were formerly of the black musical *Keep Shufflin'*.

JULY 20, 1928—Master of Ceremonies: Alderman Fred Moore, editor of *The New York Age*. Speaker: Attorney Myrtle Anderson Howard, president of the Myrtle Anderson Women's League. Music: Loretta Anthony, Merrill Dames, Ruth Ellis, Raymond Waters, Viola Anderson, and members of the Women's League, Thelma Lippins, soprano, Cecil Scott, reader, and Zorlida Wilson and Byron Smith, duet.

AUGUST 10, 1928—Master of Ceremonies: Bessye Rearden, New York representative of *The Chicago Defender*. Speaker: Eugene Gordon, journalist for *The Boston Post*.

AUGUST 17, 1928—Sponsor: The Negro Business League. Presentations: "Insurance" and "Business Women" by unknown speakers

AUGUST 24, 1928—Master of Ceremonies: Mabel Laws Horsey, New York talent booking agent. Music: Unnamed quartet and orchestra. Billy Pierce arrangement of Taps.

SEPTEMBER 7, 1928—Presentations: Various arts and crafts. Also, short sketches on African American achievement.

SEPTEMBER 14, 1928—Sponsor: YMCA.

Speaker: Caroline Bagley, author of "My Trip Thru Egypt and the Holy Land." At the time she was considered one of the most widely traveled black women. Program arranged by E. B. Weatherless, Director of the Department of Service and Activities.

SEPTEMBER 21, 1928—William Elkins was schedule to present a musical program in conjunction with the Acme Mutual Taxpayer Liability Insurance Co. There was also to be a short talk on the history of Harlem's growth. Technical difficulties at the station, however, forced the program to be rescheduled for October 5th.

OCTOBER 5, 1928—Music: William Elkins and an orchestra under his direction and the Brooklyn Choral Club. Speaker: E. B. Weatherless read a talk by Caroline Bagley who was unable to appear. Originally scheduled for September 21, the program was moved to October due to technical problems.

OCTOBER 12, 1928—Speaker: Robert Vann, chairman of the Eastern Publicity Committee for Colored Republicans. The original line-up was changed for unknown reasons. The advertised guests were: Sponsor: The Harlem Lawyer's Association. Speaker: William Eustice, attorney. Music: The Choral Art Society Glee Club, directed by John Johnson. Also, the Instrumental Trio of the S. Coleridge Taylor Art Society and piano selections by Carrie Overton and Wesley Graves. Voice selections by Essie Frierson, soprano, and Mildred Johnson, soprano. They appeared the following week.

OCTOBER 19, 1928—Sponsor: The Harlem Lawyer's Association. Speaker: William Eustice, attorney. Music: Will Vodery, arranger, composer, and song writer, and J. Berni Barbour. Vodery had written musical numbers for Klaw and Erlanger, Schubert, and Florenz Ziegfeld. Also, performances by Della Sutton and her Melody Girls Orchestra, the Choral Art Society Glee Club, directed by John Johnson, and the Instrumental Trio of the S. Coleridge Taylor Art Society. Piano selections by Carrie Overton and Wesley Graves and voice selections by Essie Frierson, soprano, and Mildred Johnson, soprano.

NOVEMBER 2, 1928—Billed as the "last in the series of the Republican Negro Achievement Hours." Speaker: George Harris, editor of *The New York News*. Music: Prof. C. F. LeCarr, director of the choir of the Mother AME Zion Church.

NOVEMBER 16, 1928—Sponsored by Omega Psi Phi Fraternity. Speaker: George Hall, attorney, on "Achievements of the Negro in Business and Music." Additional lectures by Stanley Douglas, attorney, on the history of Omega Psi Chi and Alexander Miller on the achievement projects of the fraternity. Performances arranged by Miller, keeper of records of the Zeta Psi chapter in Brooklyn. Music: William Pickens, Jr., Lydell Usher, and Clarence Johnson. Dramatic reading: Beatrice Henderson.

DECEMBER 14, 1928—Sponsor: Harlem Tuberculosis and Health Committee. Speaker: Dr. Peyton Anderson, chairman of the Medical Committee of the Harlem Committee, on the work of the Medical Committee.

DECEMBER 28, 1928—Sponsor: *The American Recorder*. Directed by Mr. Malliett of the *Recorder*.

JANUARY 4, 1929—Sponsor: The North Harlem Medical Society. Master of Ceremonies: Dr. Binga Dismond. Speakers: Walter White, assistant executive secretary of the NAACP, and Dr. Louis Wright, president of the Society.

JANUARY 11, 1929—This week's broadcast celebrated the fiftieth consecutive week of broadcasting for *The Negro Achievement Hour*. Two hours were devoted to the event which included persons and organizations that had taken part in the various programs over the past year. Participants were asked to contribute something toward purchasing a work of art depicting Negro achievement. The purchase—a painting by Aaron Douglas—was presented to Arthur Clark, WABC station director. A purse was given to Bradford Browe, the station's manager. Guest speakers included Dr. W. Alexander (medicine), Eugene Gordon (journalism,) Eugene Kinckle Jones (social service work), Harry Pace (in-surance), Anthony Overton and Charles Spaulding (business), Prof. Alain Locke (education), J. Finley Wilson (fraternal orders), and Alexander Miller (college fraternities). Artists included Eugene Kinckle Jones, the Martin Trio, Bessya Rearden, Harry Pace, Eugene Gordon, Noah Thompson, Chauncey Northern, tenor, Ivy Nugen, Ruby Green, Eugene Jackson, Dr. Channing Tobias, Empire Jubilee Quartet, Dr. Walter Alexander, Charlotte Murray, Alexander Miller, J. Bernie Barbour, Charlotte Hasa, Catherine Handy, W. C. Handy, Jr., Fats Waller, Jimmy Johnston, J. A. Jackson, Eugene Jordon, Jr. The committee of sponsors was headed by Benjamin Thomas of the Broadway Auto School.

JANUARY 18, 1929—Sponsor: The Epsilon Sigma Chapter of the Phi Beta Sigma fraternity. Speakers: H. E. Williams, attorney, and C. D. King on the history of the Phi Beta Sigma fraternity and its achievements. Also, Ruth Ellis. Music: Empire Jubilee Singers.

JANUARY 25, 1929—Sponsor: Citizens' Welfare Council, a coalition of welfare and social workers' organizations which focused on housing, employment, health education, social welfare, voter registration, and civic improvement. Speaker: Dr. Charles Butler.

FEBRUARY 22, 1929—Speaker: the Rev. George Miller, rector of St. Augustine Church in Brooklyn. Music: Luther King, singer.

MARCH 1, 1929—Sponsor: The New York Howard Club. Speaker: Dr. Mordecai Johnson, president of Howard University. Music: Arranged by Dr. Melville Charlton and included Charlotte Wallace Murray, mezzo soprano, Marguerite Kennerly Upshur, pianist, Alexander Gatewood, tenor, and Dr. Charlton, accompanist. Special songs of the university were sung by the Howard Quartet of New York headed by attorney George Hall.

MARCH 8, 1929—Multiple musician's appeared on this broadcast including featured singer Cora Green, the Wanderers Quartet, Clint and Marie of Sam Russel's *Quakertown Scandals*, W. C. Handy, Maude Russell, and Lucille Hegamin. Program arranged by Geraldyn Dismond.

MARCH 15, 1929—Sponsor: Zeta Phi Beta. Speaker: Josephine Carroll on the organization.

MARCH 29, 1929—Sponsor: The Johnson C. Smith University Club of New York. Master of Ceremonies: Club president James Allen. Speaker: Armond Scott, Washington, D.C. Smith's official representative on the program was Capt. John Edgar Smith. Music: Richard Allen, Atlantic City, Gladys Freeland, Revella McCrogrey, Elnorist Young, and a college orchestra. Dramatic reading: Gertrude Hill.

APRIL 12, 1929—Sponsor: The Clef Club Minstrel Show under the direction of Joseph J. Boris. Master of Ceremonies: Sam Patterson. The cast included singers, instrumentalists, quartet, trio, and orchestra.

The complete program was as follows: "Come Along Children" entire ensemble (opening); "Lucy" Jim Hunt (end Song); "Marie" Andrew Meade (tenor solo); "I'll Be Ready" "Peter on the Sea" Clef Club Quartet (spirituals); "Muddy Waters" Tom Bethel (end song); "Kansas City Kitty" Orchestra (instrumental selection); "Don't Be Like That" Alex Johnson (baritone solo); Comic song by Mitchell Lewis, Bert Williams impersonator; "Dat's Gwine to Be a Landslide" William Elkins (bass solo); and "Outside" Junk Edwards (end song).

APRIL 26, 1929—Sponsor: The Bordentown Manual Training School of New Jersey. Speakers: W. Valentine, school principal, and Garland Anderson under arrangement of *The Amsterdam News*. Music: The Bordentown glee club, a 25-voice mixed chorus, and a male quartet made up of Saffel Huggs, tenor, Basil Lewis, baritone, Timothy Cox, bass, and Ira Godwin, leader. All music directed by Professor Frederick Work, Fisk University. Program arranged by Lester Granger, extension worker for Bordentown.

MAY 3, 1929—Speaker: Dr. Gilber Jones, president of Wilberforce University. Music: The Wilberforce Quartet. Dramatic reading: Richard Harrison.

MAY 10, 1929—Sponsor: The Braithwaite School of Business. Speaker: I. Newton Braithwaite, founder and director of the school, on "The Negro in Business."

JUNE 14, 1929—Sponsor: The Carlton Avenue branch of the YMCA. Speaker: Alexander Miller on the organization's Camp Carlton. Program arranged by E. B. Weatherless.

JUNE 21, 1929—Sponsor: The Utopia Children's Home. Speaker: Daisy Reed, house president, on the work being done at the Home. Poem recitation: Jessale Harris, "To the Negro Child" dedicated to the Children's Home. Music: Carl Diton, Rebecca Norcom and the Utopia Glee Club, under the direction of Bertha DeaVerney.

JUNE 28, 1929—Sponsor: The Lincoln Secretarial School. Speakers: Gwendolyn Bennett and George Smith. Music: The Four Muskateers Quartet of Montclair, NJ.

AUGUST 16, 1929—Sponsor: The Monarch Band, under the direction of Lieut. Simpson. Speakers: J. Finley Wilson and Casper Holstein (introduced by Alderman Fred Moore). Music: The first documented appearance of the Negro Achievement Quartet, a group that would appear intermittently until the end of the known broadcasts. Musical arrangements by Dr. H. Binga Dismond.

AUGUST 30, 1929—This was the *Negro Achievement Hour*'s 85th and final broadcast over WABC. It moved from Friday nights to Sunday afternoons (1:45–2:45) over Jersey City's WAAT. In an attempt to bolster listenership the show began giving away prizes which included a scholarship to the Lincoln Secretarial School ($130), a radio, and a speaker.

SEPTEMBER 15, 1929—Speaker: Hubert Delany, Assistant U.S. Attorney and candidate for Congress.

SEPTEMBER 22, 1929—Speaker: Dr. William Byrd who was building a community church in Jersey City.

OCTOBER 20, 1929—Sponsor: The Columbus Hill Center. This musical program featured various individual and group performances.

The DECEMBER 4, 1929, issue of *The New York Amsterdam News* publicized the winners of the *Achievement Hour*'s popularity contest.

First prize (a Lincoln Secretarial scholarship valued at $150) was awarded to the Independent Musical Mixed Quartette of Newark, NJ. Catherine Cook of Jersey City was awarded 2nd place, a radio set. The Negro Achievement Quartette of Montclair, NJ, took 3rd prize, a radio speaker. In addition, the Bonnemere Brothers won a $500 accident policy. Other contestants included were the Golden Leaf Quartette, Mrs. Joseph Judkins of Plainfield, NJ, Prof. A. E. Nixon, Joseph Hayes, The Gay Pirateers of Brooklyn, Leonard De Paue of Jersey City, Adena Kelley, and Pearl Lawreance of Newark, NJ. The contest, which ran for eight weeks, resulted in more than 800 votes being cast.

DECEMBER 29, 1929—Four months after moving to WAAT the *Negro Achievement Hour* aired its last broadcast over the station.

MARCH 13, 1930—Three months after leaving Jersey City's WAAT the *Negro Achievement Hour* is resurrected on WRNY. The *Hour* was a presentation of the Harlem Broadcasting Corporation, an organization with studios located in the Tri-Borough Building on Lenox Avenue. The corporation's purpose, according to Joseph Boris, was to give Harlem a broadcasting voice. Rudy Horst, Jr., who had been involved with the *Hour* at both WABC and WAAT prior, announced its debut on a third station. The featured speaker was Hubert Delany, assistant U.S. attorney for the Southern District of New York, who spoke on the work of the NAACP. George Garner also gave a talk. Performers included the Negro Achievement Quartet, W.C. Handy, Cooper and Sam, Eddie Green, Louise Morgan, Sam Paige, ye Olde Neste Three, Josephine Hall, Olivia Ward Bush-Benke, and Chauncey Lee.

MARCH 20, 1930—Sponsor (first half): Theta Psi chapter of Omega Psi Phi. Speaker: Clarence Johnson, fraternity member. Program arranged by E. B. Weatherless. Music: The Harlem Studio Ensemble under the direction of Cecil Monroe. Also, a quartet from the black Broadway comedy *Sun Down*, Lucille Jackson, soloist, and Cooper and Sam, ventriloquists. Sponsor (second half): The

Lincoln Recreation Center. Speaker: Helen Henning. Music: The Jubilee Chorus, under the direction of Harry Freeman.

MARCH 27, 1930—Sponsor: The New York Educational Department in connection with the Improved and Benevolent Protective Order of the Elks of the World. Speaker: James Allen, grand auditor as appointed by New York's director of education, on educational work and a national oratorical contest.

APRIL 3, 1930—Speaker: J. Finley Wilson. Music: Arranged and directed by Immense Thespian, Inc., a theatrical agency headed by John Carey.

APRIL 10, 1930—Speaker: George Harris, editor of *The New York News*, on the newspaper. The Artists' Bureau of the Harlem Broadcasting Corp. arranged the music which featured the Negro Achievement Quartet, Ernie Ferguson's Midnight Ramblers, and Frances Miller Grant.

APRIL 17, 1930—Speaker: Roberta Ole, The Madame C. J. Walker Manufacturing Company, on "Negro women who [were] striving to better their economic conditions." Music: Virginia Garvin, a member of the "Great Day" chorus, arranged the songs, some of which were performed by the Virginia Four. The National Negro Pageant, Inc., an organization which raised money for scholarships and educational tours, contributed to the *Hour* as well.

APRIL 24, 1930—Music: Chauncey Northern, tenor, presented his Northern Vocal Art Group. The group performed several spirituals. In addition, the National Negro Pageant Association presented the New Negro Art Theatre, under the direction of Hensley Winfield. Winfield was assisted by Dr. Gertrude Fayde, Olivia Moore, Eulde Braithwaite, Inez Clough, and James Allen.

MAY 1, 1930—Music: The Brooklyn Male Choral club. Featured officers of the club were Dr. William Morcom, president, James Mitchell, vice-president, A. Jerome Loring, corresponding secretary, Phillip Carpenter, financial secretary, Henry Walker, treasurer, and Joseph Snow, manager. Also, Dr. Gertrude Fayde and Hensley Winfield presented another sketch which starred an ensemble under the direction of David Johnson.

MAY 8, 1930—For the third straight week the *Hour* focused on musical performances. The Negro Achievement Quartet headlined and award-winning students of the David Johnson Studio also played. The students, who won first place in the district contest of the New York Music Week Association, were Edwina Coker, Dorothy Marks, Raymond Waters, and Austin Hall. Wilfred Loveland, violinist, also performed.

MAY 15, 1930—Sponsor: The Alpha Phi Alpha Fraternity. Speaker: Lloyd Cofer, representative of Alpha Phi Alpha, on "Go to High School, Go to College." Music: The Northern Vocal Art Group.

The JUNE 11, 1930, edition of the *New York Amsterdam News* reports that the *Negro Achievement Hour* had moved to station WWRL and would be broadcast from the studios of the Harlem Broadcasting Corporation from 9:00 to 10:00 on Wednesday evenings. WWRL was owned by the Long Island Broadcasting Corp. and was too small to be listed in radio listings of the city's newspapers.

Negro Art Group Hour

FEBRUARY 10, 1928—Winifred Watson, soprano; Lydia Mason, piano; Ira Reid, poet; C. Carroll Clarke, baritone.

FEBRUARY 17, 1928—Winifred Watson, soprano; Lydia Mason, piano; Ira Reid, poet; C. Carroll Clarke, baritone.

FEBRUARY 24, 1928—Winifred Watson, soprano; Lydia Mason, piano; Ira Reid, poet; C. Carroll Clarke, baritone; Andrew Taylor, baritone.

MARCH 2, 1928—Winifred Watson, soprano; Edith Benjamin, reader; A. Carroll Clarke, baritone; Andrew Taylor, baritone; Lydia Mason, piano.

MARCH 16, 1928—Winifred Watson, soprano; Edith Benjamin, reader; A. Carroll Clarke, baritone; Lydia Mason, piano.

MARCH 23, 1928—Winifred Watson, soprano; Edith Benjamin, reader; A. Carroll Clarke, baritone; Andrew Taylor, baritone; Lydia Mason, piano.

APRIL 13, 1928—Winifred Watson, soprano; Edith Benjamin, reader; A. Carroll Clarke, baritone; Andrew Taylor, baritone; Lydia Mason, piano.

MAY 4, 1928—Edith Benjamin, reader; Andrew Taylor, baritone; Lydia Mason, piano.

JUNE 8, 1928—C. Carroll Clark, baritone; Lydia Mason, piano; Mrs. Norcum, soprano.

JUNE 29, 1928—Augusta Boon Handsome, piano; Sara Brown, reader; Mrs. Norcum, soprano.

JULY 6, 1928—Frank Crosswaith, speaker, "A Negro Looks at the Campaign"; W. C. Handy spoke on his own publications, assisted by his entertainers.

JULY 20, 1928—Ethelred Brown, speaker; Mrs. Zachary, soprano; Gertrude Martin, violin.

JULY 27, 1928—Charlotte Murray, soprano; Roy Lancaster, Secy. Treas. Brotherhood of Sleeping Car Porters, speaker; Lydia Mason, piano.

AUGUST 3, 1928—Beryl Onterbridge, piano; William Martin, tenor.

AUGUST 10, 1928—Helen Hagen, piano; Frank Harrison, baritone; Wm. H. DesVerney, speaker, on "Experiences of a Veteran Pullman Porter."

AUGUST 24, 1928—Charles Johnson, speaker, editor of *Opportunity* magazine; Marlon Cumbo; William Martin, tenor.

AUGUST 31, 1928—Charlotte Junius, contralto; David Johnson, violin, accompanied by David Johnson, Sr.; Ethelred Brown, speaker, on spiritual evolution.

SEPTEMBER 14, 1928—Lloyd Hickman, baritone; Marlon Cumbo, cello; readings from *Opportunity*.

SEPTEMBER 21, 1928—J. E. Allen, speaker; Charlotte Murray, contralto; Caswell Rhetts, baritone.

SEPTEMBER 28, 1928—Llewellyn Ransom, tenor; the Rev. H. H. Proctor, speaker, on "Between Black and White."

OCTOBER 5, 1928—Maurice Hunter, artists' model; Dolly Brooks, soprano; Mayme Reiley, reader.

OCTOBER 12, 1928—C. Carroll Clark, baritone; Caroline Bagley, speaker, on "A Nile Voyage"; Merritt Hedgeman, tenor.

OCTOBER 19, 1928—Lydia Mason, piano; Caswell Rhetts, baritone; Caroline Bagley, speaker, on "Peasant Life in the Holy Land."

NOVEMBER 2, 1928—William Martin, tenor; A. Phillip Randolph, speaker, "Politics and Labor"; Bertha Dea Verney and Junior Concert Company.

NOVEMBER 17, 1928—Pierce McNeil Thompson, speaker, *The Crisis* magazine; Euphoria Singers, James Woodruff, director; Caswell Rhetts, baritone.

NOVEMBER 24, 1928—Robert Bagnall, speaker, on "Modern Science and Radicalism"; Alice Carter, Soprano; Ruby Green, contralto.

DECEMBER 15, 1928—Addie Hunton, speaker; Margetson Pianists, music; C. Carroll Clarke, baritone.

DECEMBER 22, 1928—Ruby Green, contralto; James Horn, violin; Eugene Kinckle Jones, speaker, on "Social Service Among Negroes."

JANUARY 5, 1929—Hugo Borrn, piano; R. J. Douglass, reader; Doris Trotman, soprano.

JANUARY 12, 1929—Marian Ray, speaker, on "How to Make Lampshades"; Clinton Williams, tenor; Ira De A. Reid, poems.

JANUARY 26, 1929—Pierce McNeil Thompsen, biographies; Liewelyn Ransom, tenor; Dean Dixon, violin.

FEBRUARY 2, 1929—David Johnson, violin; Irma Strickland, soprano; Caswell Rhetts, baritone; Ernestine Rose, speaker, on "As Negroes Read."

FEBRUARY 20, 1929—David Johnson, violin; Pierce McNeil Thompson, biographies; Caswell Rhetts, baritone.

MARCH 2, 1929—Robert J. Elzy, speaker, executive secretary Brooklyn Urban League; Choir of Grace Congregational Church, Olyve Jeter, director.

MARCH 9, 1929—Pierce McNeil Thompson, biographies; How Hedgeman, baritone; Clinton Williams, tenor.

MARCH 16, 1929—the Rev. Robert Blay,

speaker, on "The Way of Peace"; Willie Bibbins, violin; Robert Sawyer; Florence J. Mills and Madelline E. Johnson, piano duets.

MARCH 23, 1929—Caswell Rhetts, baritone; Pierce Mcneill Thompson, biographies; Irene Innis, piano.

MARCH 30, 1929—Edward Steel, piano; Minnie Brown, speaker, on the National Association of Negro Musicians; Ruby Green, contralto.

APRIL 6, 1929—Pierce McNeil Thompson, biographies; Vivian Shurland, piano; Luther Lamont, tenor.

APRIL 13, 1929—William C. Handy and Entertainers.

APRIL 20, 1929—James Bell, tenor; Pierce McNeil Thompson, biographies; Edward Steel, piano.

APRIL 27, 1929—Eva Vaughn, soprano; Richard Harrison, reader; Northern Quartet: Felix, Robert, Ralph, Joseph.

MAY 4, 1929—Dean Dixon, violin; James Egbert Allen, speaker; C. Rhetts, baritone.

MAY 11, 1929—Hugo Bornn, piano; Harcourt Tynes; Davis Johnson, violin.

MAY 18, 1929—Marie Bates, soprano; Arthur Bates, piano; Frank Crosswaith, speaker, on "Peace and the Negro," William Martin, tenor.

MAY 25, 1929—Joseph J. Boris; Loretta Anthony, piano; Ira De Reid, poet; Caswell Rhetts, baritone. WEVD producers inaugurated a contest to determine the most popular artist or group of artists. It was open to any amateur artist or group of artists, vocal or instrumental through June 15. Listeners were asked to send in letters which would be judged. The first performers nominated for most popular artist were Eva Vaughn, WMCA Quartette, Waldine Williams, David Johnson, Jr., and Caswell Rhetts.

JUNE 1, 1929—John Perry, tenor; Pierce McNeil, biographies; Arthur Young, piano. The second contest audition featured Roberta Bosley, John Perry, Albert Thornton, Jacob Lavall, Vivienne Shurland, James Bell and Arthur Young.

JUNE 8, 1929—Popularity contest artists: Winifred Gordon, William Allen, Jr., George

Duncan, Theresa Smith, Luther Lamont. Fred Crawford, speaker, United Colored Socialists of America.

JUNE 22, 1929—Loretta Anthony, piano; William Pickens, news from the field; Caswell Rhetts, baritone.

JUNE 29, 1929—Robert Douglas, Theresa Smith, Alta Brown.

JULY 6, 1929—Helen Sherrill, piano; Merritt Hedgemann, tenor; Pierce McNeil Thompson, speaker.

JULY 13, 1929—Robert Sawyer, basso; *The New York Amsterdam News* section; James Bell, tenor.

JULY 27, 1929—Hazel Farrar, piano; Pierce McNeil Thompson, biographies; Ruby King, soprano.

AUGUST 4, 1929—Caswell Rhetts, baritone; Mary Mason, reader; T. Smith, piano.

AUGUST 10, 1929—Symphonic Trio; selections from Negro poets; J. Dewitt Spencer, baritone.

AUGUST 17, 1929—Thelma Ingram, piano; Davis Smith, reader, classic Dunbar poems; Roberta Bosley, soprano.

AUGUST 24, 1929—Hazel Farrar, piano; Vere Johns, entertainer; William Webster, tenor.

SEPTEMBER 7, 1929—Irene Innis, piano; Helmsley Winfield, director, New Negro Art Theatre, speaker, on "Negro Theatre Making in America"; Merritt Hedgeman, tenor.

SEPTEMBER 14, 1929—Victoria Whittington, soprano; Marion Pettiford, Supervisor Harlem Centre, Henry Street Settlement Nursing Service, speaker, on "Harlem's Health"; John Gateway, baritone.

SEPTEMBER 21, 1929—Hazel Farrar, piano; Beatrice Henderson, black poetry readings; Dean Dixon, violin.

SEPTEMBER 29, 1929—New Negro Art Theatre—Scene from "Wade in de Water" by Jeroline Hemsley.

OCTOBER 6, 1929—Sidney Sanders, speaker, on *Hallelujah* and other black movies.

NOVEMBER 9, 1929—Richard Harrison, reader; Bob Douglas, violin; Olyve Jeter, piano.

NOVEMBER 17, 1929—David Johnson, violin.

NOVEMBER 24, 1929—Helen Hagan, piano; Eugene Kinckle Jones, National Urban League, speaker; Alexander Gatewood, tenor.

DECEMBER 1, 1929—Choir of Grace Congregational Church, Harlem, Olyve Jeter, director; the Rev. W. Herbert King, speaker.

DECEMBER 8, 1929—Alta Drowne, soprano; White Rose Quartette; Brooklyn Urban League; David Johnson, violin.

DECEMBER 15, 1929—Joseph Douglass, violin.

DECEMBER 29, 1929—Choir of Fleet Street A.M.E.P.Z. Church; Henry Abscroft, speaker, on "Industrial Work of the Brooklyn Urban League."

JANUARY 12, 1930—W. C. Handy and company; Robert Bagnall, speaker, on "The Negro March Forward."

JANUARY 19, 1930—David Johnson Quartet; Caswell Rhetts, baritone; Dr. Wm. R. R. Granger, speaker, on "Health."

JANUARY 26, 1930—White Rose Quartet; T. Arnold Hill, director of industrial relations, National Urban League, speaker.

FEBRUARY 16, 1930—Frank Crosswaith, speaker, on "The Darker World Stirs"; Hugo Bornn, piano.

FEBRUARY 23, 1930—Ethelred Brown, speaker; Irene MacPherson, soprano.

MARCH 2, 1930—White Rose Quartette; Addie Hunton, speaker, on "Racial Aspects of the Haitian Situation"; Mabel Bergen, soprano.

MARCH 9, 1930—the Rev. Ethelred Brown, speaker, on "The Scientific Mood"; Loretta Anthony, piano.

MARCH 16, 1930—James Egbert Allen, directing. Armond W. Scott, speaker, on "Justice and Peace, the Demand of the Hour."

MARCH 23, 1930—Frank Crosswaith, speaker; Irene Innis, piano.

APRIL 6, 1930—Capt. Napoleon Marshall, speaker, on "The Haitian Situation"; Little Mt. Zion Junior Quartette.

APRIL 13, 1930—the Rev. Ethelred Brown, speaker, on "The Negro Democrat"; Loretta Anthony, piano.

APRIL 20, 1930—Bessye Rearden, speaker; White Rose Quartette.

APRIL 27, 1930—the Rev. Robert Blay, speaker; Isabelle Rogers Clayton, Sadie Rogers Wilson.

MAY 4, 1930—New Rochelle Quintet; William Andrews, speaker, on "The Negro's Fight for Freedom."

MAY 11, 1930—Hugo Bornn, piano; Carlton Moss, speaker, on "Intercollegiate Dramatics."

MAY 18, 1930—Isabelle Rogers Clayton, soprano; William Andrews, speaker, on "The Parker Case."

MAY 25, 1930—Morgan College Dramatic Club.

JUNE 1, 1930—Frank Crosswaith, speaker; Frank Crosswaith, Jr., violin.

JUNE 8, 1930—Frank Crosswaith, speaker; Frank Crosswaith, Jr., violin.

JUNE 15, 1930—Josephine Pinyon Holmes, speaker, on "Employment for Negro Girls."

JUNE 22, 1930—Loretta Anthony, piano; Ethelred Brown, speaker, on "The West Indians Among Us"; Negro Art and Discussion Hour.

JUNE 29, 1930—Eloise Uggams, soprano; Marion Pettiford, piano; Ethelred Brown, speaker, on "The Price We Pay."

JULY 6, 1930—Lydia Mason, piano; W. D. Simmons, speaker, on "Employment."

JULY 13, 1930—David Johnson, violin quartet; Ethelred Brown, speaker.

Bibliography

Books

Abbott, John C. *Yours Truly, Johnny Dollar, Volumes 1–3.* Duncan, OK: BearManor, 2010.

Abbott, Lynn, and Doug Seroff. *Ragged but Right: Black Traveling Shows, "Coon Songs," and the Dark Pathway to Blues and Jazz.* Jackson: University Press of Mississippi, 2007.

Albertson, Chris. *Bessie.* NY: Stein and Day, 1972.

Allen, Ray. *Singing in the Spirit: African American Sacred Quartets in New York City.* Philadelphia: University of Pennsylvania Press, 1991.

Altschuler, Glenn C. *All Shook Up: How Rock 'n' Roll Changed America.* New York: Oxford University Press, 2003.

Andrews, Bart, and Ahrqus Juilliard. *Holy Mackerel! The Amos and Andy Story.* Boston: E.P. Dutton, 1986.

Ansbro, George. *I Have a Lady in the Balcony: Memoirs of a Broadcaster in Radio and Television.* Jefferson, NC: McFarland, 2000.

Arsenault, Raymond. *The Sound of Freedom: Marian Anderson, the Lincoln Memorial, and the Concert That Awakened America.* New York: Bloomsbury, 2009.

Baldwin, Kate A. *Beyond the Color Line and the Iron Curtain: Reading Encounters Between Black and Red, 1922–1963.* Durham, NC: Duke University Press, 2002.

Balk, Alfred. *The Rise of Radio, from Marconi through the Golden Age.* Jefferson, NC: McFarland, 2006.

Bannerman, LeRoy. *Norman Corwin and Radio: The Golden Years.* N.p.: University of Alabama Press, 1986.

Barlow, William. *Voice Over: The Making of Black Radio.* Philadelphia: Temple University Press, 1999.

Barnouw, Erik. *The Golden Web: A History of Broadcasting in the United States, Volume II, 1933–1953.* New York: Oxford University Press, 1968.

Benny, Mary Livingstone, and Hilliard Marks with Marcia Borie. *Jack Benny.* Garden City, NY: Doubleday, 1978.

Berry, S. Torriano, and Venise T. Berry. *Historical Dictionary of African American Cinema.* Lanham, MD: Scarecrow, 2007.

Billups, Connie, and Arthur Pierce. *Lux Presents Hollywood: A Show-by-Show History of the Lux Radio Theatre and the Lux Video Theatre, 1934–1957.* Jefferson, NC: McFarland, 1995.

Blue, Howard. *Words at War: World War II Era Radio Drama and the Postwar Broadcasting Industry Blacklist.* Lanham, MD: Scarecrow, 2002.

Bogle, Donald. *Bright Boulevards, Bold Dreams: The Story of Black Hollywood.* New York: Ballantine, 2005.

_____. *Dorothy Dandridge.* New York: Amistad, 1997.

Bourne, Stephen. *Butterfly McQueen Remembered.* Lanham, MD: Scarecrow, 2008.

Bowser, Pearl, Jane Gaines and Charles Musser. Bloomington and Indianapolis: Indiana University Press, 2001.

Boyle, Sheila Tully, and Andrew Bunie. *Paul Robeson: The Years of Promise and Achievement.* Amherst: University of Massachusetts Press, 2001.

Browne, Ray B., and Pat Browne. *The Guide to United States Popular Culture.* Madison, WI: Popular Press, 2001.

Buxton, Frank, and Bill Owen. *The Big Broadcast, 1920–1950: A New, Revised, and Greatly Expanded Edition of Radio's Golden Age, The Complete Reference Work.* New York: Viking Press, 1972.

Calloway, Cab, and Bryant Collins. *Of Minnie the Moocher and Me*. New York: Thomas Y. Crowell, 1976.

Cantor, Louis. *Wheelin' on Beale: How WDIA-Memphis Became the Nation's First All-Black Radio Station and Created the Sound That Changed America*. New York: Pharos, 1992.

Carr, Ian, Digby Fairweather, and Brian Priestley. *The Rough Guide to Jazz: The Essential Companion to Artists and Albums, 3d ed.* London: Rough Guides, 2004.

Cox, Jim. *American Radio Networks: A History*. Jefferson, NC: McFarland, 2009.

_____. *The Great Radio Sitcoms*. Jefferson, NC: McFarland, 2007.

_____. *The Great Radio Soap Operas*. Jefferson, NC: McFarland, 1999.

_____. *Historical Dictionary of American Radio Soap Operas*. Lanham, MD: Scarecrow, 2005.

_____. *Music Radio: The Great Performers and Programs of the 1920s through Early 1960s*. Jefferson, NC: McFarland, 2005.

_____. *Radio Crime Fighters: Over 300 Programs from the Golden Age*. Jefferson, NC: McFarland, 2002.

_____. *Radio Speakers: Narrators, News Junkies, Sports Jockeys, Tattletales, Tipsters, Toastmasters and Coffee Klatch Couples Who Verbalized the Jargon of the Aural Ether from the 1920s to the 1980s—A Biographical Dictionary*. Jefferson, NC: McFarland, 2007.

_____. *Say Goodnight, Gracie: The Last Years of Network Radio*. Jefferson, NC: McFarland, 2002.

_____. *This Day in Network Radio: A Daily Calendar of Births, Deaths, Debuts, Cancellations and Other Events in Broadcasting History*. Jefferson, NC: McFarland, 2008.

Dance, Stanley. *The World of Count Basie*. New York: Charles Scribner's Sons, 1980.

_____. *The World of Earl Hines*. New York: Charles Scribner's Sons, 1977.

Dandridge, Dorothy, and Earl Conrad. *Everything and Nothing: The Dorothy Dandridge Tragedy*. New York: Abelard-Schuman, 1970.

Davis, Ossie, and Ruby Dee. *With Ossie and Ruby: In This Life Together*. New York: William Morrow, 1998.

DeLong, Thomas A. *The Golden Age of Musical Radio ... The Mighty Music Box*. Los Angeles: Amber Crest, 1980.

Duberman, Martin Bauml. *Paul Robeson*. New York: Alfred A. Knopf, 1988.

Dunning, John. *On the Air: The Encyclopedia of Old-Time Radio*. New York: Oxford University Press, 1998.

Ely, Melvin Patrick. *The Adventures of Amos 'n' Andy*. New York: Free, 1992.

Fein, Irving A. *Jack Benny: An Intimate Biography*. New York: G. P. Putnam's Sons, 1976.

George-Warren, Holly. *Public Cowboy No. 1: The Life and Times of Gene Autry*. New York: Oxford University Press, 2007.

Gourse, Leslie. *Louis' Children: American Jazz Singers*. New York: Cooper Square, 1984.

Grams, Martin, Jr. *The History of the Cavalcade of America*. Delta, PA: Grams, 1998.

_____. *Radio Drama: A Comprehensive Chronicle of American Network Programs, 1932–1962*. Jefferson, NC: McFarland, 2000.

_____. *Suspense: Twenty Years of Thrills and Chills*. Kearney, NB: Morris, 1997.

Haskins, James. *Black Theater in America*. New York: Thomas Y. Crowell, 1982.

Havighurst, Craig. *Air Castle of the South: WSM and the Making of Music City*. Urbana and Chicago: University of Illinois Press, 2007.

Hayes, Richard K. *Kate Smith: A Biography, with a Discography, Filmography and List of Stage Appearances*. Jefferson, NC: McFarland, 1995.

Hickerson, Jay. *The 2nd Revised Ultimate History of Network Radio Programming and Guide to All Circulating Shows*. Hamden, CT: Presto, 2001.

_____. *The 3rd Revised Ultimate History of Network Radio Programming and Guide to All Circulating Shows*. Hamden, CT: Presto, 2006.

Hiss, George. *The Joe Bostic Story: First Black American Radio Announcer*. AuthorHouse, 2006.

Jackson, Carlton. *Hattie: The Life of Hattie McDaniel*. Lanham, MD: Madison, 1993.

Jaker, Bill, Frank Sulek, and Peter Kanze. *The Airwaves of New York: Illustrated Histories of 156 AM Stations in the Metropolitan Area, 1921–1996*. Jefferson, NC: McFarland, 1998.

Keiler, Allan. *Marian Anderson: A Singer's Journey*. New York: Scribner, 2000.

Lawrence, A.H. *Duke Ellington and his World: A Biography*. New York: Routledge, 2003.

Leff, Laura. *39 Forever, Second Edition, Volume 1: Radio, May 1932–May 1942*. North Charleston, NC: BookSurge, 2004.

_____. *39 Forever, Second Edition, Volume 2: Radio, October 1942–May 1955*. Jack Benny International Fan Club, 2006.

Lotz, Rainer E, and Ulrich Neuert. *The AFRS "Jubilee" Transcription Programs an Exploratory Discography*. Frankfurt, West Germany: Norbert Ruecker, 1985.

MacDonald, J. Fred. *Don't Touch That Dial! Radio Programming in American Life from 1920 to 1960*. Chicago: Nelson-Hall, 1979.

_____. *Richard Durham's Destination Freedom: Scripts from Radio's Black Legacy, 1948–50*. New York: Praeger, 1989.

Magee, Jeffrey. *The Uncrowned King of Swing:*

Fletcher Henderson and Big Band Jazz. New York: Oxford University Press, 2005.

McClure, Rusty, with David Stern and Michael A. Banks. *Crosley: Two Brothers and a Business Empire That Transformed the Nation.* Cincinnati: Clerisy, 2006.

McLeod, Elizabeth. *The Original Amos 'n' Andy: Freeman Gosden, Charles Correll and the 1928– 1943 Radio Serial.* Jefferson, NC: McFarland, 2005.

McNeil, W. K. *Encyclopedia of American Gospel Music.* New York: Routledge, 2005.

Murray, Albert. *Good Morning Blues: The Autobiography of Count Basie as told to Albert Murray.* New York: Random House, 1985.

Nachman, Gerald. *Raised on Radio: In Quest of The Lone Ranger, Jack Benny, Amos 'n' Andy, The Shadow, Mary Noble, The Great Gildersleeve, Fibber McGee and Molly, Bill Stern, Our Miss Brooks, Henry Aldrich, The Quiz Kids, Mr. First Nighter, Fred Allen, Vic and Sade, The Cisco Kid, Jack Armstrong, Arthur Godfrey, Bob and Ray, The Barbour Family, Henry Morgan, Joe Friday, and Other Lost Heroes From Radio's Heyday.* New York: Pantheon, 1998.

Nevins, Francis M., and Martin Grams, Jr. *The Sound of Detection: Ellery Queen's Adventures in Radio.* Churchville, MD: OTR, 2002.

Newman, Mark. *Entrepreneurs of Profit and Pride: From Black-Appeal to Radio Soul.* New York: Praeger, 1988.

Paley, William S. *As It Happened: A Memoir.* Garden City, NY: Doubleday, 1979.

Passman, Arnold. *The Deejays.* New York: Macmillan, 1971.

Patterson, Lindsey, ed. *Anthology of the American Negro in the Theatre: A Critical Approach.* New York: Publisher's Company, 1968.

Payton, Gordon, and Martin Grams, Jr. *The CBS Radio Mystery Theater: An Episode Guide and Handbook to Nine Years of Broadcasting, 1974– 1982.* Jefferson, NC: McFarland, 1999.

Peterson, Bernard L., Jr. *The African American Theatre Directory, 1816–1960: A Comprehensive Guide to Early Black Theatre Organizations, Companies, Theatres, and Performing Groups.* Westport, CT: Greenwood, 1997.

Price, Michael H. *Mantan the Funnyman: The Life and Times of Mantan Moreland.* Baltimore, MD: Midnight Marquee, 2006.

Robeson, Paul, Jr. *The Undiscovered Paul Robeson: An Artist's Journey, 1898–1939.* New York: John Wiley and Sons, 2001.

Sampson, Henry T. *Blacks in Black and White: A Source Book on Black Films, 2d ed..* Metuchen, NJ: Scarecrow, 1995.

_____. *Swingin' on the Ether Waves: A Chronological History of African Americans in Radio and Television Programming, 1925–1955, Volume I.* Latham, MD: Scarecrow, 2005.

_____. *Swingin' on the Ether Waves: A Chronological History of African Americans in Radio and Television Programming, 1925–1955, Volume II.* Latham, MD: Scarecrow, 2005.

Savage, Barbara Dianne. *Broadcasting Freedom: Radio, War, and the Politics of Race 1938–1948.* Chapel Hill, NC: University of North Carolina Press, 1999.

_____ and Ruth Marie Griffith. *Women and Religion in the African Diaspora: Knowledge, Power, and Performance.* Baltimore, MD: Johns Hopkins University Press, 2006.

Scott, Michelle R. *Blues Empress in Black Chattanooga: Bessie Smith and the Emerging Urban South.* Urbana and Chicago: University of Illinois Press, 2008.

Segal, Eli. *The Eternal Light: An Unauthorized Guide.* Newtown, CT: Yesteryear, 2005.

Sies, Luther F. *Encyclopedia of American Radio, 1920–1960.* Jefferson, NC: McFarland, 2000.

Simpson, Eugene Thamon. *Hall Johnson: His Life, His Spirit, and His Music.* Lanham, MD: Scarecrow, 2008.

Singer, Arthur J. *Arthur Godfrey: The Adventures of an American Broadcaster.* Jefferson, NC: McFarland, 2000.

Sklaroff, Lauren Rebecca. *Black Culture and the New Deal: The Quest for Civil Rights in the Roosevelt Era.* Chapel Hill, NC: University of North Carolina, 2009.

Smith, Jessie Carney, and Shirelle Phelps. *Notable Black American Women.* Detroit, MI: Gale Research, 1996.

Smith, Mona Z. *Becoming Something: The Story of Canada Lee.* London: Faber and Faber, 2004.

Southern, Eileen. *The Music of Black Americans: A History, 3d ed.* New York: W.W. Norton, 1997.

Stumpf, Charles, and Ben Ohmart. *The Great Gildersleeve.* Boalsburg, PA: BearManor Media, 2002.

_____ and Tom Price. *Heavenly Days! The Story of Fibber McGee and Molly.* Waynesville, NC: World of Yesterday, 1987.

Swartz, Jon D., and Robert C. Reinehr. *Handbook of Old-Time Radio: A Comprehensive Guide to Golden Age Radio Listening and Collecting.* Metuchen, NJ: Scarecrow, 1993.

Vehanen, Kosti. *Marian Anderson: A Portrait.* Westport, CT: Greenwood, 1941.

Ward, Brian. *Radio and the Struggle for Civil Rights in the South.* Gainesville: University Press of Florida, 2004.

Watts, Jill. *Hattie McDaniel: Black Ambition, White Hollywood.* New York: Amistad, 2005.

Wertheim, Arthur Frank. *Radio Comedy*. New York: Oxford University Press, 1979.

Wintz, Cary D., ed. *Harlem Speaks: A Living History of the Harlem Renaissance*. Naperville, IL: Sourcebooks, 2007.

Woll, Allen. *Dictionary of the Black Theatre: Broadway, Off-Broadway, and Selected Harlem Theatre*. Westport, CT: Greenwood, 1983.

Articles

Barnett, David C. "Radio Show Chronicled Blacks' Harsh Realities." National Public Radio, March 3, 2008. Accessed online December 4, 2010.

Baron, Steve. "Ken-Rad and the Last Receiving Tube in the Western Hemisphere." *Mid-South Antique Radio Collectors*, Winter 1993/1994, pp. 1–3.

Dunning, John. "Poe on the Radio." *Edgar Allan Poe Review* vol. 1, no. 2 (2000): 3–9. Accessed online at *http://www2.lv.psu.edu/PSA/EAPR.html*, July 29, 2010.

Ellett, Ryan. "Amos 'n' Andy: The Chicago Defender's Response." *Old Time Radio Digest*, Winter 2010, pp. 14–20.

Funk, Ray, and Peter Grendysa. "The Southernaires." *Goldmine*, June 21, 1985, p. 16, 24, 72–73.

Hopkinson, Doug, and Ryan Ellett. "The Radio Work of Henry Moeller and Hal Gilles." *Radiogram*, April 2010, pp. 9–14.

Kennedy, Rick. "Clarence M. Jones (1889–1949) Almost Forgotten (But Not Quite)." *78 Quarterly* 9 (1999): 37–46.

Newman, Mark. "On the Air with Jack L. Cooper: The Beginnings of Black-Appeal Radio." *Chicago History* 12 (Summer 1983): 51–58.

Peterson, Pete. "The Mariners." *American Legacy* (Spring 2005): 17–24.

Porter, James, with Rick Wojcik. "Oscar Brown, Jr.." *Roctober* 15 (1996) accessed online at *http://www.roctober.com/roctober/greatness/obj.html*, July 24, 2010.

Dissertations and Theses

Delay, Theodore Stuart, Jr. "An Historical Study of the Armed Forces Radio Service to 1946." Dissertation, University of Southern California, 1951.

Edmerson, Estelle. "A Descriptive Study of the American Negro in United States Professional Radio, 1922–1953." Master's thesis, University of California at Los Angeles, 1954.

Spaulding, Norman W. "History of Black Oriented Radio in Chicago 1929–1963." Doctoral thesis, University of Illinois, 1981.

Archival Material

John Henry scripts, Deliah Jackson Papers, Manuscript, Archives, and Rare Book Library, Emory University.

NBC documents from WEAF and WJZ station records, New York City.

Magazines

(see individual entries for specific issues)

Billboard
Jet
Radex
Stand By ... On the Air
Time

Newspapers

(see individual entries for specific issues)

The Atlanta Daily World
The Baltimore Afro-American
The Chicago Defender
The Chicago Tribune
The Cleveland Call and Post
The Delta Democrat-Times (Greenville, MS)
The Herald Star (Steubenville, OH)
The Los Angeles Sentinel
The Los Angeles Times
The New York Amsterdam News
The New York Times
The Norfolk Journal and Guide
The Philadelphia Tribune
The Pittsburgh Courier
The Savannah Tribune (Savannah, GA)
The Times (Hammond, IN)
The Topeka Plaindealer (Topeka, KS)

Websites

David Goldin: www.radiogoldindex.com

Finding Aid for Canada Lee Papers, Schomburg Center for Research in Black Culture, The New York Public Library: http://www.nypl.org/.

Halper, Donna. "African Americans and Early Radio": http://www.coax.net/people/lwf/AAER.htm.

The Internet Movie Database: www.imdb.com.

Jester Hairston interview: http://www.umich.edu/~afroammu/standifer/hairston.html.

Kansas Historical Society: www.kshe.org.

New York Daily News, February 5, 2003, http://www.nydailynews.com/archives.

Papers of Countee Cullen 1921–1969: http://microformguides.gale.com/Data/Download/8350000C.pdf.

Richard Durham Papers, 1939–1999 online finding aid, Chicago Public Library: *www.chipublib.org.*

http://paramountshome.org.

http://einsiders.com/august-2004/hollywood-obituaries/august-2004-hollywood-obituaries.html.

http://www.fatswaller.org.

http://www.hillbillyheart-throbs.com.

http://www.nj.com.

http://www.targetmarketnews.com.

Index